RACE RELATIONS IN RHODESIA

A Survey for 1972-73

compiled by
DOROTHY KEYWORTH DAVIES

REX COLLINGS LONDON 1975

First published in 1975 by
Rex Collings Ltd
6 Paddington Street London W1M 3LA

Printed in Great Britain by
Biddles Ltd, Guildford, Surrey

CONTENTS

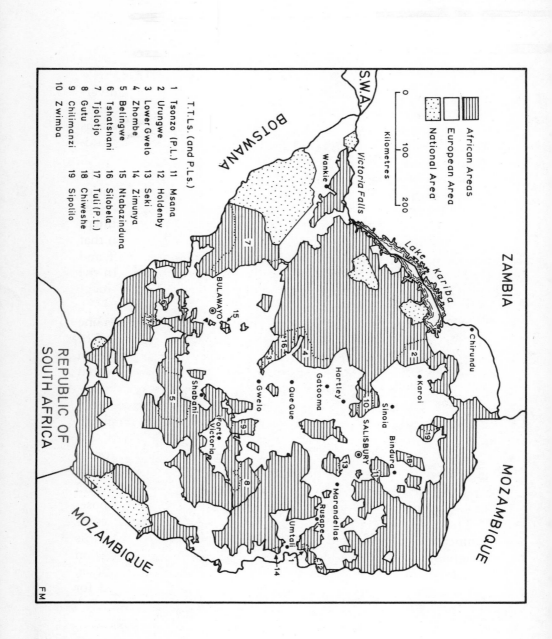

FOREWORD

MARSHALL W. MURPHREE

*Maurice Webb Professor of Race Relations and
Director of Centre for Inter-Racial Studies
University of Rhodesia*

The Centre for Inter-Racial Studies was established at the University of Rhodesia in June 1970. The Centre, created to promote research and teaching in race relations, has departmental status within the University and is located in the Faculty of Social Studies.

The establishment of the Centre followed the creation of the Maurice Webb Chair of Race Relations at the University. Maurice Webb, a former president of the South African Institute of Race Relations, left a bequest for the establishment of a Department of Race Relations at the University of Natal on the condition that admission to membership in the department, both of staff and students, be 'on the ground of merit irrespective of race'. In the event Natal was unable to accept the bequest and the endowment was offered to the University of Rhodesia.

The University was founded in 1955 under Royal Charter, one of the provisions of which is that 'No test of religious belief or profession or of race, nationality or class shall be imposed upon or required of any person in order to entitle him to be admitted as a member, professor, teacher or student of the University College or to hold office therein or any advantage or privilege thereof.' Undergraduate full-time enrolment by race in the University in 1973 was as follows: 'African' 373, 'Asian' 47, 'Coloured' 19, 'European' 469, a total of 908. The Centre thus constitutes an independently financed unit for the study of race relations in a country where race is of critical political and social significance, and is located in an institution uniquely endowed for the purpose.

The Centre operates a programme covering three areas: communication, teaching and research. One important aspect of this programme involves the identification, classification and collection of contemporary documentary data on race relations in Rhodesia. An extensive library of these materials has been developed for the use of scholars at the Centre under the direction of our Research Officer, Mrs. Dorothy Davies. To make much of this material available to a wider reading public a periodic report is to be published, of which this is the first. We are grateful to the trustees of the Maurice Webb estate for the financial support which has made this publication possible. If the dissemination of this material leads to a greater understanding of the dynamics motivating the different segments of Rhodesia's multi-racial population by readers both within and without Rhodesia's borders, we believe that Maurice Webb's objectives of 'discovering causes of tensions that may exist' between these segments and 'suggesting ways by which the causes of such tensions may be removed' will in part have been fulfilled.

SALISBURY   DECEMBER 1973

INTRODUCTION

GEOGRAPHICAL FEATURES

Rhodesia occupies an area of 389 000 sq. km in the interior of tropical south-central Africa, extending from 15°40' to 32°25' south and from 25°10' to 33°05' east. Entirely landlocked between neighbouring Botswana, Mozambique, South Africa and Zambia, it depends heavily for its overseas trade on rail and road routes to Beira and Lourenco Marques and the major South African ports.

The country lies astride high plateau land between the Zambezi and Limpopo rivers and comprises four relief divisions. The *highveld*, undulating plateau country above 1 220 m, extends across Rhodesia from south-west to north-east, where it is widest. This is the main area of European settlement and the economic heartland of Rhodesia and includes most of the principal urban centres. The *middleveld*, between 915 and 1 220 m flanks the highveld to north-west and south-east. The *lowveld*, land below 915 m (and largely below 600 m), occupies the extensive Sabi-Lundi and Limpopo basins in the south and south-east of the country, and also the narrower Zambezi basin in the north-west. The *Eastern Highlands* form a fourth and distinctive region of rugged mountainous country running from north to south along the eastern border. This narrow belt of high land, rising to 2 594 m in Mount Inyanga in the north and largely above 1 800 m in elevation, marks the uplifted edge of the tableland of south-central Africa.

Rainfall, mainly restricted to the period November-March, is the critical climatic factor. In view of the high rates of evapo-transpiration and marked unreliability, mean annual rainfall, ranging from 1 400 mm in the eastern mountainous region to less than 400 mm in the Limpopo valley, is rarely more than barely adequate for commercial crop production and in the drier areas supports at best only extensive ranching; underground water supplies are also limited. Mean monthly temperatures range from 22° C in October to 13° C in July on the highveld, to 30° C and 20° C respectively in the Zambezi valley. The clear, sunny winter months show wide diurnal temperature ranges and frosts are not uncommon on the highveld. Soils, which are highly varied, are generally secondary to climatic factors in determining farming potential.

The country has varied and rich workable mineral resources, mostly distributed on the *highveld* and flanking *middleveld*. These include coal at Wankie, and asbestos, chrome, gold, copper, nickel, tin, iron ore, limestone, iron pyrites and phosphates.

MAIN HISTORICAL EVENTS OF MODERN TIMES

Prior to the Ndebele invasion between 1838 and 1840, the territory between the Limpopo and Zambezi Rivers was largely populated by Shona-speaking people. The Ndebele tribe had been formed from warriors of the Nguni Khumalo clan who, under their leader Mzilikazi, had rebelled against their Zulu overlord Shaka (Chaka) who at that time was establishing Zulu ascendancy over the territory later called Natal. After much wandering Mzilikazi led his warriors, accompanied by women and children captured during raids, to the area subsequently known as Matabeleland. The Ndebele eventually made exaggerated claims to sovereignty over the entire area between the Limpopo and the Zambezi 'as far east as Tete, the Mazoe Valley and the mountains in the east of the Sabi River.'

Partly to satisfy Rhodes' empire building ambitions but largely to stop a link-up between the Germans in the north (Tanganyika) and the south-west (Damaraland and Namaqualand) and the Boers of the Transvaal Republic (who had recently concluded a treaty with the Ndebele) and also to check any Portuguese territorial expansion from Portuguese East Africa, Britain claimed 'an exclusive sphere of influence over all the Matabele domains'[1] in 1888, following the signing of the Moffat Treaty with Lobengula, son of Mzilikazi and king of the Ndebele.

In October 1889 Queen Victoria signed a Royal Charter establishing the Chartered Company (the British South Africa Company) giving it authority to operate in Bechuanaland (now Botswana) and beyond the Limpopo River to the west of Portuguese

1 1970: Nutting, Anthony: *Scramble for Africa: the Great Trek to the Boer War*: London: Constable.

territory for a period of 25 years. The Charter, made possible by the Rudd Concession signed by Lobengula the previous year, granted and assigned '...complete and exclusive charge over all metals and minerals contained in my [Logengula's] kingdom, principalities and dominions, together with full power to do all things they [Rudd and his associates—representatives of Rhodes] may deem necessary to win and secure the same.'[1]

In 1890 the Pioneer Column was organized by Rhodes and set off from Kimberley in the Cape Province to occupy Mashonaland. According to one biographer of Rhodes 'It was to Mashonaland rather than to the more convenient Matabeleland Rhodes sent his pioneers because he knew he had no right to the land, and preferred to argue the matter, if necessary, with the humble Mashona rather than with the arrogant Matabele.'[2] On the way to Mashonaland a part of the Pioneer Column had split off and moved east towards Portuguese territory. By means of a treaty with local Manica chiefs the B.S.A. Company's authority was extended to cover Manicaland. In 1893, following a dispute over cattle and ostensibly to stop Ndebele raids into Mashonaland, Matabeleland was invaded by the Company's armed forces. Following the defeat of the Ndebele, Matabeleland was added to Manicaland and Mashonaland to form what eventually became known as Southern Rhodesia. During 1896 both the Ndebele and the Shona rebelled against Company authority and it was not until late 1897 that the last of the Shona rebels surrendered.

At the end of the First World War (because of the war the initial Royal Charter had been extended by ten years) considerable attention was given to the future of Southern Rhodesia. In 1922 a referendum was held to decide whether the territory should be given responsible government under the British Crown or become a fifth province of the Union of South Africa. The former alternative having received an affirmative answer, an increasing degree of internal self-government was attained during the period prior to the Second World War. It was understood that full independence would ultimately ensue.[3]

---

1 1958: Mason, Philip: *The Birth of a Dilemma: the conquest and settlement of Rhodesia:* London: Oxford University Press.
2 1933: Millin, Sarah G.: *Rhodes:* London: Chatto and Windus.
3 1970: Gale, R. D.: *Rhodesia 1890-1970—Eighty Years Onwards* Salisbury: H. C. P. Anderson.

The Second World War interrupted plans for amalgamation of Northern and Southern Rhodesia and it was not until 1953 that the Federation of Rhodesia and Nyasaland was formed. (Nyasaland had been included in the plans for federation at a later date).

The Federation lasted for only ten years until, with much bitterness on the part of Southern Rhodesia, it broke up into its component parts. Northern Rhodesia, as Zambia, and Nyasaland, as Malawi, were given independence from British rule almost immediately.

Since the break-up of the Federation the pursuit of independence has dominated the political scene in Rhodesia and by early 1965 relations with Britain had deteriorated into a 'conflict over principles [which] reinforced the continued distrust between the two governments.'[1] The Unilateral Declaration of Independence (U.D.I.) was announced by Rhodesia on 11 November 1965.

LANGUAGES

The official language of Rhodesia is English. The majority of people, however, speak one of the African languages of which Shona, spoken by 3 433 960 people, and Ndebele, spoken by 706 750 people, are the two main ones.[2] Afrikaans (as a home language) is spoken not only by the Afrikaner community (estimated in 1951 to be about 13.5 per cent of all Europeans in Rhodesia) but also by some members of the Coloured community—descendants of Coloured people originating from South Africa. The majority of the Coloured people, however, speak English as a mother tongue. The Asian community, largely descendents of people of Indian origin, speak both English and one of the Indian languages. The small Greek, Italian and Portuguese communities speak their own language as well as English.

TERMINOLOGY

In order to avoid confusion the general principle has been adopted of retaining terminology in official and common usage

1 1967: Barber, James: *Rhodesia: the road to rebellion:* London: O.U.P.
2 According to the 1969 Population Census (Interim) Report. Vol. II: The African Population, p. 27.

within Rhodesia. One of the most confusing terms to anyone unaccustomed to Rhodesian (and South African) colloquial usage is the term 'European'. In Rhodesia this term is used to designate any person who is (as defined by the Concise Oxford English Dictionary) 'a member of one of the races chiefly inhabiting or having inhabited Europe, and characterized by a certain type of civilization.' For certain purposes also, principally for the franchise, Asian and Coloured persons are regarded as 'Europeans'.

The term 'Coloured' also varies from current usage abroad. In Rhodesia a Coloured person is the offspring or descendant of a union between a 'European' (or Asian) and one of the indigenous African people, who lives in a manner considered appropriate to a 'European'. Coloured persons who live in one of the tribal African societies are, however, regarded as Africans.

THE AIM OF THE SURVEY

This survey, which owes much to the admirable annual surveys of race relations in the Republic of South Africa by Muriel Horrell of the South African Institute of Race Relations, aims to record objectively a representative spread of opinion expressed in the news media. It is intended neither as a justification nor a criticism of the circumstances of daily life affecting race relations in Rhodesia but rather as an endeavour to outline the facts of the situation as seen by different sections of the people living in this country.

If any justification is necessary for relying so heavily upon press reports this may be found in the words of Colin Seymour-Ure (who wrote on the role of the national press in the British political system) 'Newspapers... are one of the many things which, over a long period of time, shape a person's attitudes towards his society and its political institutions and machinery.'[1] In the short-term it is felt that the Rhodesian press serves as a mirror which, whether it is believed that it casts a distorted image or a true reflection, provides basic information for discussion and the formation of opinion. Its reporting provides facts (in spite of its acceptance of self-imposed censorship) and its commentary at least displays

1 Ure, Colin Seymour-: *The Press, Politics and the Public: an essay on the role of the national press in the British political system: London: Methuen.*

the range of topics that were talking points at particular moments of time when they were fresh and not obscured by hindsight.

In Rhodesian society race consciousness is apparent in many aspects of day-to-day living. In writing about inter-racial relations in such a society the difficulty is not in finding topics to discuss but in deciding what to omit. The sections of this survey therefore reflect not only what are, in the opinion of the compiler, the more important aspects of the relations between the races but also follow the themes most often pursued in the national press. In following these themes the compiler is not unaware of news reports and differing expressions of opinion appearing in the news media of other English language countries but has reluctantly accepted the limitations imposed by censorship since an important objective of the survey is to collate and disseminate the material for Rhodesian readers. If certain topics are under-represented and important documentation inadvertently omitted the Centre for Inter-Racial Studies would welcome criticism and constructive suggestions for future issues.

When this survey was initially projected it was considered that it should be based upon a calendar year as in the South African survey. However, owing to the necessity to fill in the background of many of the current topics, which made it a much larger and more time consuming undertaking than was originally anticipated, it was decided to update the material to the middle of 1973. This decision was reinforced by the fact that annual government reports, from which most recent statistics can be obtained, are only published in mid-year after their presentation to parliament.

ACKNOWLEDGEMENTS

A survey such as this would be impossible without numerous newspaper reports and editorials to draw upon. From the preponderance of references to the *Rhodesia Herald* and the *Sunday Mail* it will be noted that a particular debt of gratitude is owing to these newspapers, which, although acknowledging a degree of self-imposed censorship, make every effort to place before their readers facts and opinions in a way which embodies the high standards of other responsible news media. To the editors of *Moto* also my thanks and appreciation are extended for placing before the public in a responsible manner the topics and opinions with which many African readers, in particular, are able to identify.

My thanks are also due to the Director of the Centre for Inter-Racial Studies, Professor Marshall Murphree, for his patience and encouragement and for valuable suggestions; to Dr. Philip Warhurst for reading the whole of the manuscript and commenting thereon; to Messrs. Ashley Dixon and Peter Harris and to Dr. Elizabeth Hendrikz for reading and commenting upon parts of the manuscript; to Chief Technician, Mr. R. G. Wheeler and his assistant, Mr E. Muchenga of the Department of Geography for the map which forms the frontispiece; to Mrs. Audrey Portman for typing the manuscript; and lastly to Dr. D. Hywel Davies for his constant encouragement and invaluable editorial guidance.

CHRONOLOGICAL TABLE OF EVENTS
IN MODERN RHODESIAN HISTORY

c. 1838-40 Ndebele invasion of Mashonaland.

1859 First permanent European settlement started with the founding of the Inyati Mission.

1888 Signing of the Moffat Treaty and consequent proclamation of a protectorate over Matabeleland by Britain.
Signing of the Rudd Concession.

1889 Signing of the Royal Charter forming the Chartered Company (The British South African Company) to exploit the Rudd Concession.

1890 The Pioneer Column organized in Kimberley. Arrives in Mashonaland, raises the Union Jack at Fort Salisbury and takes possession of the territory.

1891 A British Order in Council declares a British Protectorate over Bechuanaland (now Botswana), Mashonaland and Matabeleland.

1893 War on the Ndebele authorized by Britain.

1896 *(March)* Ndebele Rebellion.
(June) Shona Rebellion.
(August) Rhodes' *indaba* with Ndebele Chiefs.

1897 Mashonaland, Matabeleland and Manicaland become officially known as Southern Rhodesia.
The Municipalities of Salisbury and Bulawayo created.
(October) Shona Rebellion ended.

1899 Legislative Council for Southern Rhodesia.

1917 Union of Northern and Southern Rhodesia proposed but rejected by Southern Rhodesian Legislative Council.

1922 Referendum on question of responsible government or becoming a fifth province of the Union of South Africa.
Majority for responsible government.

1923 Southern Rhodesia becomes a self-governing colony under the British Crown. Independent Legislative Assembly established.

1931 Land Apportionment Act passed.

1949 Preliminary conference to discuss the federation of Southern and Northern Rhodesia and Nyasaland.

1952 White Paper on proposed federation tabled in Southern Rhodesian Legislative Assembly.

1953 *(April)* Referendum in Southern Rhodesia for federation.
Majority in favour.

1956 Sir Roy Welensky becomes Prime Minister of the Federation.

1957 Sir Edgar Whitehead invited to become Prime Minister of Southern Rhodesia.

1959 Widespread riots and disorders in Northern Rhodesia and Nyasaland. Southern Rhodesia arrests African nationalist leaders.

1960 Monckton Commission formed to consider future of the Federation. Kariba Hydro-electric scheme opened.

1961 New constitutional proposals for Southern Rhodesia accepted in Referendum.
Widespread intimidation, arson, unrest, cattle-maiming in rural areas.

1962 Mr. Winston Field becomes Prime Minister in Southern Rhodesia's first Rhodesian Front Government.
New constitutions, allowing majority rule, granted to Northern Rhodesia and Nyasaland.
Unrest and disorder spread to urban areas.
Nyasaland given right of secession from the Federation.

1963 Federal and Northern and Southern Rhodesian governments send representatives to London for discussions on the future of the Federation.
Continuing reign of terror by African nationalist parties.
Northern Rhodesia given right of secession from the Federation.
(July) Conference on the break-up of the Federation.
(December) The Federation officially comes to an end.

1964 Mr. Field resigns and is replaced as Prime Minister by Mr. Ian D. Smith.
Southern Rhodesia becomes Rhodesia when the newly independent Northern Rhodesia becomes Zambia.
Rhodesian Prime Minister goes to Britain to discuss independence terms.
Domboshawa *Indaba* (Conference of Rhodesian African chiefs near Salisbury. Boycotted by British Government). Votes unanimously for independence from Britain.
Referendum on new constitution shows large majority in favour of independence although not necessarily unilaterally.
Rhodesian African Nationalist parties banned and leaders placed in detention.

1965 *(January)* Rhodesian Prime Minister goes to Britain for talks with British Prime Minister Harold Wilson.
(April) Rhodesian Government issues White Paper on the economic aspects of a possible U.D.I.
Guerrillas infiltrate from bases in Zambia and conduct a terrorist campaign.
(May) General Election. Rhodesian Front party wins large majority.
An African M.P. (for first time in Rhodesia's history) becomes Leader of the Opposition.
(October) Rhodesian Prime Minister with two Cabinet Ministers fly to Britain for talks on independence.
British Government announces five-point plan for Rhodesian independence.
Break-down of Anglo-Rhodesian talks.
British Prime Minister Harold Wilson flies to Salisbury.
Offers to appoint a Royal Commission to evolve a settlement scheme.
(November) Unilateral Declaration of Independence declared by Rhodesia.
Rhodesia expelled from sterling area and assets in Britain frozen.

(December) British Government introduces sanctions against Rhodesia including an oil embargo.

1966   *(May)* Rhodesian Prime Minister and colleagues meet British Prime Minister Wilson on H.M.S. Tiger.
New proposals for independence settlement rejected by Rhodesia.
British Government announces new point to be added to previous 5-point plan—NIBMAR (No Independence Before Majority African Rule).
Members of banned nationalist parties set up headquarters in Lusaka.

1967   Constitutional (Whaley) Commission appointed.
Many foreign countries join in embargoes against Rhodesia.

1968   United Nations Security Council adopts resolution calling for mandatory sanctions against Rhodesia.

1969   Referendum held to approve republican status and adoption of the new Constitution.

1970   Rhodesia becomes a republic and adopts new constitution. Mr. Clifford Dupont becomes the first President of the new Republic.
At the general election the Rhodesian Front wins all 50 European seats in the House of Assembly.
Rhodesian currency is decimalized.

1971   Proposals for a settlement agreed between the Rhodesian Prime Minister and Sir Alec Douglas Home, the British Prime Minister.
Proposals to be subject to a Commission reporting on acceptance of the terms by the people of Rhodesia as a whole.

1972   Pearce Commission conducts test of acceptability.
Pearce Report records overwhelming African rejection of the settlement terms.
(November) Britain renews Sanctions Order-in-Council.
Intensification of guerrilla infiltrations.

1973   *(January)* Rhodesia closes posts on Zambia-Rhodesia border
(February) Rhodesia re-opens border but Zambia keeps her side closed.

I
THE CONSTITUTIONAL
DISPUTE

THE ANGLO-RHODESIAN SETTLEMENT 1971-1972

As in previous years informal contact between the British and Rhodesian governments was maintained during 1971: a series of more formal talks was initiated in Salisbury in April and continued throughout most of the year. On November 15th these talks culminated in official negotiations between Mr. Ian D. Smith, the Prime Minister of Rhodesia, and Sir Alec Douglas-Home, the United Kingdom Secretary of State for Foreign and Commonwealth Affairs. An agreement on proposals to end the constitutional dispute was signed on November 24th 1971 by both parties.[1]

The proposals, which were subject to a test of acceptability by the people of Rhodesia as a whole, were mainly based upon recognition of the Rhodesian 1969 Constitution with certain modifications.[2] These modifications were: to increase African parliamentary representation, to introduce specially entrenched clauses with an agreed procedure for future amendments, and to effect the justiciability of the Declaration of Rights and the subsequent abolition of the Senate Legal Committee. Other proposals included the setting up of a commission, (terms of reference being set out in the proposals) to consider ways of progressing towards ending racial discrimination; a review of cases of detainees; plans for the development of the Tribal Trust Lands and other land for African occupation; the elimination of racial discrimination in the Public Service by the acceptance of merit and suitability as the only criteria for employment; and recommendations for ending the State of Emergency.

THE 1969 CONSTITUTION

In May 1969 a White Paper was published setting out proposals for a new republican constitution which was to be the subject of a referendum later in the year. The White Paper explained why the government believed it necessary for a new constitution to be introduced; namely, that the Constitution then in force contained a number of 'objectionable features' principally that 'it provides for eventual African rule and, inevitably, the domination of one race by another and... does not guarantee that government will remain in responsible hands.'

The proposed new constitution would ensure that government would remain in 'responsible hands' and would provide Africans with the right to play an increasing role in the government as they earn it by increased contributions to the national exchequer.[3]

The new republican constitution came into force on 2nd March 1970, following its acceptance by voters in a referendum in June 1969. Legislative power was vested in the President and in Parliament, the latter comprising the Senate and the House of Assembly.

SENATE

The Senate is composed of 23 persons, qualified on general grounds of age, length of residence, citizenship, etc. It comprises ten Europeans elected by an electoral college of European members of the House of Assembly; ten African chiefs (five from Mashonaland and five from Matabeleland) elected by an electoral college of chiefs who are members of the Council of Chiefs; and three other persons appointed by the President. Senate is empowered to recommend amendments to money bills, but not to delay them; to prevent enactment of bills to amend the Constitution or the entrenched provisions of its accompanying Electoral and Land Tenure Acts; to delay other bills for 180 days unless certified by the Prime Minister that they are urgent; and to appoint a Senate Legal Committee to examine statutory instruments and to report whether or not any of their provisions are inconsistent with the Declaration of Rights. The Senate Legal Committee, in effect, replaced the former Constitutional Council, an independent multi-racial body.

THE HOUSE OF ASSEMBLY

The House of Assembly consists of 66 members. Fifty European members elected by persons enrolled on the European voters' rolls (in the Constitution the term 'European' means any person not an African). Sixteen African members, of whom eight are elected on the basis of four each by Africans on the Mashonaland and Matabeleland African roll constituencies and eight elected on the basis of four each by electoral colleges comprised of chiefs, headmen and elected councillors of African Councils in the Tribal Trust Lands. Provision for an increase in African representation is made on the basis of income tax contributions. When the contribution of Africans exceeds 16 sixty-sixths of the total income tax contribution of both Europeans and Africans the procedure for increasing African representation will come into effect: African members will then be increased (two at a time by the electoral colleges and by voters on the African rolls alternately) in direct proportion to the increase in tax contributions in such a manner that when the contribution of Africans amounts to half the total contribution of Europeans and Africans combined the number of African members will be equal to the number of European members. Qualfications and electoral procedure are laid down in the Electoral Act.[4]

Qualifications for the European and African Rolls are the general ones of adult status (over 21 years of age), citizenship, residence, knowledge of English and ability to complete enrolment forms. Specific qualifications are—

For the European Roll:
a) Income for previous two years of not less than $ 1 800 *per annum* OR ownership of immovable property worth not less than $ 3 600;
b) Income for previous two years of not less than $ 1 200 *per annum* OR ownership of immovable property worth not less than $ 2 400 AND completion of four years of secondary education of a prescribed standard.

For the African Roll:
a) Income for the previous two years of not less than $ 600 *per annum* OR ownership of immovable property worth not less than $ 1 200;
b) Income for previous two years of not less than $ 400 *per annum* OR ownership of immovable property worth not less

than $ 800 AND 2 years secondary education of a prescribed standard.

For both rolls married women are deemed to have the same means qualifications as their husbands except, in the case of Africans, only the first wife would be eligible.

THE DECLARATION OF RIGHTS

The Declaration of Rights forms the second Schedule of the Constitution and provides the rights and freedoms, duties and responsibilities of citizens as set out in the preamble:

> Whereas it is desirable to ensure that every person in Rhodesia enjoys the fundamental rights and freedoms of the individual, that is to say, the right, whatever his race, tribe, political opinions, colour or creed, to life, liberty, security of the person, the enjoyment of property and the protection of the law, and to freedom of conscience, of expression and of assembly and association, and to respect for his private and family life;
>
> And whereas the exercise of these rights and freedoms gives rise to duties and responsibilities and should be subject to such formalities, conditions, restrictions or penalties as are prescribed by law and are necessary in a democratic society in the interests of national security, territorial integrity or public safety, for the prevention of disorder or crime, for the protection of health or morals, for the protection of the reputations, rights and freedoms of others, for preventing the disclosure of information received in confidence or for maintaining the authority and impartiality of the judiciary:
>
> And whereas, in particular, it is the duty of every person to respect and abide by the Constitution and the laws of Rhodesia and to respect the rights and freedoms of others and the public interest;
>
> And whereas loyalty to Rhodesia is a fundamental duty of every citizen;
>
> Now, therefore, the following provisions of this Schedule shall have effect for the purpose of prescribing the rights and freedom, duties and responsibilities for the purposes of this Constitution...

With reference to the Declaration of Rights, Section 84 reads: 'No court shall enquire into or pronounce upon the validity of any law on the ground that it is inconsistent with the Declaration of Rights.'

THE ENTRENCHED CLAUSES

The entrenched provisions of the 1969 Constitution relate to the composition of and election to the Senate and the House of Assembly; the constitution and powers of the High Court and Chief Justice; the appointment, qualifications, tenure of and removal from office, renumeration, oath of loyalty and judicial oath of judges; the definitions of laws to be administered; definitions and requirements for the passing of constitutional bills; and amendments to the entrenched provisions of the Electoral and Land Tenure Acts.

THE PROPOSALS FOR THE ANGLO-RHODESIAN SETTLEMENT

The proposals for a settlement provide for the creation of a new African Higher Electoral Roll with the same qualifications as those for Europeans in the 1969 Constitution and add four more categories to the African Lower Roll qualifications, *viz* :

1. Income of not less than $ 300 in the two years preceding the claim for registration OR ownership of immovable property to the value of $ 600 AND completion of 2 years secondary education of a prescribed standard;
2. Persons over 30 years of age with—
   a) an income at the rate of not less than $ 300 for the two years preceding application for enrolment OR ownership of immovable property to the value of not less than $ 600 AND completion of a course of primary education of a prescribed standard;
   b) income of not less than $ 430 for two years preceding the application OR ownership of immovable property worth not less than $ 400;
3. All kraal heads with a following of 20 or more families.

INCREASED AFRICAN REPRESENTATION

The proposals provide for the system of African representation, on the basis of the aggregate of income tax assessed on both Europeans and Africans, to be replaced by a system depending on the numbers of registered voters on the African Higher Roll. The present 16 African seats would remain and when the number of voters registered on the African Higher Roll equals 6 *per cent* of the number of voters registered on the European Roll, two additional African seats would become available. With each such proportionate increase of African voters further African seats would be created; two at a time elected in rotation by direct vote and by electoral colleges until there is equal representation in the House of Assembly.

When there are equal numbers of Africans and Europeans in the House (i.e. the present eight African members elected by the African Lower Roll, plus 18 members elected on the African Higher Roll and 24 members indirectly elected by the tribal electoral colleges), a referendum of African voters on both Rolls would be held to decide whether seats held by indirect election should be replaced by seats held by direct election by voters on the African Higher Roll.

Following the first general election after parity is reached, a Common Roll would be created from both the European and the African Higher Rolls to elect ten additional members, unless a special, independent commission on the question of representation, (with membership and terms of reference laid down in the agreement) should recommend a different arrangement acceptable to all the people of Rhodesia. Membership of Senate would remain as in the 1969 Constitution.

THE DECLARATION OF RIGHTS

A return to the pre-1969 right of enforcement of the Declaration was proposed. However, the provisions of an Act or statutory instrument which had been in force for a period of at least ten years prior to the enactment of the proposed 1972 Constitutional Amendment Act could not be pronounced as *ultra vires* on the grounds that its provisions are inconsistent with the Declaration. The section on preventive detention, without a Declaration of a State of Emergency, was to be retained but with a reduction in the period during which a person could be detained without ministerial order or review by the special Tribunal.[5] The formation of the Tribunal was to be subject to legal process and its members were no longer to be chosen by the President. The section on deprivation of property was to be amended to ensure that reasonable notice would be given and rights of compensation and of

the United States; Sir Maurice Dormer, a former Governor-General of Malta; Sir Glyn Jones, a former Governor of Nyasaland (and Governor-General when that country became Malawi); and Sir Frederick Pedlar, a former Colonial Office official in West Africa and an acknowledged expert on that part of Africa. The last-named, however, resigned shortly before the Commission was due to arrive in Salisbury.

During the interval before arrival in Salisbury 16 Commissioners were appointed and a booklet was prepared setting out a simplified version of the White Paper in English, Shona and Ndebele. It was proposed that these booklets be distributed in all the main centres and that the 16 Commissioners would be sent around the country to explain the proposals before the actual task of collecting evidence was begun.

Before the Commission arrived in Rhodesia both signatories to the Agreement took the opportunity of voicing their views on the question of modifying the proposals. Sir Alec Douglas-Home was quoted as saying that 'it is not possible, as some in Rhodesia have canvassed, to re-open negotiation. These proposals themselves, taken as a whole, represent the best that could be obtained by negotiation. If they are rejected, that will be the end of it. There would be no possibility of trying again.'[17] While Mr. Smith, in his New Year radio and television message said 'Let me make it quite clear that the terms signed on November 24th represent the limit of the concessions which we are prepared to make, and there will be no going back on these.'

The Commission, composed of its Chairman, three deputy chairmen, and some of the 16 commissioners, together with various officials charged with practical arrangements, arrived in Salisbury on the 11th January 1972. As an introduction to its work the Commission issued a press statement inviting individuals and organizations to state whether or not they regarded the settlement proposals as acceptable. Views in writing were invited in the first instance. The Commission announced that it was in Rhodesia to satisfy itself that the proposals, as set out in the British White Paper, had been 'fully and properly' explained and also 'to ascertain by direct contact with all sections of the population whether the people of Rhodesia as a whole regard these proposals as acceptable as a basis for independence; and to report back to the Foreign and Commonwealth Office accordingly.'[18]

At an introductory press conference shortly after his arrival Lord Pearce outlined plans for gathering the necessary information. Lord Pearce and his Deputy Chairmen would gather information, at the Commission's headquarters in Salisbury, from national organizations such as political parties, the Christian Council of Rhodesia and the Council of Chiefs, and would also make occasional field trips to observe the teams of commissioners at work. The commissioners would be divided into seven investigating teams to tour the country for an initial ten days according to a published itinerary, mainly to gather opinion from Africans in the tribal areas.[19]

THE TEST OF ACCEPTABILITY

In an editorial welcoming Lord Pearce and his team, the *Herald* discussed the task before the Commission and, in particular, the question of deciding whether freedom of expression would be available to all who would wish to give evidence. The newspaper was commenting on an interview that Lord Pearce had given to Mr. J. Orokoro, the diplomatic correspondent of *Africa Features* (a feature agency specialising in the African market), on the day before he left London. Mr. Orokoro had queried whether, in view of what leaders in Black African countries considered to be the lack of free expression in Rhodesia, it would not be very difficult for the Commission to ascertain the true opinions of the people. Lord Pearce had replied that he and the members of his commission were well aware of this difficulty and would do their best to overcome it.

The *Herald* considered that this seemed to imply that Lord Pearce believed that freedom of expression was lacking and that the biggest obstacle to frankness would be victimization by the Rhodesian authorities. It was not in question that there were existing inhibitions to freedom of expression, the editorial continued, but far more relevant would be the kind of mass intimidation practised in the early sixties by Africans against Africans, of which the whole country had bitter memories.[20]

Testing of opinions among persons living in the rural areas started on the 18th January with the stationing of two commissioners in each of the seven Provinces to hold meetings to explain the settlement terms to the people of the area. The commissioners, however, had to report that meetings at Fort Victoria, in the Tsonzo Purchase Area (near Umtali) and in the Urungwe Tribal Trust Land (near Karoi) were rowdy and undisciplined and meetings had had to be cancelled. The next day sporadic violence was reported at a meeting in Fort Victoria's Mucheke Township where police used tear gas to disperse small groups of rioters and it was reported that people giving evidence in Lower Gwelo Tribal Trust Land were intimidated by members of a singing and chanting crowd.[21]

Against a background of more serious disorder towards the end of the week it was necessary for Mr. Mark Patey, one of the commissioners, to warn the Que Que branch of the African National Council that less weight would be given to the views of people shouting 'No' at meetings where there was rowdyism. Mr. Patey also cautioned crowds at a meeting in Zhombe Tribal Trust Land (to the west of Gatooma and Que Que) that if he found any cases of intimidation he would ignore their votes. The *Herald* found it timely to comment at this stage that 'in their meticulous and efficient way, the commissioners are making it pretty plain to the whole country that it is the open hand held up at a meeting, rather than the clenched fist holding a rock, that will speak for Rhodesia.'[22]

In early February Bishop Abel Muzorewa, chairman of the anti-Settlement African National Council (A.N.C.), spoke of a 'grave, explosive intimidation of Africans by both the Government and European employers.'[23] Meanwhile, in Britain, the *Daily Express* spoke of a 'terror dossier', allegedly compiled by British officials working independently of Rhodesian intelligence services in Salisbury, which had been submitted to Whitehall and was said to reveal an 'operation well organized—and closely linked with outside "liberation movements"' and reporting that the African National Council was allegedly involved with other nationalist movements banned in Rhodesia.[24]

While denying that the Pearce Commission had been involved in the alleged reporting of professed A.N.C. participation in terror tactics, a spokesman for the Commission said that the British government had been requested to send two more commissioners to concentrate on investigating allegations of intimidation and interference in the expression of opinion. The two special commissioners, Mr. Aldhelm St. John Sugg (a former police officer and provincial commissioner in Northern Rhodesia) and Mr. Anthony Whitfield (a senior assistant in the British department of Public Prosecutions) were reported to be 'working ten hours a day sifting through hundreds of allegations of intimidation submitted by political parties, organizations, individuals and members of the Pearce Commission'. A summary of alleged government and European-employer intimidation of Africans handed to them by a six-member delegation from the African National Council received particular notice from the Press. It was claimed that the summary was a preliminary to the Council's 100-page dossier which would be handed over to the Pearce Commission within a week, and would contain letters, pamphlets, posters and other documents which, the A.N.C. claimed, indicated the degree of intimidation which Africans had suffered during the Pearce Commission's inquiry.[25]

On the same day another African group presented a memorandum to the Pearce Commission, this was the pro-Settlement Rhodesian Progressive Liberal Forum, which stated that 'the truth has been twisted by extremists who have advocated total rejection of the terms. They are using all kinds of hooligans in the urban African townships who are willing tools in the hands of extremists prone to violence and intimidation.' The Forum then went on to describe three groups who were, in its opinion, opposed to the settlement terms: 'Right-wing Europeans, who are just a small group of misguided white extremists; African extreme nationalists whose hopes and dreams of power would be completely destroyed if the proposals are accepted and put into practice [and] the opposition from church leaders...'[26]

At this stage it was surmised that the highly public method of presentation was not conducive to obtaining a satisfactory conclusion to the test of acceptability and it was reported that one of the Commissioners, Lord Harlech, who had flown to London, was discussing the possibility of using market research methods with the British Prime Minister and Foreign Office. This assumption was later denied by the Commission.[27]

INTIMIDATION

On the 7th April the local press published a *résumé* of the 26-page memorandum on intimidation which the Rhodesian government had sent to the Commission before its departure. It said, firstly, that 'the January riots throughout the country conditioned Africans to submit to African nationalist instructions. Intimidation therefore was completely effective'. It reviewed the history of African nationalism in Rhodesia and the reasons for banning certain African political parties. It then went on to link the African National Council with the intimidation and violence which had occurred during the sitting of the Pearce Commission, and alleged that widespread intimidation and 'other unlawful activity' followed the start of the anti-Settlement campaign initiated by the African National Council. It detailed numerous incidents occurring in the centres where violence had taken place and said 'these incidents were similar to those perpetrated by the African nationalists in the 1960's. The planned effect of the riots was to create a climate of fear in the mind of the Africans'. The memorandum further stated that 'There was a wealth of evidence showing that threats were made against people who voted "Yes", gave evidence to the Pearce Commission in private, failed to attend mass meetings organized by the nationalists, patronized beer-halls, failed to carry "No" cards on certain buses and who failed to display "No" stickers on their homes. Failure to respond [to the wholesale intimidation] was dealt with by murder, assault or burning of schools, churches, dipping tanks or private houses or malicious damage to property or stock—all of this directed against the innocent law-abiding Africans both in the towns and the rural areas.'[28]

Later in the month reports in the British press discussed a dossier of alleged intimidation by the Rhodesian authorities drawn up by a team of British lawyers in Salisbury, financed by the International Defence and Aid Fund. It was stated that the British lawyers, who had been in almost daily contact with the Commission, 'gathered a catalogue of detentions, arrests and threats to Africans and pressures on chiefs and headmen by District Commissioners... and in the private sector dismissals by European employers of workers who were known to have opposed the proposed settlement terms'.[29]

The attitude of the Pearce Commission members was summed up in the Pearce Report: 'The Rhodesian Government can fairly argue that there was a shadow of fears still lingering from the early 60's which it might be easy to bring back. On the other hand these fears were not entirely one-sided. There was also the fear of authority to counterbalance it in some measure. We do not regard the incidents of alleged intimidation, some without substance, some true, some probably true, some possibly true, as part of an overall political design. We believe them to be sporadic outbreaks of unjustifiable pressure to compel a minority to consensus and solidarity.'[30]

DISORDERS

The week before the arrival of the Pearce Commission, a meeting was held to discuss the settlement terms at the Humbani rest camp in the south-east of the Belingwe Tribal Trust Land.[31] The gathering apparently became restless when the police arrived on an errand not connected with the meeting and a riot ensued. A community adviser and a chief's messenger were severely injured and the two police vehicles were stoned; action which was followed by eleven arrests on charges of attempted murder, stoning and assault. This event was said to be the first political disturbance reported in Rhodesia for more than six years.[32]

At this time Mr. R. T. D. Sadomba, M.P. for Nemakonde, was quoted as saying that political feeling on the proposals was running pretty high in the African townships,[33] a warning which was soon borne out by reports of disturbances in Bulawayo and Gwelo townships over rumours of watered beer and poisoned sweets.

More serious trouble developed from the labour dispute at the Shabanie Mine which started as a dispute over the dismissal of several workers. The striking men rampaged through the African townships of Kodondo, Maglas and Nil, looting shops and destroying furniture and amenities in the beer-halls, mine offices and restaurants. At the height of the disturbance the police opened fire, one youth was killed and nine men were taken to hospital suffering from gunshot wounds, none being severely injured. It was reported in the press that the strike leaders were adamant that the disturbances were non-political, but the fact that the strike started on the day the Pearce Commission arrived in Salisbury gave rise to fears that the violence would escalate.[34]

Mr. T. H. P. Bashford, president of the Centre Party, considered it his duty 'to warn responsible Rhodesians that there is more than an even chance that the settlement proposals will be turned down unless action—I stress the word action—is taken to allay genuine African fears that they are being sold down the river', for he considered that mistrust was being fostered by the absence of any declaration in support of the proposals on the part of the six Rhodesian Front divisional chairmen.[35]

On the 16th January, the day before the Pearce Commissioners were due to begin their work of opinion testing, 'the most violent African demonstrations in Rhodesia since U.D.I. six years ago' erupted in the African townships of Gwelo. Most of the violence occurred in Monomotapa township but the disturbance is said to have manifested itself simultaneously in all three of the Gwelo townships of Monomotapa, Ascot and Mambo. Beer-halls, houses and shops were stoned and looted, an African church, motor vehicles and goods and passenger trains were stoned and a beer-hall and a newly-completed youth centre were badly damaged by fire. Police reservists and regular police armed with riot guns and shields, later backed by African and European army units, with automatic weapons, confronted the crowd aided by a spotter plane. Two volleys of tear and irritant gas shells were fired to disperse the mob but it was reported that 'by daylight it was apparent that crowds were being persistently harangued by hooligans to continue the pattern of unrest.' Several arrests were made.[36]

The disturbances at Monomotapa Township lasted for three days and the township was described as 'looking like a battle-field, with the streets littered with rocks and broken bottles and two buildings in flames'. Late in the afternoon of the third day a locomotive was derailed a short distance from the township. During the disturbances an African youth died from chest wounds reported to have been received by tripping over a log while running away from the police, two alleged looters received gunshot wounds and forty-two arrests were made, seven of which were for arson, public violence and allied offences. It was later estimated that damage during the three days of violence had cost more than $250 000.

In its editorial on the same day as the report on the violence at Gwelo, the *Herald* commented that 'normal political activity is one of the conditions agreed to by the Rhodesian Government. But there is nothing normal about what is happening in Gwelo. It is organized disruption. It would almost seem that its purpose —or a part of its purpose—is to make it impossible for the Pearce Commission to operate—to test opinion in conditions remotely resembling normal. ...it places not only the Pearce Commission in a dilemma, but the Rhodesian Government also.'[37]

By the evening of the 19th January the violence had spread to Salisbury's Harare Township. Gangs rampaged through the streets stoning vehicles and shops and setting fire to buildings and overturned cars. At one stage the rioting reached the edge of the city itself and shops along Charter Road had their windows smashed. Several Europeans and Asians who happened to be in the vicinity of the disturbances were injured. Later reports said that there were four deaths in the riots.[38] Minor disturbances were also reported at Salisbury's Tafara Township and Que Que's Amaveni Township.

A day later violent disturbances occurred in Umtali's Sakubva Township and it was reported later that eight Africans had been killed and 14 wounded. Twenty-four arrests were made following the stoning of police vehicles, the tearing up of a section of the railway line and attempts to invade Umtali's industrial sites.[39] Prompt action by the police averted other attempts at disturbances in Fort Victoria and Que Que, and by the end of the week all was reported to be peaceful.[40]

On the 21st January, Harold Pakendorf, reporter of the weekly *Rhodesian Financial Gazette*, considered that the outbreak of disorder that accompanied the Pearce Commission 'made it abundantly clear why the British and Rhodesian governments decided not to have a referendum as test of acceptability. The violence and intimidation Rhodesia would have seen then from those who want to have power now, is too appalling even to consider.'[41]

On the 16th February in his statement on the disorders, the Prime Minister said that 14 people had died and 1,505 people had been arrested during the riots. 'Of those arrested 278 are awaiting trial on specific charges; 415 have been convicted on various charges and 712 have been acquitted or released without trial. A further 100 cases are still under investigation.'[42]

Later in the year, in its report, the Pearce Commission summed up its impressions of the riots: 'No doubt the outbreak at Gwelo on 16th January lit the fuse which started a similar series of mass violence in other areas during the ensuing six days. But we have been given no convincing evidence that there was deliberate planning or political direction by the A.N.C. at the back of these outbreaks. It seemed to us that they were more likely to be spontaneous

uncontrolled outbursts than carefully organized violent demonstrations.'[43]

DETENTIONS

On the 10th December 1971, a government spokesman announced
that the government was actively engaged in processing the release
of the 31 detainees mentioned in Section IV of the White Paper
on the Settlement Proposals.[44]

On the 19th January it was reported that Mr. R. S. Garfield
Todd, a former Prime Minister of Southern Rhodesia, had been
arrested, together with his daughter Judith, the previous day in
terms of the Law and Order (Maintenance) Act.[45] Early protests
expressing 'deep concern' were made by Lord Pearce and the
World Council of Churches, while concern was expressed in
British government circles that the arrests would call into question
the whole basis of the conditions under which the Pearce Commission was operating.[46] A few days later it was announced that Mr.
J. Chinamano, the National Treasurer of the African National
Council, together with his wife, had also been arrested and placed
in detention.[47]

Two weeks later, having had 'no satisfactory explanation' from
the Rhodesian government about the detained persons, Lord
Pearce stated that because of 'the failure either to prefer charges
against them or to release them, the commission must infer that
the purpose of their detention is to inhibit the free expression
of their opinion. If this is the case the commission takes the view
that it constitutes an infringement of the provisions given in the
proposals agreed between the British and Rhodesian Governments
that ...during the test of acceptability normal political activities
will be permitted ... provided they are conducted in a peaceful
and democratic manner. So far as those taken into custody by
the police are concerned, the commission are still pursuing their
inquiries.' Lord Pearce also informed the government that he had
asked for the appointment of two more commissioners to investigate charges of intimidation, pressure and obstruction of the holding of meetings.[48] According to the Pearce Report 'No further
explanation was given by the Rhodesian Government nor were
any charges preferred up to the time we left Rhodesia.'[49]

On the 28th February, however, a Review Tribunal was set

up in terms of the Declaration of Rights in the Constitution. The regulations do not specifically give a detainee the right to appear personally before the Tribunal; in practice, however, detainees have always been given the opportunity to do so or to have a legal representative. During a three-day sitting held in camera the Tribunal, composed of Mr. Justice H. E. Davies, a High Court Judge, and Messrs. A. M. Bruce-Brand and M. C. Hagelthorn, heard witnesses and had personal interviews with the two African detainees. The two European detainees declined to appear on the grounds that 'there are aspects of the machinery of the review procedure which inhibit the Tribunal from arriving at a fair and just conclusion.'[50] The Tribunal members were unanimous in their recommendations and were satisfied that the continued detention of all four detainees was necessary in the interests of public safety and order. The reports however, because they contained security information, were not published.[51]

Members of the Pearce Commission referred to the detainees in their final report:

> The expression of their views to us was in no way interfered with since we were given ready access to them in detention... We have no evidence that they were planning disorders... although we are conscious that we may not have the full facts we feel compelled to infer that these detentions were an interference with normal political activities. But we do not think that they had any marked effect. Indeed we are inclined to think that they were counter-productive.[52]

REACTIONS TO THE TEST OF ACCEPTABILITY

EUROPEAN POLITICAL PARTIES AND ORGANIZATIONS

The Rhodesian Front

Shortly after the arrival of the Pearce Commission in Salisbury the *Sunday Mail* devoted its main editorial to a comment on the 'strange silence' of the 48 Rhodesian Front (R.F.) Members of Parliament and the R.F.'s office bearers. For, with the exception of the Prime Minister and the Minister of Foreign Affairs, Mr. J. H. Howman, who had both publicly undertaken to make the proposed new constitution work, no official statement had been made on behalf of the party. The editorial appealed to R.F.

members to 'speak out now, for there are still many who find it difficult to believe the party as a whole sincerely intends to back the Government's solemn undertakings.'[53] Later, following a radio appeal by the Prime Minister for public expressions of support for the proposals, seven R.F. members of parliament publicly expressed their support, although more than one of them indicated (as had the Prime Minister) their preference for the 1969 Constitution. The *Herald* considered that this line had played directly into the hands of the anti-settlement forces for 'this public hankering after the 1969 Constitution cannot fail to reinforce the suspicion that promises of different principles would be forgotten once British sanctions were removed and recognition given.'[54]

The Pearce Report commented: 'Indeed, one thing which struck ourselves and our Commissioners was how little had been done to commend the proposals to the population... No-one else stepped in to fill the vacuum created by the absence of any attempt by the administration to mount a campaign in favour of the Proposals. Little seems to have been done in the African areas by ministers, or the Rhodesian Front.'[55] By the end of January, however, the *Herald's* political reporter forecast a more active role by R.F. members following a parliamentary caucus meeting when concern was expressed about the trend of events.

In the same issue of the newspaper it was reported that Mr. A. S. Holland, M.P. for Salisbury North, addressing a party meeting, had accused the Pearce Commission of 'arrogance' in not accepting local advice on how best to test African opinion, and of precipitating the riots through ignorance of local conditions.[56] The Prime Minister was reported to have sent a 'strongly-worded letter' to the British Foreign Secretary also criticizing the Pearce Commission. These actions were later censured by Centre Party leader, Mr. Bashford, as showing that the R.F. was anticipating a 'No' vote and trying to exculpate itself in advance for 'the Rhodesian Front seeks to blame the British Government—and indeed everyone but the true culprit—the R.F. party itself. Is not the R.F.'s failure to conduct a campaign for acceptance of the settlement proposals a tacit admission of defeat?'[57]

The R.F. chairman, Mr. D. Frost, together with the deputy chairman and three of the six divisional chairmen, met the Pearce Commission in private on 4th February 1972. Mr. Frost's statement, later handed to the press, began by describing the support which the electorate had given in the last election when 77 *per cent* of all votes cast by European Roll voters had been for the R.F., which had won all 50 European seats in the House of Assembly. The statement then went on to say that government had explained the proposals to all six of the R.F.'s divisions and that, although reservations on certain points had been expressed, they had come to the conclusion that as the proposals were part of a package deal they could accept them in the best interests of the country.

The statement then went on to criticise the Pearce Commission saying that the delay in its arrival had 'resulted in agitators and self-seekers intimidating the African to such an extent that the progress and good relations that have been built up between the European and African over the last decade has suffered a serious set-back, I may say to the detriment of the African.' It concluded with an expression of regret at having to say to the Pearce Commission 'as visitors to our country... that the sooner your commission completes its task and returns to England the sooner we shall be able to return to the peace and tranquillity that Rhodesia has enjoyed for the last decade.'

Editorial comment the same day considered that the Rhodesian Front's evidence hardly gave unequivocal support for the settlement terms. On the contrary, it was 'carping and complaining'. Nor did the Party pledge itself to implement the terms in both letter and spirit, which would have been 'of the utmost importance at this stage in the Pearce Commission's proceedings.'[58]

The Prime Minister's press conference a few days later evoked criticism that he was unconvincing in his attempt to explain what Mr. Frost and his fellow party office-bearers had said to the commission. This in turn had led to the conclusion that basic differences existed between the government and the R.F.[59] As a magazine article by Gordon Ross put it 'the R.F. Government, once the epitome of solidly-based Right-wing opinion, finds itself in a wretched dilemma. It is under fire from the Left, from the African as represented by the A.N.C., for promising too little and too late— and for being likely to give even less than it is promising. And it is under fire from the Right, the white Right, for giving away too much, too soon—and, indeed, for giving away anything at all'.[60]

At the time when the settlement agreement was signed the other European parties consisted of the Republican Alliance and the

Rhodesia National Party. There were also pressure groups such as the Conservative Association, the Conservative Group and the Candour League. Later, in February 1972, the United Front was formed.

The Republican Alliance

In mid-December 1971 the *Sunday Mail's* editorial, entitled *Speak Now or Never*, posed certain questions and commented upon them. 'What can have happened to the far right-wing of Rhodesian politics? The settlement proposals contain a whole arsenal of weapons the white supremacists could fire, yet they have been remarkably silent. Why are they silent, when men of other persuasions are freely putting their views? It is certainly not because they find the proposals acceptable.'[61]

Commander C. W. Phillips, chairman of the Republican Alliance (R.A.), was the first to respond when he drew attention to the fact that, on November 30th, political correspondents of the press had been handed a factual written statement of the R.A.'s stand against the proposals. Commander Phillips asked the newspaper to make an 'honourable reparation', for ignoring this statement, and to publish it in full without amendment.

As Commander Phillips had requested the newspaper printed the statement in full. It began by outlining the 'true purpose' for which the Rhodesian Front had been formed and then went on to claim that the Republican Alliance 'has held and will hold to the R.F.'s original purpose... to preserve all Rhodesians of all races from the tyranny inevitable under Black rule' and that 'also like the R.F. the Republican Alliance believes that the African must be given a fair chance to develop himself and his own areas but that this does not mean the European should destroy himself and his civilization to achieve it.'

The statement continued with the R.A.'s interpretation of the White Paper which it described as resembling 'a contract drawn up by two clever lawyers, each of whom desired that the subjects of the contract should have the greatest difficulty in understanding what they were letting themselves in for' and then went on to criticise the section dealing with the test of acceptability which stated that radio and television time would be made available only to political parties represented in the House of Assembly, coming to the conclusion that as 'former African nationalist parties now banned do not legally exist... the exclusion was not aimed at them... [and] must have been designed to hinder the conservative element of the European population in making their fellow Rhodesians aware of the dangers implicit in the proposals.'

With regard to the effects of the new Higher electoral roll, the R.A. considered that this, combined with the African development programme, would mean that progress towards parity in the numbers of European and African M.P.'s would be 'progressively accelerated'. The R.A. could foresee, therefore, that once parity was reached a stalemate would ensue when 'the only way the deadlock can be broken and an operating government be formed is for a European who sides with the Africans to win a European seat. That the contrary should happen is more than unlikely because there are more liberals among the Europeans than conservatives among the Africans. The Rhodesian Government would then consist of 50 African M.P.'s and one European M.P. which is government by Africans without further argument.'

The sections dealing with the Entrenched Clauses in the Constitution Electoral Act were described as being 'designed by the British to prevent any alterations to the constitution or franchise qualifications which might impede the progress towards majority rule' and comments were made on the Declaration of Rights; the review of the Land Tenure Act; the commission to make recommendations on ending racial discrimination; the government's intention of making more land available for Africans when the need arose; and employment on merit in the civil service.

The statement concluded with a discussion of the erosion of sanctions and the effect of the British entry into the Common Market on their effectiveness, and ended with the comment—'under these circumstances it remains a mystery why the R.F. leaders now tell us we must give up the fight when we have already paid such a heavy price over the last six years to gain the true purpose for which the Rhodesian Front was formed.'[62]

On the 6th February 1972, Commander Phillips presented the Pearce Commission with the R.A.'s rejection of the settlement terms on the grounds that if they were implemented European civilization in Rhodesia could not be. preserved.[63] The Pearce Report says that it had been decided that the hearings should start with taking the views of those political parties represented in the House of Assembly and of the African National Council. However, during this series of hearings the commissioners also heard from two other parties; the Republican Alliance and the Congress National Union. On the Republican Alliance the Pearce Report comments that the R.A. explained that its 'over-riding principle was the preservation of European civilization in Rhodesia. They could find nothing in the proposals to support these principles and accordingly rejected them. We read in the press of other bodies who took the same view. But these took their opposition to the point of not recognizing our enquiry.'[64]

The Rhodesia National Party

According to *Herald* reporter John Kelley the Rhodesia National Party (R.N.P.) is 'a very small group—the total membership of which is kept a secret'. He describes its leader's message as a direct one—'that the Rhodesian Front is about to hand over the country to the black man' and his policy as 'stark simplicity—for the continuance of white rule for Rhodesia and an end to what he sees as Britain's plan for a total black Africa'.[65]

As early as 24th December 1971, the *Financial Gazette* commented that, following the announcement of the settlement terms, there was new life on the Right and that if there was to be opposition to the ruling Rhodesian Front party by Europeans it would 'most probably be at its most effective if it does come from the Right'.[66]

However, it was not until the 10th February 1972 that right-wing parties held the first of a series of public meetings to enable right-wing leaders to put their views to the public. The first meeting, in Salisbury, was chaired by a former Cabinet Minister and former founder member of the Rhodesian Front, Mr. W. R. Harper. The three speakers were Mr. L. Idensohn, the R.N.P. leader, Dr. I. Anderson of the Candour League, and Mr. J. Redmond, the president of the Republican Alliance.

The three speakers were described by a monthly periodical (which describes itself as 'entirely independent' but is widely held to be a proponent of *ultra* right-wing views) as being 'not as effective as the occasion demanded [but] just three citizens with the guts to say what they and we feel'—the latter sentiment being a quotation from a member of the audience.[67]

At the meeting Mr. Idensohn said that he considered the Pearce Commission was in Rhodesia as a kind of 'Trojan Horse' to collect classified information as to the effect and evasion of sanctions, mineral exports and local industry.[68] At a later meeting Mr. Idensohn gave his reasons for not joining the recently formed United Front Party and went on to say that 'I wish to make it quite clear that the R.N.P. as a party still stands and will continue to stand as the only right-wing party in Rhodesia.'[69]

The Candour League sponsored another right-wing public meeting on the 9th March. Mr. L. Idensohn was one of its four speakers and, according to the *Herald,* drew the loudest applause when 'he donned a black gauntlet, raised his fist in the black power salute and said black power had never taken away white rule in Africa—it had been the white hand in the black glove'.[70]

The Rhodesia National Party is not mentioned as having given evidence in the Pearce Report.

The Conservative Association

The chairman of the Conservative Association, Mr. A. Hubbard, resigned to join the Rhodesia National Party early in January and was replaced, as acting chairman, by Mr. P. Young, a Salisbury businessman, at a meeting of the Association's executive committee. At the same time the committee passed a resolution calling upon its members to reject the proposals on the grounds, as reported in the press, that 'The Rhodesian Government had no right to discuss a settlement but only to negotiate recognition. The association did not consider the proposals to be in the national interest. The proposals negated U.D.I. [and that] in a matter of such importance as the survival of Western Christian civilization our Government should not be afraid to hold a referendum based on the electoral roll.'[71]

On the 3rd February the Association announced its rejection of the proposals giving as its reasons the view that they 'legally bound Rhodesia to a political ideology constitutionally directed towards African majority rule' and that the proposals 'removed the principle of free democratic elections by removing from the electorate the free right of choice of government and vested in the constitution veto powers over legislation.'[72]

The Conservative Group

The Conservative Group was organized by Mr. J. Whiting who, even before the settlement terms were announced, resigned as vice-president of the Republican Alliance in order, as he said, 'to assist in the re-organization of conservative opinion in Rhodesia'. This action was seen by the *Sunday Mail* as indicative that 'the ultra-Rightists hope to repeat the early history of the Rhodesian Front.'[73] In a later interview with the press, Mr. Whiting spoke of the possibility of a new right-wing party being formed, but added that it was important that the conservative vote should not be split, since the organization of right-wing opinion was essential if election strategy was to be formulated in time.[74]

By March, however, reporter Paul Juhl, commenting in the *Mail* on the possibility of a general election in the near future, stated that 'little has been heard recently of the Rhodesian Conservative Group initiated by Mr. Jack Whiting, the Salisbury city councillor and defector from the Republican Alliance... Mr. Whiting tried to get a new political party off the ground, but if he succeeded he must be a member of the most secretive party in the country. It appears that he has not joined forces with the United Front.'[75] Mr. Juhl, however, was taken to task, in the following week's issue of the *Mail*, by Mr. E. R. Wright of the United Front's press relations office who said 'the fact, which could have been ascertained by Mr. Juhl with a little trouble, is that Mr. Whiting's party, the Conservative Group, unanimously decided, at the inaugural meeting which formed the United Front to join the U.F.'[76]

The Candour League

Dr. I. Anderson became chairman of the Candour League in 1965 after resigning as branch chairman of the Rhodesian Front party. He stood as an independent candidate in the three-candidate by-election at Mabelreign in August 1971 and was only narrowly defeated (by 68 votes) by the Rhodesian Front candidate, Mr. J. C. Gleig. The election was later described by the Centre Party leader, T.H.P. Bashford, as being significant because 'more votes were cast against the R.F. than for it.'[77]

On the 26th January, the League made a statement on its attitude towards the settlement proposals which said that as it believed the British government had no standing in Rhodesia it would not give evidence to the Pearce Commission. In a further statement on the 7th February the League forecast that if the settlement proposals were accepted Black majority rule would be in force within a period of ten years.[78]

A few weeks later the League made another statement reiterating that the proposals would not provide independence for Rhodesia. The following day it was responsible for another meeting in the series given for right-wing leaders to put their views before the public. At this meeting Dr. Anderson denied reports of disunity among right-wing groups.[79]

The United Front

The decision to form a new right-wing party was taken at a meeting on the 17th February 1972, at which several right-wing organizations and parties were represented. The resolution, for which there was unanimous support, stated in part that 'a new party called the United Front be formed tonight containing the overriding principle that the white man's position must be supreme for all time.'[80] The following Sunday, the *Mail* commented that the newly-formed party seemed to be a sort of 'mini-*broederbond*'.[81]

On the 9th March the United Front was represented at one of the series of meetings of the right-wing leaders. *The Financial Gazette* saw this meeting as 'underscoring the point' of white uneasiness about the proposals for 'they accept it because it is a package deal but very many are by no means wholeheartedly behind it. They argue that they have been doing quite well so far and see little advantage for themselves in the proposals and a great deal for the Africans.'[82]

Shortly afterwards it was reported in the press that two U.F. party meetings planned for the Wankie constituency had been cancelled on the instructions of the Ministry of Internal Affairs in terms of the Emergency Powers regulations.

The following week the *Financial Gazette* again criticized the new party for being 'strong on emotion but weak on logic' and, in view of its stated aim of keeping the white man's position supreme for all time, enquired 'how 250 000 people (not even remotely united...) are going to remain supreme in a country where they are outnumbered 21 to one'. The newspaper then answered its own question by saying that 'until the United Front can tell Rhodesians how it intends the White man to remain 'supreme' in Rhodesia with justice to all racial groups, we shall consider their objective unbelievable and unattainable.'[83]

THE MULTI-RACIAL CENTRE PARTY

The November 1971 issue of the Centre Party's newspaper *Centrepoint* devoted about half of its contents to speculations by various people on the prospects for a settlement. An article by the Centre Party (C.P.) president, Mr. T. H. P. Bashford, commented that 'even assuming that a termination of the Anglo-Rhodesian quarrel is "in the bag", will whatever is agreed upon between Mr. Smith and the British Government provide a genuine settlement? The one certainty that has arisen from U.D.I. is that Rhodesians of all races must look to themselves for a resolution of their country's problems.'[84]

In the next issue of *Centrepoint* Mr. Bashford considered that his party was feeling a sense of anti-climax, for the proposals appeared to have been 'lifted' in large measure from Centre Party policy. He warned, however, that 'settlement proposals are meaningless unless people of all races are prepared to accept them in good faith on their face value and consciously strive to make them work.' He also cautioned Africans not to repeat their mistake of the previous decade when they had boycotted the 1962 elections for which 'they have paid... with ten years of political, social and economic stagnation—even retrogression.'

In its editorial in the same issue *Centrepoint* hoped that the C.P. would be forgiven for 'waxing less than lyrical' about some aspects of the proposals, but 'in commending the package with all its defects to our supporters, we are satisfied that it is the best that can be expected in the circumstances.'[85]

In a Christmas Eve article, the *Financial Gazette* attempted a forecast. With regard to the Centre Party, a difficult period was envisaged in the near future, for the newspaper considered that 'it has almost no support from the White electorate and made a fairly good showing at the last election among African voters mainly because it was the best organized group in the field. With ex-detainees now beginning to shout—once again—their all-or-nothing demands, it is foreseeable that the C.P. will also lose out among African voters.'[86]

In the January 1972 issue, *Centrepoint* took the opportunity of drawing up a balance sheet on the settlement proposals in response, as it stated, to the many requests it had received. The balance sheet was particularly addressed to the African people for, as the article said 'they, unlike the Europeans, have not been represented

in the negotiations.' Before examining the various points in details
the article drew attention to, what the C.P. considered to be, two
important points:

1. This is a compromise settlement. It is necessary to look at
   all the good points, and all the bad points, balance them
   against each other, and then decide whether the whole package deal is a good thing or not.
2. We do not have a choice between this particular settlement
   and some other settlement... the question is 'Is this compromise settlement better than no settlement at all?'

In the same issue the editorial regarded the settlement terms as
a challenge; in it the C.P. declared that it made 'no apology for
insisting that mere passive acquiesence... is not sufficient. Much
more is needed. Progress ought by now to be well under way—and
ought to be seen to be well under way—in the dismantling of
the shabby edifice of racial discrimination that has been built up
over the past decade. On another page the C.P. stated that it would
be failing in its duty to the nation 'if it did not point out that
the whole settlement may be prejudiced by lack of vision on the
part of the Prime Minister and his colleagues. The take-it-or-leave-
it attitude currently displayed by the Rhodesian Front Government is unfortunate... it is vital that the Government should reas-
sure Africans by making an immediate gesture of good faith.'[87]

Even before the arrival of the Pearce Commission the C.P. began
to press for the recall of Parliament for, as its leader said, 'only
in the glare of publicity surrounding the proceedings of Parliament
can the government obtain a platform to establish and show its
sincerity in implementing the promises contained in the proposals.'[88]

In mid-January six of the party M.P.'s (all of whom are Africans)
had a two-hour meeting with the Prime Minister who gave them
an assurance that the government intended to honour both the
letter and the spirit of the proposed settlement constitution. When
reporting this meeting later, however, a C.P. statement reiterated
that it remained 'convinced that the best forum in which African
doubts regarding the good faith of the Government can be allayed
is Parliament.'[89]

The campaign to recall Parliament, however, was unsuccessful
for, although Parliament was recalled, as scheduled, on the 29th
February, it sat for only one and three-quarter hours at the end

of which the Minister of Justice, Mr. D. W. Lardner-Burke, moved that the House be adjourned until 2nd June. In introducing the motion the Minister said that he believed that it might be necessary for a recall of Parliament at an earlier date, depending upon the information which would, in due course, be received from the British government and that he was moving the adjournment as 'my colleagues have indicated to me that they have nothing of such urgency as to cause it to sit at the moment.'

On the 19th January, Mr. R. T. D. Sadomba, political secretary of the Centre Party, announced his resignation. He explained that this action had been taken in response to calls from his constituency, in order that he might campaign for a rejection of the proposals. In commenting upon Mr. Sadomba's resignation, the Party leader said that the decision had not come as a surprise for, in his opinion, 'the ground was literally cut from beneath the feet of our M.P.'s when the Prime Minister refused to recall Parliament... By this refusal Mr. Smith deprived our M.P.'s of their constitutional rights to lay before the House of Assembly the doubts and fears of their constituents concerning the settlement proposals.'[90]

Later in his evidence to the Pearce Commission, Mr. Sadomba is reported to have said that the Africans in his constituency overwhelmingly rejected the proposals because 'we cannot afford to legalize our perpetual subjugation. It will be a sin to go against our own conscience and it is evil to commit our future generations to this unsatisfactory and deceitful document arranged by the two White Governments without any regard for our African race's opinion.'[91]

On the 26th January a party delegation, led by Mr. Bashford, gave evidence to the Pearce Commission. In explaining why the C.P. accepted the proposals 'under duress' the statement given to the press outlined some of the points made: 'The Centre Party exists because we are convinced that there can be no racial peace in Rhodesia except under a genuine non-racial meritocracy. We support the Settlement proposals, with reservation, because we believe they are a small step towards this end. We are only too aware of the tenuous value of an agreement that represents a complete reversal of R.F. principles and policies which has neither been debated in Parliament, nor indeed ratified by a congress of the Rhodesian Front Party.'[92]

In mid-February the C.P. held a public meeting to discuss the proposals, which was timed to coincide with the C.P.'s radio and television broadcast, which had been the subject of heated exchanges between Mr. Bashford and the Rhodesia Broadcasting Corporation over the interpretation which the Corporation's Board of Governors had placed upon the White Paper's reference to broadcasting time for political parties 'represented in the House of Assembly'. The Board's decision had been to allow broadcasts by Members of Parliament only while the C.P. insisted upon its right to nominate whomsoever it chose to represent it.

The C.P. political broadcast took place during the public meeting, which had as its theme *deeds to end deadlock*, and was relayed to it. Mr. Bashford took the opportunity of outlining the political, economic and social dangers facing Rhodesia if the settlement proposals were rejected. The meeting as a whole was told why the Centre Party supported the proposals and the chairman, Mr. N. J. McNally, supported by Mr. Bashford, said that 'If the Pearce Commission finds it impossible to say that the settlement proposals have been found to be acceptable, then I believe that the Conservative Party and the Rhodesian Government must have the courage to implement the settlement proposals.'[93]

The meeting was followed up in an article by Mr. Bashford in *Centrepoint*. Mr. Bashford considered that the implementation of the proposals would be the only politically safe course for the country to take and, in commenting upon the polarization of opinion, asked 'can anyone read into African non-acceptance of the proposals a preference for the *status quo?* Dare we read into the overwhelming European acceptance of the proposals a rejection of the 1969 Constitution as it stands?'[94]

AFRICAN POLITICAL PARTIES AND ORGANIZATIONS

The African National Council

The African National Council (A.N.C.) was formed, according to its chairman, Bishop Abel T. Muzorewa, in response to the African call for a united front to oppose the settlement proposals and to represent the voice and will of the silent African majority. One of its main aims was 'to explain, advise and expose the dangerous implications that would result if they [the African people] accepted the Anglo-Rhodesian constitutional settlement proposals.'[95]

On the day following the launching of the A.N.C. a rally was held in Harare African Township in Salisbury and the crowd was invited by the speakers, 'all of whom were under some form of restriction which prevented their names from being published, to reject the proposals and to spread the word in the townships, the beer-halls, the compounds and the Tribal Trust Lands.' The speakers urged the crowd 'to act responsibly and not to get involved in anything that could be construed as intimidation.'[96]

In early January the *Financial Gazette* devoted an article to an interview with Bishop Muzorewa. The Bishop was reported as saying that if the Pearce Commission was objective, it would find that the overwhelming majority of Rhodesians was opposed to the settlement proposals. He claimed that the settlement proposals were 'a constitutional rape of Africans' by both the Rhodesian and British governments and that the proposals themselves were nothing but a 'vicious and subtle device by the British for the recognition of U.D.I.'[97]

In mid-January the A.N.C. organized a further meeting at Harare Township where a crowd of more than one thousand people 'shouted their approval when A.N.C. speakers condemned Sir Alec Douglas-Home, Ian Smith, the British Government and the Rhodesian Front.' When asked by the A.N.C. organizing secretary, Mr. John Cherisa, whether they accepted the proposals he was answered by a roar of 'NO-NO-NO'. Mr. Cherisa said that it was 'totally wrong, unchristian and ungodly' of Sir Alec to discuss the issue without Africans being represented and reminded his hearers of events in South Africa after 1909 when a minority independence had been granted to South Africa. Mr. Cherisa ended his speech by an appeal to his listeners to avoid all violence and intimidation.[98]

During the same week-end it was announced in the press that a London lawyer, Mr. Bernard Sheridan, had arrived in Salisbury to advise the A.N.C. on the drafting of its views on the settlement proposals for submission to the Pearce Commission. Mr. Sheridan said that he had been instructed by the International Defence and Aid Fund for Southern Africa to carry out this task. He was originally to have accompanied Sir Dingle Foot but the latter had been denied entry into Rhodesia.[99]

Following reports of the disorders at Belingwe, Fort Victoria, Shabani and Gwelo, Bishop Muzorewa and the national deputy chairman, the Rev. Canaan Banana, issued a joint statement attributing the events to a spontaneous reaction to frustration by the African people and claiming that it was not until the police had intervened that the people had become violent.[100]

At the end of January, Bishop Muzorewa led a delegation of A.N.C. members at a two-hour session with Lord Pearce and his deputy chairmen. The Bishop, as chairman of the A.N.C., presented a formal statement giving a detailed rejection of the settlement terms while other members of the delegation criticized particular aspects of the proposals, describing them as 'a political conspiracy to assassinate the political future of the Africans now and for all time.'[101]

Shortly afterwards the Bishop flew to England where he was scheduled to give a press conference at the House of Commons; to address a meeting at Ruskin College, Oxford; and to speak at a mass rally in Trafalgar Square.[102] He then paid a ten-day visit to New York, where he addressed a special meeting of the United Nations Security Council. It was reported that the Bishop called for an intensification of sanctions; accused white officialdom and employers in Rhodesia of using intimidatory tactics during the test; suggested that the large sums of money promised for African development in the tribal areas be used instead for the repatriation of whites who would not want to co-exist with Africans in a Rhodesian state under majority rule; and reiterated the A.N.C.'s hopes for a constitutional conference in place of the settlement proposals.[103]

At the end of February the *Sunday Mail* reporter, Charles Catchpole, wrote an article on Bishop Abel Muzorewa, who had decided to accede to requests to lead the A.N.C. because he considered the settlement proposals were unjust. In his article, entitled *ANC leader : reluctant politician,* Mr. Catchpole outlined the Bishop's views on the current situation. Describing him as 'no spluttering demagogue, no skilful rabble-rouser', Mr. Catchpole quoted the Bishop as saying 'I am not a politician. I am not concerned with politics, I am merely engaged in seeing through an issue which I consider to be a completely moral one. One hears a lot about the "benefits" of the settlement deal. I don't want something that will benefit Africans, something that will benefit whites, or something that will benefit any particular section of Rhodesian society. My only desire is for a settlement that is just. If there is justice for all men in the proposals, that's fine. If there is not then they must be rejected.' Going on to refer to the disorders which had taken place at the beginning of the Pearce Commission's enquiry the Bishop said 'I am a non-violent man and I renounce any kind of violence. For the Pearce Commission to pack up and go home because of the work of trouble-makers would be a disaster for the A.N.C. and the African people. We want nothing more than for them to conclude their task and report the honest, peacefully expressed opinions of the people of Rhodesia.'

With regard to the report that he had advocated the repatriation of Rhodesian whites when majority rule had been achieved, the Bishop said that the report had been incorrect, he had suggested that if there were any Europeans who felt that they could not live under a black government or work with Africans they should be financially compensated and repatriated if that was what they wanted.

Mr. Catchpole then took the opportunity of asking the Bishop what he thought of 'White liberals in Rhodesia [who] were baffled and hurt by the A.N.C. rejection of the settlement proposals because they considered them to be an advancement on the 1969 Constitution, and a symbol of hope for the African?' The Bishop answered that he was 'just sorry that they do not see the dangers we see. We look at the history of this country and we see liberal laws that have been whittled away. That is our over-riding fear.'[104]

The A.N.C. was formally reconstituted into a political organisation on the 10th March 1972.[105] Bishop Muzorewa remained as its leader and said that one of its main aims would be to advocate the calling of a constitutional conference in which elected African representatives would participate.

The Banned African Nationalist Parties

Following the signing of the Smith-Home Agreement, journalist Justin Nyoka reported in *Moto* that African leaders condemned the proposals. He quoted a statement by a former leader (now restricted to the Salisbury area) of the Zimbabwe African Peoples' Union (Z.A.P.U.) which said that the proposals erred against the basic democratic principle of majority rule and also criticized the

proposed test of acceptability on the grounds that political meetings could not be held while leaders of the African nationalist parties were in either detention or restriction and that no genuine
assessment of opinion could be held 'under the shadow of a state
of emergency and fear of reprisal...' Another statement, made by
Mr. Michael Mawema, a former member of the Zimbabwe African
National Union (Z.A.N.U.), postulated that the proposals not only
failed to meet the African demand for majority rule but also failed
to meet the five principles as laid down by Britain. He advised
Africans not to believe that the banned parties would ever return
and urged them therefore 'to consolidate and reconstitute ourselves
and meet the challenge.'

Two weeks later *Moto* reported the formation of a nationwide
organization to be known as the African National Council. It gave
details of the membership of the national executive which, besides
Bishop Muzorewa and the Rev. C. Banana, included former top
executive members of the banned parties, three of whom were
still under restriction and could not be named, the others being
Messrs. M. Mawema, A. Chadzingwa, C. C. Ngcebetsha and the
Rev. H. H. Kachidza.[106]

Later in written evidence to the Pearce Commission, Mr. Joshua
Nkomo, former leader of Z.A.P.U., (whose memorandum was
reported in the Pearce Report as representative of documents submitted by other detainees interviewed by the Commission) itemized the reasons why he considered the proposals should be
rejected 'in the strongest possible terms'. He appealed to Lord
Pearce 'to impress upon the British Government to abandon these
proposals and summon a constitutional conference at which leaders
of all sections of our population will take part.'[107]

The Rhodesia African Party

Early in the new year the *Herald* reported that Mr. E. Mhlanga,
president of the Rhodesia African Party and vice-president of the
4 000-strong Rhodesian National Voters' Association, had stated
that the proposals offered the African people opportunities for
employment, improved education, progress and 'general well-being'. He criticized 'certain people and organizations who were
engaging in anti-settlement activities' and said that these were only
a 'small voice' consisting mainly of urbanized Africans and he won-
dered whether they realized the effect a rejection would have on

the chances of African progress. He queried whether 'these people [are] perhaps hoping that rejection of the proposals will result in greater power for themselves?'[108]

Towards the end of the month Mr. Mhlanga appealed to 'the five million Africans of Rhodesia' not to be misled by nationalists and warned them against repeating the mistake they had made in the 1962 general election when nationalists had urged them not to allow their names to go on the voters' rolls in order that Sir Edgar Whitehead's United Federal Party would lose the election to the Rhodesian Front 'which would in turn be toppled by Britain'. Mr. Mhlanga went on to say 'if there is not a settlement on the basis of these proposals the 1969 Constitution will stay with us. Is this what Africans really want? I beg them to think for themselves and to accept these proposals while there is still time.'[109]

The National Peoples' Union

In the 1970 general election the National Peoples' Union (N.P.U.) was the only all-African party to have a member elected to the House of Assembly. He was the late Mr. J. M. Gondo, M.P. for Kunyasi and acting-president of the N.P.U. At the beginning of 1972, however, Mr. L. Mbanga, secretary general of the N.P.U., announced that steps were being taken to expel Mr. Gondo from the party because he, unlike the majority of other members of the party, was in favour of the settlement. Mr. Mbanga also said that plans were in hand for merging with the African National Council.[110] Mr. Gondo, however, said he had no intention of resigning either from the N.P.U. or from his parliamentary seat. He then dismissed five members of the executive committee of the N.P.U.[111]

This action produced a curious situation later in January when a four-man delegation to present evidence to the Pearce Commission on behalf of the N.P.U. was found to contain two of the 'sacked' officials. The delegation read a prepared seven-page statement putting forward the views of the N.P.U. and recording the party's total rejection of the proposals.[112] During the second week in March Mr. L. Mbanga announced the dissolution of the N.P.U. and urged members to support the African National Council.

The Rhodesia Electoral Union

The eight African M.P.'s, who were elected in 1970 by electoral colleges, shortly after election organized themselves into a party political caucus under the leadership of Mr. R. C. Makaya, M.P. for Lowveld, and took the name of the Rhodesia Electoral Union (R.E.U.). By the middle of 1971 it was estimated that the R.E.U. had about sixty branches throughout the tribal areas.

During January 1972 it was reported that Mr. D. M. Namate, M.P. for Tuli, was to explain the settlement proposals to African chiefs and their followers in Tshatshani Tribal Trust Lands (in Matabeleland). Mr. Namate explained that he himself was not satisfied with the proposals for they did not go far enough—'the time to achieve majority rule is too long'—but that he would not advise the people to accept or reject the proposals although, from previous meetings on the subject with his constituents, he had gained the impression that they also were not satisfied.[113]

Following the disorders during the test of acceptability, the R.E.U., at a party meeting with the Pearce Commission on 24th January, called for the suspension of the test. The R.E.U. delegation also submitted a memorandum which the Commission afterwards printed in full in its final report. In its preamble the statement read: 'We, the members of the Rhodesia Electoral Union, who are Representatives of 5 1/2 million people in Rhodesia are giving the views of the majority of Africans who have not been able to say "No", in the presence of the Commissioners.' The statement then went on to detail nine reasons why the R.E.U. was 'emphatically' rejecting the proposals.[114]

ORGANIZATIONS ARISING OUT OF THE TEST OF ACCEPTABILITY

Apart from the rise of two political organizations (the African National Council and the United Front) the period of the test of acceptability gave rise to other non-political organizations such as the People Against Racial Discrimination (P.A.R.D.); the Committee to Organize Support for a Settlement (C.O.S.S.); and two African-led pro-settlement groups—the African Progressive Council and the Rhodesian Progressive Liberal Forum. With the exception of the African Progressive Council these organizations all started their activities following the period of initial violence which accompanied the arrival of the Pearce Commission, a period which, as the *Herald's* London Bureau said, 'has shocked the Europeans out of a mood of potential hope into one of mistrust, doubt, suspicion... There is now an almost desperate fear that the settlement with Britain will break down.'[115]

P.A.R.D. was formed on the 15th February 1972, 'to counter racial discrimination and to promote African acceptance of the settlement proposals', under the chairmanship of Mr. K. Mew, who outlined the organization's plans and later announced that the group would give evidence to the Pearce Commission in support of the settlement. Mr. Mew said that the settlement terms provided 'the instrument for the removal of racial discrimination in Rhodesia [and] where and when necessary P.A.R.D. would exert pressure to ensure as far as possible that the terms referring to racial discrimination—both implicit and implied—would be implemented.' When he visited the Commission Mr. Mew produced certain leaflets which he claimed the A.N.C. had distributed among the African population and which 'like all propaganda contained elements of truth and large amounts of fantasy.'[116]

On the 26th January, Mr. R. Cary, chairman of C.O.S.S., referred to 'categorical assurances' given by the Minister of Foreign Affairs that the government would honour the spirit and letter of the proposals and said that C.O.S.S. intended to do everything possible to ensure that the government of the day kept to this pledge. To this end members of the organization inserted advertisements in the local press explaining that C.O.S.S. had been in touch with many thousands of organizations and individuals and that the one consistent response of each African they had contacted was that 'the terms would be acceptable—if only we could trust the Europeans to carry them out'.

C.O.S.S. had, therefore, come to the conclusion that what was needed was a 'clear, solemn declaration by Europeans young and old, by individual Companies and Associations that, if the settlement goes through, they will do everything possible to see that the terms are agreed to in the spirit and the letter.' To achieve this aim the advertisement carried declaration forms addressed to C.O.S.S. which could be filled in by a person, company or association 'solemnly undertaking to do this'.[117]

The formation of the pro-settlement African Progressive Coun-

cil was announced on the 7th January. It was to be headed initially
by Mr. B. M. N. Phiri, a former member of the Federal parliament. Its aims were to support the proposals 'as a vital first step
to the creation of mutual understanding between the races of the
country' with the objective of attaining a parity government in
which 'one [race] is not subordinate to the other and where mutual
objectives can be achieved... which will lead to a strong and unified
nation.'[118]

The Rhodesian Progressive Liberal Forum presented the Pearce
Commission with a memorandum which was reported to have said
that since the signing of the agreement 'responsible Rhodesians
both black and white, of moderate outlook had welcomed the
opportunity for a settlement. But the truth has been twisted by
extremists who have advocated total rejection of the terms.' The
memorandum went on to give a description of the three groups
who were opposing the proposals—'Right-wing Europeans who
are just a small group of misguided white extremists. African
extreme nationalists whose hopes and dreams of power could be
completely destroyed if the proposals are accepted and put into
action', and opposition from church leaders—'These so-called
champions of Christianity [who] cannot even combine to eradicate
poverty, superstition and prostitution.'

The Progressive Liberal Forum described the settlement proposals as 'a new path to partnership in Rhodesia' and said that if
the proposals were rejected it would amount to an 'admission that
there was no hope of survival for any multi-racial society in the
African continent.' Its memorandum ended with the prophecy that
it would be a tragedy if the proposals were allowed to fail and
'the proposed new road to partnership is closed.'[119]

OTHER SECTIONS OF THE COMMUNITY

TRADE UNIONS

P.S. Harris, of the Department of Economics at the University
of Rhodesia, described the nature of the trade union organization
in Rhodesia when he wrote that the Industrial Conciliation Act
of 1959 (substantially revised in 1971) 'reinforced the division of
the labour movement along lines of skill differential.' He explained
that although unions may not restrict membership on the basis

of race the principles behind the Act 'have had the effect of segregating the industrial labour movement on the basis of the level of skill within particular industries. The membership of the 'skilled' unions is predominantly white... [they] are white led, are organizationally strong, enjoy active sponsorship from the governing political group... the 'unskilled' unions [are] almost exclusively African both in terms of membership and leadership... [and] are required to oppose not only organized employer groups, but also workers of a higher order of skill who view the development of African trade unionism as a potential threat to the stability of the white working class.' [120]

'Unskilled' Trade Unions
The split in the 'unskilled' or predominantly 'African' trade union movement between the National African Federation of Unions (N.A.F.U.) and the African Trades Union Congress (A.T.U.C.) occurred in 1965 when a break-away movement from the A.T.U.C. formed a congress of unions which was later banned and replaced by N.A.F.U. The split is at national level and the two organizations often sponsor rival unions within particular industries.

Shortly after the signing of the settlement agreement the vice-president of N.A.F.U., Mr. S. P. Hlongwane, said in Bulawayo that the terms should be rejected for they fell far short of democratic principles, while Africans should not accept terms which had not been discussed with African leaders. The Mashonaland region of N.A.F.U. then arranged a meeting at which the settlement terms were described as a 'sell-out' in that they fell far short of majority rule.

The statement issued at the meeting read 'Only a popular government established through majority rule can permanently ensure peace and economic prosperity for the people of this country.' It went on to condemn the test of acceptability procedure, for N.A.F.U. considered that any method outside a country-wide referendum 'smacked of arbitrary action... and was open to suspicion.' The delegates at the meeting asked N.A.F.U. to take the initiative in calling a special convention of African leaders to mobilize African opposition to the terms. [121]

In January 1972 the President of the A.T.U.C., Mr. P. F. Sithole, called upon the government to implement the settlement, without waiting for the test of acceptability, as an act of faith so as to convince the rest of the world that there had been a change of heart by the Rhodesian government. Later when Lord Pearce visited Bulawayo he was visited by a seven-man delegation who claimed that A.T.U.C. represented mainly African workers from 14 affiliated trade unions and was speaking on behalf of 60 000 employees. These delegates criticized the proposals as not meeting the requirements of democratic procedures—'the elementary right of electing or being elected to Parliament was severely limited to fewer than one *per cent* of the African people.'[122]

The Pearce Report later noted that, although both N.A.F.U. and the A.T.U.C. strongly opposed the proposals and had suggested a joint delegation to meet the Pearce Commission, this meeting had never materialised. The Report also commented that 'the African Trade Union Congress and the National African Federation of Unions also claimed to speak for all their members in expressing their root and branch opposition to the Proposals which they claimed would not benefit their members. The extent to which there had been detailed consultation with their membership or in some cases the effective strength of the individual unions remained in doubt.'[123]

'Skilled' Trade Unions
On the 23rd January 1972, the Trades Union Congress (T.U.C.) of Rhodesia adopted a resolution which read: 'The general council of the T.U.C. of Rhodesia, being aware that it cannot direct the affiliated organizations, nevertheless advises that a settlement is necessary and recommends that the proposals be accepted as a basis for the future progress of all the peoples of Rhodesia.' The T.U.C. president, Mr. H. Bloomfield, added that the resolution was based primarily on economic reasons.[124] On the 21st February Mr. Bloomfield, in an interview with *Herald* reporter Alun Vaughan, outlined the views of established labour on the effect of the settlement proposals on industrial relations. Speaking of race relations in industry he said 'if any person has the qualifications and ability for a particular job he should be paid the agreed rate for that job. If these principles—the rate for the job and the maintenance of standards—are upheld then there is no reason why Europeans and Africans cannot work side by side.'

When asked whether the trade unions would make a similar pledge to that given by employers, namely to honour the spirit as well as the letter of the proposals, Mr. Bloomfield was reported as saying that 'the T.U.C. member unions have no restrictions on their constitutions, intentions or actions that discriminate against anyone on the basis of race, colour or creed... we will not make the pledge because we have none to make.'[125]

In its report on evidence given by the trade unions the Pearce Report concluded by stating that 'we would be unwise to accept at face value claims by the Trade Unions to represent the views of their members. Our Commissioners in the field came to the same conclusion.'[126]

The provisions of the Industrial Conciliation Act cover all workers except those in domestic service, agriculture, the public service and the Rhodesia Railways. These categories of workers are represented by such bodies as the African Farmers' Union (A.F.U.); the Rhodesia National Farmers' Union (R.N.F.U.); the Rhodesia Railway Workers' Union (R.R.W.U.); and the Railway Associated Workers' Union (R.A.W.U.).

The African Farmers' Union

The African Farmers' Union, with a membership of about 9 000, represents the interests of the private farmers of the African Purchase Areas.[127] Shortly after the signing of the agreement on settlement terms its president, Mr. W. H. Kona, urged African leaders to call a convention on a non-party political basis to consolidate African opinion before the test of acceptability. He was quoted as saying that 'the whole thing is a fuss and a political swindle of the highest order.'[128]

In mid-February Mr. Kona met Lord Pearce and his deputy Sir Maurice Dorman and explained the reasons why A.F.U. was rejecting the terms—'We reject the terms in order to keep Britain committed in the dispute between black and white as the custodian of African political advancement towards African self-determination.' It was reported that several African National Council officials were present among an orderly crowd of about 40 people which attended the hearing.[129]

The Rhodesia National Farmers' Union

The Council of the Rhodesia National Farmers' Union announced on the 19th January that it would give evidence to the Pearce Commission supporting the proposals and that it was urging its members, their families and their employees to give evidence whatever their views. As the president of R.N.F.U. said 'It would be tragic if farmers allowed this final chance to slip because of their failure to give evidence.' In its statement the Council stated that the 'maintenance of a viable agricultural industry was essential for national survival. Acceptance of the settlement proposals was the best way of ensuring this.'[130]

The Rhodesia Railway Workers' Union

The Rhodesia Railway Workers' Union represents the higher railway grades and has predominantly European membership. According to the *Herald*, on the 16th January the president of the 7 000-strong R.R.W.U., Mr. J. Kinley, appealed to railwaymen to accept the proposals for, as he said, 'the vast numbers of people of all races desire a settlement. My advice to them is to stand up and be counted before mischief makers stir up more trouble and we find ourselves in a political vacuum.'[131] On 2nd February the president and the secretary of R.R.W.U. gave evidence to the Commission saying later that they had accepted the proposals mainly on economic grounds.

DOMESTIC SERVANTS

The Pearce Report comments that there was one section of the population from which only a very few opinions were received. These were domestic servants which, according to the Report, comprise, in Salisbury alone, about 40 *per cent* of adult Africans, the numbers of which, living in the European areas, outnumber the European residents.[132]

EMPLOYERS' ASSOCIATIONS

At the end of January it was announced that the Confederation of Rhodesian Employers (C.O.R.E.), which comprises groups and associations of employers and single employers such as the Rhodesia Railways and the Rhodesian Iron and Steel Company (but not those in the agricultural sector) had accepted the proposals as being 'in the best interests and for the well-being of all Rhodesians.' The president of C.O.R.E., Mr. C. J. Freer, explained that it was solely on the economic and social aspects of the proposals that their unreserved acceptance had been given.[133]

Shortly afterwards a C.O.R.E. deputation presented Lord Pearce with a pledge from about 560 employers promising to honour the spirit as well as the letter of the proposals; to support and promote the expansion of training and educational facilities for all employees; and to consider, where practicable, appointments and promotions on the basis of merit at wages related to the job irrespective of race. Mr. Freer, who led the deputation, said that C.O.R.E. believed that employers as a whole would want to go further than this and 'eliminate not only economic discrimination but also the petty social irritation which in the past has been based on colour.'[134]

Towards the end of February the Associated Chambers of Commerce of Rhodesia (A.C.C.O.R.) representing (according to its president, Mr. A. G. Calder) about 2 000 individual members employing about 40 000 Europeans and about 74 000 Africans, told the Pearce Commission that it firmly believed that acceptance of the settlement proposals would lead to more work for non-Europeans in the commercial sector. A.C.C.O.R. would ensure that in future, merit and not colour would be an over-riding factor in employment.[135]

In its report, the Pearce Commission commented that 'economic arguments generally loomed largest especially from the leaders of industry and the business associations' and quoted one of its commissioners as saying 'The most forceful and determined support for the Proposals came from people in commerce and industry... all industrialists, commercial managers and businessmen admitted that expansion was being prevented because of lack of capital while some even admitted that economic stagnation was a real threat if no Settlement was reached.'[136]

THE ASIAN AND COLOURED COMMUNITIES

A few days after the settlement agreement was signed both Asian and Coloured leaders announced plans for holding meetings in all main centres to ascertain the attitudes of their communities towards the proposals.

The Coloured Community

Mr. G. Raftopolous, the leader of the National Association for Coloured People (N.A.C.P.), announced on the 26th January

1972, that the Association's executive committee had urged acceptance of the proposals but was leaving the final decision to the
coloured community as a whole, for plans for a meeting of Coloured
representatives from all over the country were being made.

A deputation representing the Bulawayo Coloured community
gave evidence to the Commission on 2nd February and urged the
Commission to make an enquiry into racial discrimination in Rhodesia. They told the Commission that the Coloured community
accepted the settlement proposals 'but with reservations, grave
concern and doubt' for they doubted whether the settlement terms
would be implemented in letter and spirit. The deputation added
that the Coloured community prided itself on being 'first-rate
citizens with the culture and standards of Europeans [but they]
were still afforded fourth-rate citizenship status in all matters.'[137]
In the Pearce Report it was noted that the Coloured community
'took the view that the proposals did not go far enough to eliminate
the discrimination against them. Nevertheless they thought that
if there were no settlement their situation would get worse rather
than better.'[138]

The Asian Community

Like the Coloured community the Asians were critical of the proposals for not doing enough to end racial discrimination, but according to the Pearce Report opinion was divided and therefore
their Association did not present evidence at a national level. It was
understood that most Asians gave their evidence personally in writing because they wished to avoid the appearance of taking one
side or the other. The Pearce Report stated that most witnesses
'accepted the Proposals as a compromise, a new chance for stability
and for dismantling racial discrimination, a possibility of progress
for all, or at least an improvement on the present impasse.'[139]

THE CHURCHES

During the final week of the talks leading to the signing of the
settlement agreement the Roman Catholic Cathedral in Salisbury
held special prayers 'For God's help and guidance that the talks
may reach a successful conclusion establishing peace and justice
for all races.'

Church Organizations

The African Ministers' Fraternal, representing all the major denominations in the city, issued a press statement in Salisbury during December 1971 stating that the proposals must be rejected since, as they stood, they were wholly unacceptable to Africans. At the same time the multi-racial Christian Council of Rhodesia (C.C.R.) severely criticized the proposals in a statement entitled *Think Again*. The C.C.R. followed this up by organizing a meeting at which sixteen churches and other Christian organizations (covering almost every non-Roman Catholic church in Rhodesia) were represented with Roman Catholic observers present. The Rev. A. Ndhlela, General Superintendent of the Methodist (U.K.) Church, took the chair and said afterwards that attendance at the meeting was divided almost equally between Africans and Europeans—delegates attending on a basis of the membership strength of their churches. The meeting adopted a motion to reject the settlement terms by 25 votes to 9. Later the Rev. Ndhlela was reported as saying that 'there was no block voting. Different delegates from the same church voted against each other. Some Europeans voted for the motion, to reject the settlement terms, and at least one African voted against it, in favour of the terms.'[140]

Shortly afterwards the C.C.R. issued a pamphlet entitled *Guide to the Settlement Proposals*. This pamphlet aroused a certain amount of ill feeling, particularly as the document was issued before being approved by a majority of the C.C.R. members. The *Herald* voiced the feelings of many when its editorial queried whether 'a document that by design sets out to emphasize what are considered defects [can] truly be called a guide?' and concluded that 'the pamphlet was prepared by people hostile to the proposals.'[141] In mid-February an unsuccessful attempt was made at the C.C.R.'s annual meeting to persuade the Council to withdraw its opposition to the settlement terms, an action attributed to members of the newly-formed Rhodesia Christian Group.

The Rhodesia Christian Group was organized by a group of Anglican clergymen, together with a body of European supporters from the main churches, 'to counter attempts to use the Churches and church bodies as instruments of revolutionary policy.'[142] The Rev. A. R. Lewis, Rector of Rusape, was the Group's chairman and was reported later to have said that he had moved the resolution at the annual C.C.R. meeting and that during the ensuing debate 'the arguments against were almost entirely emotional. No-one seemed to bother about logic, or the practicalities of the situation.'[143]

The Anglican Church

Writing in their respective diocesan journals—*The Link* and *Contact*—the Bishops of both Mashonaland and Matabeleland agreed that the proposals merited acceptance. Bishop Mark Wood commented: 'it is obvious that the successful implementation of the proposals will depend on the sincerity of those in power. No legal documents can create sincerity. It is at this point that the Christian Churches of Rhodesia will have a task to perform and will have the clear duty and right to recall to future Governments the spirit as well as the letter of the proposals.' The Anglican church as a whole, however, did not feel it desirable that the churches should try to influence opinion in the matter of acceptance or rejection, regarding this as a matter for individual conscience.[144]

The Rev. A. R. Lewis disagreed with this attitude, for he felt that the period of the test was such a crucial one that the churches should provide a positive leadership based on the Gospel for 'if the churches are ever to offer leadership in the country's affairs (and they did not hesitate on the Land Tenure Act) surely now is the time to speak: to say to people of all races, "This may be the last chance in Africa of building a country where the races can live together in peace and understanding." '[145]

The Roman Catholic Church

At the end of January, following the annual meeting of the Roman Catholic Bishops' Conference, a pastoral message was issued itemising criticisms of the proposals and urging Catholics to make a personal decision and to make their views known. The statement signed by the 5 Roman Catholic Bishops objected strongly to the fact that Africans had been placed in the position of saying yes or no to an agreement about which they had not been properly consulted and went on to say that 'the Catholic Bishops have carefully studied these proposals. They share the disappointment felt generally by their people that the hopes which were widely entertained have not been fulfilled.' In the statement the Bishops asked Catholics to take into account a number of considerations, which they listed, when determining their attitude on the proposals for, the Bishops warned 'neither choice fully accords with Christian moral principles. Each person has therefore to judge under which of the two choices there is a better chance of working towards the fulfillment of these principles.'[146]

The Chichester Club in Salisbury (a 93-member organization of Roman Catholic professional and businessmen strongly opposed to Communism and representing conservative Catholic opinion) reacted strongly to the Bishops' statement by calling an emergency meeting, after which they announced that the Club disassociated itself completely from the statement. The Club considered that the proposals were in the best interests, both spiritual and material, of all the people of Rhodesia and urged that they be accepted.[147] The Salisbury Association of Conservative Catholics also disagreed with their Bishops' stand and issued a statement that they accepted the proposals as being in the best interests of the country as a whole and that 'we are joining the mounting forces of Catholic lay opinion in expressing our dissatisfaction at the Catholic bishops' lack of leadership at this critical time.'[148]

The *Financial Gazette,* on the 18th February, saw the disagreement as a polarization along racial lines with African Catholics (reported as outnumbering their European counterparts by over 360 000) coming out strongly in support of the Bishops and European laymen dissenting in strong terms.

The Methodist Church

There are two branches of the Methodist Church in Rhodesia, the United Methodist Church, of American origin, which began its work in Rhodesia in the 1890's, and the Methodist Church in Rhodesia which was founded by British Methodists, also in the 1890's.

The Methodist Church (U.K.) held its annual synod in Salisbury on the 5th January 1972, and was addressed by its General-Superintendent, the Rev. A. Ndhlela, who said that the Church to-day should not remain silent on matters of political and social issues, but 'ought to point to and expose those things which are unjust.' At a later meeting the Rev. Ndhlela deplored the exclusion of the African people from the negotiations and the presentation of the proposals as 'something that must be accepted or rejected without alteration.' The synod finally expressed its unwillingness either to accept or reject the terms and passed a resolution recommending

that each member of the church should express his own judgement
to the Commission.[149]

The United Methodist Church, at its conference in Umtali, was
reported as calling for a rejection of the terms 'because they are
a device intended to legalise U.D.I. and perpetuate minority rule.'

Government ministers had reportedly taken exception to the involvement of clergymen in political matters. Mr. M. H. H. Partridge,
Minister of Local Government and Housing, spoke of the difficulties which Rhodesia was facing and accused the clergy of vanity
and pride in believing that they could sit in judgement on the
governments of the United Kingdom and of Rhodesia 'on such
difficult and controversial matters as constitutional reform in a
plural society. Mr. D. W. Lardner-Burke criticized those religious
people who were endeavouring to 'achieve their own ambitions
from their position in the Christian world.'[150]

Such criticism was answered by a number of church leaders
and others including the Principal and Vice-Chancellor of the
University of Rhodesia, the Rev. Professor R. Craig, who defended
Christian involvement in politics and concern in race relations in
a public lecture (since published in pamphlet form as *Politics and
Religion : a Christian view*), and the Rabbi of the Bulawayo Hebrew
Congregation, who said that Mr. Partridge's remarks probably
arose because of opposition to the settlement proposals and went
on to say 'we ministers of religion should not in any way try to
prejudice or impede the outcome of the proposals.'[151]

THE CHIEFS

In early January 1972 the *Herald's* political reporter, Ian Mills,
reported on a 'routine' meeting of the Council of Chiefs attended
by the Minister of Internal Affairs, Mr. L. B. Smith, and the Secretary for Internal Affairs, Mr. H. Nicolle. Following this meeting
a statement was issued from the office of the Prime Minister saying
that the Council had announced that it 'was unanimous in its support of the proposals [and] voiced its pleasure that the quarrel
between Britain and Rhodesia had been settled in such an amicable
manner... [it] strongly recommended the proposals for the approval of all Africans who had the interests of their people at heart
[and] deplored the attempts by certain people to mislead Africans
into rejecting the proposals. It is confident the African people will

appreciate that the correct and only answer is yes, because the proposals are clearly in their interests.' The statement concluded by recommending that 'in the knowledge of intimidatory tactics seen in the past... views expressed to the Commission by individuals and groups should be treated... as confidential.'[152]

In commenting upon this statement by the Council of Chiefs, the *Sunday Mail* considered that the statement lacked credibility primarily because the meeting was held in secret, and pointed out that not only is secrecy foreign to African tribal procedure but that it breeds suspicion.[153]

Later in January it was reported that an African crowd (including four chiefs) at a meeting in the Tjolotjo Tribal Trust Land (a large area to the west of Bulawayo) had torn up copies of the simplified version of the White Paper to demonstrate their disapproval of the terms. In the Gutu Tribal Trust Land (a large area east of Gwelo) a group of about 30 chiefs and tribal leaders who were to have met the Pearce Commissioners declined to do so without their followers and later joined the crowd in a unanimous 'No' vote. During February it was reported that Chief Chilimanzi had led his followers in turning down the proposals when the Commissioners visited the Chilimanzi Tribal Trust Land (a smaller area east of Gwelo and west of Gutu T.T.L.). On the other hand there were reports also of chiefs who accepted the proposals. In the Zwimba Tribal Trust Land, near Sinoia, both Senator Chief Chirau and Chief Zwimba, with their councillors and headmen, gave a unanimous 'Yes' vote while Chief Msana of Msana Tribal Trust Land (south of Bindura) was shouted down by his followers and was reported to have joined with his tribesmen in rejecting the proposals.[154]

As *Moto* commented in its editorial on the 12th February: 'It is a fact that on many occasions the Chiefs have been blanketly accused of being government stooges, and unrepresentative of the wishes of their people. The blanket accusation no longer stands. Since the arrival of the Pearce Commission many chiefs have come out in the open and stood with their followers to condemn what they all regard as an unfair constitutional arrangement.' The newspaper went on to make the point that any chiefs who found themselves out of line with the administration should remember that their people would be behind them.[155]

In the Pearce Report a whole chapter was given to the Chiefs.

It describes the position of chiefs in historical perspective and goes on to remark that the Commission 'appreciated at the outset that one of the most important questions... was: "How far could the Chiefs and other tribal leaders be said to voice the opinions of the tribesmen in the Test?"' In answering this question the Commission quoted from the Report of the Secretary for Native Affairs and Chief Native Commissioner for the year 1961 which reads:

> ... and in the political field chiefs should be able to express their views and Government should attach as much importance to those views as it does to any other responsible and organized representative group such as the Chamber of Mines or Commerce, but in no way substitute for or exclude normal political expression and other representative African thinking.

and stated that this was what the Commissioners had endeavoured to do. In section 182, the Report gives figures analysing the response of the chiefs:

> There are 206 substantive Chiefs, 33 acting Chiefs and six vacancies making a total of 245. Of these 184 were seen by the Commission. Forty-four accepted the proposals, 87 rejected them and 53 either said they did not know what answer to give, or abstained altogether from giving an opinion. In addition we received 20 letters from Chiefs, six in favour and 14 against the proposals.

and in the following section commented that 'many Chiefs seemed to be acutely embarrassed by the demand that they should express a political opinion at all. Except in Matabeleland where the majority accepted the proposals, the majority of the Chiefs with their people rejected them or declined to give an opinion.'[156]

Following the announcement of the Pearce Commission's verdict and the publication of the Pearce Report a Motion to take note of the Report was moved by the Prime Minister. In his introductory speech he stated 'unfortunately some chapters of the Pearce Commission report could leave a completely wrong impression in the minds of the public. I refer in particular to the chapter on chiefs. I am satisfied that, with a few exceptions, the chiefs acquitted themselves well under very difficult circumstances. I and my Government continue to retain the confidence we have always had in the chiefs.'[157]

FOREIGN REACTIONS

As early as June 1970, following the Conservative victory in the British general election, conjectures by various eminent politicians had been voiced in Rhodesia regarding the chances of coming to a settlement with the British government. The Prime Minister, Mr. Ian D. Smith, commented that now Rhodesia was independent the outcome of the British election no longer influenced political events in Rhodesia. However, a former Cabinet Minister, Mr. W. R. Harper, pointed out that whilst in opposition the Conservative Party had pledged itself to make a final attempt to reconcile the impasse between the two governments and that the Conservative victory had given Rhodesia what might be the last chance to reach a negotiated settlement. The leaders of the Centre Party called upon the government to take immediate steps for an all-party consultation which would lead to an all-party conference and all-party negotiations at 'this moment of great opportunity.'

By December 1970 the British Foreign Secretary had initiated the 'last effort' to try and settle the Rhodesian issue and the early part of 1971 saw much conjecture by politicians and others on how the requirements of the two interested parties—Rhodesia and Great Britain—could be reconciled.

In July 1971 the *Herald Africa News Service* commented on the attitude of Zambia towards a settlement of the Anglo-Rhodesian dispute, saying there was a considerable body of opinion which saw Britain compromising with her 'kith and kin' in Rhodesia. But 'Zambia's fears are not entirely based on altruistic feelings... there is a very real fear here [in Lusaka] that a withdrawal of sanctions could strengthen Rhodesia's position to the detriment of Zambia.'[158] In September Sir Seretse Khama, President of Botswana, was reported as saying that the Black African States would welcome an early settlement of the Anglo-Rhodesian dispute but only on the terms of satisfying the five principles laid down by Britain.

On the 19th November 1971, Britain rejected a motion presented to the United Nations General Assembly's 13-nation Decolonization Committee to request the United Nations to reaffirm that any Rhodesian settlement must be 'worked out with the fullest participation of all nationalist leaders representing the majority of the people of Zimbabwe... and must be endorsed by the people on the basis of universal adult suffrage.'[159]

In the South African newspapers much interest was taken in the Rhodesian settlement issue and it was believed possible that South Africa had already exerted pressure upon the Rhodesian government to do everything in its power to reach an 'honourable settlement'. A settlement that might differ somewhat from that which many Rhodesians were contemplating for, as South Africa's Prime Minister, Mr. B. J. Vorster, had outlined, on a number of occasions, South Africa's main interest was the removal of the unresolved issue between Rhodesia and Britain, which was seen as a threat to the stability of the whole of Southern Africa.

Immediately the news of the signing of the agreement was released, on the 24th November 1971, the South African Prime Minister congratulated both governments. The leaders of both the United and the Progressive Parties of South Africa made press statements welcoming the news. Washington was reported also to have welcomed the news of the agreement for the settlement of the issue had come to be seen as a stabilizing factor in an area where the United States wanted stability and also because the prospect of a settlement was seen as checking a drift towards apartheid policies in Rhodesia. Moscow was reported as describing the agreement as a 'betrayal of the interests of the African majority' and *Tass* was quoted as saying that the accord reached between Rhodesia and Britain would go down in history as 'an undisguised and shameful collusion between the imperialists and their racist henchmen in Africa.'[160] In New Zealand and Mozambique the news of the agreement was welcomed but Zambia, Tanzania and Kenya considered that the terms were almost certainly a 'sell-out'.

On the 21st December the United Nations General Assembly approved by 94 votes to 8 (with 22 abstentions) a resolution rejecting the proposals, calling the terms of the agreement a 'flagrant violation of the inalienable rights of the African people of Zimbabwe [Rhodesia] to self-determination and independence.' The text of the resolution reaffirmed that no settlement which did not conform strictly to the principle of NIBMAR (No Independence Before Majority African Rule) was acceptable to the United Nations.[161]

The appointment of the Pearce Commission was critized by one British Sunday newspaper which considered the 'Rhodesian affair... a tiresome charade... [for] Black majority rule was the inevitable outcome... which current negotiations would neither hasten nor delay' and said that in its opinion the Pearce Commission "was no better equipped to test the acceptability of the proposals than a posse of United Nations" officers would have been.' It further commented that a team composed almost entirely of past and present government officers, all white, 'seems to hark back to the vanished age of colonial paternalism. If no African was invited to join it, an important propaganda point was missed. If none accepted, the implications are even more disturbing.'[162]

Later in the month several other British newspapers criticized the validity of the exercise, and it was reported that a delegation of British M.P.'s had announced their intention of visiting Rhodesia to assess the degree of freedom the Rhodesian government was affording the Pearce Commission. The delegation was later found to be a mission from the British Labour Party on behalf of that party's national executive. The reaction in Rhodesia was not encouraging and the *Herald* took the opportunity of pointing out that a Labour M.P., Mr. M. Foley, and a Conservative M.P., Mr. N. Fisher, were already in the country conducting the kind of survey that 'Mr. Healey was thumping the table about' and asking that it should be made plain to the Labour Party spokesman, Mr. Healey, 'that the situation in Rhodesia is tricky enough—indeed, extremely sensitive—without the extension of British party political in-fighting.'[163] In order to counter British parliamentary criticism of the handling of the test of acceptability, especially following the news of disorders and detentions after the arrival of the Pearce Commission, the British Foreign Secretary sent a special observer to Rhodesia, Mr. P. Mansfield. Described as head of the Rhodesia Section at the Foreign and Commonwealth Office, Mr. Mansfield spent five days in Rhodesia.

On the 26th January 1972 an emergency debate was held in the British House of Commons. Sir Alec Douglas-Home was reported as making 'a passionate defence of the provisional settlement.' The opposition Labour Party spokesman, Mr. D. Healey, made four demands of the Foreign Secretary—that he must insist that the Rhodesian Prime Minister give full details of the reasons for the detentions and, in the event that the persons had been detained merely to silence them, must demand their release; must insist that the African National Council be given permission to hold political meetings in the Tribal Trust Lands; must ensure freedom for opponents of the settlement to use radio and television to put forward their case; and must secure the freedom for British public figures, whether inside or outside Parliament, to visit Rhodesia. Mr. Healey said that if there was no satisfaction on these four points, then 'normal political activity as provided for in the agreement was not being permitted and... it was the Government's duty to withdraw the settlement... and the Commission.'[164]

On the specific demands made by Mr. Healey, Sir Alec said that they amounted to asking him to intervene, over the heads of the Commission, to impose political terms. Circumstances which made this necessary might arise in the future but they were not so at the present time. Sir Alec disagreed with sending a delegation of British M.P.'s to Rhodesia, since 'The test of acceptability did not envisage under normal political activity that the Westminster parties should transfer their own squabbles to Rhodesia.'

On the 29th January the Rhodesian Prime Minister announced that the British Labour Party would not be allowed to send an observation team to Rhodesia because, at its Conferences of 1970 and 1971, the Labour Party had passed resolutions supporting 'terrorist' movements. Mr. Smith also stated that a British Liberal M.P., Mr. D. Steel, would not be allowed in Rhodesia as he was an outspoken critic of Rhodesia and supported 'terrorist' organizations. Mr. Smith added, however, that 'the Rhodesian Government have agreed to the British Government's request for a small all-party delegation of M.P.'s to come to Rhodesia in order to observe the workings of the Pearce Commission' with the proviso that the delegation should include no persons on record as having aided or encouraged 'terrorists'.[165]

At the United Nations Security Council meeting in Addis Ababa, African members were reported as being adamant that the Security Council should call for the withdrawal of the Pearce Commission. At the same meeting the Soviet Union's chief U.N. delegate, Mr. J. Malik, called upon the Security Council to tell Britain to eliminate the Rhodesian government and bring about an immediate transfer of power to the African majority. Commenting on the eventual vote on the resolution (which Britain vetoed) the *Herald* concluded that 'in effect to abstain is to vote for the unpopular view without admitting it.'[166]

When the names of the members of the all-party delegation from the British parliament were announced it was found that both the Labour and Liberal Parties had included nominees who had already been declared *persona non grata* by the Rhodesian government. Mr. Ian Smith had therefore refused to allow the delegation to visit Rhodesia. This had led to a 'brief but lively' exchange in the House of Commons with 'many Conservatives as well as Labour and Liberal M.P.'s resenting what was seen as an affront to the House of Commons.'[167] The refusal also led to speculation in the House that if the Rhodesian government had refused to accept this 'quite modest' demand what would be the likelihood of it honouring any bargain with the British government? The decision was also criticized in Salisbury, not only for itself but for the week's delay in returning an answer, for, queried the *Herald*, if there had to be a delay instead of a decisive No, why not delay until the end of the Pearce Commission's work at the end of the week? 'Procrastination is sometimes justified. In this instance it would have kept the delegation out but without causing the direct affront that many Members of both Houses of the British Parliament will see in the Rhodesian stand.'[168]

The members of the Pearce Commission left Rhodesia on 11th March 1972. On the eve of his departure Lord Pearce said on the Rhodesia Broadcasting Corporation service that he hoped 'there would be no lingering doubts about the independence of the Commission' and that the Commission would work as fast as it could to finish its report, which, he hoped, would be in the hands of Sir Alec Douglas-Home by the latter half of April. 'Our analysis will be completely impartial,' he assured his listeners.

In Salisbury, the *Herald* took the opportunity of praising the Commission for deserving credit on two counts: 'it quickly adjusted its approach to the realities. And it has never wavered in its determination to finish the job.'

Following the first two weeks of the sitting of the Pearce Commission with its attendant disorders throughout the country, there was much speculation both in Rhodesia and in other countries as to the future course of action if the outcome of the test of acceptability was a negative one. In the House of Commons questions on this theme were parried by the Foreign and Commonwealth Secretary but in a report from Britain it was postulated that there appeared to be only two official pointers to this question. 'There will be no second Pearce Commission if this one brings back a negative answer. And there will be no attempt to negotiate a fresh agreement with Mr. Smith.' Articles in the British press were quoted as pointing out that on the whole if there was a rejection it would show that Britain was powerless to do anything about Rhodesia. Britain's Prime Minister, Mr. E. Heath, was also questioned in the House of Commons about the Government's intentions if the Pearce Report was negative, but he refused to comment beyond saying that the outcome of the Pearce Report must be awaited.

THE INTERVAL BETWEEN THE TEST OF ACCEPTABILITY AND THE PEARCE REPORT

On the day that Lord Pearce arrived back in London, the Labour Party's shadow Foreign Secretary made a statement which appeared to indicate a major change in Labour policy on Rhodesia. Mr. Healey said that if there was a negative response to the test of acceptability then 'The five principles must go overboard. Any future settlement must be negotiated with representatives of the African majority.'[169]

A public opinion poll conducted by the Opinion Research Centre for the London *Sunday Times* was quoted as showing that there was a lot of confusion in Britain about Rhodesia. A 45 *per cent* vote was recorded in favour of another attempt at negotiating another agreement more acceptable to the Africans but it also showed that about half the people interviewed had said that the British government should not be responsible for the future of Africans in Rhodesia.[170]

In Rhodesia the general opinion seemed to be that when the detailed reports had been studied the Pearce Commission must return a 'No' verdict, but that it would be a qualified verdict. The rumours were that this 'not proven' verdict would lead to further talks between the British Foreign Secretary and the Rhodesian Prime Minister on a new independence deal with modifications. It was contended, however, that many British M.P.'s would insist that fresh negotiations must include an African representative, and that the Rhodesian Prime Minister would not only have to contend with right-wing pressure groups but also with the A.N.C. in any fresh negotiations.

Mr. T. H. P. Bashford, the leader of the Centre Party, considered that during the sittings of the Pearce Commission there had been 'an atmosphere of emotionalism and confused thinking' and that in such an atmosphere a clear-cut 'Yes' or 'No' could hardly be expected. He also considered that 'the implementation of the British fifth principle has brought to light hitherto unknown factors that make it virtually impossible for Rhodesia to return to square one.'[171] He defined 'square one' as retention of the 1969 Constitution and the hope of a gradual erosion of sanctions.

Early in April, Mr. Bashford challenged the Rhodesian government to implement the settlement proposals unilaterally, a move suggested earlier by the Chairman of the Johannesburg Consolidated Investment Company and former Federal High Commissioner in London, Sir Albert Robinson, who considered that such a move would mean that 'meaningful contact between the races would be made without undue delay and within our parliamentary system, but on a more representative basis than is the case at present.'[172]

The United Front, however, took the opposite view for they considered that Sir Albert was advocating the destruction of a principle laid down by Rhodesia's founder, Cecil John Rhodes, 'that as long as the chiefs supported the white government of the day the authority and influence of the chiefs over their own people would be upheld'. The U.F.'s spokesman added that the proposals were specifically geared for majority rule and if they were implemented it would be the 'final betrayal' of the white man and the chiefs. A reminder was added that for the government of a constitutionally independent country to reach an agreement with a foreign power to change its constitution could be construed as treason.[173]

At the end of April the Centre Party president led a C.P. delegation to London with the aim of trying to prevent the settlement from coming 'unstuck', and correcting the misapprehension in London that the continuance of sanctions would produce further concessions from the Rhodesian government. Mr. Bashford said that the Centre Party view was that continued sanctions would push Rhodesia into apartheid.[174]

On the 10th March the African National Council was reconstituted into a political organization so that 'with a common voice our cry can be heard and our aspirations reached', as its leader, Bishop A. Muzorewa, said when he read out the organization's manifesto. The Bishop also said that a constitutional conference was now one of the party's main aims and that he hoped it would take place soon after publication of the Pearce Report.[175]

On the 26th April it was announced that the A.N.C. had sent two delegates to Britain to ask the British government to hold a Rhodesian constitutional conference. The two delegates, the Rev. Canaan Banana, the A.N.C.'s vice-president, and Mr. Ronald Sadomba M.P., formerly of the Centre Party, were to meet Bishop Muzorewa (who had been attending a church conferencce in America). The Rev. Banana said that they hoped to meet the British Foreign Secretary and possibly the British Prime Minister and that the A.N.C. would represent Rhodesian Africans. It was reported that the two delegates hoped to hold talks with the U.N. Committee on Decolonization in Addis Ababa on the way to London.

Whilst in London the delegation met Sir Alec Douglas-Home and, according to the Rev. Banana, explained the position of the Rhodesian African to him. 'We suggested to Sir Alec that a constitutional conference would be the only way to solve the Rhodesian political crisis.' The Rev. Banana also claimed that he had cleared up 'certain misconceptions' at his meeting with Sir Alec and had told him why the proposals were unacceptable. Mr. Sadomba reported that the delegation had met with a 'tremendous response' from the British public and an 'unexpectably good' response from the British government.[176]

On the 30th April, Mr. Ian Smith said that 'while the Government was hoping for the correct answer, a "Yes", it had been considering Rhodesia's future in the event of a "No".' He referred to the question of the continuation of sanctions against Rhodesia and warned against over-simplification of the question of their removal —'it is not simply a question of removing sanctions now, Rhodesia must ensure that with the removal of sanctions she retained her "way of life" and Western civilization [which] was what the Rhodesian Government was trying to do in its agreement with Britain.'[177]

On the 5th May it was announced that the Pearce Report had been handed to Sir Alec Douglas-Home who was quoted as saying that he would make a statement of the British government's future policy towards Rhodesia simultaneously with publication of the report. On the 8th May the Rhodesian Prime Minister held a radio and television press conference. He said that he considered that if the Pearce Report gave a 'No' verdict it would mean the end of the road in the Anglo-Rhodesian settlement search, but he added that the Rhodesian government would be 'quite happy' to implement the agreement if the British government did likewise. In answer to a question as to whether he considered that the Pearce enquiry had been a fair test of Rhodesian opinion Mr. Smith answered 'I think it was a complete and utter farce. We warned the British Government of this and advised them against carrying out this test. But they knew more about Rhodesia than we did and decided to go on with it.'[178]

When the members of the Centre Party delegation returned from London the C.P.'s vice-president, Mr. N. J. McNally, reiterated Mr. Bashford's call on the Rhodesian government in May, to implement the settlement unilaterally. He said that if the Pearce Report recorded a 'No' vote then 'it would be up to Rhodesians to initiate moves to settle the problem.' Mr. McNally emphasized that it was important to realise that the 'real problem is not an external settlement, but an internal one... black and white have somehow to live together in this country... Rhodesians should start talking about whether it was a good idea to implement the proposals unilaterally or to appoint a commission on racial discrimination.'[179]

An article in the *Herald* on the 15th May, by a reporter writing from Britain, speculated on the attitude of British M.P.'s when the Pearce Report and the British government's statement on future policy towards Rhodesia was laid before the House of Commons. Unofficially it was considered that M.P.'s were discussing two possibilities: first, the introduction of a bill into the House of Commons renouncing sovereignty over Rhodesia and leaving it to the United Nations to administer the sanctions policy; or second, without any relinquishment of sovereignty, the government should shelve the problem as Labour Prime Minister Harold Wilson had done after the second failure to reach agreement.

The two Rhodesian political party delegations to Britain and their proposals were also discussed. The article considered that the Centre Party's proposal for implementation of the proposals despite the Pearce verdict would 'run smack into a series of immoveable objects' for the successful passing of a test of acceptability had always been a condition of any agreement. It would harm Britain's relations with the United Nations and the Black African states and would also run into solid opposition from a substantial minority of Conservative M.P.'s who would be prepared to vote against their government in company with Liberal and Labour M.P.'s. The A.N.C.'s proposal for a constitutional conference was also considered to be a non-starter for although 'a broadly-representative Rhodesian constitutional conference, including A.N.C. delegates, would suit almost all parties in Britain... it would presumably be unacceptable to Mr. Smith.'[180]

THE PEARCE COMMISSION REPORT

The Pearce Report was handed to the Rhodesian Prime Minister on the 17th May. Despite Whitehall denials that the British emissary, Sir Denis Greenhill, was not in Salisbury to re-open negotiations, both the British and Rhodesian press conjectured that the standing of the men commissioned to deliver the Report indicated a desire to continue communication between the two governments. The belief that the British government had some solution to the impasse was also strengthened by the announcement that Britain had sent envoys to Washington, Canada and Nigeria for talks on Rhodesia.

The Pearce Commission Report was published in Britain on the 23rd May and its publication was accompanied by a statement from Sir Alec Douglas-Home on the Report and his government's attitude towards it. In Salisbury the news of the 'No' finding was published in a special edition of the daily newspaper which summarised the Commission's findings—firstly that the Commission was fully satisfied that the proposals were 'fully and properly explained to the population' and secondly that the Commission was satisfied that although the proposals were acceptable to the great majority of Europeans, they were rejected by a majority of Africans and therefore, in the Commission's opinion 'the people of Rhodesia as a whole do not regard the proposals as acceptable as a basis for independence.'[181]

CONTENTS OF THE PEARCE REPORT

The Report on the Commission on Rhodesian Opinion under the Chairmanship of the Right Honourable the Lord Pearce (to give its full title) was published as a British Command Paper on 23rd May. It consists of 207 pages plus a map of Rhodesia showing the density of population, excluding urban communities, based on the 1956 Census. The map shows places which were visited by Lord Pearce and/or his deputy chairmen as well as the areas covered by the teams of commissioners.

The Report begins by describing why the Commission was set up and explaining its composition and the practical arrangements made to facilitate its work. In Chapter 7 there is a discussion of the possible use of a sample survey as 'a valuable addition to other methods' and of the practical difficulties of organizing such a survey.[182] In ensuing chapters the problems of assessment; the position of the chiefs; the question of intimidation; the meaning of 'normal political activity'; and the detentions under the Emergency Powers legislation are discussed.

The report states that out of 206 substantive and 33 acting chiefs, 184 were seen by the Commission and 20 letters from chiefs were received. Out of these, 50 were in favour of the proposals, 101 rejected them and 53 'either said they did not know what answer to give or abstained altogether.' The Report concludes by saying—

We understand the deep significance of Chieftainship to be a binding together of the tribesmen into a community and this demands that there should be general agreement throughout their ranks before any important decision is taken affecting the welfare of the tribe. But politics in the modern sense are divisive and thus tend to split tribal solidarity; hence partly the reluctance of Chiefs to speak on political matters and the resentment of many of their people of the Government's policy of so involving them. [183]

The Question of Intimidation

In chapter 12 of the Report,[184] the Commission considered that an attempt should be made to differentiate the charges under the heading of intimidation, for 'when people in Rhodesia were talking about intimidation this covered a broad band of activities, varying at one end from violence, running through threat of violence, undue influence or pressure, implied threat of unpleasant consequences or simply threatening attitudes, to normal political activities at the other end of the scale, where propaganda, persuasion and organization were also thought to be intimidatory and particularly if deployed to advocate a course opposed to one's own convictions.'

Serious allegations had been made against the Rhodesian government of using intimidatory tactics to induce Africans to accept the terms, but the Commissioners were agreed that they did not believe this. Employers, mainly Europeans, had been accused of actively influencing employees to accept the proposals. The special commissioners instanced cases which, in their view, illustrated the weakness of such allegations for they found 'little if any evidence of senior management exercising any persuasion or offering any guidance to employees which it was not perfectly proper for them to give... pressure, such as it was, from employers had little effect.' Thirdly African nationalists had been accused of intimidating Africans to reject the proposals. The Commissioners reported that 'we found it improbable, if not impossible, that with such a tight security system which has existed in Rhodesia for several years, a minority could dominate a majority by intimidation in a few weeks.' The chapter concluded by saying 'the actual number of cases of intimidation were... very small when one considers the size of the country and the five million or so African inhabitants... it is our considered view that, had there been no intimidation, there would still have been a substantial majority against the proposals.'

Definition of 'Normal Political Activity'

With respect to 'normal political activity' the Commissioners felt that the phrase 'has to be read in the context of Rhodesia, it has an objective meaning and is not to be interpreted according to the specialities of Rhodesian law.' The commissioners had the discretion to decide what was, in their view, 'normal political activity' and they determined that 'the vigorous expression of political views either orally or in writing in order to persuade people to answer "Yes" or "No" to the Commission, and canvassing to this end was therefore permitted, but that violence and intimidation were not.'

During the test the members of the Commission found that 'it never became necessary to attempt to solve particular complaints about denials of meetings, since it became almost immediately obvious that there was great political activity throughout Rhodesia.' In discussing the detentions the Commission considered that 'the case must go by default against the Rhodesian Government and although we are conscious that we may not have the full facts we feel compelled to infer that these detentions were an interference with normal political activities. But we do not think they had any marked effect. Indeed we are inclined to think they were counter-productive.'[185]

Assessment of Evidence

In assessing the evidence, the Commissioners considered first whether the proposals had been fully and properly explained to the population and concluded that: 'European, Coloured and Asian witnesses were in general well informed in the meaning and implications of the Proposals... we have no hesitation in affirming that the Proposals were fully and properly explained to this section of the population of Rhodesia.'

With regard to the African people the Commission commented fully on the fact that 'the Rhodesian authorities had limited their efforts to distributing the Proposals in full and in summary form and to briefing the Chiefs... otherwise had left it to the Chiefs to publicise them in the rural areas and had themselves refrained from any direct attempt to influence opinion.' The Commissioners were struck with 'how little had been done to commend the Proposals to the population.' On the other hand the Commissioners found 'In marked contrast to this... the African National Council... had been actively canvassing against the Proposals in nearly all the African areas we visited,' with the result that the Commissioners found 'when they reached an area that many were already seized of the disadvantages of the Proposals but had not always been given an objective explanation.' They did find, however, that A.N.C. activities were not uniform throughout the country, they were almost total in areas of greater political consciousness and very limited in remote areas. Nor did they generally penetrate into communities on European farms or at some mines.

In conclusion the Commissioners reported that 'Clearly there were many Africans who at the end of our labours had at best a limited understanding of the Proposals... But all our teams of Commissioners, except one (Matabeleland North) concluded that the majority of Africans whom they met sufficiently understood the basic principles and implications of the proposals to pass a valid judgement on them... in this sense the Proposals were fully and properly explained to the population of Rhodesia'.[186]

Conclusions

The Commissioners outlined their conclusions in chapter 13:

> We are satisfied on our evidence that the Proposals are acceptable to the great majority of Europeans. We are equally satisfied, after considering all our evidence, including that on intimidation, that the majority of Africans rejected the Proposals. In our opinion the people of Rhodesia as a whole do not regard the Proposals as acceptable as a basis for independence.

Appendices to the Report include biographical notes; selected memoranda and letters from individuals and organisations; lists of groups heard by the chairmen; population tables based on the 1969 Census; summaries of Commissioners' reports; an analysis of written evidence; an analysis of reasons for rejection given by Africans in written evidence; extracts from Commissioners' reports and other material relating to intimidation; and extracts from correspondence on normal political activity.

REACTIONS TO THE PEARCE REPORT

The Rhodesian Government

In the same late edition of the Salisbury daily newspaper publishing the findings of the Pearce Commission a statement, outlining the government's preliminary views on these findings, was printed. This was later given in full in a pamphlet issued by the Ministry of Information which also included the text of the Prime Minister's broadcast.[187]

The statement commenced by explaining that the Pearce Commission had been appointed by the British government in terms of the requirement of the British 'fifth principle'; namely, that the terms providing a basis for the recognition of Rhodesia's independence should be acceptable to the people as a whole. The government accepted that the task of the Commission was a difficult one but found this not to be surprising for 'the Rhodesian Government have never been convinced that complex constitutional proposals should be the subject of an exercise of this nature.' The statement then continued by detailing reasons why 'certain aspects of the Report are unsatisfactory and certain conclusions do not carry conviction.'

First, with regard to African opinion, the government considered that the Commission had given insufficient weight to the question of intimidation and that the Commission's finding, that the majority of the African tribesmen had understood the Proposals, was of doubtful validity. With regard to the Commission's estimate that the Commissioners saw 6 *per cent* of the adult population of the Tribal Trust Lands, the statement goes on to say that 'it will therefore be appreciated that there was an enormous silent majority in the Tribal Trust Lands, amounting to 94 *per cent* of the adult population, which did not express an opinion.' Moreover, as the A.N.C. had claimed that there was no part of Rhodesia to which their canvassing had not reached, the Government considered that it was 'significant that in spite of the vigorous and extensive A.N.C. campaign, 94 *per cent* of the adults in the Tribal Trusts Lands remained silent... it is evident that the views of the majority of the tribesmen, who comprise the greater part of the African population, remain unknown.'

Secondly, the government doubted the Commission's finding that the proposals had been 'fully and properly' understood. The dominant reason for rejection—namely mistrust of the government—'illustrates, in so far as it relates to the implementation of the proposals, that they do not seem to have been understood... [for] the proposals provide that it is only *after* the Rhodesian Government has given effect to the constitutional changes... that the British would carry out their part in implementing the agreement.'

'Firstly, there is a basic improbability that unlettered African tribesmen can understand and assess complex constitutional matters even though explained in simple terms. Secondly, account must be taken of the intimidation found by the Commission to have been present. Thirdly, according to the Report, all political activity in the Tribal Trust Lands was carried on by the anti-settlement element whose aim... according to the Commission, was to achieve "an appearance of solidarity intended to convince the Commission that Africans spoke with one voice". The anti-Settlement element could hardly have achieved this aim by exposition and logical persuasion in the short time at their disposal; they could only have done so by methods which tended to stifle discussion and explanation, by dragooning people into conformity or by appealing to the emotion.'

The statement went on to criticize the acceptance of the quantitive test which the Pearce Commission had decided should be applicable. For the Commission had accepted as 'No' votes those who had rejected the proposals because they distrusted government intentions or disapproved of government policies rather than because they had disapproved of the Proposals themselves. 'It would seem that this unqualified acceptance of 'No' votes for reasons not relevant to the Proposals is not consistent with the rejection of votes given by mistake or with the aim of the test, which was to determine whether or not the Proposals were acceptable.' The statement also found that the manner in which the majority of the Commission dealt with the question of intimidation was 'not at all convincing' for, apart from what the government considered to be a mistaken attitude towards the effects of the riots and disorders which took place at the beginning of the Commission's tour the Commission had had no experience of the events of the 1960's which had shown to what extent, in a politically tense situation, a minority could dominate a majority in a few weeks by intimidation. It also found that the reasoning, in the statement that the Commission had found the actual number of cases of intimidation very small considering the size of the country and its 5 million or so African inhabitants, entirely unconvincing on the grounds that due allowance was not made for 'the fear of intimidation [being] as powerful a factor as intimidation itself'; that the size of the country was irrelevant considering there had been reports of intimidation in all the Provinces; and that there was an inconsistency in saying that the numbers of cases of intimidation were small compared to a population of 5 million when for the sake of assessing the proportion of the population they saw, the Commissioners referred only to adult Africans and the figure given was just over 2 million.

The statement concluded that
1. The Report itself clearly showed that the views of the overwhelming majority of African adults were not obtained;
2. Two of the teams of Commissioners were satisfied that intimidation amongst Africans was on such a large scale and the level of comprehension of the Proposals so low that it was not possible to assess the views of Africans;
3. The reasons given by the remaining Commissioners for concluding that intimidation was not by a minority against the majority and that there was an adequate degree of comprehension amongst Africans were unconvincing;

4. It was unreasonable not to discount the weight of the votes of those who were not rejecting the Proposals but were expressing disapproval or distrust of the Government.

At the end of the statement the government said that 'for these reasons' it was unable to accept as being correct the conclusions reached by the Pearce Commission.

In his broadcast, the same evening, the Prime Minister announced that there would be a full debate on the Report when Parliament reassembled in June and then said that he 'would not have credited that any report could contain so many misinterpretations and misconstructions of the true position.' He then went on to give detailed examples and figures from the Report to illustrate what he meant:

Out of slightly more than 100 000 Europeans, 98 634 said 'Yes', 1 790 said 'No': in other words, more than 98 *per cent* said 'Yes'. In the case of the Coloured people, 391 said 'Yes', while only 10 said 'No': in excess of 97 *per cent* in favour.
Dealing with the Asian community, 624 said 'Yes', 21 'No': more than 96 *per cent* in favour.
Dealing with the Africans, the report concedes that the Commissioners saw less than 6 *per cent* of the adult African population. Accepting that the majority of these were opposed to the terms, however specious the reason, what about the other 94 *per cent* of African opinion?

The Prime Minister then stated that 'when all this is added up (and there is much more similar evidence) I submit there is only one conclusion: The Pearce Commission had the wool pulled over its eyes.'

Mr. Smith then went on to speak of the future. He said that he had informed the British government that the Rhodesian government was prepared to implement the Agreement if the British would do so but there was to be no question of a unilateral implementation of the terms; that there would be no more negotiations with a view to changing the terms of the agreement; that the Rhodesian government, in the event of a rejection of a mutual implementation of terms would continue to govern firmly in terms of the existing Constitution.

On the following day the *Herald's* editorial said that 'both Governments—the British as well as the Rhodesian—have some hard lessons to learn from the Pearce *debacle*... the first is that it is dangerous to depart from the principle that in our and in the British system, governments are elected to govern. The British fifth principle—the test of acceptability— was a grave error of judgement. The second lesson is that on the Pearce Commission's own showing the veto was accepted as effective though it was exercised by only a fraction of the African adult population—less than 6 *per cent*... The third lesson is one particularly for the Rhodesian Government to learn. Whether Mr. Smith likes to admit it or not, he must recognise if progress is to be made that human relations in this country are bedevilled by mistrust... The initiative for remedying the situation—and it is urgent that a remedy be found—must come from the Government.'[188]

Foreign Reaction

In South Africa, the Prime Minister, Mr. B. J. Vorster, viewed the verdict of the Pearce Commission as a 'tragic shock' and considered that its consequences would be difficult to foresee. However, he assured Rhodesia that South Africa's relations with, and its attitude towards, Rhodesia would remain unchanged. The leader of the opposition United Party, Sir de Villiers Graaff also commented, saying that all friends of Rhodesia in South Africa were deeply disappointed.

The Canadian Minister of External Affairs said that the confidence of outside observers had been upheld by the Commission's verdict and that Canada would continue to support 'democratic majority rule... [and]... to refuse to recognise the illegal regime.' Canada would also continue to uphold United Nations obligations and maintain existing sanctions against Rhodesia.

Among the Black African states, Emperor Haile Selassie of Ethiopia praised the 'objective report reflecting the genuine feeling of the African majority in Zimbabwe' and urged Britain to call a constitutional conference and to tighten sanctions against 'the rebel regime'. In Ghana, the *Ghanaian Times* commented that the rejection of the terms had come as no surprise for only 'racists and big business interests ever nursed any false hopes that the proposals would be countenanced by the Rhodesian Africans.' The newspaper also went on to say that 'the absence of Rhodesian Africans during the negotiations... reinforces the view that British economic interest was the over-riding factor.' It urged the Organization for African Unity (O.A.U.) and all nations 'who cherish human dignity to raise their voice and urge Britain to pile up pressure against Smith and his henchmen.' In Kenya, the Foreign Minister, Dr. Mungai, expressed his government's satisfaction 'on the impartiality of Lord Pearce and his Commission', while in Uganda, President Amin was quoted as saying on Radio Kampala that for the sake of good race relations the British government should press Mr. Smith to establish general elections based on one man, one vote and to accept the majority verdict. In Zambia, the *Zambia Daily Mail* (the government newspaper), said that the 'No' verdict 'was the most honest assessment of local opinion that had come out of that unhappy country for many years' and went on to advise the British government to take the A.N.C.'s advice seriously and call a national convention of all leaders in the country to try and solve the country's political problems. The *Malawi News* commented that in view of the fact that the 'No' verdict was largely registered by the African majority it must be interpreted to mean that 'if an amicable, honourable solution is to be found... it is, by and large, the Africans whose will must be taken into account.'[189]

In Britain, Sir Alec Douglas-Home presented the Pearce Report to the House of Commons saying that the British government now believed that 'it is up to the Rhodesian people as a whole to produce their own ideas for a constitution which would achieve independence'. He confirmed that the *status quo* as regards sanctions would continue. In commenting the next day, in its editorial, the *Daily Telegraph* said 'Whatever argument there may be about the Pearce Commission's justification for finding that the Home-Smith proposals were unacceptable to Rhodesian Africans, one thing is obvious: the famous fifth principle—that any settlement must be acceptable to the people of Rhodesia as a whole—is dead beyond hope of revival [for] the inescapable conclusion must be that mass opinion, however tested, will always reflect the view of the African nationalist politicians.'

The debate on the Pearce Report took place in the House of Commons on the 15th June 1972. In his address Sir Alec Douglas-Home appealed to Rhodesian Africans to re-consider their opposition to the settlement proposals for he did not believe that it would be practical to negotiate better terms. He also said that it was 'fair to conclude that "No" related less to the actual proposals than to distrust of the Rhodesian Front Government' and said that the

Rhodesians must be given time for saner reflection. At the end of the debate Sir Alec confirmed that the Beira patrol (to stop oil being supplied to Rhodesia through the port of Beira) would continue to operate and that any new proposals for a settlement would be within the five principles.

The next day the *Daily Telegraph* printed an article in which the debate was commented upon. 'The occasion itself was supposed to be an Opposition attack on Government policy in the wake of the Pearce Commission Report... the contribution by Mr. Callaghan [Labour M.P. and Shadow Foreign Secretary] can only be described as bombastic fatalism. There were all sorts of ringing declarations about Britain's responsibility, followed by a rather lame admission that Britain could not discharge it.'[190]

Parliamentary Debate on the Report

When the House of Assembly re-assembled on the 6th June 1972 the Prime Minister opened the debate on the Pearce Report. In Rhodesia it was felt that the debate would provide a barometer of Rhodesian Front feelings in the aftermath of the Report and also provide a pointer towards future Rhodesian relations both with Britain and South Africa.

The Prime Minister prefaced his speech with reference to the talks which had led up to the settlement proposals. He said that the British negotiators had given the impression that 'the exercise [of testing the acceptability of the proposals] would be a quiet testing of responsible opinion and that the emphasis would be on ascertaining whether the proposals were acceptable in the light of the alternative of retaining the *status quo*.' Much importance had been placed on a minimum of delay in proceeding with the test. It was therefore with 'considerable disquiet' that the government learnt that the Commission would not arrive in Rhodesia until the second week in January and that the Test would take about two months to complete. The Rhodesian government had pointed out the danger of delay increasing 'the chances of opposition to the settlement being generated through intimidation', for it was anticipated that nationalist extremists would be bitterly opposed to proposals that would end their hopes of attaining majority rule immediately. The Prime Minister also gave details of organizations in Britain which had been given time to mount campaigns against acceptance of the proposals.

In discussions with the Commission's secretariat regarding the procedures to be adopted during the test, government officials had been 'gravely concerned by their plans which were far removed from the quiet testing of responsible opinion we had been led to expect.' The British officials 'were warned that if the test was to be carried out on the lines proposed it would be impossible to create an atmosphere free from tension and disturbance necessary for obtaining an accurate and genuine expression of African opinion.'

Mr. Smith also quoted from a letter he had sent to Sir Alec Douglas-Home on the 26th January in which, without implying criticism of the Commission, he had pointed out that the Commission 'had been wrongly advised in regard to the methods used' and that the methods had 'given both opportunity and encouragement to intimidators.' The Prime Minister went on to make two general observations, firstly, that 'The entire operation must provide one of the very few occasions in history when the least responsible elements of a community have been able to influence the future of their country merely by shouting "No" sufficiently loudly and often. It also provides the remarkable situation of the British government virtually binding itself in advance to accept the findings of a Commission of Inquiry even though those findings might be clearly contrary to the interests of the people and country concerned.'

Secondly, on the question of intimidation, the Prime Minister said 'perhaps nowhere else in the Report have the Commission so completely destroyed the credibility of their findings and so starkly revealed their ignorance of the stresses and strains to which Africans become subject during times of tension and unrest.' He then went on to give instances of what he meant by inconsistencies and 'curious features' of the Report, and to illustrate the extent to which intimidation had permeated throughout the whole operation.

Mr. Smith continued by criticizing the basis of evaluation used by the Commission, which he found less than fair. He instanced the Africans employed in the European areas—about 250 000 farm workers and about 116 000 domestic servants—who were either not tested or not reported upon. He summed up by saying that 'the views expressed by 114 534 Africans with whom the Commission had either direct or indirect contact are the views of those

Africans and no others. However, the Commission has concluded that the opinions of the majority of the Africans in Rhodesia are those expressed by less than 6 *per cent* of their number and it is the views of that proportion which have decided the outcome of the test.'

Turning to relations between the two governments, the Prime Minister said that in the latter part of February it had become increasingly clear that the British government had had a change of heart. The visit of one of the Deputy Chairmen, Lord Harlech, to Britain in early February and the remarks that he had made on his return to Salisbury 'seemed to indicate that already the [negative] result was a foregone conclusion, even though the test was still in progress and, more significantly, even though the two special Commissioners sent out from the U.K. to assess the effects of intimidation had barely commenced their investigations.' Mr. Smith continued by giving further instances which seemed to him indicative of the British government's change of mind. He concluded by commenting 'as the picture unfolds it certainly reveals an astonishing story which must compel people to speculate why the British suddenly changed course in mid-stream.'

Towards the end of his speech the Prime Minister referred to what he considered the most important of all the problems requiring urgent attention—the promotion of harmonious race relations—and urged the people of Rhodesia to try and solve this problem in such a way as to 'minimise friction [and] acknowledge human feelings and the dignity of man.' He also promised that the government would be fair but would also be strong and firm.

In conclusion Mr. Smith said that it appeared that the British government seemed to have lost the will to settle and that the bitter lesson which Africans in Rhodesia must learn from the 'abortive Pearce Commission' is that 'the British government has no power to influence further the course of events in Rhodesia.'[191]

Commenting upon this speech the *Herald's* editorial the next day said: 'It is a sorry story of mismanagement and misjudgement—and not only by the Commission. It is another example of the futility of thinking about and for Africa and Africans in Westminster terms.'[192]

Following the Prime Minister's speech, Mr. D. Fawcett Phillips, M.P. for Hillside (Bulawayo), found it surprisingly illogical that the British government 'should enter into an agreement which specifically excludes unimpeded progress to majority rule and yet, on the other hand, set up a commission to test the acceptability of the settlement proposals on the basis of universal suffrage.' Another speaker, Mr. M. M. Bhebe, M.P. for Ntshonalanga, said 'I am one of those who supported the proposals very genuinely, not because I was supporting the Rhodesian Front Government... but I thought it was a national issue... I do not think, and I will never ever believe, either in my bones or in my brain, that a single African in this country could have afforded refusing these proposals were it not for the distrust they had in the Government.' Mr. Bhebe then continued by discussing the traditional non-political role which the chiefs had played in the past: saying that in his opinion, the government had erred in not recalling Parliament during the Commission's visit so that the proposals and the government's intentions could have been properly explained to the people; he also censured the government for not allowing African M.P.'s to broadcast in the vernacular. Mr. Bhebe finished his speech by urging the government to implement the settlement terms unilaterally.

Two other African M.P.'s, Mr. L. Masenda and Mr. J. M. Khabo, M.P.'s for Mabvazuwa and Pagati respectively, spoke of the confusion they felt over the government's attitude towards the proposals: they had heard other M.P.'s say that they would be happy to retain the 1969 Constitution, but now they were saying they were sad that the Africans had rejected the proposals. Mr. Khabo considered that what the Africans wanted was for 'the African and the European to work together and find solutions which will bring the two races to mutual understanding which does not exist in this country today.'

Another African, Mr. R. T. D. Sadomba, thought that Africans had good reasons for mistrusting the proposals, for not only had the Prime Minister 'assured the white electorate that the Rhodesian way of life would not change' but during the Test the chairman of the Rhodesian Front Party had, on two occasions, said that the Land Tenure Act would remain as it was and that the government would go ahead with its policy of provincialization.' Mr. Sadomba considered that the 'No' vote was a 'spontaneous reaction by the Africans and a clear disapproval of government policy.'

Mr. C. A. R. Savory, M.P. for Matobo, said that he believed

that the government was out of touch with African thinking and that the failure to recall Parliament during the Test was 'a great opportunity lost'. Mr. Savory went on to give instances in which he disagreed with the Prime Minister's criticism both of the Pearce Commission and the British government. In particular he did not agree with the Prime Minister's allegations that the British government had had a change of heart half-way through the sitting of the Pearce Commission.

Mr. J. A. Newington, M.P. for Hillcrest (Salisbury), who continued the debate, considered that the European point of view had not been given a fair hearing and pointed out to his listeners that the period had been 'a point in Rhodesian history when there was great willingness to co-operate and this [had been] lost by the African.' Mr. Newington found it hard to believe that any government could have gone to such lengths to agree on terms 'which it believed provided both social and economic advances and that were fair and reasonable and then... allowed their reasoned planning to be negated by the opinion of drop-outs and rabid hooligans, agitators and the like, the fools and the primitive mob.'

The late Mr. Gondo, M.P. for Kunyasi, believed that the opportunity for a settlement was still present and that the Prime Minister should not be afraid to find out the true opinion of the Africans 'regarding where amendments or where changes could possibly be made' and went on to appeal to the Prime Minister to get 'to the people and [find] out whether something can be done about the acceptance of these proposals.'[193]

The debate was adjourned until the following afternoon to enable the Prime Minister to study previous speeches and to prepare his reply. Prefacing his speech by saying that although, understandably, there had been wide differences of opinion during the debate, there had been an interesting revelation in the wide measure of agreement on a number of the broad issues involved. There seemed to be general agreement 'that the Commission was totally misguided in the procedures it had adopted' and no contradiction of the government's view that the Commission had 'compounded its errors by basing its conclusions on a quantitative evaluation... the test... thereby [being] reduced to a counting of heads operation.' Another issue in which Mr. Smith found no fundamental disagreement from M.P.'s was on the 'validity or otherwise of the conclusions drawn by the Commission from the evidence set out in their Report' for there was general agreement that the conclusion reached was totally unjustified.

Referring to the British government's apparent change of mind during the sitting of the Commission, Mr. Smith said he was interested to see that this had been noticed by a number of members and he had noted the suggested reasons they had advanced for this apparent change of direction. 'I was not attacking the British Government for deciding that a "No" from the Pearce Commission would be easier to handle than a "Yes". The British government have a number of intractable problems on their hands which, they told us, were of greater importance than the Rhodesian issue. For example, at that time the passage of the Common Market legislation through the House of Commons had reached an extremely delicate stage and at the same time they had, and still have, the problems of Ulster and of industrial unrest. The point I am making and the lessons which Rhodesians of all races must draw is that the British policy on Rhodesia is dictated, not necessarily by what is in the best interests of Rhodesia, but rather by what is seen by the British government to be in the best interests of Britain.'

The Prime Minister 'rejected out of hand' the various claims that the government's refusal to recall Parliament had meant that people had not been 'given an authoritative lead on the merits of the proposals and the advantages to be gained from their acceptance,' and went on to outline measures which the government had taken to recommend the proposals to the people. 'As a result of these endeavours we were accused, in certain circles, of putting undue pressure on Africans... partly to avoid giving the impression of excessive government influence and also so as not to add to the political fervour and excitement that had been aroused we decided not to recall Parliament'.

The Prime Minister also referred to Chapter 12 of the Pearce Report saying that the eighteen paragraphs entitled *Intimidation of Africans by the Rhodesian Authorities to gain Acceptance* showed that, if the government had been as inactive as alleged, there would have been no need for all these paragraphs. Mr. Smith added that members of the Commission supported the government in these views.

Finally Mr. Smith summed up by saying:

The Pearce Commission was a British Commission appointed by the British Government and composed entirely of Britishers. Its terms of reference were laid down by the British Government without consultation with my Government. They decided on their own *modus operandi* and in doing so they ignored very largely the advice of Rhodesian officials and others who know Rhodesia and know the Rhodesian Africans. The Commission did not, in any way or at any time, consult us in regard to how to assess African opinion. We believe that their verdict was a wrong one for the following reasons: firstly, because the overwhelming majority of three of the four racial groups and of all responsible bodies, who together make up the running of the country, were in support of the proposals. Secondly, because of the way they carried out the test, the effects of intimidation made it impossible for them to make a fair assessment of African opinion. Thirdly, because a large proportion of the Africans, who they say rejected the settlement, either had no knowledge or understanding of the implications of the proposals themselves, or else they were rejecting the settlement for irrelevant reasons, such as their dislike of the Government, their dislike of dipping their cattle, of digging contour ridges etc. Fourthly, because they arrived at their conclusion on a purely quantitative basis instead of the qualitative basis which they themselves admit would have been in the best interests of Rhodesia.[194]

Following the debate in the House of Assembly, the Senate began its debate on the Report on the afternoon of 13th June. Senator S. E. Morris (a former Secretary for Internal Affairs who had given specialist advice to the Pearce Commissioners) criticized the Commission's failure to act upon this advice and in particular for having undermined, in the way that they had conducted meetings in the tribal areas, the authority of the chiefs and other tribal authorities. He also criticized African members of the House of Assembly for their expressed views on the role of chiefs in tribal society.

The debate was resumed the next day when Chief Sigola (a Senator from Matabeleland and the oldest chief in the Senate, a member of both the Monckton and Whaley Commissions)[195] expressed his dismay at the Report and said (in a speech translated from Ndebele) 'What I do not understand is this—when a man arrives at another person's house, is it customary for that traveller to ask the road from the children, or from the elders? Now, it appears that England defied custom and spoke with the children, leaving out the opinion of the elders.' The Chief continued by discussing what he had said to the Pearce Commissioners and said that he had questioned 'whether in their own country did they consult children and the ordinary man in the street on issues of importance? In the case of the Common Market did you approach the man in the street or was it dealt with by responsible people?'

Senator G. F. Fraser said that he considered that the Report 'flouted basic principles of law and justice for the assessing of evidence... incorporated... in English law, particularly in relation to undue influence... the first example of which is intimidation, force and fear.' The Senator then went on to quote definitions of undue influence from Halsbury: *Laws of England*[196] and summed up by commenting that intimidation 'ran right round the country and hung like a miasma over the whole land... [but] the Commissioners failed to see it or chose not to'. He queried whether 'the basic principles of law, good sense and justice, within which it [the Pearce Commission] was presumably supposed to act, gave it the right in those circumstances to arrive at an outright verdict at all, particularly a verdict of "No"?' Senator Fraser added that 'The verdict at which it arrived was, of course, the verdict which the intimidation was designed to secure; which makes it all the more incomprehensible and reprehensible that it should have arrived at that verdict.'

The following day Senator W. H. Whaley, chairman of the Senate Legal Committee and chairman of the Constitutional Commission (which bears his name) in 1968, gave his views on the Report. With regard to the demand from some quarters that there should be a unilateral implementation of the terms, Senator Whaley said that he considered this would be ingenuous and naive for it would put Britain in the position of being able to say that this was an earnest of Rhodesia's good faith but new circumstances had arisen and it was not now sufficient. Senator Whaley also referred to the question of discussions with the A.N.C. to work out a compromise settlement and said that 'if there is to be any consultation between racial groups on the one hand and the Government on the other, the racial groups concerned must then be prepared to step down off their perch, abandon many of their preconceived notions... and walk along the road towards the Government extending the hand of friendship instead of spitting hatred and venom.' The Senator added that the A.N.C. manifesto had features which revealed 'antagonism, arrogance and an unyielding determination not to give way or to compromise.'[197]

Comment other than from Government

Comment from extra-governmental circles mainly came from political parties and the press. The multi-racial Centre Party considered that the Pearce 'No' verdict was an implicit condemnation of the Rhodesian Front and that Rhodesians 'of all races have to work out their own salvation.' In an article in the C.P. newspaper, *Centrepoint*, the C.P. vice-president, Mr. N. J. McNally, said 'We Whites have really got to make up our minds. Either this is a white country in which Africans have no rights and no human dignity or it is a complex, multi-racial country in which both race groups must work out their joint future.'[198] On the other hand the African National Council saw, in the action of sending the Rhodesian government an advance copy of the Pearce Report and not sending the A.N.C. one, 'something deplorable' and warned the British government that 'it is this practice of excluding African leaders at the initial stages of considering issues that defeated the settlement proposals', adding that in any future negotiations African leaders should be consulted in advance for 'in order for any future negotiations to succeed the three major parties in this issue—the British Government, the Rhodesian Government and the African National Council—should come together.'[199]

On his return from visiting Britain and the United States the A.N.C. leader, Bishop Muzorewa, said that he had fully expected the 'No' verdict and regarded it as a victory for the A.N.C. The Bishop considered that there should now be a lull to allow things to cool down.

In June the monthy *Property and Finance* headlined its main article *The Nation's Narrow Escape: P.M.'s Future: R.F.'s Last Chance: Public Demands Clean-up*. The newspaper explained that the headline *Nation's Narrow Escape* had first been used by *Property and Finance* in 1966, after the Prime Minister's agreement with the British Prime Minister on H. M. S. Tiger had been successfully resisted by certain members of the Prime Minister's own Cabinet. In the article, the Pearce Commission was criticized for its long initial delay which had enabled ex-detainees to organize resistance; the composition of the Commission was described as 'a microcosm of men adept at selling the white man down the

African river'; and comment was made that 'the Pearce "No" on the basis of the Black veto warranted nothing more than dignified contempt.'[200]

In July the same periodical commented 'It is now clear that most Africans shouted "No" because they did not believe the Prime Minister would implement the terms; and that most Whites said "Yes" because they believed exactly the same thing.'

Moto considered that 'the Pearce Report is by no means entirely negative but also had positive implications important enough to act as guidelines of future policy regarding Rhodesia. First of all it is clear that the African people of Rhodesia have a political awareness which was unsuspected... The African National Council and its leaders were thrown up by the masses...' *Moto* then went on to outline its own ideas for the future and concluded by saying 'the British Government... should by now have learned the lesson that only Africans who are accepted by Africans can speak for Africans, and that it must base its future policy for Rhodesia on this fact... what must be sought is not just a settlement but a just settlement.'[201]

POST-PEARCE PLANNING

On the day the Pearce Report became available to members of the public, the A.N.C. held an open-air press conference at Salisbury's Highfield African Township at which its plans for settling the impasse over the failure of the acceptability of the settlement proposals were announced. The A.N.C. spokesman outlined the plans for a national convention to be held in the near future to which would 'be invited... the whole of the A.N.C. executive, 25 delegates from the Rhodesian Front, up to six delegates from each of the other Rhodesian political parties, all trade unions and employers' organizations, organized commerce and industry, the churches, local authorities [and] African chiefs' as well as a number of prominent Rhodesians, including some who were in detention, and, in an advisory capacity, heads of all government ministries, heads of the armed services and the judiciary. It was also hoped that observers would be present from 'all the British political parties, the United Nations, the Organization for African Unity, the World Council of Churches and other church groups.' The speakers said they expected 'that this convention [would] pass a resolution calling upon the British Government, the Rhodesian Government, the African leaders and leaders of other recognized parties to bring about a constitutional conference'. Bishop Muzorewa considered that the convention plan would be a 'valued and positive approach... to resolve the Rhodesian constitutional deadlock'.[202] The next day however, the Prime Minister, Mr. Ian Smith, gave his views on the A.N.C. proposals saying that his government would neither sponsor a dialogue between Rhodesians on the settlement issue nor would he see A.N.C. leaders for, he said, 'they present to me a picture of a bunch of unscrupulous politicians who have hoodwinked the poor African into going in a direction which may be of advantage to those few politicians but obviously to the disadvantage of the African. They would have to prove themselves a lot more responsible and show that they do speak on behalf of the African people before I will have any truck with them.' As regards plans for the future, Mr. Smith said that he did not envisage any more initiative from, or talks with, Britain in the near future. Rhodesia would carry on as she had been doing since U.D.I. 'concentrating on her own home affairs, irrespective of the rest of the world.'

Comments on the A.N.C. proposals were varied: in an editorial the *Herald* agreed that it was clear that Rhodesians must get together to discuss their differences and that there must be a willingness to compromise, to get together and try to appreciate the other man's point of view, from all sides. It did, however, consider that the A.N.C.'s plans for a convention, to include observers from British political parties, the United Nations, the Organization for African Unity and the World Council of Churches would be impertinence for they had 'no place, or any right to a place, in Rhodesian domestic affairs.' The newspaper concluded with the comment, as a last point, 'let no-one claim when the A.N.C.'s present "initiative" is rebuffed that this is proof once more of White intransigence. For the A.N.C. knew when they made it that the proposal was a non-starter.'[203]

The Centre Party held the view that it would 'agree to any representative discussion on the country's constitutional future, whether convened by the A.N.C. or anybody else.' It would not agree, however, to 'any outside participation or even to the presence of outside observers.' Both the Rhodesian Front and the United

Front parties refused comment but the leader of the Rhodesia National Party, Mr. L. Idensohn, said that he had expected this move 'because the R.F. have lost the initiative and it is now with the black man... It means that the British Government has forced the situation where the only step forward is to instant black rule.'

The Associated Chambers of Commerce offered no comment on the issue and the President of the Association of Rhodesian Industries felt that, as it was a political matter, his Association should not get involved with it. Spokesmen for the churches throughout the country refused to comment except for a spokesman for the Anglican church who said that as it was to be a political convention the church could not become involved but 'this is not to say we are not interested. We are very interested in the affairs of this country and feel that justice should be done for all races.'

Commenting on these various views, the *Herald's* political reporter, Ian Mills, said 'Statements made this week by both sides show that the wedge driven into Rhodesian politics by the test of acceptability is biting deeply... in forcing the Government and the governing party to reject publicly its proposals for solving Rhodesia's problems the A.N.C. has thrown down the gauntlet and possibly set a pattern of racial political confrontation.' [204]

SETTLEMENT DEVELOPMENTS DURING 1972-3

By early July 1972 there was much conjecture about a new settlement. 'Informed sources' in Britain were quoted as saying that if responsible African opinion would indicate that the November proposals were acceptable an immediate end to the deadlock could be found. Three specified fields of responsible African opinion were mentioned; African church leaders, African trade union leaders and African teachers. Sir Alec Douglas-Home was quoted as saying that the settlement proposals were 'still on the table [but] the next move must come from the Rhodesians.'

Various Rhodesian government ministers gave their views on whether a settlement could be obtained and the A.N.C. vice-chairman, the Rev. Canaan Banana, said that the situation now called for 'positive attempts at working out a new formula, together with African leadership, that would bring a lasting solution.' On the 15th July, in announcing plans for the first A.N.C. public meeting in a European residential area, Bishop Muzorewa said that the

A.N.C. wanted a settlement but 'there has to be a compromise between Europeans and Africans... [a] compromise [which] must be between "never majority rule" and "majority rule now".'[205]

On the 25th July it was announced that a new group had been formed in Salisbury to encourage Africans to support the 1971 settlement terms. Known as the Rhodesian Settlement Association, this would, according to its chairman, Mr. W. M. Munangatire, 'work to establish branches in all main centres... for the personal opinions of many Africans have yet to be heard. Our Association will give them voice to express support for a prompt settlement.' The Association's aims were to ensure that the settlement terms were fully explained and to try to convince people who had rejected the settlement that, if implemented, the terms would ensure that Rhodesians as a whole would have a happier and more prosperous future. Mr. Munangatire added that the Association 'would try to gain support from leaders of different societies (both in urban and rural areas), such as trade unions, African chiefs, church leaders, politicians, businessmen, farmers and social organisations.' The constitution of the Association emphasized that there would be no links with political organisations which did not accept the settlement terms.[206] Later in the year the Rhodesian Settlement Association merged with the pro-settlement Rhodesian Progressive Liberal Forum to form the Rhodesian Settlement Forum.

A new European-led organisation was formed at the beginning of August—the Settlement Council—dedicated towards obtaining African acceptance of the terms. Its chairman, Mr. R. Cary, in an article in the *Herald* said that the Settlement Council had been formed to provide 'an African rallying point—an African movement which, by its reasonableness and wide appeal [would] become credible both here and in Whitehall as a real expression of African opinion.'[207]

During the debate in the House of Assembly on 10th August, on the Revenue Vote for the Prime Minister, African members took the opportunity to criticize Mr. Smith for what they considered to be his lack of communication with Africans. Mr. Smith replied to these criticisms and in answer to a question as to what the government and the Prime Minister intended to do next, said 'I believe I have made the position quite clear... The only thing for us to do now is to face up to the facts of life. The facts of life are that these terms were rejected by the Africans and so we have accepted the position as it is now. We are going to get on and govern Rhodesia firmly under the 1969 Constitution to the best of our ability.'[208]

On the 29th September it was reported that an unofficial envoy from Britain, Mr. J. A. Hutter, a prominent member of both the Anglo-Rhodesian Society and the Conservative Monday Club, had arranged unofficial talks between the Minister of Internal Affairs, Mr. L. A. Smith, and representatives of African political groups, including the A.N.C. At the same time Sir Alec Douglas-Home announced, at a press conference, that although the sanctions order would be renewed in November he hoped that the Rhodesian government and Rhodesian Africans would soon be able to agree on some compromise formula for progress towards majority rule.[209]

By the 2nd October, however, the scheduled second meeting between the Minister and representatives of the A.N.C. had been cancelled and Mr. L. A. Smith denied that he had been holding talks with the A.N.C. as such. He issued an official statement reading: 'A great deal of publicity has been given in the last few days in the Press to a meeting which I had with Mr. Hutter... and certain Africans whom Mr. Hutter had expressed a desire to see... At no time have discussions taken place with the A.N.C. as such, nor are there likely to be any. The A.N.C. has been described previously as an irresponsible body, and Government sees no merit in having discussion with them. The fact that individual members, as Africans with a problem, wished to come forward and meet me is something I have always accepted and am always prepared to accept in future. However I do not intend to pursue discussions with these individuals any further.' The A.N.C. secretary-general, Mr. C. C. Ngcebetsha, however, stated that talks had been held between the Minister and three A.N.C. leaders who had reported to the executive committee that they were satisfied that the talks were going in the right direction.[210]

The following day, Ian Mills, commenting on the cancellation of the meetings, said in the *Herald* that 'it appears that there is a move to let things cool down and to remove the talks from the glare of publicity. Another factor is believed to have cropped up in the form of complaints from the African chiefs, who are understood to have expressed fears about the Government talking to the A.N.C.'[211]

In 1972 the annual congress of the Rhodesian Front was held in closed session, partly, it was conjectured, so that the Prime Minister could have 'a frank discussion with party delegates of the continuing needs for a settlement'. It was expected that 'the outcome of this week's congress—the success enjoyed by the Prime Minister in swaying his party's hardliners to his views—will have an important influence on the prospects of renewing dialogue in the months ahead... and of reaching a settlement.'[212] Later it was reported that the Prime Minister's views and wishes had dictated the whole tone of the congress and that the options were to be kept open on the settlement issue.

By November Ian Mills considered that 'as Rhodesia enters her eighth year of independence, settlement prospects could be poorer now than they have been since November 11th 1965. Until a year ago a settlement was a matter for the Rhodesian and British Governments [but] those days have gone by. The Pearce Commission and its aftermath [have] produced today's changed and unenviable situation... the Pearce Commission gave Rhodesian Africans a voice in the reckoning and British Government policy since Pearce has kept them there.'[213]

In the House of Assembly on the 22nd November two African Centre Party M.P.'s, Messrs. E. G. Watungwa and L. A. Ndhlovu, moved a private member's motion asking the House to deplore the Government's handling of the Anglo-Rhodesian dispute. The Speaker of the House, Mr. A. R. W. Stumbles, considering that a restriction should be placed on the debate because it might otherwise cover 'a wide and almost impossible range of discussion', ruled that during the course of the debate only topics which had taken place since the debate on the Pearce Report in June should be discussed.

Mr. Watungwa, M.P. for Harare (Salisbury), said he would like to offer the Government the opportunity 'to begin the initiative which Britain will accept' that is, to initiate discussion with African leaders. Mr. Watungwa warned, however, that although the African people were 'quite prepared to take a gamble and we are quite prepared to compromise... we are not going to be subdued into accepting a document which was signed by two Scotsmen to be imposed on the African people of this country.' Mr. Ndhlovu, M.P. for Insukamini, also felt that 'it is time now for the Government to take whatever steps they can to bring the African people together with the European people as Rhodesians and confront the British Government with an already drafted agreement which has already been proved acceptable to us in Rhodesia as a whole.' Another African, Mr. N. A. Gandanzara, M.P. for Manica, criticized the Prime Minister for not taking the initiative in summoning African leaders for consultation. He considered that the Ministry of Information, by continuing to say that Africans had now changed their minds, was depriving the government of the opportunity 'of seriously attempting and asking and persuading the Africans to come to settlement.' Mr. M. M. Bhebe endorsed what had been said by the other speakers in the debate and said that he considered it to be 'highly essential that both sides, not only the government but also the Africans who have refused the settlement, must swallow their pride.' He suggested that there must be 'a bartering of some kind. The Africans, and particularly the A.N.C., should be prepared at this stage to barter their "one man one vote" for the settlement and, of course, the Government must also be prepared to barter its status.'[214]

The debate lasted for only one hour and twenty minutes and the *Herald* commented 'As might have been expected, Government M.P.'s did not support the motion, but neither did they oppose it... in fact, there appeared to be a Government boycott. At one stage only four Government members were seated, and one of these was asleep. The Government Front Bench was also bare and for about thirty minutes not a single Cabinet Minister was in his seat. The Prime Minister... left his seat before the debate began.'[215]

The debate was continued on the 7th December when the Prime Minister said that he had studied the contributions made previously but found 'there is not a great deal to comment on because much of what was said was not really related to the subject of the motion.' Mr. Smith went on to examine the African claim that they had not been consulted during the negotiations which was one reason given for rejection of the proposals. He said that nobody other than the government had been consulted for 'the negotiations were conducted in the only possible way, that is, on a confidential government to government basis.' The Prime Minister went on to outline the benefits which would have accrued to Africans if the settlement terms had been accepted and he queried whether there ever was 'a more apt example of the expression "cutting off your nose to spite your face"?... does not this irresponsible behaviour prove how unworthy they are of consultation?'

The Prime Minister continued by stating 'there can be no question... of a national convention or any other gathering to discuss variations of the settlement terms because... the terms of the agreement are not negotiable.' He suggested that the time had come for a 're-appraisal of the situation by the African leaders [but] it must be appreciated once and for all that the choice lies between remaining under the 1969 Constitution or moving to the proposed new Constitution. There is no third alternative and anyone who attempts to persuade the Africans otherwise is doing them a grave disservice.' The Prime Minister concluded his speech by saying 'What we are suggesting is that those Africans who, in the emotional heat engendered by the Pearce Commission, rejected the settlement because they were not consulted beforehand, or because they do not like the Government or because they thought they might get a better offer, these people should now face up to the facts of life, and accept that those reasons have nothing to do with the question before them.' The Motion was put to a division and was denied.[216]

On the 22nd December Bishop Muzorewa held a press conference at the party headquarters in Highfield at which he said he hoped that settlement talks would begin some time in January, with the A.N.C. opening negotiations with the Rhodesian Front if there was a general response from the government. The talks would take place at Ministerial level but, added the Bishop, 'when any negotiations between the two parties begin, we shall be going there as the African National Council and not as individuals.'[217]

The early part of 1973 was largely occupied in attempting to find ways by which it could be demonstrated to the British government that the majority of Africans, despite the findings of the Pearce Report, actually did accept the 1971 proposals.

Towards the end of January the national executive of the A.N.C. met to draw up a statement on its official policy towards the settlement issue in readiness for any 'serious and meaningful talks' with the government. The Prime Minister, however, in an interview on British television warned Africans that what had to be decided was whether the 1971 terms were acceptable, for there could be no question of further negotiations.[218]

The closure of the border with Zambia on the 9th January was seen in Britain as increasing the odds against a settlement. As the London *Times* commented 'the circumstances that led to the closing of the border—infiltration by guerrillas which had considerable support from within Rhodesia—hardly suggests that the Africans are now ready to reverse their earlier verdict.'[219]

In mid-February, the Prime Minister, appearing again on British television, stated that before having talks with the A.N.C. he would have to be assured that there would be an agenda and some constructive discussion. As the *Mail* pointed out, however, it would be unwise to expect too much of such a meeting for 'both men have truculent supporters... Mr. Smith has his right-wing racialists, whom he has tried to placate in recent months... Bishop Muzorewa has his racialists—familiar faces from past nationalistic capers who will accept nothing short of majority rule.'[220]

At about the same time, however, the 'political staff' of the *Financial Gazette* considered that the A.N.C. had had a change of heart, 'undoubtedly... influenced by the formation of two pro-settlement groups formed by Africans generally outside the political spectrum.' This was a reference to the Rhodesian Settlement Forum and the African Settlement Convention 'which is concentrating its efforts on swinging opinion among urban Africans.' The A.N.C. publicity secretary, however, did not see these two groups as posing a threat to the A.N.C. He considered them to be 'just little groups with no message for the African people.'[221]

In late February it was announced that both the pro-settlement groups were to send delegations to London. The Forum claimed to have the signatures of more than 80,000 Africans, including those of about 80 chiefs, accepting the 1971 settlement proposals. The Convention (which had concentrated upon the organisation of small meetings in the urban areas) reported strong support for their pro-settlement line.

Plans for talks between the A.N.C. and the government were halted when two senior members of the Council's national executive were detained under the Emergency Powers Act. It was not until mid-March that Bishop Muzorewa announced that, although no satisfactory reply regarding the detentions had been received from government sources, the A.N.C. would be available to talk with anyone 'who is sincerely and genuinely determined to try and solve the present impasse.' Ten days later, however, the *Herald's* political reporter, Ian Mills, was commenting that moves to reconcile differences between the government and the Council were again faltering. He reported that the government was 'understood to be adamant in insisting that the settlement terms must be accepted as they are... and that the terms are not negotiable [while] the A.N.C. will not accept this stipulation.'[222]

Early in April Mr. E. G. Watungwa asked the Prime Minister in the House if an agreement had been reached with the A.N.C. on an agenda and if negotiations had begun. The Prime Minister confirmed that the government had been in contact with the A.N.C. but refused to give any further information. The following day, during the resumed debate on the security situation, the Prime Minister intervened 'to look into the future and to indicate the course which we intend to pursue.' Mr. Smith said that he considered that the security situation was aggravated and inflamed by 'the uncertainty over British intentions regarding the implementation of our constitutional agreement.' He went on to say that another opportunity, to convince the British government that the settlement was not only in the best interests of Rhodesians but also acceptable to them, had presented itself. He warned, however, that thought must be given to what would happen if, on completion of the exercise, it was found that the British government was not prepared, because of outside pressures, to implement its side of the bargain.[223]

A few days later the British Prime Minister, in answer to a question in the House of Commons regarding the trial and sentence of journalist Peter Niesewand, spoke of the damage done to Rhodesian hopes of a settlement by this action. Hopes of progression out of the impasse were further dampened when Bishop Muzorewa revealed that in his opinion talks between the government and A.N.C. representatives had not produced anything more than an attempt to induce the A.N.C. to accept the 1971 proposals.[224]

A week later Sir Alec Douglas-Home used the platform of the golden jubilee dinner of the South Africa Club to put across what the Herald's London Bureau reported as being regarded in London as 'his most important pronouncement on Rhodesia since the Pearce Report.' Sir Alec urged both sides to co-operate in trying to achieve 'an agreed basis for legal independence' and warned that it was no longer possible for either race to avoid the choice between 'persuasion and the gun'.[225]

Rhodesian opinion generally saw in this speech a plea for further negotiations and for concessions on the 1971 agreement. The Prime Minister, however, reiterated, in a press interview, that the 1971 terms were not negotiable and warned that 'if there were people who believe that by re-opening the talks they would get the Government to give more, they would be sadly disillusioned.' On this point he was criticized by both the A.N.C. and the Rhodesia National Party (at the other extreme). The A.N.C. warned that if Mr. Smith slammed the door on further negotiations 'it would have serious consequences for all the races in Rhodesia', while the R.N.P. considered the assumption that Rhodesian Europeans were still willing to implement the terms smacked 'of a dictatorial attitude by a government that has grown arrogant with too much power for too long.'[226]

In early May Sir Alec again called for an evolutionary political settlement in Rhodesia. This was followed by an A.N.C. statement which urged the government to negotiate towards the end proposed by Sir Alec and postulated that it was 'no longer political realism to stick to the rejected 1971 Anglo-Rhodesian proposals.' Later that month an exchange in the House of Commons was reported in the *Herald*. Mr. Harold Wilson, the leader of the opposition Labour Party, asked whether it should not be made clear that the settlement agreement did not still lie on the table and that it would require substantial amendment as well as African approval. In reply the British Prime Minister said that he could see no point in removing the agreement altogether, it would be better to use it as a basis for discussion. As the *Herald's* editor commented 'it emerges clearly from Mr. Heath's answer that the British Government has abandoned the position that the Home-Smith proposals are inviolable—that they are a package deal and cannot be changed. That is not Mr. Smith's view...'[227]

At the opening of the fourth session of the 12th Parliament in mid-June, the President, Mr. Clifford Dupont, began his speech by referring to the Anglo-Rhodesian situation. He prefaced his remarks by stating that the Rhodesian government still viewed a settlement with Britain as an important objective, but added 'it has become obvious that, because of political and economic considerations unrelated to Rhodesia, the British Government no longer have the same determination to resolve the issue that was evident when the agreement was signed in November 1971... If the British Government are not prepared to implement the 1971

Proposals my Government believe that the people of Rhodesia must reconcile themselves to this position.'[228] In the ensuing debate, both in the House of Assembly and in the Senate, the settlement issue was a dominant theme.

Towards the end of June it was reported that three British officials had been in Salisbury for four days and had been holding talks with Rhodesian officials. The British team was led by Sir Denis Greenhill, Permanent Under-Secretary at the Foreign Office, and he was accompanied by Mr. Miles Hudson, Sir Alec Douglas-Home's political secretary, and Mr. Robin Byatt, head of the Rhodesian Political Section at the Foreign Office. It was postulated that the visit had been expected in Rhodesian circles, for the British government was known to want the issue settled one way or the other before the forthcoming Commonwealth Prime Ministers' Conference. Furthermore, the A.N.C. leader had said that he considered that a visit by British officials would help in overcoming the deadlock.[229]

Following this visit Sir Alec Douglas-Home made a statement in the House of Commons. He emphasized that Sir Denis Greenhill had taken no new proposals with him nor had he brought any back and explained that 'the purpose of the visit was to provide me with an assessment of the present position in Rhodesia.' He appealed for both sides in Rhodesia 'to come together in the spirit of mutual compromise.' According to the *Telegraph's* reporter in Salisbury the British team 'paid particular attention to the views and findings of the two pro-settlement African groups.' It was noted, however, that the British officials motored 250 miles to ascertain the views of Bishop Muzorewa, who was now thought 'to be holding out for immediate parity of representation in the Rhodesian Parliament with swift transition to African majority representation.'[230]

At the end of June the Prime Minister, Mr. Ian Smith, speaking at the end of the debate on the President's speech referred to calls for talks with the A.N.C. He reminded members that the government had been in constant contact with African opinion 'through the Chiefs, both in the Senate and in the Council of Chiefs; through African members of Parliament in this House; through the leaders of various African organisations and by means of formal contacts with African businessmen and others.' He added that there had been direct contact with the African pro-settlement groups and that there had been discussions with the A.N.C. on two occasions, first with Bishop Muzorewa and secondly with two or three of the Bishop's senior supporters.

With reference to his meetings with the A.N.C. leaders the Prime Minister said that it had soon become clear that 'the fundamental objective... was to enter into formal negotiations with the Government with a view to drawing up a completely new settlement.' He then went on to detail the changes which the A.N.C. spokesmen had stated were necessary. These were: a substantial broadening and lowering of the franchise qualifications relating to the African Higher Roll; an increase in African membership of Parliament to bring about immediate parity in numbers of M.P.'s; an indication that the British Parliament be given the power to veto amendments to certain sections of the constitution; a new declaration of rights to apply to all existing laws which, if discriminatory, were to be repealed within 12 months; the recommendations of the proposed commission on racial discrimination to be wholly binding; the repeal of the Land Tenure Act, but with the retention of the Tribal Trust Lands for exclusive African use; all appointments to Ministries and the armed forces to be on the basis of equal racial quotas; and immediate release of all detainees with an amnesty for all members of 'terrorist' organisations outside the country.

Mr. Smith went on to say that it was hardly necessary for him to state 'that these demands of the A.N.C. are totally and absolutely unacceptable, individually and as a whole.' He stated 'quite categorically, that in the present circumstances the prospects of an acceptable settlement appear to be remote and we should adjust our thinking accordingly.'[231]

In reply to the Prime Minister's speech the A.N.C. denied that it had made 'heavy and unrealistic demands' and stated that its proposals were 'still secret and will remain a secret until negotiations begin.'[232] *Moto,* in its editorial comment, remarked upon the fact that the A.N.C.'s demands had not been published and urged the Council 'to have the courage to bring their views into the open and not add to the national confusion.'[233]

NOTES

1 *Anglo-Rhodesian Relations : Proposals for a Settlement : Presented to Parliament by the Prime Minister on 25 November 1971 :* Cmd. R.R. 46-1971 : Salisbury: Government Printer.
2 Constitution Act No. 54 of 1969.
3 C.S.R. 32-1969: *Government Gazette Extraordinary :* 21 May 1969.
4 Electoral Act No. 56 of 1969.
5 The powers and composition of the Tribunal form paragraphs (6), (7) and (8) of the Declaration of Rights in the Second Schedule of the 1969 Constitution:

> (6) A tribunal ... shall be established by law and its members shall be appointed by the President and shall include at least one person who is or has been a judge of the High Court of Rhodesia or is qualified in terms of section *sixty-five* for appointment as a judge of the High Court. (A person qualified as a judge of the High Court must be or have been a judge of a superior court, in Rhodesia or in a country in which the common law is Roman-Dutch and English is the common language OR is or has been for not less than ten years qualified to practise as an advocate in Rhodesia or in a country in which the common law is Roman-Dutch and English is the common language).

> (7) The authority by whom the detention was ordered is obliged to act in accordance with any recommendations of the aforesaid tribunal unless the President directs otherwise.

> (8) Where the President has directed that the authority referred to in (7) above shall not act in accordance with any recommendation of the aforesaid tribunal that authority shall cause to be published in the *Gazette* a notice that the President has so directed.

6 *Rhodesia Herald* (afterwards referred to as *R.H.*) 26 November 1971.
7 *The Observer :* (London) 3 December 1971.
8 *The Guardian :* (London) 26 November 1971.
9 *The Times :* (London) 26 November 1971.
10 *Moto :* Vol. 13, No. 22. 4 December 1971.
11 *R.H.* 27 November 1971.
12 *Sunday Mail* (afterwards referred to as *S.M.*) 28 November 1971.
13 *R.H.* 7 December 1971.
14 As quoted in *R.H.* 3 December 1971.
15 *R.H.* 26 November 1971.
Lord Pearce, a distinguished legal authority, was called to the Bar in 1925 and served as a judge of the High Court and as Lord Justice of Appeal. In 1951 he was chairman of the Royal Commission on Marriage and Divorce and in 1962 was created a life peer.
16 *S.M.* 28 November 1971.
17 *R.H.* 8 January 1972.
18 Advertisement published in *R.H.* 15 January 1972.

19 *R.H.* 13 January 1972.
20 *R.H.* 12 January 1972.
21 *R.H.* 19, 20, 21, 22 January 1972: *S.M.* 23 January 1972.
22 *R.H.* 22 January 1972.
23 *R.H.* 4 February 1972.
24 As reported in *R.H.* 4 February 1972.
25 *S.M.* 20 February 1972.
26 *R.H.* 22 February 1972.
27 *R.H.* 24 February 1972.
28 *R.H.* 7 April 1972.
29 *R.H.* 21 April 1972.
30 Rhodesia: *Report of the Commission on Rhodesian Opinion under the chairmanship of the Right Honourable the Lord Pearce.* London: H.M.S.O. Misc., No. 19 (1972) Cmnd. 4964 (Afterwards referred to as the *Pearce Report*).
31 The Belingwe Tribal Trust Land is, with other tribal lands, roughly centred around Shabani.
32 *S.M.* 9 January 1972.
33 *R.H.* 10 January 1972.
34 *R.H.* 15 January 1972.
35 *S.M.* 16 January 1972.
36 *R.H.* 18 January 1972.
37 *R.H.* 19 January 1972.
38 *R.H.* 20 January 1972.
39 *R.H.* 22 January 1972.
40 *S.M.* 23 January 1972.
41 *Rhodesian Financial Gazette* 21 January 1972 (afterwards referred to as R.F.G.)
42 *R.H.* 17 February 1972.
43 *Pearce Report*, p. 102.
44 Section IV reads—The Rhodesian Government stated that 23 detainees have been released since the end of March 1971, leaving 93 detainees and two restrictees (excluding 34 detainees who have been released on conditions). It is the Rhodesian Government's intention to release a further 31 detainees as soon as the necessary arrangements can be made. (p. 7).
45 *R.H.* 19 January 1972.
46 As reported in *R.H.* 20 January 1972.
47 *R.H.* 22 January 1972.
48 *R.H.* 8 February 1972.
49 *Pearce Report*, p. 40.
50 *S.M.* 27 February 1972.
51 *R.H.* 3 March 1972.
52 *Pearce Report*, p. 40.
53 *S.M.* 16 January 1972. Information about Rhodesian political parties is given in the next chapter.
54 *R.H.* 24 January 1972.
55 *Pearce Report*, p. 55.
56 *R.H.* 27 January 1972.
57 *S.M.* 30 January 1972.

58 *R.H.* 5 February 1972.
59 *S.M.* 13 February 1972.
60 *Illustrated Life Rhodesia.* Fortnight ending 8 March 1972
61 *S.M.* 12 December 1971.
62 *S.M.* 19 December 1971.
63 *S.M.* 6 February 1972.
64 *Pearce Report,* p. 25.
65 *R.H.* 23 March 1972.
66 *R.H.G.* 24 December 1971.
67 *Property and Finance* No. 193, March 1972.
68 *S.M.* 13 February 1972.
69 *R.H.* 19 February 1972.
70 *R.H.* 10 March 1972.
71 *R.H.* 17 January 1972.
72 *R.H.* 4 January 1972.
73 *S.M.* 31 October 1971: The reference is to the time when the Rhodesian Front Party first came to power in the general election of 1962.
74 *R.H.* 9 November 1971.
75 *S.M.* 19 March 1972.
76 *S.M.* 26 March 1972.
77 *R.H.* 6 August 1971.
78 *R.H.* 17 February 1972.
79 *R.H.* 10 March 1972.
80 *R.H.* 18 February 1972.
81 *Broederbond:* An Afrikaans word meaning literally—band of brothers. It is the name of a South African secret organization formed in 1918 with the aim of uniting all Afrikaners in a single brotherhood. It has since been regarded as a very strong political pressure group behind the South African Nationalist Party.
82 *R.F.G.* 18 February 1972.
83 *R.F.G.* 25 February 1972.
84 *Centrepoint:* Vol. 2, No. 1, November 1971.
85 *Centrepoint:* Vol. 2, No. 2. December 1971.
86 *R.F.G.* 24 December 1971.
87 *Centrepoint:* Vol. 2, No. 3, January 1972.
88 *R.H.* 10 January 1972.
89 *R.H.* 18 January 1972.
90 *R.H.* 20 January 1972.
91 *R.H.* 22 February 1972.
92 *Centrepoint:* Vol. 2, No. 4. February 1972.
93 *R.H.* 16 February 1972.
94 *Centrepoint:* Vol. 2, No. 5. March 1972.
95 As quoted in *R.H.* 18 December 1971.
96 *S.M.* 19 December 1971.
97 *R.F.G.* 7 January 1972.
98 *S.M.* 16 January 1972.
99 *R.H.* 18 January 1972.
100 *R.H.* 20 January 1972.
101 *R.H.* 29 January 1972.

102 *R.H.* 8 February 1972.
103 As reported in *R.H.* 18 February 1972.
104 *S.M.* 27 February 1972.
105 *R.H.* 11 March 1972.
106 *Moto:* Vol. 13, Nos. 22, 24. 4, 18 December 1971.
107 *Pearce Report,* pp. 141-6.
108 *R.H.* 7 January 1972.
109 *R.H.* 25 January 1972.
110 *S.M.* 2 January 1972.
111 Mr. J.M. Gondo, M.P. died in a car accident on 27th October 1972.
112 *S.M.* 23 January; *R.H.* 28 January 1972.
113 *R.H.* 17 January 1972.
114 *Pearce Report,* pp. 117-8.
115 As quoted in *R.H.* 19 January 1972.
116 As quoted in *R.H.* 2 March 1972.
117 *S.M.* 13 February 1972.
118 *R.H.* 8 January 1972.
119 *R.H.* 22 February 1972.
120 By kind permission of the author: P.S. Harris: *Industrial Legislation, Government Policy and Industrial Relations in Rhodesia:* unpublished m/s read at a seminar on Industrial Relations: University of Rhodesia: 30 October 1972.
121 *R.H.* 11 December 1971.
122 *R.H.* 7 February 1972.
123 *Pearce Report,* pp. 28, 70.
124 *R.H.* 24 January 1972.
125 *R.H.* 22 February 1972.
126 *Pearce Report,* p. 70.
127 There is no privately owned land in the Tribal Trust Lands. All land is held communally by the tribe.
128 *R.H.* 10 December 1971.
129 *R.H.* 17 February 1972.
130 *R.H.* 20 January 1972.
131 *R.H.* 17 January 1972.
132 *Pearce Report,* p. 22.
133 *R.H.* 31 January 1972.
134 *R.H.* 18 February 1972.
135 *R.H.* 23 February 1972.
136 *Pearce Report,* p. 75.
137 *R.H.* 3 February 1972.
138 *Pearce Report,* p. 58.
139 *Pearce Report,* p. 79.
140 *S.M.* 2 January 1972.
141 *R.H.* 5 January 1972.
142 According to the Group's chairman, African clergy and laymen were not invited to join the group because of fears that they would be intimidated.
143 *R.H.* 20 February 1972.
144 *Contact* December 1971.

145 *R.H.* 18 December 1971. Article entitled *Opportunity for Christian Lead* by Rev. A.R. Lewis.

146 As quoted in *R.H.* 22 January 1972.

147 *S.M.* 23 January 1972.

148 *R.H.* 24 January 1972.

149 *R.H.* 4, 8 January 1972.

150 *R.H.* 14, 23 March 1972.

151 Craig, Robert: *Politics and Religion : a Christian View.* Salisbury: University of Rhodesia. *R.H.* 15 March 1972.

152 *R.H.* 6 January 1972.

153 *S.M.* 9 January 1972.

154 *R.H.* 25, 26, 27 January; 4, 6 February 1972.

155 *Moto :* Vol. 14, No. 7, 12 February 1972.

156 *Pearce Report,* pp. 44-51.

157 *Hansard :* Vol. 81, No. 2. 6 June 1972: Col. 28.
    All *Hansard* references are to House of Assembly Debates unless otherwise indicated. References which give numbers as well as volumes indicate that the information and quotations given are from the uncorrected reports and not from the bound copies which have been corrected and only give the volume number.

158 *R.H.* 6 July 1971.

159 *R.H.* 20 November 1971.

160 *R.H.* 21 November 1971.

161 *R.H.* 22 December 1971.

162 *Sunday Telegraph* (London) as quoted by *R.H.* 27 January 1972.

163 *R.H.* 28 January 1972.

164 As reported in *R.H.* 27 January 1972.

165 *S.M.* 30 January 1972.

166 *R.H.* 7 February 1972.

167 *R.H.* 3 March 1972.

168 *R.H.* 4 March 1972.

169 *R.H.* 13 March 1972.

170 *R.H.* 13 March 1972.

171 *R.H.* 14 March 1971.

172 *R.H.* 7 April 1972.

173 *R.H.* 8 April 1972.

174 *R.H.* 4 May 1972.

175 *R.H.* 11 March 1972.

176 *R.H.* 14 May 1972.

177 *S.M.* 30 March 1972.

178 *R.H.* 9 May 1972.

179 *R.H.* 13 May 1972.

180 *R.H.* 15 May 1972.

181 *R.H.* 23 May 1972 (Late Edition).

182 *Pearce Report,* pp. 34-6.

183 *Pearce Report,* pp. 44-51.

184 *Pearce Report,* pp. 88-111.

185 *Pearce Report,* pp. 37-40.

186 *Pearce Report,* pp. 54-6.

187 *The Pearce Commission Report. Broadcast Statement by the Prime*

Minister, The Hon. I. D. Smith, and a Statement by the Rhodesian Government, 23 May 1972; Salisbury: Ministry of Information.

188 *R.H.* 24 May 1972.

189 As quoted in *Africa Research Bulletin :* Vol. 9, No. 5. June 1972. Cols. 2485-6.

190 *Daily Telegraph* (London) 15, 16 June 1972.

191 *Hansard :* Vol. 81, No. 2. 6 June 1972: Cols. 10-36.

192 *R.H.* 7 June 1972.

193 *Hansard :* Vol. 81, Nos. 2, 3: 6, 7 June 1972: Cols. 37-110, 117-204.

194 *Hansard :* Vol. 81, No. 4: 8 June 1972: Cols. 205-21.

195 The Monckton Commission convened in 1960 was an advisory Commission on a review of the Constitution of the Federation of Rhodesia and Nyasaland. The Whaley Commission was convened in March 1967 'to examine the provisions of the 1965 Constitution and to advise the Rhodesian Government on a constitutional framework best suited to the sovereign independent status of Rhodesia.'

196 Halsbury: *Laws of England :* London: Butterworth.

197 *Hansard : Senate Debates :* Vol. 3, Nos. 5, 6, 7, 9. 13, 14, 15, 20 June 1972: Cols. 108-291.

198 *Centrepoint :* Vol. 2, No. 8. June 1972.

199 *R.H.* 19 May 1972.

200 *Property and Finance :* No. 196, June 1972.

201 *Moto :* Vol. 14, No. 25, 17 June 1972.

202 *R.H.* 25 May 1972.

203 *R.H.* 26 May 1972.

204 *R.H.* 27 May 1972.

205 *S.M.* 16 July 1972.

206 *R.H.* 26 July 1972.

207 *R.H.* 9 August 1972.

208 *Hansard :* Vol. 81, No. 27. 10 August 1972: Cols. 2352-434.

209 *R.H.* 29 September 1972.

210 *R.H.* 3 October 1972.

211 *R.H.* 4 October 1972.

212 *R.H.* 20 September 1972.

213 *R.H.* 10 November 1972.

214 *Hansard :* Vol. 83, No. 2. 22 November 1972: Cols. 112-39.

215 *R.H.* 23 November 1972.

216 *Hansard :* Vol. 83, No. 11. 7 December 1972: Cols. 905-11.

217 *Moto :* Vol. 14, No. 53. 30 December 1972.

218 As reported in *R.H.* 29 January 1973.

219 The *Times* (London) 1 February 1973.

220 *S.M.* 25 February 1973.

221 *R.H.* 23 February, and as reported in *S.M.* 25 February 1973.

222 *R.H.* 20, 31 March 1973.

223 *Hansard :* Vol. 83, Nos. 18, 19. 4, 5 April 1973: Cols. 1288-9, 1399-47.

224 As reported in *R.H.* 11 April 1973.

225 As reported in *R.H.* 18 April 1973.

226 As reported in *R.H.* 20 April 1973.

227 As reported in *R.H.* 14 May 1973.
228 *Hansard:* Vol. 84, No. 1. 14 June 1973: Col. 2.
229 *R.H.* 26 June 1973.
230 *Daily Telegraph* (London) 28 June 1973.
231 *Hansard:* Vol. 84, No. 9. 29 June 1973: Cols. 637-54.
232 As reported in *R.H.* 30 June 1973.
233 *Moto:* Vol. 15, No. 27. 7 July 1973.

II

POLITICAL PARTIES

EUROPEAN

THE RHODESIAN FRONT

The Rhodesian Front Party (R.F.) held its inaugural congress at the beginning of May 1962. According to the *Herald's* political reporter, Ian Mills, in a recent article, it 'brought a new force into Rhodesian politics—a unified and determined Right-wing faction that believed it was fighting for its life.'[1] It was organized as a consolidation of three main right-wing parties to form a united front against Sir Edgar Whitehead's United Federal Party and to contest the December 1962 general election. The 1962 election campaign centred largely around racial issues, for it was the first general election under the new 1961 Constitution which enabled Africans to sit in the Southern Rhodesian parliament.

The three components of the Rhodesian Front were the Southern Rhodesian Dominion Party led by Mr. William Harper; the Rhodesian Reform Group led by Mr. Ian D. Smith; and the Federal Dominion Party led by Mr. Winston Field the latter being accepted as the interim leader of the new party.

The election platform which the new party adopted was 'to uphold the principles of the Land Apportionment Act;[2] to reject enforced racial integration; to foster equality of opportunity and justice for all; to promote the full economic development of Southern Rhodesia with the full co-operation of all its peoples; and to seek the willing co-operation of the other Federal countries[3] while preserving Federal aspects that were of mutual benefit.' The Rhodesian Front won the 1962 election by a narrow margin of five seats.

In December 1963 the Federation was dissolved and in the following year Britain recognized the independence of Rhodesia's two erstwhile partners, Malawi and Zambia. In 1964, too, after lengthy negotiations on independence for Rhodesia Mr. Ian D. Smith replaced Mr. Winston Field as Prime Minister and leader of the R.F.

During 1965 attempts to reach a settlement on the terms for independence were continued. Early in the year two British ministers, Mr. Bottomley, the Commonwealth Secretary, and Lord Gardiner, the Lord Chancellor, visited Rhodesia to hold discussions with all sections of the Rhodesian public. According to Barber (writing in 1967) 'almost everywhere they... met intransigence and fixed attitudes [and] failed to resolve the deadlock between the two governments.'

Negotiations were continued centering around the five main principles as laid down by the British government—

1. The principle and intention of unimpeded progress to majority rule, already explained in the 1961 Constitution, would have to be maintained and guaranteed.
2. There would also have to be guarantees against retrogressive amendments of the Constitution.
3. There would have to be immediate improvement in the political status of the African population.
4. There would have to be progress towards ending racial discrimination.
5. The British Government would need to be satisfied that any basis proposed for independence was acceptable to the people of Rhodesia as a whole.[4]

During the closing months of the year the Rhodesian Prime Minister visited London and was followed on his return to Salisbury by Mr. Harold Wilson, the British Prime Minister at that time, discussions between the two Prime Ministers being based on the 1961 Constitution, which, according to Barber, represented 'to the Southern Rhodesian Government... a dangerous and over-liberal concession to African extremist's claims [and] to the British Government... represented the first but not the last step to increased African participation in government.' Mr. Wilson, however, 'achieved no substantial shift of attitude' by... 'the very real and obvious power of the R.F. Government, and the suppressed but potentially enormous power of the African nationalists.'[5]

By this time the Rhodesian Front government had received the 'overwhelming support' of the electorate (in the earlier general

election it had won all fifty seats on the 'A' roll and had not contested the fifteen seats on the 'B' roll) and considered that there
was no reason to make further concessions. According to Mr. D.
Lardner-Burke, the present Minister of Justice, 'It became finally
and absolutely clear that if Rhodesia was to take her rightful place
on the road to further prosperity and maintain the standards she
had set herself by her own endeavours during forty-two years of
self-government she would have to leave the path laid down for
her by Britain. Rhodesia could no longer, by her inaction, allow
indecision and doubt to continue until she was demolished, as
was the Federation of Rhodesia and Nyasaland. This was the
spectre that hung before her, and thus it was that Independence
was declared on 11 November 1965.'[6]

Following publication of the Whaley Commission Report early
in 1968 the party became involved in setting out its own ideas
for a new constitution in preparation for the 1968 annual party
congress, which was described by the *Herald's* political correspondent as 'for all concerned... the most vital the party has had
since its inception.'[7]

In early July it became evident that there was dissension among
members of the party when following a parliamentary caucus meeting it was reported that certain elements had, in opposition to
the Prime Minister and his supporters, announced their preference
for a phasing out or whittling away of African representation in
Parliament. This had culminated on 5th July in the Prime Minister requesting and receiving the resignation of Mr. W. J. Harper
from his Cabinet post. Mr. Harper later resigned his seat in the
House of Assembly (he had also been leader of the House) and
from the Rhodesian Front. A few other party members also
resigned, including Mr. Winston Field, who was understood to have
said in his letter of resignation that he was dissatisfied with the
party leadership and the seeming lack of resolve in carrying out
the party's principles and policies. He denied that his resignation
had anything to do either with Mr. Harper's resignation or constitutional affairs.

A meeting of the R.F. executive committee followed and the
Prime Minister was given a vote of confidence. It was later reported
that the Prime Minister had said that the reason why Mr. Harper
had been asked for his resignation was because he was a security
risk.[8]

At the congress, which opened on the 5th September 1968, the Prime Minister received a 'resounding ovation' when he rose to speak. In his speech the Prime Minister said that the government and party had certain commitments to all Rhodesians and that their 'responsibility to black Rhodesians should be uppermost in the minds of delegates since none were at the congress'. He urged delegates to keep their heads in view of the tremendously important decisions they would have to make.

A two-stage plan for the franchise, commonly known as the Yellow Paper, was accepted at the congress but was later superseded by a one-stage plan. The 1969 Constitution, which was subject to a referendum on the 20th June 1969, gave Rhodesia republican status and came into effect on the 2nd March 1970. In describing this Constitution the Prime Minister explained that it was 'a racial not a racialistic' constitution for there is a 'big and fundamental difference' between the terms. 'A racialistic constitution would be most undesirable. A racialist believes that he is above other races; a superior sort of person. He practises his philosophy to the detriment of others. That is wrong. I am not one, and never have been. And I hope I never will be one. But a racial constitution; that is different... The aim of our new Constitution is to ensure that there will be no domination of one race by the other.[9]

In the 1970 general election campaign the R.F. announced that it would ensure the government remained permanently in responsible hands and the right of all individuals, within the framework of the law, to private ownership, freedom of worship, speech and association as well as the opportunity to develop their abilities to the full and to receive reward and recognition entirely on merit. It would also ensure 'the permanent establishment of the European in Rhodesia' and to this end would encourage European immigration and would uphold the principles of the Land Tenure Act.

In its pre-election pamphlet, the R.F. also stated that 'The party opposes compulsory [racial] integration and believes that the peaceful co-existence of people can only be achieved when communities have the right and opportunity to preserve their own identities, traditions and customs and therefore recognises the obligation of Government and respective communities, where necessary, to ensure the provision of such separate facilities as will make this possible.' It was also announced that the R.F. would protect the standards of skilled workers against exploitation by cheap labour and said that the fourth of its vital objectives was 'the preservation of the existing peace and good order, with continuing racial harmony and understanding.'[10]

In the election the R.F. contested all 50 European seats. Opposition came from the Centre Party which had 16 candidates, from the Republican Alliance with 14 candidates and from 14 Independents. The result was a landslide victory for the R.F. which won all 50 seats; a record number of other candidates losing their deposits (20 out of 44).

In August 1971 an important by-election was held at Mabelreign (Salisbury) which had traditionally been an R.F. stronghold since 1962. The R.F. candidate, Mr. J. Gleig, won by a narrow 68-vote majority which was seen by certain political observers as being significant for the future as more votes had been cast for opposing candidates than for Mr. Gleig. Dr. Ian Anderson of the Candour League (standing as an Independent) gained 456 votes and Mr. W. Weedman of the Centre Party gained 158 votes. R.F. experts put this result down to apathy (there had been only a 59.5 *percentage* poll) but some party members asserted that there was evidence in the loss of 456 right-wing votes that the Mabelreign voters did not consider the R.F. to be sufficiently right-wing.[11]

Developments during 1972-3

In the early months of 1972 political activity was confined largely to the Settlement Proposals and the Test of Acceptability (see pp. 20-38).

In March the party was criticized by the 'resurgent extreme right-wing' on the grounds that the settlement proposals meant a complete change in the R.F.'s approach to Rhodesia's problems. This was countered by party chairman, Mr. D. Frost, who said that there was 'no reason why the principles of the R.F. should be altered—our principles remain inviolate'[12]

During April the Prime Minister made a 'whistle-stop' tour explaining the settlement proposals to R.F. branches throughout the country. *Sunday Mail* reporter, Paul Juhl, regarded this tour as a 'crucial one for the Rhodesian Front.' As he explained in detail, 'the reasons for the electorate's disenchantment are many and varied.' In its editorial the next day, the *Herald* considered that 'in the past year dissidence with the R.F. has been sharpened first by hush-hush negotiations (which generated great uneasiness and much suspicion among the hard core), then by the Home-Smith talks and the Settlement proposals to which they led, and last by the Pearce Commission and the events that accompanied it.' A few days later the *Herald* concluded: 'Mr. Smith has received a number of votes of confidence during his tour of the branches throughout the country. But the branch and constituency council meetings [in preparation for the R.F.'s annual congress] will provide a much more critical forum for reviews of the Government's and Mr. Smith's performance in the last year.'[13]

After the publication of the Pearce Report the R.F. chairman was interviewed by the *Herald*. Mr. Frost outlined the R.F.'s post-Pearce policy as being largely to concentrate on internal policies and 'measures to remove racial friction and the advancement of the African areas by expansion of community development to provincial level.'[14]

The July issue of the R.F. newspaper, *The Rhodesian Forum*, noted that 'in the wake of the Pearce Report, Rhodesians are seeking a firm indication of their constitutional future and the question posed is "where do we go from here?"' The answer to this question was seen by the R.F. as an 'early and vigorous implementation of our provincialization programme'. The article then went on to look at the practical implementation of this policy in depth, defining its aim as 'to decentralise on an evolutionary pattern the administration of the Tribal Trust Lands to provincial authorities... These provincial councils or assemblies would be an arm of Government interspersed between central Government and the local government area or district councils... The relationship of provinces to central government may be analogous to that of the cantons and federal government in Switzerland... [and] will provide an excellent training ground in the art of government and an avenue for responsible political ambition... National policy in matters... of health, education, local government and housing, agriculture, internal affairs, labour and social welfare, commerce and industry, local roads, land, game parks and water development... will emanate, of course from central government and the provincial authorities will be required to work within the framework of this policy and under the direction of the appropriate central Government ministry... These authorities will participate in and assist in the implementation of our development programmes for the Tribal Trust Lands, which are designed to bring these areas into the cash economy and to maximise the job opportunities for African professional, business, skilled and semi-skilled persons at a pace and in an atmosphere suited to their traditional requirements.'[15]

In mid-August the party's executive committee decided that the three-day annual congress would be held in private, the press being completely barred for the first time in many years. Ian Mills commented in the *Herald* that 'The move to close the congress tends to confirm the view in political quarters that the R.F. plans to take a hard critical look at itself, its past performance and what it plans to do in the post-Pearce hiatus.'[16]

In June, the *Herald's* political reporter revealed that a special party committee had been preparing a statement of official party policy for publication prior to the annual congress in September, when it would be debated. The statement was made available to the press in late August and the *Herald* provided a summary of its main provisions with the reminder that it would be subject to amendment at the congress.

Starting with the acknowledgement that Rhodesia had been built on the mutual interdependence of all races, the statement went on to say that accordingly the party believed each race to be as much part of the nation as another, but also believed that the members of each racial group 'are desirous of preserving their own identities, traditions, customs and ways of life'. Therefore, because of the party's respect for these differences, it would create conditions 'conducive to the peaceful co-existence of all races' and accord to each race the 'opportunity of developing to its fullest extent in its own area and in accordance with its own social structure, without intrusion upon its privacy and rights by any other race.' Accordingly, it would set an example to the public by providing 'separate facilities for the different races in State offices and institutions.' The statement went on to say that the party further aimed 'to engender, between the races, the mutual confidence and respect that will encourage the fullest participation of persons in their own development and so enable all to contribute to the overall growth of the nation.' It also referred to the policy of provincialization and said that this would be introduced to allow each race to control many of the matters affecting the daily lives of its people.

With regard to party policies the statement went on to detail these under 29 sub-heads.

In its editorial the following day the *Herald* commented that 'the drafters cannot deny that "providing separate facilities for the different races in State offices and institutions" is South African apartheid and nothing less.' It went on to state that 'In our view the national interest dictates that every available dollar should be spent where it can increase productivity—which we believed to be R.F. policy—or improve the country's infrastructure and social services: developing the country's potential. Every dollar taken from that national drive to provide unnecessary and unproductive Government or municipal facilities for each of the four races is a dollar handed to those people who would bring Rhodesia crashing to economic ruin.'[17]

Shortly before the congress it was announced that Lord Graham,[18] a vice president of the party, had stated that he would not be available for the vice presidency. This action was seen as an attempt to unseat Mr. Smith from his position as Prime Minister and president of the R.F. for Lord Graham had indicated that in his view it was not democratic of the Prime Minister to hold both positions.

The congress opened on the 21st September and it was announced that selected details of the proceedings would be given to the press by the congress' press officer, Mr. A. S. Holland. The Prime Minister set the tone of the congress from the beginning in a speech which the *Herald* described as hard-hitting and 'geared towards moderation and a warning against losing the trust and co-operation of the African people in the face of the terrorist and Communist threat.' In his speech, Mr. Smith made it clear that although the government wished to keep its options open this did not mean there would be any further negotiations with Britain—'there is no question of yielding on our principles'. Mr. Smith also gave examples to refute accusations from what he referred to as 'the so-called right-wingers' that the R.F. and the government had given way on its principles to effect a settlement. A large part of his speech, as reported, consisted of references to 'petty racial issues' for, as he said, 'We must not deliberately create conditions that make local Africans our enemies... whereby our Africans have no option but to become our enemies... We would be foolish to be provocative unnecessarily and lose the trust we have built up. On the contrary, our policies that we are now forming will do quite the reverse.'[19]

The *Herald* leader the next day considered that this speech held 'More sound sense... than we have heard from any Rhodesian politician for a very long time'; the Prime Minister was 'laying his Government's policy on the line with a vengeance.' He had made it quite clear that he and the government wanted a settlement and that nothing would be done to jeopardize the chances for one or to 'create conditions whereby our Africans have no option but to become our enemies.' The *Herald* went on to conjecture that 'it must seem that those members of the party—including some M.P.'s—whose first priority is petty apartheid must change either their principles or their party if they are to retain credibility' and concluded by saying that 'Rhodesians who believe as we do that racial peace and racial co-operation form the first essential to a liveable and prosperous Rhodesia will want to judge that claim [that party policies formed at the Congress would do nothing to estrange black Rhodesians] for themselves, although proof will come from events. On the face of it, however, Mr. Ian Smith has done what no other Rhodesian Prime Minister has done; faced with discontent from the Right, he has stuck to his ground and not quelled a "rebellion" by joining it.'

In the same issue it was reported that Lord Graham had withdrawn his nomination for the presidency of the party, in what the *Herald* called 'the first ever [challenge] made to topple Mr. Smith from the post.' Lord Graham was quoted as saying that he had withdrawn his name because he had previously thought that the conflict with Britain was over but since the Prime Minister had made it obvious that settlement options were still open, with the backing of the congress, he had withdrawn his name. The press officer was quoted as saying that 'Lord Graham's statement had been taken as a gesture to maintain party unity' and that the decision had been made by Lord Graham in the 'light of Mr. Smith's advice that Rhodesia should not do anything provocative and so endanger settlement prospects.'[20] At the election for office bearers for the coming year Lord Graham was replaced as vice-president of the R.F. by the Minister of Agriculture, Mr. David Smith.

In his analysis of the congress proceedings Ian Mills said in the *Herald* that 'the settlement failure had left the party rank and file in a bit of a quandary. The congress was the place for them to be reassured on both the party's future and how the Government was going to handle things... From what I have been told, few delegates really believe a settlement is possible but in exchange for action on domestic issues they were happy to leave the issue to Mr. Smith... Given the party mood and expectations before the congress Mr. Smith gave a masterful performance... In fact, the Rhodesian Front is probably now more united than it has been for years and the various factions that once made up the party have now... been moulded into a singular, cohesive whole.' [21]

The following Friday the *Financial Gazette's* reporter, Harold Pakendorf, also concluded that the congress had been a personal triumph for the Prime Minister, for, apart from the issues of keeping the options on the settlement open and the question of party policies, 'Mr. Ian Smith once again confirmed his total mastery over his followers... party members now know exactly how far the R.F. under Mr. Smith will go on the issue of segregation—and it is not a lot further than has been the Rhodesian custom all along.' [22]

In November the R.F.'s executive committee complained about the government's failure to issue a full public explanation of the imposition of the African bar curfew (see below) which led the *Herald* to comment that 'It is encouraging to find it has at last dawned on the Rhodesian Front machine, at least, that silence is not always golden and doesn't necessarily pay... It will have an even harder time persuading its Government members that there is something worse than stubborn silence.' [23] The *Financial Gazette* also commented on this issue by saying that 'The party has in the past been notoriously shy about criticising the Government in public, and this statement illustrates the frustrations being felt within the R.F. about how little it is being told. The Government's handling of several recent measures—such as the *Situpa* Bill and the bar curfew—has disturbed sections of the party. While most agree in principle for the need for such measures, they feel the Government's apparent attitude of remaining silent and hoping the measures will go through unnoticed, is causing grave damage to the country's image.' [24]

In late November, the *Mail's* editorial discussed what appeared to be a discrepancy between what the Prime Minister had said at the congress, about the need to avoid 'irritating apartheid laws',

and the various Bills which the government had introduced at
its end-of-year parliamentary session. In particular the *Situpa*,
or to give it its proper title, the Africans (Registration and Identification) Amendment Bill—was commented upon. 'It is true there
isn't much in the controversial "*situpa* bill" to get excited about.
No revolutionary changes are proposed; and there may well be
good reasons for tightening up the old arrangements. But it is
nakedly discriminatory. Its very title makes that clear. As such
it is not only damaging to Rhodesia's image and most embarrassing
to decent Rhodesians; it is also completely contrary to Rhodesian
Front policy—and almost guaranteed to spoil the chances of ever
completing a settlement with Britain... Who can reconcile it all
with the Prime Minister's publicly stated desire to avoid irritating
apartheid laws, and to press on to clinch the settlement?'[25]

Criticism of the R.F. came from *Property and Finance* in
October, from the African National Council in November and
from the Centre Party in December. *Property and Finance* summed
up the main implications of the Prime Minister's intervention at
the R.F. congress and said that 'on his resumed gamble for a
settlement, and by rejecting key provisions in the Party's revised
policies, Mr. Smith has at last accepted personal and public
accountability for the present policy of turning a blind eye to the
enforced racial integration that the Party itself has tried to oppose.
The integration is specifically evident in the loss of White jobs,
rights and amenities. The R.F. is no longer the White-unity movement that it was... the political situation has therefore reverted
to the U.F.P. [United Federal Party] Dominion Party struggle
before the merger of the two parties ten years ago.' The periodical
concluded that 'All in all, therefore, the whole stage-managed
affair, including the secrecy of the conclave (but not of the voting)
was as brilliant a piece of political engineering as the country has
seen since the salesmanship that preceded the Federation.'[26]

In mid-November, addressing a crowd of about 1 400 Africans
in Gwelo's Monomotapa Township, the Rev. Canaan Banana (vice-
president of the A.N.C.) said that 'as long as the R.F. continued
to treat Africans as political hostages they would destroy any
remaining chance of goodwill between the races.' The new legislation was a 'grievous insult to the African's integrity and a humiliat-
ing affront to human dignity.'[27]

The Centre Party's newspaper, *Centrepoint,* in an article entitled

Hell-Bent for Apartheid queried where it would all end for 'the Government is now doing precisely the opposite of what was envisaged in the settlement. Instead of carrying out his solemnly agreed intention to make progress towards ending racial discrimination Mr. Smith is now piling it on so thickly that he had his own supporters gasping,' and it went on to comment that 'the settlement foundered on the rocks of an almost pathological mistrust; but far from assuaging African doubts the R.F. have simply confirmed them.'[28]

The 1973 By-Elections

The anticipated by-election in the Victoria constituency[29] was viewed by the right-wing monthly, *Property and Finance,* as a test for the government for it saw one candidate, Mr. Wynn Starling of the United Party (formerly a founder-member of the R.F.), as 'standing four-square on the R.F.'s original principles and policies as the electorate understood and voted for them.'[30] The *Herald* also saw the by-election as a test for the governing party, commenting that 'the post-Pearce situation has fired Right-Wing elements with new resolve and together with the Rhodesia Party, the United Front and Rhodesia National Party are itching for a chance to test their strength and popularity against the R.F.'[31]

The appointment of Colonel G. H. Hartley as Speaker of the House was announced on the 30th March together with a proclamation ordering an election to fill the ensuing vacancy in the House of Assembly.[32] The R.F. announced its candidate as Mr. Gordon R. Olds who was described as a founder-member of the R.F. with an active career in local government. Shortly afterwards Mr. Olds announced that the R.F. had planned a full campaign and that the Prime Minister would himself address two meetings.[33] It was announced later that Messrs. Peter S. Hingeston and Len Idensohn would stand as candidates for the Rhodesia Party and for the Rhodesia National Party respectively.

Although the other by-election, in the African seat at Matojeni, was not of direct concern to the R.F. (the R.F. does not have African party members for they cannot vote for European constituencies) the outcome of both elections was seen by the *Herald* as potentially significant for the R.F. It was predicted that the Victoria election would show whether the R.F. had 'kept its grip on and the loyalty of the voters in this traditionally conservative constituency' while the outcome at Matojeni (where 7 candidates were standing but only one had a party affiliation—Mr. Pfumojena of the Centre Party) would show 'whether or not African natio-alism has continued to grow since Pearce.'[34]

Two weeks before polling day at Victoria the Chairman of the R.F., Mr. D. Frost, urged voters not to be apathetic. He com-mented upon the poor attendances at R.F. meetings and forecast that there would be large crowds at meetings where the Prime Minister was scheduled to speak. The *Herald's* political reporter commented that, although clear-cut issues had not yet emerged, the R.F. theme of urging continued support for the Party and for voters to examine the government's success in 'combating sanc-tions and facing world criticism over U.D.I.' would underline whatever else was said during the campaign.[35]

The Prime Minister's commitment of speaking at eight private and public meetings during the last few days of the campaign was seen as clearly illustrating the importance which he and the Party attached to the by-election. After the first public meeting which the Prime Minister addressed, reporter Chris Reynolds expressed the opinion that Mr. Smith 'had turned what was an important, but pretty dull, political affair into a major cut and thrust exer-cise.'[36]

By the eve of the election day the consensus of opinion seemed to be that the field had narrowed down to two main protagonists—the Rhodesian Front and the Rhodesia Party—although the pre-sence of the two Right-wing candidates presented a prospect of votes being lost to the R.F. In fact on election day, the 17th May, the R.F. gained a landslide victory. In a percentage poll of 67.5 the R.F. candidate, Mr. Gordon Olds, gained 985 votes (71 *per cent*) while the Rhodesia Party candidate gained 305 votes (22 *per cent*). The other two candidates, Mr. Len Idensohn and Mr. Wynn Starling, gained 45 and 43 votes respectively and lost their depos-its.[37] These results were seen by the *Herald* as a personal triumph for the Prime Minister; as the newspaper's reporter commented, 'from the moment he set foot in the Province and started his barn-storming display of political wizardry the result was inevitable... the landslide vote in his favour has indicated that the Victoria electorate, traditionally a conservative stronghold, is behind the Prime Minister's renewed bid for a settlement.'[38]

A fortnight later, when the result of the Matojeni by-election was announced, the same reporter commented that it was a 'severe setback for Prime Minister Ian Smith in his bid to convince the British Government that the majority of Rhodesian Africans now accept the 1971 proposals.' The result of the 47 *per cent* poll was that Mr. Lot Dewa, a self-confessed supporter of the A.N.C., gained 133 votes and his fellow A.N.C. supporter gained 85 votes. Mr. Pfumojena of the Centre Party narrowly missed having to forfeit his deposit with 30 votes and all the other candidates lost their deposits.

Prior to the Victoria by-election there had been conjecture in the news media about the possibility of forthcoming Cabinet changes. Although denials had come from his own office that changes were being contemplated, the Prime Minister held a press conference on the 23rd May to announce changes and new appointments which would become effective on the 1st June. The *Mail* expressed itself as disappointed with the changes on the grounds that 'the moves suggest that, far from contemplating any new approaches to old problems, the Prime Minister is quite happy with things as they are. Grooming some juniors for future Cabinet jobs—which is obviously what he is doing in appointing three deputy ministers—suggests that he expects to stay happy for some time to come. This is a pity, for surely the one thing that might help to solve the most critical political issue of the day is some fresh thinking in the Cabinet.'[39]

THE UNITED FRONT

Shortly before the settlement terms were announced in 1971 the *Sunday Mail* reported that 'secret attempts are being made to form a strongly Right-wing group which would oppose any settlement Mr. Smith might reach with Britain.' This story was based on the announcement by the vice-president of the Republican Alliance, Mr. R. James, that he was resigning from that party to assist in 'the re-organization of conservative opinion' in Rhodesia.[40]

By early February 1972 it was reported that there would be a meeting of Right-wing groups in an attempt to form a coalition. The decision to form the United Front (U.F.) was taken at this meeting, the convenor of which, Dr. J. Redmond of Gwelo (former president of the Republican Alliance) was reported to have said that the party's 'overriding principle [was] that the white man's position must be supreme for all time.'[41] The president of the Rhodesia National Party, Mr. L. Idensohn, announced that his party was not associated with the new party and would continue to stand as the only Right-wing party in Rhodesia. The chairman of the Republican Alliance, Commander C. Philips, stated that Dr. Redmond, together with a colleague from the R.A.'s executive, had both been automatically expelled from the Republican Alliance when they had joined the new party. Commander Phillips also said that the Republican Alliance would have nothing to do with the United Front.

On the 27th February the new party placed an advertisement in the press calling upon everyone 'to safeguard all our futures and to support the United Front'; setting forth its aims as being 'to ensure white rule in the European areas while providing for political advancement of the African in his own areas', and stating that 'Mr. Smith's Government wants you to accept Black Majority Rule'. In March two scheduled meetings of the United Front, to be held in the Wankie Constituency, were cancelled in terms of the Emergency Powers Regulations and rumours of an early general election were strengthened when one of the U.F. leaders announced that all prospective candidates for the Mashonaland constituencies had been selected at a meeting of the party's Mashonaland co-ordinating committee.

In mid-April the U.F. held its first public meeting in Salisbury. It was recorded the next day that fewer than 50 people were attracted to it. 'There was no heckling, no vitriolics from the platform, no fiery atmosphere which might suggest that the Rhodesian Front Government was cracking up in the face of a white backlash', commented a *Herald* reporter, and went on to say 'ironically enough, the United Front principles, as stated in the pamphlets distributed to the middle-aged audience, appeared not to go far enough for most people in the hall.'[42]

In early May the U.F. challenged the Prime Minister to obtain a mandate from the electorate, through a referendum, to give the settlement proposals a legal basis in terms of the 1969 Constitution. In May it issued a statement on Mr. Smith's press conference (held about ten days before the publication of the Pearce Report) stating that 'Mr. Ian Smith has done a double U.D.I.—first against the Queen and against the British Government in 1965 and now, with the signing of the Smith-Home agreement, he is attempting to pull off his second U.D.I., but this time it is against the people of Rhodesia.' It went on to query 'if governments are empowered... to come to agreements with foreign powers on matters affecting the constitution of an independent country, why did he [the Prime Minister] use U.D.I. to glorify his own position when he could have reached the same agreement with Britain without U.D.I. or sanctions?'[43]

Following the closure of the border with Zambia the U.F., in early January 1973, claimed that the Prime Minister's reluctance to take even sterner action against Zambia was influenced by big business interests. It called upon the government to switch off electric power supply from Kariba to Zambia and to ban overflights from Zambia and other hostile countries.[44]

In early February 1973 it was announced that the U.F.'s interim chairman, Dr. J. Redmond, and two other members of the executive committee had resigned from the U.F. In a press statement Dr. Redmond explained that he and his two colleagues had been holding informal talks with a member of another party (Dr. Morris Hirsch of the Rhodesia Party—according to the *Herald* one of the country's leading constitutional experts) and that certain other members of the U.F. executive had taken violent exception to this. A motion to expel Dr. Redmond had been passed by the U.F.'s Midland division under the chairmanship of Mr. Wynn Starling.[45] In a letter to the Press, the U.F.'s national executive secretary, Mr. L. E. King, explained that the 'United Front is a Right-wing party and its members have no desire for political talks or negotiations of any kind with Left-wing parties.' Mr. King also announced the appointment of a party public relations officer.[46]

The United Front was the first party to announce that it would be contesting the Victoria by-election. Mr. Wynn Starling, the national organizing secretary, a former Dominion Party M.P. and a founder-member of the Rhodesian Front, had his nomination accepted in April, when he was quoted as saying that the 'United Front's policies are exactly the same as those of the original Rhodesian Front. But the Rhodesian Front has changed and swung to the Left.' Mr. Starling said he would fight the election on the original R.F. principles.[47]

In the election both Right-wing candidates lost their deposits, Mr. Starling, with 43 votes, coming at the bottom of the poll.

As a post-election comment he was quoted as saying that the Victoria voters 'have shown the country that they want a settlement on the 1971 terms. What else can this result mean? We say those terms mean majority black rule. We shall continue to fight against it.'[48]

THE REPUBLICAN ALLIANCE

The Republican Alliance (R.A.) was formed in 1969 as a splinter group from the Conservative Association. A founder member, Mr. R. James, M.P. for Salisbury City, had been expelled from the Rhodesian Front caucus and suspended from the party itself for six months. He was later expelled from the R.F. party but continued to sit in the House of Assembly as an independent member until 1970. The R.A. fought the general election in 1970 putting up 14 candidates but all failed to gain enough support for election. Following the defection of two of its leaders, Mr. Robin James and Dr. J. Redmond, to the United Front in early February 1972 the R.A. was further weakened when a majority of its Mashonaland Divisional Council demanded a merger with the United Front. In April, after a financial dispute with Mr. R. James, the party chairman, following a poll among members of the party's future, announced the dissolution of the R.A.

In early May, Commander Phillips announced the formation of a new party to be called the Democratic Party, which was 'to provide a home' for those who did not wish to join the Rhodesia National Party, the United Front or the Rhodesian Front, with the 'first and over-riding principle that the white man and his civilization in Rhodesia shall be preserved. All other principles and policies shall be subordinate to this principle.'[49]

THE RHODESIA NATIONAL PARTY

The Rhodesia National Party (R.N.P.) was formed in March 1968.[50] Its chairman at that time, Mr. L. Idensohn, had been the most senior of the Rhodesian Front's divisional chairmen but had resigned in order to form a new party, whose aim, he was quoted as saying, was to put an end to 'the clandestine racial integration' taking place under Mr. Smith's government. The Johannesburg *Sunday Times* commented, over a year later, that 'the R.N.P. never became a significant force... it nevertheless illustrated the demands

from the ultra-conservatives for a firmer race policy.'[51] Although
the R.N.P. did not contest the 1970 general election it did field
a candidate in a by-election shortly before who had been defeated
by the Rhodesian Front candidate.

Early in March 1972, Mr. Idensohn was a speaker at the meeting
organized by the Candour League 'to show the Pearce Commission
the size of the white backlash.' Later in the month, *Herald* reporter
John Kelley, in a short biographical article, commented that 'Idensohn's policy has stark simplicity. It is for the continuation of
white rule for Rhodesia and an end to what he sees as Britain's
plan for a total black Africa "with the co-operation of Mr. Ian
Smith, the Prime Minister".'[52]

At the end of March Mr. Idensohn addressed a meeting at Hartley, where he was reported as saying that the proposals for the
settlement were a 'sell-out'. Later in the year Mr. Idensohn continued his attacks on the Rhodesian Front and in September he
wrote in his party newsletter, according to the *Herald*, that the
government 'having failed to hand over the country to the
A.N.C.—is now trying to sell its second evil: the hastily prepared
provincialization plan... [for] Black rule in Rhodesia would come
a lot quicker under... the plan... [which] would mean that while
black areas were run exclusively by blacks, the white areas would
be run by a Parliament with a steadily increasing ratio of black
M.P.'s.'[53] At the end of November Mr. Idensohn said that his
party, 'encouraged by an increase in membership during the past
year, had decided to fight the next election' because, as he
announced, the Rhodesian electorate had for too long faced an
uncertain future—'This uncertainty must be removed... the
R.N.P. will put forward a genuine separate development programme at the next election. Separate development of the races
is the only way the present racial friction can be eliminated.'[54]

Early in the New Year 1973 the R.N.P. joined the two other
opposition parties in expressing its condemnation of the government for what it called its 'weakness and lack of initiative in protecting Rhodesia from terrorist attacks.' It called for the destruction
of 'terrorist' camps in Zambia and for a mandatory death sentence
for all acts of terror.[55]

A few days later the R.N.P. announced that it would most definitely be contesting the Victoria by-election. Not until the third
week in April 1973, however, did the party name its candidate

as Mr. Len Idensohn. In announcing Mr. Idensohn's nomination, the party chairman, Mr. F.C. Nel, said that the R.N.P. was 'contesting the election because it believed Victoria constituents should be given the chance to vote for white or black rule.' [56] He later claimed that 'We are the only genuine Right-wing party in the field and I am confident that our candidate will win a lot of support. We have a real chance here.' [57]   ·

At his first public meeting of the campaign Mr. Idensohn called the settlement proposals a 'sell-out' and warned his audience of about 30 people that by returning an R.F. candidate they would be confirming the solidarity of the electorate for a settlement on the 1971 proposals.[58] Earlier Mr. Idensohn had addressed a public meeting in Salisbury at which his speech had been taken as an indication of the stand he would take during the by-election campaign. Describing the 1971 proposals as a 'Pandora's box full of Trojan horses' he warned that the box should never be opened.[59]

After the by-election Mr. Idensohn, who gained only 45 votes and forfeited his deposit, indicated that he might be leaving politics by saying that 'I have got the message. The country is just not interested.'[60] Mr. Nel, however, claimed that the R.N.P. was 'three times as strong now' and that all had agreed to work three times as hard.

THE RHODESIA PARTY

In mid-March 1972 the *Mail* speculated that Rhodesian farmers were planning to challenge the Rhodesian Front at the next general election by the formation of a new political party and that Mr. C. A. R. Savory, who had recently resigned from membership of the Rhodesian Front, had been approached to lead it. The next day, however, Mr. Savory denied any such approach while the president of the Matabeleland Rhodesia National Farmers' Union, which had been described as the most anxious for such a party to be formed, refused to speak to the press. By July, the rumours still persisted and *Centrepoint's* reporter interviewed the Centre Party's vice-president, Mr. N. J. McNally, about the speculation that he had been discussing, with others, the formation of a new party. Mr. McNally confirmed that he had been holding talks with a number of people outside the Centre Party for 'there are a lot of Europeans who think that we need a dynamic European party in opposition to the Front; a party that can be trusted and respected by the African people, but which is answerable directly to the European electorate. Alongside such a party they would hope to see the emergence of a moderate African party, answerable in its turn to its own African electorate, but brave enough to say that it will work within the realities of power in Rhodesia.'[61]

During the second week in August the *Mail's* reporter, Chris Reynolds, claimed to have seen the confidential manifesto of the new party, which was expected to announce its official formation at the end of September, the delay being, it was suspected, to allow time for the Rhodesian Front Congress to come and go. In commenting upon the new party's policies, Mr. Reynolds said, 'The party's outlined policies are less socialistic than those of the Rhodesian Front. If anything, they are Right—in the original political sense of the word—of the R.F. But in the racial context, the party is determined to stamp out petty racialism'.[62]

The Rhodesia Party was officially launched at the end of October.[63] It had an interim steering committee headed by Mr. R. Ashburner, a farmer from the Raffingora district, who had stood as an independent candidate in the 1970 general election and lost to a member of the Rhodesian Front. Other members were Mr. C. A. R. Savory, Independent (although elected under the R.F. ticket) M.P. for Matobo, and Dr. M. I. Hirsch, who had been a United Federal Party M.P. from 1958 until defeated by a R.F. candidate in the 1962 general election.

In an article based on a press conference held with the party's interim office bearers, the *Herald's* reporter quoted Dr. Hirsch and Mr. Savory as saying that the R.P. was at present all-European but that Africans would not be barred if they wished to join. African membership, however, would not be encouraged for under the present Constitution voting was along racial lines. Party principles were outlined as being for the retention of the government and administration of Rhodesia in the hands of those 'with the education, income and possessions to give them an interest in stability and to qualify them for such responsibility.' On racial matters the R.P. would uphold the principle that 'the sensitivities of the various groups should be respected in their private lives but in their public lives the objective should be the elimination of discrimination between all Rhodesians on the grounds of colour'. To these ends the party adopted three main guidelines: freedom of association in the private sphere and freedom from discrimination in public life; differentiation on grounds of race to be continued only where there was sound and just reason for it (the party believes that such differentiation may be either advisable or unavoidable, because of major differences in social and judicial systems, values, habits, attitudes and affluence until such time as development and time would change these factors); and the introduction of a Land Standards Act to govern all land occupation and use, the party opposing 'a rigid, permanent, racial apportionment of land [as] not only unrealistic but dangerous.'

Commenting on the formation of the R.P. the Rhodesian Front chairman stated 'I am sure that our basically conservative electorate will not be fooled by these people who, in the last general election tried to cover their political philosophies by calling themselves independents... one thing is obvious: the only stumbling block to their amalgamating with the Centre Party must be disagreement on a commonly acceptable leader.' An A.N.C. spokesman said that he welcomed the formation of the new party, for the R.F. had 'outlived its purpose' and was 'bogged down'. 'A new European party, which does not practise petty discrimination... is necessary.' The A.N.C. secretary-general, however, was quoted as saying that 'the new party perpetuated white minority rule and was therefore worse than the R.F.' The *Mail* felt that the new party had courage and that its 'emergence... at least serves to enliven a political scene grown turgid and spiritless through long years in the cold, clammy grip of the Rhodesian Front.'[64]

Early in the New Year 1973 the Rhodesia Party joined its voice to that of two other opposition parties in criticizing the government for the partial closure of the border with Zambia. The party stated that while it would at all time 'support fully any tough, positive, well-planned and intelligent anti-guerilla warfare programme' it had severe doubts about the wisdom of this present action, for Rhodesia had always condemned sanctions as a tool of international politics and was now applying partial sanctions against Zambia.[65]

In late January the R.P. held the first in a series of public meetings in different parts of the country to publicise and explain the party's policies. Speakers at this meeting in Que Que (which attracted about 300 people) were Mr. C. A. R. Savory, Dr. M. I.

Hirsch and a local lawyer, Mr. L. Bennett. Mr. Savory spoke of the security situation and in particular of the recently introduced regulations under the Emergency Powers Act, which empowered district commissioners to impose collective punishment such as fines and payment of compensation on communities who deliberately co-operated with guerrillas. Mr. Savory said that he considered that the regulations were 'appalling in their implications' and that Parliament should be recalled to debate and signify its approval of this action. Mr. Savory also spoke critically of the closure of the border with Zambia. Dr. Hirsch spoke on the settlement and constitutional issues and Mr. Bennett appealed to Rhodesians to reject petty apartheid and create racial harmony as a pre-requisite for a stable future. Ian Mills commented in the *Herald* that 'if the Que Que audience is a valid cross-section of Rhodesian public opinion, which it appeared to be, then a questioning attitude is again prevalent among Rhodesians... this attitude could easily make the Rhodesia Party the most formidable threat the Rhodesian Front has faced since it came to power more than 10 years ago.'[66] On the 21st February the R.P. drew a multi-racial crowd of about 900 to its first public meeting in Salisbury.

Even before Colonel Hartley vacated his Victoria seat to become Speaker of the House, there was much discussion about the forthcoming by-election in that constituency. Mr. Savory made it clear that he would not resign his own seat at Matobo to contest the Victoria seat, but the R.P. would definitely put up a candidate. The Victoria seat was regarded as a safe one for the R.F. (Colonel Hartley had been returned unopposed at the two general elections following the 1962 election) but this time it was to be contested by four parties and would be the first public test for the Rhodesia Party. The R.P. candidate, Mr. Peter Hingeston, reiterated the party's announcement that the campaign would mainly focus on the settlement issue.

Towards the end of the campaign the *Financial Gazette* commented that the 'Rhodesia Party is proving less effective in operation than had been anticipated, and its campaign has not been greatly helped by the inexperience of its candidate.'[67] The results of the election showed that Mr. Hingeston had gained 305 (22 *per cent*) of the votes cast. Summing up the election results the *Herald* commented that until the Prime Minister had stepped into the campaign the R.P. election workers 'had begun to persuade themselves that they could actually win... [but] everywhere he went Mr. Smith hammered home one point—the need for unity. And he hung the dread label "leftist" on the Rhodesia Party... Nonetheless, with the election over, the Rhodesian Front was not as jubilant as might have been expected... With the smoke of battle dying away, one hard fact remained—305 voters in a highly conservative constituency had resisted the blandishments of Mr. Smith himself and voted R.P.'[68]

Having conceded defeat at the by-election the R.P. nevertheless felt that the results showed that they could confidently plan for the next general election. This decision was welcomed by the *Mail*, which commented 'Taking all into account, it might be fair to say that the R.P. could if it really tried, take half a dozen seats. Even half a dozen faces in opposition would be very good for Parliament.'[69]

According to the editor of the *Financial Gazette* the R.P. occupied itself, after the by-election, in a critical self-evaluation. Its immediate needs were seen as a necessity to appoint a responsible national leader to master-mind its campaign and to establish a competent executive to organize its first national congress later in the year.[70]

THE CANDOUR LEAGUE

Although not a political party the Candour League was active in rallying support for the European campaign against the settlement proposals. Its president, Dr. Ian Anderson, had stood as an independent candidate in the Mabelreign by-election and received only 68 votes less than the R.F. candidate.

At the Right-wing rally which the League sponsored in March 1972 (to which the audience had been asked to 'roll up and show the Pearce Commission the size of the white backlash') Dr. Anderson warned of the dangers of 'international finance' which was trying to take over Rhodesia as a stepping stone to South Africa.[71] Earlier the League had made a statement criticizing the settlement proposals saying that Rhodesians were being asked to surrender 'life, liberty and property for nothing concrete.' The League said that because it believed that the British government had no standing in Rhodesia it would not give evidence to the Pearce Commission.[72]

Later in the year the League called upon members of the Rhodesian Front to ensure, at their forthcoming congress, that a motion was passed rejecting the settlement proposals 'for all time'. The League also challenged the government to hold a full public debate on the proposals.[73]

AFRICAN

THE AFRICAN NATIONAL COUNCIL

Although the African National Council[74] has not become a formal political party it became one in all but name on the 10th March 1972. It was launched in mid-December 1971 as an African-led organization in response to the African 'call' for a united front to oppose the settlement proposals. Its chairman, Bishop Abel T. Muzorewa, head of the United Methodist Church in Rhodesia, when announcing the formation of the new group confirmed that all the members of the executive committee were under some form of restriction. He himself was not allowed to enter the Tribal Trust Lands. The Bishop said that 'European support for the organization would be welcomed if it had the same aims.'[75]

In February 1972 the A.N.C. made a public statement denying claims in the British press that a banned Rhodesian African nationalist party in exile was represented within Rhodesia by the A.N.C. Later during his visit to London, Bishop Muzorewa, commenting upon this report, that the A.N.C. was 'well organized and closely linked with outside "liberation movements",[76] categorically denied that the A.N.C. had any links with agencies outside Rhodesia.

Following his address to the United Nations Security Council in New York, the Bishop reiterated the A.N.C.'s plea for a constitutional conference in place of the current settlement proposals. If the idea of a constitutional conference was rejected, he said, the measures his organization envisaged included a campaign of civil disobedience.[77] At a later conference, however, the Bishop said that the A.N.C. had no positive plans for such a campaign.

After Bishop Muzorewa's return to Rhodesia, the *Sunday Mail* published a profile of the Bishop entitled *A.N.C. Leader: the Reluctant Politician* and quoted him as saying 'My only desire is for a settlement that is just. If there is justice for all men in the proposals, that's fine. If there is not, then they must be rejected.'[78]

The announcement that the A.N.C. was considering forming itself into a political organization led the *Herald* to comment that this plan came as no surprise for 'its leading figures, with the exception of Bishop Muzorewa, have been active African nationalist politicians before'. 'A responsible, efficiently-organized well-led African political party, pledged to operate constitutionally and within the law, and genuinely representative of Rhodesian African aspirations, could cause no objection. Indeed it might be a good thing. [However] the African National Council has shown only too clearly that it is looking to influences outside this country... Other manifestations too are not reassuring. Despite the African National Council's avowed dislike of violence, there is evidence that many of those who disagreed with its attitude toward the settlement proposals came to be afraid... Some of the A.N.C.'s spokesmen, in public, have made it abundantly clear that they are as intolerant now as they were in 1961 of any proposals that do not offer them immediate power... They are interested only in "power to change the Government"... In other words their policy is all or nothing. It is uncompromising and, whether by calculation or not, must lead to conflict. We condemn it as fully—and for the same reasons—as we condemn the policies of the white supremacists at the other extreme.'[79]

In March it was announced that the National Peoples' Union (N.P.U.) had dissolved itself and that all its members were being urged to join the A.N.C., an action which had been taken without consultation with the N.P.U.'s only M.P., Mr. Josiah Gondo. Later in the month a Swedish student, Mr. Klas Erling Soderstrom, who had been an active member of the A.N.C. since its formation, was served with a deportation order.

Towards the end of March the A.N.C. National Executive was reported to be meeting to plan strategy in the months ahead regarding the organization of branches, individual and group functions, Mr. Soderstrom's deportation, and a massive recruitment campaign which, it was hoped, would get under way the next day with the sale of membership cards to augment party funds.

The government, however, promptly prohibited both the sale and possession of the cards in terms of Section 18 of the Law and Order (Maintenance) Act. According to a Ministry of Information statement, the government was of the opinion that the cards would be used as weapons of intimidation, for the sale of membership cards by African political parties had, in the past, 'led to wide-spread intimidation of members to buy them and show them on demand by party officials and gangs of thugs [leading] to intimidators knocking on doors at night and calling out innocent householders to produce membership cards. There were also serious threats of injury to life and property and actual physical violence.'[80]

The prohibition of membership cards led to rumours of a total ban on the A.N.C., and it was reported at the end of March that President Kaunda of Zambia had issued an invitation to Bishop Muzorewa to go to Lusaka and form a 'government in exile' in the event of the party being banned. This led to conjecture that President Kaunda's motive was 'to persuade the Bishop... that his loyalty would be to re-organize the Rhodesian terrorist factions in Zambia into a responsible body.'[81] The A.N.C., however, denied this and said that in any case the majority of A.N.C. leaders would not accept this idea, for a government in exile could not affect the realities of the political scene in Rhodesia. The Zambian government also denied that such an approach had been made, but in April, the *Financial Gazette* reported that the Bishop was to meet two senior Zambian diplomats in New York to discuss the setting up of a 'Zimbabwean' government in exile in Lusaka.

In April the A.N.C. sent two representatives to London to meet Bishop Muzorewa on his way back from the United States (where he had been attending a church conference). Mr. R. T. D. Sadomba, the former Centre Party M.P., and the Rev. Canaan Banana, the A.N.C. vice-president, hoped to join the Bishop to form a three-man delegation to see Sir Alec Douglas-Home and possibly the British Prime Minister to try and persuade the British government of the necessity for holding a constitutional conference.

Following publication of the Pearce Report, the A.N.C. announced plans for a national convention to examine the desirability of a settlement and for convening a constitutional conference to which members of the Rhodesian Front and other political parties in Rhodesia would be invited. The A.N.C. also announced that it would ask British political parties, the United Nations, the Organization for African Unity and the World Council of Churches to send observers.[82] The Prime Minister, Mr. Ian Smith, was emphatic that he would have nothing to do with the A.N.C. The latter part of the statement (referring to the observers) met with wide-spread criticism since most people felt that Rhodesia's problems should be solved without outside interference.

Early in June the government issued a new regulation under the Emergency Powers Act. Designated the Emergency Powers (Prohibition of Foreign Aid to Designated Political Parties) Regulations it enabled the government to designate a particular organization as a political party and to prohibit it from obtaining funds and other assistance from external sources if 'by past conduct either of the party itself or its members it appears likely that the receipt of such external funds will result in activities likely to cause an interference with public safety, the maintenance of public order and the preservation of peace.' The regulations also prevented the entry of goods and funds from external organizations by people 'who have identified themselves with African terrorist organizations or have supported banned Rhodesian organizations.' Accompanying the notice in the *Government Gazette* was a further Notice which read that 'under these regulations the Minister of Law and Order declares the African National Council to be a designated party for purposes of the Act'.[83] A government spokesman was reported as saying that the Minister had designated the A.N.C. under the regulations because 'the A.N.C. or its members had, in his opinion, been responsible for actions which interfered with the peace, order and good government of Rhodesia.'[84]

On the 16th June the Minister of Justice and of Law and Order, Mr. D. W. Lardner-Burke, moved that the House declare an extension to the State of Emergency for a further period of twelve months. The Minister referred to the threat from outside Rhodesia's borders and went on to say that 'within Rhodesia the recent disorders have demonstrated... that in the field of security we must not be too complacent... the African National Council attracted to its ranks many dissident elements including a majority of individuals who have been associated with subversive political organizations in the past... it seems improbable that the A.N.C. can for long pursue a policy of non-violence... So it is only prudent that the Government maintains a strict surveillance on the activities of this party, its office bearers and members... the Government must be ready to act without hesitation the moment this organization endangers the public safety of Rhodesia.'[85]

At a press conference in July Bishop Muzorewa spoke of a forth-coming meeting which would be the first of a series to be held in European areas. The Bishop said that at this meeting he would 'make it clear whether Africans want majority rule now or in the future. I believe that what I am going to say will make it clear we are not pressing one way or the other.' The *Sunday Mail* commented that 'the Bishop's statement is regarded by political observers as a significant step towards ending the deadlock to the Anglo-Rhodesian dispute' while the *Herald* saw the forth-coming meeting as the first open sign that 'European liberal elements in Rhodesia are making a positive bid to save the settlement situation.' [86]

Shortly before the meeting was due to take place, two senior members of the A.N.C. left the country precipitately. They were Mr. M. Mawema, who was due to speak at the meeting, and another man who was under conditional restriction. After their arrival in Lusaka *en route* to London, the Zambian press was quoted as saying that the two men had been afraid that they were about to be arrested and that is why they had left the country so suddenly. This supposition was denied in Rhodesia and it was pointed out that the fact that the men had been able to leave the country unhindered was proof that the government had no intention of arresting them. Later in the month it was announced that Bishop Muzorewa had given instructions that the two men were not to be regarded as speaking for the A.N.C. and that when they arrived in London, A.N.C. representatives there must guard against their giving the impression that they reflected official A.N.C. thinking. [87]

The meeting, which took place in the Harry Margolis Hall in the Milton Park suburb of Salisbury, was chaired by Mr. H. H. C. Holderness (a former M.P.). Mr. Ken Mew and Bishop Muzorewa both addressed the crowd. Bishop Muzorewa first outlined what the A.N.C. was—'It is not the continuation of any previous organization. It is not a group of political agitators, dictating to five million Africans what they should think or do. It is not organized or controlled by anyone outside the country. It is not made up of hooligans, bent on destruction and violence. It is not responsible, as has been made out, for hostile acts that have occurred in recent months. It is not anti any racial group... It is a spontaneous grass-roots movement... It is the embodiment of the hopes and aspirations of the vast majority of the people of this country as a whole... It has the support of other prominent members of the country such as a majority of Chiefs and African M.P.'s... [It] champions the cause of the full rights of all people—Africans, Asians, Europeans, Coloureds. Its membership is wide open to all racial groups.'

The Bishop then went on to discuss the A.N.C.'s manifesto, which claims that the A.N.C. is 'the one sole voice of the African masses of Zimbabwe and all people of good will in their just and normal struggle for national emancipation from the yoke of a racist and oppressive minority rule'. In terms of doctrine, the Bishop said that the A.N.C.'s manifesto laid down that it was to 'strive to create a nation where black and white can live as children of the One Almighty God' and that the A.N.C. had pledged themselves to work for the attainment of democratic rule by non-violent means.

After disclaiming responsibility for organizing violence during the sitting of the Pearce Commission, the Bishop examined 'the main reasons why the vast majority rejected the proposals'. He said that 'First and foremost, we rejected the agreement because it was based on the 1969 Republican Constitution... a settlement based on this Constitution was nothing but a legalization of U.D.I. which the majority regard as their No. 1 enemy... Secondly, the proposals do not affect, with any significance, the racially segregatory and discriminatory legislation which constitutes the basic structure of apartheid in Rhodesia, which itself is the cornerstone of all our racial injustice... Thirdly we rejected the proposals because of our lack of confidence and trust in the R.F. Government.'

With regard to the future, the Bishop deplored what he called the trend by the government to use the chiefs in an attempt to reverse the African rejection of the settlement terms. He considered that using the chiefs in this way was ' prostituting the traditional role of the chiefs, by making them a mouthpiece of the Government instead of a spokesman for their people.' He continued by speaking to 'My fellow white countrymen,' (for the meeting had been called to put the A.N.C. point of view to a largely white audience) and attempting to allay fears that once majority rule had been achieved there would be no place for Europeans. The Bishop then enumerated the reasons why he believed that 'an orderly transition to democratic rule with peace and prosperity for all' could be achieved. He considered firstly that, in Rhodesia, 'we have the advantage of a greater educational advancement than that existing·in most states to the north of us. Already we have 2 000 African university graduates.[88] Second, 'we have achieved a level of economic development which means that an increasing number of our people have a stake in a growing economy... Third, a high percentage of our people have an understanding of and commitment to the Christian faith. Fourth, there is a deep aversion to violence in the culture of the African people and a desire to solve differences, no matter how great, through consultation rather than by bloodshed. Fifth, the diversity of our tribal groups... is practically nil here... Sixth, the whites... here... are citizens by birth or otherwise. No sane, responsible leader would want to expel its citizens. Democratic rule will also provide for the protection of the minority and their property.'

To end his speech the Bishop considered that settlement could be achieved by Rhodesians coming together to iron out their differences 'by calling upon Mr. Ian Smith to take the words of Lord Goodman seriously, to treat Africans as human beings and be willing to listen and to enter into constructive dialogue with them and all peoples.'

He then appealed to the government to take the lead in convening a national convention leading to a constitutional conference 'to seek common ground for a just and honourable settlement.'[89]

Reporting the Bishop's speech the *Herald* commented that 'Bishop Muzorewa clearly disappointed Europeans at the meeting by consistently refusing to say what the A.N.C. demands would be at a constitutional conference or to disclose the A.N.C.'s attitude towards majority rule. ...The Bishop's speech also indicated that the A.N.C. has rejected advice it has received in talks with European liberal elements on how to conduct its campaign for European recognition and the promotion of talks with the Rhodesian Government.'[90]

On the following Sunday the *Mail's* editorial commented that the meeting had been 'a sad waste of time [for] listeners had expected a constructive attempt to end the settlement deadlock; instead the Bishop gave them a display of intransigence that must have delighted the Rhodesian Front... he... fell back on the old demands he knew would not be met, and thereby achieved nothing.' In an accompanying article by reporter Chris Reynolds

it was postulated that there had been a difference of opinion in
the A.N.C. leadership which had led to the departure of the two
men prior to the meeting. Mr. Reynolds speculated that both Mr.
Mawema and the Bishop had intended to speak on the subject
of forgetting majority rule for the time being in favour of promoting
a settlement. 'The arrest story—it has strongly been denied by
security branch officers—is regarded as a calculated move to
obstruct talks that have been taking place in Salisbury in recent
weeks... These talks... attended by Bishop Muzorewa and Mr.
Mawema... [were on] ...ways of finding an African "Yes" within
the terms agreed last November.'[91]

At the beginning of August, when the Bishop returned from
visits to several African countries, he issued a press statement refuting rumours of a split in the A.N.C. referring to the challenge
for a round-table discussion and asking whether 'this genuine hand
of friendship, extended by moderate Africans, [would be] refused?
If so, one can only fear that this reasonable line of thinking, if
not heeded by those in power will be replaced by a more militant
one.'[92]

Early in September the passports and other travel documents
of both Bishop Muzorewa and his deputy, the Rev. Canaan
Banana, were confiscated under the new Departure from Rhodesia
(Control) Amendment Act which became law on the 1st September.

Later in the same month it was reported that London-based
members of the A.N.C. were to send a delegation to address the
United Nations Security Council. An A.N.C. spokesman, however, denied that the A.N.C. had official representation outside
Rhodesia, saying 'we have no knowledge of an official delegation
and we have not appointed anyone in London as an official A.N.C.
representative.' The 'disowned' A.N.C. in London, however,
issued the text of a 2 000-word draft to the press calling on the
Security Council to make four major changes to existing economic
sanctions. In October the A.N.C. in Rhodesia announced that it
was appointing four external representatives in order to 'prevent
variance in statements and action between our officials outside
and the leadership here.' The delegates were named as Mr. Eshmael
Mlambo, Mr. Klas Soderstrom (who had been deported from Rhodesia earlier in the year), Miss Judith Todd (who had been detained
during the sitting of the Pearce Commission and allowed to leave

the country only on the understanding that if she returned she
would be placed back in detention) and a fourth person—the man
who had fled the country with Mr. Mawena.[93]

At the end of September, it was reported that the Minister of
Internal Affairs and leaders of the A.N.C. had made contact and
later that another meeting would take place after a forthcoming
A.N.C. executive meeting. This meeting however was cancelled
by the Minister, who denied that he had been holding talks with
the A.N.C. as such. In his statement the Minister, Mr. L. B.
Smith, said 'At no time have discussions taken place with the
A.N.C. as such, nor are there likely to be any... The fact that
individual members as Africans with a problem wished to come
forward and meet me is something I have always accepted and
am always prepared to accept in the future.' The A.N.C. however
said that talks had been held and that 'A.N.C. leaders [had]
reported to the executive committee... and we are satisfied that
the talks were going in the right direction.' In commenting upon
this the *Herald* said that talks 'will be resumed in private when
each side has digested progress and the chiefs have been re-assured
that they are not being sold down the river to the politicians.'[94]

The Bishop held another press conference just before Christmas
when he announced his hopes that there would be a meeting at
ministerial level after the end of the festive season. He rejected
'recent claims by the Prime Minister, Mr. Ian Smith, that Africans
no longer had time on their side... and "had to come to their senses"
and reverse the rejection of the settlement proposals.' He added
that recent repressive legislation, such as the *situpa* bill and provincialization, had been rushed through Parliament and had only justified and confirmed the deep fears and suspicions which led to
earlier rejection of the proposals'. In Bulawayo, after Christmas,
the Rev. Canaan Banana said that 'nothing is being done at present
about the expected talks... [but] A.N.C. officials will not talk to
anybody as individuals.' He explained that the A.N.C. held three
cardinal points: that it was the indisputable spokesman of African
political aspirations; that the overwhelming rejection of the Smith-
Home proposals was genuine and there could be no going back
to them; and that there could be no settlement without the A.N.C.
participating on equal terms with the Rhodesian Front at the negotiating table.[95]

Developments during 1973

During the early weeks of 1973 three officials of the A.N.C. were charged under the Law and Order (Maintenance) Act with uttering subversive statements 'likely to engender or promote feelings of hostility or expose to contempt, ridicule or dis-esteem a group or section of the community commonly called white or European.' Two of the men were eventually given suspended sentences and the other was sentenced to four months' hard labour but allowed bail pending an appeal.

At the end of February three senior members of the A.N.C. were detained, in terms of the Emergency Powers regulations, for security reasons. This action led the Council to announce that it had abandoned plans, which were fairly well advanced, for talks with the Prime Minister. *Moto's* editor sympathized with this action but warned A.N.C. leaders that 'serious preparatory work for talks must be stepped up without more delay.' He commented that there had been rumours that the 'A.N.C. leadership is frightfully uneven: strong at the top but weak in the lower cadres' and said that the National Executive Council had not yet met as a body with full representation, this being one of the reasons confirming such a rumour. [96]

In mid-April Bishop Muzorewa addressed a large crowd in Bulawayo's Mzilikazi Township. The meeting was held shortly after the Bishop had issued a statement announcing that the Council was again prepared to call for further constitutional talks. In his address at the township Bishop Muzorewa pointed out 'We want to belong. We are not racial segregationists. We do not cry for expulsion of the whites, but we do not want to be excluded from the privileges of the country either. We want to be first class fellow citizens with them rather than being treated as third class citizens victimized by our good sun-proof colour. We do not want to live on rationed education, employment, housing, businesses, etc. We want to be responsible and contribute to the country's economy.' The Bishop continued by warning the government and its supporters that 'if they refuse our contribution of non-violent, peaceful means of solving the most depressing situation Rhodesia faces today, they will live to regret it if they do not respect our non-violent approach to the problem, for other forces beyond their control could take over.' [97]

During April, Centre Party M.P. Mr. E. G. Watungwa asked

the Prime Minister whether he and the A.N.C. had yet agreed
on an agenda for constitutional talks and whether such talks had
in fact taken place. The Prime Minister confirmed that contact
had been made with a number of African political organizations,
including the A.N.C., but he declined to give any details for he
said that he regarded such talks as confidential.[98] A few days later
the *Financial Gazette* discussed reports of a split in the A.N.C.
Bishop Muzorewa, reputedly the head of a more moderate faction,
was understood to have offered his resignation but to have been
persuaded to withdraw it to avoid letting in more militant individuals. The militant elements, reportedly led by the Rev. Canaan
Banana, were believed to be pressing for much more stringent
terms for a settlement. The *Gazette* considered that 'the moderates
won this first power struggle; the Bishop will stay in office; and
the official policy of continuing the endeavour to negotiate with
the Government will continue.' Bishop Muzorewa, however, later
condemned this report.

In the same article the *Financial Gazette* also discussed the rivalry
between the A.N.C. and the two African pro-settlement groups
and asked who really represented informed African opinion for
'Both sides claim overwhelming support but the evidence is difficult to judge.' The newspaper concluded that the forthcoming
by-election at Matojeni would supply an answer, for, although
the African Settlement Convention had announced that it would
not put up a candidate, the African Settlement Forum had already
announced that it would do so and A.N.C. sources were understood
to have announced that, while they would not put up an official
candidate, they would put their resources behind a candidate who
was an A.N.C. supporter.[99]

The following month it was announced that the Rev. Canaan
Banana and another A.N.C. official had fled the country illegally.
Both men later announced from Botswana that they had left Rhodesia in order to travel to the United States to study for higher
university degrees.[100]

There were seven candidates in the Matojeni by-election (the
seat had been left vacant following the death of Centre Party M.P.
Mr. W. S. Moraka). Two of them were A.N.C. supporters. When
the result was announced it was found that the two A.N.C. supporters had received most votes, the winning candidate, Mr. Lot
Dewa, gaining 133 votes and his colleague, who came second, 85

votes. The significance of this victory for the A.N.C. was seen by Moto's reporter, Menard Masvingise, as 'clear evidence that Bishop Abel Tendayi Muzorewa still has his grip firmly on the African population' and as being 'definitely a blow for the Rhodesian Government [which was] believed to have been waiting for a victory of one of the pro-settlement elements.'[101]

In early June, in his annual report, the Secretary for Law and Order explained why it had been found necessary during 1972 to ban A.N.C. membership cards—'a weapon of intimidation'—and to designate the A.N.C. as a political party in order that funds and other assistance from outside sources should not be available to it. It was considered that 'furthering the interests of that political party would be likely to result in activities likely to interfere with public safety, the maintenance of public order or the preservation of peace.' The Report also noted that 'the delay in the arrival of the [Pearce] Commission provided time in which extremists were able to obtain financial support from anti-Rhodesian organizations overseas and in which they were able to organize themselves on a country-wide basis. As a result violence against persons and property occurred.'[102]

Towards the end of the debate on the President's speech, the Minister of Justice and of Law and Order stated that the government was satisfied that some members of the A.N.C. had associated with and supported 'terrorists'. He warned that if 'sufficient individuals of an organization identify themselves with an unlawful purpose the inference must be drawn that the organization itself is also linked with an unlawful purpose... the whole organization... is of course under our surveillance and we will not hesitate to act if this becomes necessary.'[103]

THE NATIONAL PEOPLES' UNION

Competing for the eight seats on the African Roll in the 1970 general election, 22 candidates represented 5 different parties while eleven stood as independents. Of these candidates seven were elected from the Centre Party and one from the National Peoples' Union (N.P.U.). During 1969-70 four all-African parties were formed, the N.P.U. being formed early in 1969 by a merger of the United Peoples' Party (which had been the official opposition in the previous parliament) and the Democratic Party.[104] During the 1970 election campaign, the N.P.U.'s president at that time,

Dr. Gordon Chavunduka, put the party's aims succinctly—'we are not anti-white, anti-coloured or anti anybody else. What we oppose are certain aspects of Rhodesian Front policies.'

At the beginning of 1972 it was announced that the N.P.U. was taking steps to expel their leader and only M.P., Mr. Josiah Gondo, and to merge with the A.N.C. on the grounds that the N.P.U. was anti-settlement while Mr. Gondo had been urging acceptance of the settlement terms. Following the announcement in March that the A.N.C. had become a political organization, the N.P.U. dissolved itself and urged all former members to join the A.N.C. Mr. Gondo, who had been Leader of the Opposition in 1965 (the first African to reach such a position), continued to sit in the House of Assembly as an Independent until he was killed in a car accident in late October. In the ensuing by-election, out of six candidates, only one was a member of a political party—Mr. Percy M'Kudu—although the name of another candidate was linked with the A.N.C. The A.N.C. however, denied that it was officially contesting the seat. In a quiet poll, with a percentage of 39.8, an Independent, Mr. T. T. Zawaini, was elected.

THE RHODESIA ELECTORAL UNION

Of the sixteen seats for Africans under the Electoral Act No. 56 of 1969, eight seats are reserved for candidates to be elected by the Tribal Electoral Colleges. Candidates are allowed to lobby the Colleges and to address College meetings but, at the time of the general election in 1970, a government spokesman, Mr. W. H. H. Nicolle (at that time Secretary for Internal Affairs) said that he hoped that the tribal M.P.'s would take 'a non-party political line and that they will act, as the chiefs have requested, in the national interests... but... the attitude to be adopted by the tribal representatives... was something they would have to decide for themselves.'[105]

On the 28th April 1970, however, the formation of a new all-African party was announced by Mr. Ranches Makaya, the only former M.P. to be elected by the tribal colleges. He was quoted as saying 'we are for gradualism towards majority rule.' The new party, called the Rhodesia Electoral Union (R.E.U.), included the other seven tribally elected members and it hoped that it would be called upon to form the official opposition in the House of

Assembly. A hope that was not fulfilled for the Leader of the House of Assembly, Mr. D. W. Lardner-Burke, stated in a press interview that the reason why an official opposition would not be recognized was because 'all the African M.P.'s had been elected to represent Africans either on the African rolls or those in the Tribal Trust areas. So how can they be called the Opposition? I think it would be entirely wrong to create an Opposition based entirely on race.'[106] By mid-1971 it was announced that the party had about 60 branches throughout the Tribal Trust Lands.

During the sitting of the Pearce Commission the R.E.U. sent written evidence itemizing the reasons why the tribal M.P.'s rejected the proposals. Following publication of the Pearce Report, which the R.E.U. welcomed as a 'valid and true' reflection of Rhodesian views, the Minister of Internal Affairs, speaking at the Senate debate on the Report, spoke of increasing the powers of the chiefs 'to ensure that the tribal authority which they head has more adequate and more responsible representation in the House of Assembly.'[107] The leader of the R.E.U. saw this as an attempt to 'muzzle' African opinion and Ian Mills of the *Herald* commented 'It has been known for some time that the Government does not regard them [the tribal M.P.'s] as being truly representative of the African tribesmen. The fact that individually elected tribal members later formed themselves into a party also annoyed the Government because it was completely contrary to what had been expected of them.'[108]

MULTI-RACIAL

THE CENTRE PARTY

Throughout the early months of 1968 discussions were held on the formation of a new political party to be re-formed out of two political associations—the Centre Group and the Rhodesia Constitutional Association. The Centre Party (C.P.) was formally announced at a press conference on the 29th August 1968 by its chairman, Mr. T.H.P. Bashford, a prominent farmer from Karoi who had been an unsuccessful candidate for the Rhodesia Party[109] in the 1965 general election.

The C.P.'s policies were later outlined as being 'To create a strong and united Rhodesia in which race is no barrier to rights ... [and] to achieve a recognized and lasting independence for Rho-

desia. The maintenance of a single parliament for all Rhodesians
... [with] general advancement on merit, ... [and] good race relations ... The maintenance and improvement of administrative and
other services; ... [to] bring greater opportunity for employment
...[and] economic development.' [110] The following day the *Herald*'s
editorial found that 'the new party's policy contains some seeming
anomalies. The party gives the impression of being, if anything,
a little to the Right of the Centre Group ... It has been dubbed
Left-wing by those whose view is limited by the confines of a self-
made laager: on any other view it is conservative. But ... for the
first time for years, there is a party which offers an alternative
direction and which can be an active source of a focus for European
political opposition.' [111]

In September of the same year it was announced that two Coloured men and an Asian were among the *ad hoc* interim committee
of the southern division of the Party. The chairman of the southern
division announced that 'there are also many Africans who have
indicated their willingness to serve and the sooner we get Africans
on to the committee, the happier I shall be.' [112]

The C.P.'s inaugural congress during 1969 was regarded by
observers as significant for, as the *Herald* commented, 'it represents
the coming together of an active country-wide opposition for the
first time since U.D.I.' [113]

The Centre Party announced in 1970 that it would contest 14
of the 50 European seats and all eight of the African Roll seats
in the forthcoming general election. Its aim would be to provide
a strong and effective opposition to the Rhodesian Front. The
result of the election was that all the C.P.'s European candidates
were defeated but it lost only one African seat (to the National
Peoples' Union Party). The *Herald* commented 'Friday's voting
is indicative of European willingness to sacrifice the two-or-more
party system in order to safeguard white political control. Hence-
forth, no matter how unsatisfactory the Government record may
be when it has to go to the country, support for any rival European
party is liable to be nervously and hesitantly given for fear of divid-
ing white representation and giving black representation greater
leverage ... And what of the Africans? History has repeated itself;
once again a party under European management has won several
seats for Africans and none for its white candidates ... But if history
repeats itself in greater detail—as it probably will—the African

M.P.'s will want to develop their own policies free of European direction and perhaps under a new party name to emphasize their independence.'[114]

During 1971 the C.P. put up a candidate for the Mabelreign by-election in which the Rhodesian Front won a very narrow victory over an Independent Right-wing candidate. The Centre Party candidate only gained 158 votes out of a total of 1 138 votes. In December C.P. members welcomed the settlement but said that they hoped they would be forgiven 'for waxing less than lyrical over some of the aspects of the settlement package.'[115]

On the 20th January 1972 one of the party's African M.P.'s who was also its political secretary, Mr. R. T. D. Sadomba, resigned from the party because 'he had found that the vast majority of his constituents appeared to be against the settlement [and] he felt he had to put forward their views—which directly opposed the Centre Party's policy.'[116] Mr. Sadomba retained his parliamentary seat as an independent member and shortly afterwards joined the African National Council.

In March the C.P. announced that it would send a delegation to Britain with the intention, as reported, of attempting to steer Conservative Party opinion towards an implementation of the settlement even if the terms were rejected. In answer to critics of this action Mr. Bashford, in an article in the party newspaper, said 'reaction to the Test has created a new situation insofar as the practicability of the British fifth principle is concerned ... [the Test] has in fact demonstrated what we in the Centre Party have always known—that no conceivable package deal acceptable to the R.F. would satisfy African nationalists ... this was the lesson of 1961 and attitudes have even hardened since then.'

The delegation, including two M.P.'s, went to London on the 28th April and on their return were interviewed by *Centrepoint*. In answer to the question whether the delegation's objectives had been accomplished they said: 'we think we achieved our objectives more completely than we imagined possible. We saw everyone we wanted to see ... we were listened to with great attention and even political extremists admitted there was more to be said for seeking ways to implement the settlement than they had thought.'[117] The delegation, however, returned with the conviction that the Pearce answer would be a negative one and that there would be a deadlock in the settlement situation.

Following publication of the Pearce Report the C.P. parliamentary caucus called upon the government to implement the proposals as a means of breaking the deadlock. Mr. Bashford, however, saw 'no hope of anything happening to break the impasse unless there was a complete political reshuffle ... or the African National Council admitted it had made a mistake in rejecting the settlement proposals.' He added that 'instead of being asked if they [the Africans] accepted the settlement proposals, they should have been asked whether they preferred them to the 1969 Constitution.'[118]

In July rumours started about resignations and a split in the party. On the 15th September the C.P.'s vice-chairman and executive committee member, Mr. N. J. McNally, announced his resignation but despite rumours that he was about to join the newly formed Rhodesia Party denied that he had any connection with it. Mr. McNally was reported as saying that although he supported the C.P.'s non-racial structure, he believed it had proved ineffective.[119]

The party's annual congress took place towards the end of October and it was announced that the congress would be asked 'to accept a resolution that the party's most useful role is to persuade black and white leaders in Rhodesia to make "meaningful concessions from their present deadlocked position".' At the congress Mr. Bashford outlined reasons why he believed the Centre Party had a vital role to play in bringing about a settlement and why all-party discussions should be held on ways of breaking the settlement impasse.

Following criticism that the poor attendance at the congress had shown that liberalism was ailing in Rhodesia, Mr. Bashford commented on what he considered to be the party's future. 'Liberalism needed a home in Rhodesia and the Centre Party could provide it.' He went on to say that 'he rejected the idea that liberalism was dead in Rhodesia ... [because] there was a strong body of liberal opinion among young people.' Mr. Bashford then announced that the C.P. planned to create a youth wing of the party.[120]

In mid-February 1973 the Centre Party parliamentary caucus met the Prime Minister to discuss the new regulations on collective fines and to protest against detention without trial. In a statement issued later the C.P. said that the Prime Minister had rejected the party's contention that the system of collective fines was immoral and counterproductive; in answer to the plea for detainees to be brought before the courts or released the Prime Minister had pointed out that all cases of detainees were reviewed by a tribunal and therefore there could be no question of a miscarriage of justice. [121]

On the 7th March Mr. W. S. Moraka, Centre Party M.P. for Matojeni, died suddenly at his home. For the ensuing by-election the C.P. announced that it would put up a candidate, Mr. M. I. B. Pfumojena, to oppose the other six candidates, all of whom stood as Independents although individually backed by the A.N.C. and by the two African pro-settlement groups. Mr. Pfumojena, like the other candidates, met constituents personally to explain his election manifesto. This had African education as its primary clause.

At the by-election Mr. Pfumojena came third in the 47 *per cent* poll and only narrowly missed having to forfeit his deposit. The *Herald* commented that 'Observers see the election results as symptomatic of [a] more nationalistic trend in African politics and the rejection of the multiracial Centre Party and those elements supporting a settlement with Britain on the 1971 terms.' [122] *Moto's* reporter also saw the result as 'a blow to multiracial politics in this country' and forecast that 'African nationalist politics is bound to gather momentum as more and more Africans convince themselves that a less efficient African government is better than an efficient government under alien rule.' [123] This statement was commented upon by Mr. Bashford in the second issue of the C.P's newsletter: 'The seemingly raw racialistic intent revealed in this last commentary will no doubt be seized upon by fearful Whites as fully confirming their worst presentiments. Those of us who know the African people, know also that this cry for majority rule is really a cry of abject despair. It comes from a people who can see no other way of erasing the stigma that the R.F. has attached to every black skin.' [124]

In early March subscribers to *Centrepoint*, the Centre Party newspaper learnt of its demise. The party executive had decided that the money set aside for subsidizing the journal would be better spent upon alternative methods of projecting the image of the C.P., for it had long been felt that *Centrepoint* had only been preaching to the converted. It was replaced in April by a cyclo-styled monthly newsletter.

Early in 1973, while awaiting a reaction from the Prime Minister regarding the C.P.'s threatened withdrawal of support for the efforts being made towards the constitutional settlement, the C.P. announced its own four-point plan for an internal settlement. The Party's press statement announced that the 'failure of the settlement and the subsequent white backlash, the resurgence of terrorism and the closing of the border (and its effect on our friendly neighbours) and the worst drought in the country's history have created a situation in which Rhodesians of all races have no alternative but to pull together.' The points which the C.P. put before the public were that there must be no further dissembling about the gravity of the situation; that immediate steps must be taken to improve economic opportunities for urban Africans; that plans for the immediate, as well as the more distant future, be drawn up to offset the effects of the drought in the rural sector; and that the 'chains of racial discrimination' which bind the economy must be loosened. [125]

In March, having received no assurance from the Prime Minister, that in the event of a settlement the racially discriminative legislation passed during 1972 would be repealed, the C.P's leader announced the withdrawal of the Centre Party's support on the settlement issue. Mr. Bashford said he considered that all that could now be done was to make a final effort to get the Rhodesian Front and the African National Council talking even 'if only to demonstrate to the general public and to the world at large that the last possible approach to a settlement under the R.F. has been explored.' [126]

During the debate following the President's speech in June, Mr. M. M. Bhebe, Centre Party M.P. for Ntshonalanga, made what the *Herald* described as his strongest attack on the government in his parliamentary career. [127] He reproached the government for its arrogance in criticizing the British government for losing its enthusiasm for settlement. He said that the President had sounded as though it must be the British government which would have to take the initiative, when it was well known that unless an internal settlement was made there could be no hope of ending the constitutional dispute in a manner which would be respected. He advised the government to 'bring together all the parties concerned, to discuss a real solution ... and then they can go forward ... and present something which is of our own making.' [128]

NOTES

1 *R.H.* 14 December 1972.
2 The Land Apportionment Act (No. 30 of 1930) divided the total land area of Rhodesia (approximately 96 million acres) into 49 million acres for European ownership and use and 29 million acres for Africans, the rest being unallocated or reserved for national park and forest land. By 1962 the area had been divided (according to the Report of the Secretary for Internal Affairs) into 40 240 000 acres for African use (Tribal Trust Land and African Purchase Areas); 35 750 400 acres for European use (there were 1,5 million Africans living in the European farm areas or in the urban areas) and 16 609 600 acres unreserved or national park and forest land. Under the Land Tenure Act No. 55 of 1969 the area was divided into 44 950 000 acres for each racial group and 6 620 000 acres unallocated or for national park and forest. (see p. 259).
3 The other Federal countries were Northern Rhodesia (now Zambia) and Nyasaland (now Malawi).
4 *Southern Rhodesia : Documents relating to the negotiations between the United Kingdom and Southern Rhodesia Governments. Nov. 1963—Nov. 1965.* Cmnd. 2807: London: H.M.S.O.
5 1967: Barber, James: *Rhodesia : the road to rebellion :* London: O.U.P.
6 1966: Lardner-Burke, Desmond W.: *Rhodesia : the story of the crisis :* London: Oldbourne.
7 *R.H.* 5 September 1968.
8 *R.H.* 5, 6, 7, 10, 11, 12, 15 July 1968.
9 *R.H.* 27 March 1970.
10 Rhodesian Front Party pamphlet: *Rhodesia and You in the Super-70's :* Salisbury: Rhodesian Front (undated).
11 *R.H.* 6 August 1971.
12 *R.F.G.* 17 March 1972.
13 *S.M.* 16 April, *R.H.* 17, 19 April 1972.
14 *R.H.* 27 May 1972.
15 *The Rhodesian Forum* July 1972.
16 *R.H.* 17 August 1972.
17 *R.H.* 25, 26 August 1972.
18 Lord Graham, 7th Duke of Montrose: former Minister of External Affairs and of Defence. A co-signee of the declaration of independence: resigned his Cabinet post on 11 September 1968 just after the Rhodesian Front congress for that year had accepted the 1969 Constitutional proposals. He was quoted as saying, in an interview on the day of his resignation, that he saw no point in raising the issue of republican status.
19 As reported in *R.H.* 22 September 1972.
20 *R.H.* 23 September 1972.
21 *R.H.* 25 September 1972.
22 *R.F.G.* 29 September 1972.

23 *R.H.* 14 November 1972.
24 *R.F.G.* 24 November 1972.
25 *S.M.* 26 November 1972.
26 *Property and Finance*, No. 200. October 1972.
27 *S.M.* 19 November 1972.
28 *Centrepoint*, Vol. 3, No. 2, December 1972.
29 The Victoria seat had been held by Colonel G.H. Hartley, the Deputy Speaker since 1962. He was appointed Speaker when the House re-assembled on 27 March 1973.
30 *Property and Finance*, No. 203. January 1973.
31 *R.H.* 5 January 1973.
32 A second Proclamation was issued in the *Government Gazette* on the same date announcing a by-election at Matojeni. The vacancy being caused by the death of Centre Party M.P. Mr. W.F. Moraka.
33 *R.H.* 13 April 1973.
34 *R.H.* 26 April 1973.
35 *R.H.* 3 May 1973.
36 *R.H.* 13 May 1973.
37 A candidate forfeits his deposit if he secures less than 20 *per cent* of the votes cast for the succesful candidate.
38 *R.H.* 19 May 1973.
39 *S.M.* 27 May 1973.
40 *S.M.* 31 October 1971.
41 *R.H.* 18 February 1972.
42 *R.H.* 21 April 1972.
43 *R.H.* 10 May 1972.
44 *R.H.* 11 January 1973.
45 *R.H.* 2 February 1973.
46 *R.H.* 8 February 1973.
   Later in the year it was announced that Dr. Redmond had joined the Rhodesia Party.
47 *R.H.* 7 April 1972.
48 *R.H.* 19 May 1973.
49 *R.H.* 9 May 1972.
50 Not to be confused with the Rhodesia National Party which in 1963 succeeded to the United Federal Party and in turn gave way to the Rhodesia Party under Sir Roy Welensky in 1964.
51 *Sunday Times* (Johannesburg) 9 November 1969.
52 *R.H.* 23 March 1972.
53 *R.H.* 12 September 1972.
54 *R.H.* 30 November 1972.
55 *R.H.* 11 January 1973.
56 *S.M.* 22 April 1973.
57 *R.F.G.* 4 May 1973.
58 *R.H.* 8 May 1973.
59 *R.H.* 26 April 1973.
60 *R.H.* 19 May 1973.
61 *Centrepoint*, Vol. 2, No. 9. July 1972.
62 *S.M.* 13 August 1972.
63 Not to be confused with the previous Rhodesia Party led by Sir

Roy Welensky from 1964 and then by Mr. David Butler (who was killed in a car accident in 1972). This party was dissolved after the 1965 general election.

64 *R.H.* 2, 3 November; *S.M.* 5 November 1972.
65 *R.H.* 11 January 1973.
66 *R.H.* 27 January 1973.
67 *R.F.G.* 1 May 1973.
68 *R.H.* 19 May 1973.
69 *S.M.* 20 May 1973.
70 *R.F.G.* 1 June 1973.
71 *R.H.* 10 March 1972.
72 *R.H.* 29 January 1972.
73 *R.H.* 23 August 1972.
74 The initials A.N.C. are also used to designate the banned African National Congresses of Southern Rhodesia and South Africa and the defunct African National Congress of Zambia.
75 *R.H.* 18 December 1971.
76 As reported in *R.H.* 8 February 1972.
77 *R.H.* 18 February 1972.
78 *S.M.* 27 February 1972.
79 *R.H.* 10 March 1972.
80 *R.H.* 28 March 1972.
81 *R.F.G.* 30 March 1972.
82 *R.H.* 25 May 1972.
83 *Government Gazette Extraordinary* 6 June 1972.
84 As reported in *R.H.* 7 June 1972.
85 *Hansard:* Vol. 81, No. 9. 16 June 1972: Cols. 668-76.
86 *S.M.* 16 July; *R.H.* 17 July 1972.
87 *R.H.* 22 July 1972.
88 e.g. when Zambia attained independence she had less than 100 African graduates.
89 Bishop Abel T. Muzorewa's speech *Return to Legality* given at the Harry Margolis Hall, Salisbury, 20 July 1972 (cyclo-styled).
90 *R.H.* 21 July 1972.
91 *S.M.* 23 July 1972.
92 Text of statement given to the press by Bishop Abel T. Muzorewa, 3 August 1972 (cyclo-styled).
93 *R.H.* 20 October 1972.
94 *R.H.* 3, 5 October 1972.
95 *R.H.* 23, 29 December 1972.
96 *Moto:* Vol. 15, No. 10. 10 March 1973.
97 *Moto:* Vol. 15, No. 12. 24 March 1973.
98 *Hansard:* Vol. 83, No. 18. 4 April 1973: Cols. 1288-9.
99 *R.F.G.* 6 April 1973.
100 *R.H.* 24, 25 May 1973.
101 *Moto:* Vol. 15, No. 22. 2 June 1973.
102 *Report of the Secretary for Law and Order for the year ending 31 December 1972.* Cmd. R.R. 17-1973: Salisbury: Government Printer.
103 *Hansard:* Vol. 84, No. 8. 28 June 1973: Col. 605.

104 Not to be confused with the Democratic Party formed in May 1972 by Commander Phillips formerly of the Republican Alliance.
105 *R.H 16 April 1970.*
106 *R.H.* 25 July 1970.
107 *Hansard : Senate Debates :* Vol. 3, No. 5. 13 June 1972: Col. 112.
108 *R.H.* 7 July 1972.
109 Not to be confused with the new Rhodesia Party formed in 1972.
110 *R.H.* 30 August 1968.
111 *R.H.* 31 August 1968.
112 *R.H.* 4 September 1968.
113 *R.H.* 12 April 1969.
114 *R.H.* 13 April 1970.
115 *Centrepoint :* Vol. 2, No. 2. December 1971.
116 *R.F.G.* 21 January 1972.
117 *Centrepoint :* Vol. 2, Nos. 7, 8. May, June 1972.
118 *R.H.* 20 May 1972.
119 *R.H.* 16 September 1972.
120 *R.H.* 21, 31 October 1972.
121 *R.H.* 23 February 1973.
122 *R.H.* 26 May 1973.
123 *Moto :* Vol. 15, No. 22. 2 June 1973.
124 *Centre Party Newsletter,* No. 2, June 1973.
125 *R.H.* 31 January 1973.
126 *S.M.* 11 March 1973.
127 *R.H.* 20 June 1973.
128 *Hansard :* Vol. 84, No. 2. 19 June 1973: Cols. 22-35.

III

RELATIONS WITH FOREIGN GOVERNMENTS AND AGENCIES

Since Rhodesia declared her independence and particularly since 1970 when Britain's representative at the United Nations Security Council moved the motion that 'all member states of the U.N. shall refrain from recognizing the illegal regime or from rendering any assistance to it' her relations with the outside world have received much attention both within and outside the country.

In late 1971 and early 1972 it was, of course, relations with Britain that received most attention because of the settlement agreement and the Pearce Commission and Report. The early months of 1973 brought the closure of the border with Zambia and relations with that country, with Britain, South Africa and Portugal became predominant.

THE CLOSURE OF THE BORDER WITH ZAMBIA

At 10 p.m. on the 9th January 1973 the Rhodesian customs and immigration posts at Victoria Falls, Kariba and Chirundu on the Rhodesian-Zambian border were closed to all road and rail traffic. The next day a special issue of the *Government Gazette* gave notice of this action and set forth the new regulations under the Emergency Powers (Closing of Border Posts) Regulations which empowered the government to take this action.[1]

Explaining why this proceeding had been adopted a government spokesman said that Rhodesia had given Zambia numerous warnings (extending over the period April 1965 to November 1972) of the counter-measures that would be taken if Zambia continued to allow African nationalist organizations to mount guerilla operations from her territory against Rhodesia, but all these warnings had been ignored. He added that the border closure was not intended to impede the movements of international travellers and

147

that special instructions had been given to officials at these border posts to exercise discretion with regard to persons travelling in passenger vehicles, Zambian residents travelling south, Rhodesian residents travelling north and school children. Empty goods vehicles would be allowed to return to Rhodesia but loaded ones would not be permitted in either direction. It was announced later that it had been decided to allow the transportation of Zambian copper via Rhodesia.

Following the border closure the *Herald* warned its readers that more militant elements in Rhodesia might consider this action was insufficient and press for more drastic action. It recommended that people should bear in mind that there was no cause for rejoicing because Rhodesia had had to resort to a form of sanctions against Zambia. It pointed out that the border closure meant 'that the confrontation with the African nationalist terrorists has entered a new and more serious stage.'[2]

RELATIONS WITH GREAT BRITAIN

During 1972, following publication of the Pearce Report, the presence of the British 'caretaker' diplomat, Mr. A. Ward (who had been in Rhodesia since the settlement terms had been drawn up) was the subject of conjecture that he might be allowed to remain. Mr. Ward, however, was withdrawn following a request by the Rhodesian Prime Minister that Rhodesia be allowed reciprocal representation in Britain. In November Britain renewed the Order in Council on sanctions for the seventh year in succession.

BRITISH REACTION TO THE BORDER CLOSURE

In early January 1973 following a Note of protest regarding the border closure from the Zambian government to the British Foreign Office (described as 'a reminder that Britain is still regarded as the sovereign power responsible for Rhodesia'), the British Foreign Office declined to comment except to say that it regretted any development which would increase tensions or cause hardship in the area. A few days later the London *Times* reported that Zambia's permanent representative at the United Nations had been instructed to prepare for an emergency debate on the border closure. The *Times* pointed out that this move appeared to observers in Lusaka 'to raise the spectre of renewed Afro-Asian demands for Britain to intervene more effectively to crush the 7-year-old Rhodesian rebellion.'[3]

By mid-January the *Herald*'s London Bureau was writing that 'the prevailing impression in Whitehall now is that the Rhodesian Government burnt its fingers in the border dispute ... the unofficial assessment is that President Kaunda is likely to emerge from the episode considerably stronger, especially politically, than he was before.' The article considered that President Kaunda had been given a 'God-given opportunity to show how justified he had been in introducing one-party rule' (he had previously stressed that the security situation had made a one-party state a necessity). It was also noted that Zambia, which had often expressed a desire to re-orientate her economy away from the White South and had been deterred by the cost of such an exercise would now be able to do so probably with outside assistance.[4]

The *Times* later reported that Zambia's High Commissioner in London had questioned Sir Alec Douglas-Home about British government views on the situation. The newspaper commented that Britain's reaction was to be seen in the light of a previous statement by Sir Alec that the aim of his government's policy towards Southern Africa was to prevent the development of racial confrontation and conflict; it was in this context, therefore, that Britain had been taking a line designed to cool down the situation.[5]
At the end of January the *Daily Telegraph*'s Lusaka correspondent reported President Kaunda's speech at the opening of a conference of Commonwealth Ministers responsible for youth affairs. In his speech the President referred to the recent deaths and injuries caused by land-mine explosions on Zambian territory and said that the situation had been caused by Britain's refusal to take effective measures against the Rhodesian 'rebellion'.[6]

In early February, following a press conference by the Rhodesian Prime Minister during which he had said that prospects for a constitutional settlement with Britain were fair and that Africans were now beginning to support the government, the *Times* commented that Mr. Smith was mistaken if he thought the border closure would have no effect upon settlement prospects. It was also pointed out that the renewed guerilla activities (which had led to the border closure) did not provide a good reason for thinking that Rhodesian Africans had changed their minds on the Pearce verdict.[7]

During this press conference Mr. Smith had also intimated that he would be prepared to open the border if he received a satisfactory assurance that Zambia would dissociate herself from assisting 'terrorists' and had implied that another country was acting as a mediator in the dispute. President Kaunda, however, was reported to have rejected what he called 'British moves to create a dialogue between him and Mr. Smith.' In its editorial the *Telegraph* considered that the Rhodesian Prime Minister had given an impression of 'uncertainty of purpose' and it advised him 'to revoke closure of the border—under whatever face-saving formula he can find—concentrate on catching infiltrators, and then turn himself seriously to the task of re-building friendly relations across the Zambezi.'[8]

When the Rhodesian Ministry of Information announced the re-opening of the border on the 3rd February the *Herald*'s political reporter, Ian Mills, commented that 'the re-opening ... bears the stamp of heavy British pressure and influence on both sides in the dispute.'[9] Shortly afterwards, in a radio and television interview, the Rhodesian Prime Minister gave details of the events leading to the re-opening of the border and spoke of a 'third party' (whom he afterwards referred to as an 'honest broker') who had acted as a mediator between Zambia and Rhodesia and had relayed the assurance, regarding Zambia's attitude towards guerillas, which the Rhodesian government had announced as being requisite before Rhodesia would re-open her side of the border. Mr. Smith also said that in the message he had received it had been stated that President Kaunda would deny that any such assurance had been sent. Both Mr. Smith and the British Foreign Office refused to confirm or deny whether the 'honest broker' had been a representative of the British government.[10]

During March Britain, as well as the United States, abstained from voting on a Security Council resolution declaring that self-determination and independence for the people of Rhodesia was the only solution for the 'grave situation' caused by the Rhodesian-Zambian border closure. An earlier draft resolution, calling upon Britain to convene a constitutional conference to enable the inhabitants of Rhodesia to exercise self-determination and independence, was criticized by Britain's U.N. representative who was quoted as saying 'whether such a resolution is necessary or desirable is, in the view of my delegation, very doubtful.'[11]

The following week it was announced that Britain would make a contribution of £1 million, as an interest-free loan, towards the cost to Zambia of diverting her trade away from Rhodesia. Announcing this loan, Britain's Minister of State for Foreign and Commonwealth Affairs, Lady Tweedsmuir, said that this loan would be in addition to the existing British aid to Zambia which amounted to some £7 million annually.[12]

BRITISH REACTION TO THE DETENTION OF PETER NIESEWAND

In April the Foreign and Commonwealth Office issued a statement on Peter Niesewand, a Rhodesian journalist, sentenced to two years' hard labour on a charge under the Official Secrets Act after a trial held in camera. The statement was followed by a letter from Sir Alec Douglas-Home to Mr. Ian Smith expressing great concern over the secrecy of the trial and pointing out that this secrecy would be bound to lead to adverse conclusions. Sir Alec asked that the detention order on Niesewand be lifted so that he could leave the country.[13] The following day Mr. Harold Wilson, leader of the opposition Labour Party, brought the matter to the attention of the House of Commons by urging that the British Attorney-General be sent to Rhodesia to protest against Mr. Niesewand's trial. In reply, however, the British Prime Minister pointed out that although Britain would naturally wish to make the strongest representations on this matter 'we have to be realistic and recognize that we cannot do this unless there is co-operation from the authorities in Rhodesia.' Mr. Heath, nevertheless, reiterated Sir Alec's plea that Mr. Niesewand be released from detention and allowed to leave the country. The *Telegraph* considered that Mr. Heath was right to insist that it was the secrecy of the trial which was most objectionable and caused the most concern in Britain and commented that what 'the Niesewand case has crystallised is a deep concern, fairly wide-spread—a feeling that Rhodesia herself is being changed, and made to accept as commonplace, processes and methods which are un-Rhodesian.' The newspaper urged that the case be heard on appeal.[14] Mr. Niesewand's case had already been set down for appeal and his sentence was eventually quashed.

The Minister of Law and Order released him from detention and he left the country for Britain.

BRITISH LABOUR PARTY POLICY TOWARDS RHODESIA

Late in May a policy document, drawn up for submission to the Labour Party's annual congress later in the year and approved by the national executive of the Party, was released for publication. It detailed the Labour Party's plans for ending the Anglo-Rhodesian dispute should it be called upon to form the next British government. The document called for an end to constitutional talks which did not include Rhodesian Africans; the scrapping of the 1971 settlement proposals; a reiteration of NIBMAR (No Independence Before Majority African Rule); a referendum on a one-man-one-vote basis before implementation of any settlement; and the extension of the Beira blockade to cover the port of Lourenco Marques. The document went on to say that the Labour Party had finally rejected the 1971 settlement proposals for it believed that 'independence should not be granted to Southern Rhodesia until there is majority rule ... based on universal adult suffrage.'[15] Writing from London later, the *Herald*'s correspondent Denis Sargeant, considered that 'if Labour does win a general election held some time between now and June 1975 ... it is likely to be rather more disposed than the last [Labour government] to treat conference resolutions seriously. This is because the old moderate and Right-wing elements of the Labour Party which used to be a very powerful part of the Parliamentary party and of any Labour cabinet have been seriously weakened.'

VISIT TO BRITAIN OF NIGERIA'S HEAD OF STATE

In mid-June the *Herald* saw, in the State visit of General Gowon of Nigeria to Britain, 'not so much a turning point as a reinforcement of Britain's determination to retain influence in Black Africa in both the trading and the political spheres.' It also warned that the visit had deep significance for Rhodesia because, as the Prime Minister, Mr. Ian Smith had warned on more than one occasion, there remained the possibility of Britain being influenced by Nigeria's attitude in any assessment of Rhodesian Africans' attitudes towards the settlement.[16] In Nigeria an article in a news magazine earlier in the year, in an allusion to the *détente* between Nigeria and Britain, commented that 'the beginning of the thaw was without doubt the publication last May of the report by Lord Pearce's Commission. Any new attempt by the British to produce a settlement in Rhodesia would bring on the icicles again.'[17]

RELATIONS WITH ZAMBIA AND MALAWI

Not only are Zambia and Malawi Rhodesia's closest Black African neighbour states but, as Northern Rhodesia and Nyasaland, they were once in a closer relationship as partners in the Central African Federation. Malawi's attitude towards Rhodesia is determined by President Banda's policy of dialogue with the white south. President Banda has stated more than once that Rhodesia should be left alone to solve her own problems. During 1972, however, President Banda reacted to allegations in the two Salisbury newspapers, that Frelimo guerillas were using Malawian territory in their drive to control the Tete district of Mozambique, by banning them.

Zambia, on the other hand, reacted sharply to Rhodesia's U.D.I., calling repeatedly to Britain to provide an armed force to put down the 'rebellion' and entering into a policy of disengagement with the South. Having close economic links with the white-ruled southern States Zambia felt herself not only to be in a highly vulnerable position strategically but also in the vanguard of the movement for the 'liberation' of southern Africa. When Rhodesia banned Z.A.P.U. and Z.A.N.U., the two African nationalist parties, in 1964, members of these parties who had fled the country subsequently established themselves in Lusaka, where they became active in assisting in the recruitment of 'freedom fighters' for the penetration of Rhodesia. Subsequently Zambia also allowed the setting up of training and transit camps for guerilla activities.

On the 20th April 1972 President Kaunda, addressing the United Nations Decolonization Committee, said that as long as the 'minority regimes' failed to respect the right of the majority and also continued to violate Zambian air space his country would never 'back away from its support for freedom fighters'.

In early June 1972, however, politics gave way to humanitarian feelings when Zambia sent miners from the Copperbelt to help in rescue operations after the Wankie Colliery disaster; the following Sunday prayers were said in churches throughout Zambia for the disaster victims. About 91 of over 400 miners who lost their lives in the Wankie tragedy were Zambians.

ZAMBIA'S REACTION TO THE BORDER CLOSURE

In Lusaka early reaction to the January 1973 border closure was the calling of an emergency Cabinet meeting after which it was stated that Rhodesia's decision to close her side of the border was 'desperate and ludicrous' and designed 'to boost the low morale of the white community in Rhodesia.' Although copper exports had been specifically excluded from the embargo on exports through Rhodesia from Zambia, a Zambian government spokesman announced shortly afterwards that Zambia would not take advantage of this concession but would re-route its copper exports either via the Benguela railway route to Lobito Bay (on the west coast) or by road to the east coast Tanzanian port of Dar-es-Salaam. It was also announced that the Zambian government had frozen payments on all goods in the pipeline from Rhodesia, South Africa and Mozambique.[18]

By mid-January it was reported that Zambia had been holding talks with the governments of Tanzania and Malawi and that help would be forthcoming from these two countries in allowing Zambia to use routes to ports in East Africa and Mozambique. The economic correspondent of the *Financial Gazette*, however, considered that it was impossible to assess how effective such divergent routes would be. He did point out that one effect would be loss of revenue for Rhodesia Railways at a time when the railways already faced a deficit in respect of the year 1972/3, with prospects of a larger deficit during 1973/4.[19]

RHODESIAN-ZAMBIAN BORDER INCIDENTS

At about the same time Zambian authorities disclosed that arrests had been made in connection with three land-mine incidents which had taken place close to the Zambian-Rhodesian border. The Zambian Minister of Home Affairs claimed that a land-mine which had killed a man and injured a woman near Kasengula (a border-post facing both Rhodesia and Botswana) had been placed there by Rhodesian troops. Rhodesia stoutly denied this allegation and pointed out that guerillas were known to be active in the areas where mines had exploded.[20]

At the end of the month a Rhodesian-born African man, arrested earlier in connection with a land-mine explosion near the Chirundu border-post, appeared in the Lusaka Magistrate's Court. In giving evidence the accused man said that he had not taken part in the laying of the mine but that he had watched mines being laid by Rhodesian whites along the road near his house. At the same time it was reported that five men, including an M.P. and a former Mayor of Livingstone, were to appear in the High Court in Lusaka on charges of treason.[21]

A few days earlier Rhodesian and South African security forces were shot at on three separate occasions from the Zambian bank of the Zambezi River between Kariba and Chirundu. A Rhodesian Ministry spokesman said that the shots had been fired by persons identified as Zambian army personnel. No casualties and very little damage had been sustained and at no time had the shots been returned.[22]

Also at the end of January Zambia called upon the Security Council to send a special representative to assess the political and military situation on the border with Rhodesia. The Zambian representative asked the Security Council to condemn what he called the 'wanton aggression, including economic blackmail and military threats, of the illegal regime of Ian Smith against the Republic of Zambia' and also put forward a twelve-point programme of action which he recommended for the Council's consideration. The programme included tightening sanctions against Rhodesia and re-affirmation of the principle of NIBMAR.[23]

A few days later at a press conference attended by representatives of some of the world's better-known newspapers the Rhodesian Prime Minister was asked to explain the circumstances under which the border would be re-opened. In reply Mr. Smith made it clear that the border would be re-opened as soon as he had received a satisfactory message from the Zambian government regarding the curbing of 'terrorist' incursions from Zambia. A day later it was reported that Zambia had closed the posts on its side of the border and that armed troops had already turned back a number of cars (of Zambian residents) awaiting re-entry into Zambia.[24]

On the 2nd February the Security Council resolved to send a four-member team to Zambia to assess the situation and (assisted by six experts) to estimate Zambia's needs for the diversification of her export traffic. A day later it was announced that as a result 'of messages which have been received the Rhodesian government is now satisfied that their objectives in closing the border with Zambia have been achieved. Accordingly the border will be re-opened from 6 a.m. tomorrow.'[25]

In Lusaka President Kaunda, at an airport conference before leaving for talks with the Presidents of Zaïre and Tanzania, said that he did not accept the re-opening of the border as genuine and therefore he would not open the posts on his side of the border. He added 'I want to say to the whole world ... that I have given no undertaking to the Rhodesian Prime Minister, Mr. Ian Smith, and at no time have I been in contact with him, either directly or indirectly.' While in Tanzania President Kaunda was reported as saying that as far as he was concerned the border with Rhodesia would remain closed, for he would not use Rhodesian routes for his exports because, as he said, 'the only thing that would persuade us to go back to the Rhodesian route would be the settlement of the rebellion by the British Government. If they did that and there was a government more reliable than Mr. Smith's government—a majority government ... based on one-man-one-vote—we would consider.'[26]

Only a week after the re-opening of the Rhodesian border-posts a Rhodesian angler was killed by machine-gun fire from the Zambian bank of the Zambezi near Chirundu. The man, 28-year-old Mr. W. F. Austen, had been on a fishing trip with two companions, both of whom were wounded in the incident. A Rhodesian Ministry of Information spokesman said that there had been eye-witness accounts of the shooting which had provided positive proof that a unit of the Zambian army was solely responsible. In Lusaka a Zambian government spokesman denied that one of its army units had been involved.[27] At an inquest held in Karoi later in the year expert evidence, regarding a spent bullet found in the abandoned boat, found that the bullet came from a gun of the same calibre as was used by the Zambian army. It did not have the same characteristics as bullets used by guerillas. The magistrate found that Mr. Austen had probably been killed by shots from Zambian armed forces while the boat in which he was travelling was on the Zambian side of the invisible international river boundary between Rhodesia and Zambia.[28]

In mid-February, following the visit to Zambia of a special U.N. mission, sources close to the mission were quoted as estimating that Zambia would need about U.S. $80 million to enable her to keep her side of the border closed. The leader of the mission, Mr. C. A. Seni (the Indonesian representative at the U.N.) was reported as saying that while visiting London prior to their journey to Zambia permission had been requested for the mission to visit Rhodesia. The British government, however, had said that they could give no assistance over such a visit for there was no British representative in Rhodesia.[29]

It was only a few days after the U.N. mission's visit that it was reported that units of the Zambian army had prevented a doctor from taking a seriously ill Zambian African woman across the border to the nearest hospital in Kariba. The soldiers had also resisted attempts to obtain blood transfusion equipment and supplies of plasma from Rhodesia, although Zambian customs and immigration officials had given permission for this. The woman subsequently died on the journey to Lusaka, more than 160 km. from Lake Kariba.[30]

Towards the end of February the railway-line from Rhodesia to Zambia was closed following the seizure of a Rhodesian railway-man, Mr. J. Smith. The procedure since the original closure of the border had been for trains crossing the Victoria Falls bridge to be shunted half-way across and then collected by the drivers of the opposite country's railway. Mr. Smith had been connecting up his engine and had accidently crossed the white line which demarcated the border-line. He had then been arrested by Zambian troops and was understood to have been taken to prison in Livingstone. A few days later two elderly West German tourists were arrested at gun point by Zambian police after straying over the white line on the Victoria Falls bridge. The engine driver was released by Zambian authorities on the 6th March after the Director of Public Prosecutions in Lusaka had announced that he had not found sufficient evidence to prosecute him. The next day it was announced that the elderly tourists had been released from jail in Lusaka and handed over to the West German Ambassador.[31]

The shooting of the Rhodesian angler, the arrests at the Victoria

Falls bridge and army interference with attempts to obtain aid for a seriously ill woman at Kariba aroused conjecture as to whether the Zambian army was properly under the control of its government. The question became even more pertinent when it was reported from Gaberones in Botswana that Zambian troops had stopped the Zambian-owned ferry from crossing the Zambezi at Kasengula, Botswana's only land-link with Zambia. Shortly afterwards an exchange of fire between South African police and Zambian troops was reported from the same area.[32]

MURDER OF TOURISTS AT THE VICTORIA FALLS

On the 16th May the Rhodesian government sent a protest note to Zambia regarding the shooting and killing of two Canadian girl tourists and the wounding of an American man at the Victoria Falls the previous day. The note stated that there was 'irrefutable proof' that Zambian troops were responsible and that there was no question of guerilla involvement.

Rescue teams were hampered in their efforts to recover the body of one of the girls, and to find the other girl (who was presumed to have been killed) by the delay in receiving an assurance from the Zambian government that troops would not interfere with their movements. It was not until three days after the shooting that the Zambian government issued a statement described in the *Herald* as 'Zambia's first firm comment on an incident which has aroused international interest in the Zambian-Rhodesian confrontation.' The Zambian statement admitted that a Zambian sentry, on guard duty at the power station across the river from where the girls had been shot, was responsible and went on to explain that he had fired on the tourists because 'they appeared to be on their way to attack a vital Zambian power station.' The statement claimed that the tourists had started to swim across the Zambezi and were in Zambian waters at the time the shooting occurred. It concluded by declaring that 'the responsibility for the death of these innocent Canadian nationals and the wounding of the American rests squarely upon the rebel regime in Salisbury.'[33]

The same day the London *Daily Telegraph* argued that the 'Zambian Government's tardy explanation is weak and does not even fit the facts. It also leaves it clear that the Zambian troops either are given far too bloodthirsty orders or themselves act irresponsibly.'[34] The previous day the *Times* also queried whether the troops had opened fire on their own authority or sought orders, and received them, from Lusaka. It considered that if the Zambian troops had acted without orders then President Kaunda 'needs to get worried over the discipline in his army' and if permission had been given from Lusaka then President Kaunda 'needs to know who in Lusaka is making his foreign policy for him.'[35] The Rhodesian *Sunday Mail* found Zambia's attempted 'explanation' totally unacceptable as it 'blandly contradicts the evidence of eye-witnesses.' The *Mail* considered that the murders were 'not the first indication that the Zambian army has a reckless will of its own.'[36] Following a report of further firing from the Zambian bank of the Zambezi at roughly the same spot, the *Herald* commented that this could indicate either that the Zambian troops were out of control or that their 'actions are a continuation of deliberate Zambian policy.' It concluded that the latter hypothesis was perhaps the most likely for President Kaunda, having insisted on keeping the border closed, needed to show the U.N. and other bodies that 'his road and rail links with Rhodesia, although open to him, cannot safely be used.'[37]

A week after the shootings the U.N. Secretary-General visited the Victoria Falls. Commenting upon this visit a Rhodesian government spokesman declared 'One would have thought that even the Secretary-General of the United Nations would indicate some sort of revulsion at the wanton killings at the Victoria Falls. Instead Dr. Waldheim has misdirected his thoughts and expressed sympathy for Zambia.' The *Herald* recommended Dr. Waldheim to read the factual report of the American couple who had survived the tragedy.[38] Towards the end of May, at the commissioning of three powerful Chinese-supplied radio transmitters, President Kaunda referred to the Victoria Falls murders and accused Rhodesia of having 'shepherded' the two Canadian girls to their deaths for propaganda purposes just before Dr. Waldheim's visit to Zambia.[39]

During June Mr. Oscar Drijber, the father of one of the murdered Canadian girls, crossed over the border into Zambia for a personal interview with President Kaunda. After two days spent in the Zambian capital he returned to Rhodesia and said that he completely rejected the Zambian version of the killings. He also indicated that in his opinion 'President Kaunda did not know the truth of the Victoria Falls incident.'[40]

RELATIONS WITH SOUTH AFRICA

On the day after Rhodesia declared her independence the late Dr. Verwoerd, then the Prime Minister of the Republic of South Africa, said that the problems that had arisen between Rhodesia and Britain should remain a dispute between those governments only and that South Africa would refrain from intervention or comment. He also said that South Africa would not participate in boycotts or sanctions. Shortly afterwards, Mr. B. J. Vorster, succeeded Dr. Verwoerd and he confirmed that his attitude was the same as that of his predecessor.

Friendly contact has been maintained between the two countries and after Rhodesia became a Republic in 1970 South Africa became, with Portugal, the only country in the world to retain representation in Rhodesia. South Africa was one of the first countries to announce its pleasure at the news of the agreement between Rhodesia and Britain in November 1971 and to congratulate both countries.

At the end of February 1972 the Rhodesian Prime Minister, Mr. Ian Smith, visited Cape Town to fulfil an engagement made in 1971 previous to the final round of negotiations with the British representatives. Commenting upon Mr. Smith's speech, while opening the Goodwood Show in Cape Town, the *Herald* advised its readers to make careful study of his words 'for they show his thinking more clearly than many of his speeches'. The essence of Mr. Smith's speech was that the Prime Ministers of the two countries had been discussing economic integration in a free trade area, with the possibility in time of a common market and political links.[41]

In October South Africa's Minister of Defence, Mr. P. W. Botha, and the Commandant General of the South African Defence Force arrived in Salisbury for a four-day visit. The *Herald* commented that the visit was timely following as it did on Mr. Smith's trip to Portugal for what was presumed to be talks on the escalation of guerilla activities in the Tete district of Mozambique and its effect on Rhodesia.[42]

SOUTH AFRICAN REACTION
TO THE BORDER CLOSURE

Following the closure of the Rhodesian-Zambian border in early January 1973 editorial comment in the South African press was described in Rhodesia as 'widely sympathetic over what was seen as an inevitable answer to continued terrorist activity.' The South African Minister of Economic Affairs was reported as saying that Zambia was responsible for the closure and, although South African exports to Zambia would be affected, he believed that Zambia would be the hardest hit.[43]

Early in the following week, John D'Oliveira, writing in the *Herald* from South Africa, discussed the implications of what he considered to be the major conflicting elements in a situation which had placed the South African government on the horns of a dilemma. On the one hand South Africa as a 'bitter opponent of terrorism' must support 'any action aimed at making Zambia realize that harbouring terrorists is not in her own best interests.' On the other hand 'the closure of the border injects fresh heat into a situation which South Africa has been trying to cool since Rhodesia's Declaration of Independence—and possibly even before this time.' Mr. D'Oliveira agreed with many South African newspapers that the situation called for an official statement from the government regarding South Africa's position.[44]

The awaited statement from South Africa's Prime Minister was issued on the 19th January. Mr. Vorster prefaced his statement by saying 'from experience I know that Rhodesia did not seek this confrontation. Zambia, on the other hand, had done nothing to prevent it or to promote good neighbourly relations and must throughout have realised that its actions and the granting of passage to, and the harbouring of, terrorists would sooner or later lead to trouble.' Mr. Vorster went on to say that South Africa had not been a party to the decision and although 'one can expect divergent speculation as to the wisdom or otherwise of this step' South Africa would treat the matter in accordance with four basic principles 'which have been repeatedly stated by us'. Mr. Vorster concluded his statement by recommending that, in the interests of South Africa, developments should be awaited calmly and nothing should be done to make matters worse.[45]

At the end of the month the Rhodesian Prime Minister, answering a series of questions on the border closure and its effect on relations with South Africa and Portugal, said that he considered that this decision not to consult those two countries prior to the closure was a correct one for it 'would have been a diplomatic blunder ... and would have caused acute embarrassment to our neighbours.' In South Africa, however, press criticism of Rhodesia's action was mounting. *Rapport*, with the largest circulation of any Afrikaans newspaper in South Africa and reputedly having a close link with South African government circles, was reported as pointing out that, although South Africa had always understood Rhodesia's problems and considered there was 'brotherly attunement ... this cannot be a blank cheque for all Rhodesia's decisions which affect us as well. Rhodesia's interests are not necessarily ours.' [46] The *Herald* inferred from this statement 'that the South African government considers there should at least have been diplomatic exchanges before the border was closed.' It drew the attention of its readers to the fact that 'Apart from trade and its wider African policies, South Africa has policemen on the Zambezi helping our troops' and considered that 'in the circumstances it is difficult to understand Mr. Smith's claim that consultation would have been a diplomatic blunder and an embarrassment'. [47] The *Financial Gazette*, however, pointed out that 'Southern African discussion of Rhodesia's action ... is losing sight of the main fact: that it was a defensive action taken in the face of considerable provocation' and commented that 'the three countries are in constant contact but are certainly not privy to one another's policy decisions. Prior consultation in a policy decision would not only divide responsibility but would oppose a basic belief: that no country should interfere with another nation's internal affairs.' [48]

In his weekly article from South Africa, John D'Oliveira reported later speeches by the South African Prime Minister and by the Leader of the Opposition, Sir de Villiers Graaff. He observed that 'South Africa's Southern African ... objectives extend way beyond the immediate problem of helping to sustain the present Rhodesian set-up' and said that against this background the two speeches together summed up South Africa's current attitude towards Rhodesia. Both Mr. Vorster and Sir de Villiers had indicated that South Africa believed there should have been prior consultation over the border closure, not only because South Africa's own interests were involved, but also because 'it might have been possible for South Africa to use her own African and other international contacts to de-fuse the terrorist situation sufficiently to have obviated the border closing.'[49]

VISITS OF SOUTH AFRICAN GOVERNMENT MINISTERS

During April the *Herald* wrote of the visit of the South African Minister of Defence, Mr. P. W. Botha, and the Commandant-General of the South African Forces, Admiral Biermann, to Rhodesia during October 1972 and stated that, although there had been no official comment at the time, there had been wide speculation that the talks they had had with Rhodesian government officials had concerned the extent of co-operation between the defence forces of Rhodesia, South Africa and Portugal. Interest in the topic was re-opened after a speech by Mr. Botha in the South African parliament a few days earlier in which he said that 'the state of stability and order in neighbouring countries had a direct bearing on South Africa's security. Consequently should requests for assistance be made by those countries, South Africa would consider them'. The *Herald* considered that this was a comfortable thought for Rhodesia as 'Mr. Botha's statement opens the door to much wider participation by South African forces in defence measures to preserve stability and maintain order in Rhodesia.'[50]

A few days later it was announced that South Africa's Deputy Prime Minister and Minister of Transport, Mr. Ben Schoeman, was making an unannounced visit to Rhodesia during which he would talk with several Rhodesian Ministers. Describing Mr. Schoeman as one of South Africa's most senior and shrewdest politicians, the *Financial Gazette* considered that joint problems such as the guerilla situation and the settlement of the Anglo-Rhodesian constitutional dispute were likely to be the main reasons for the visit.[51] Both the Rhodesian and South African authorities stressed that Mr. Schoeman's visit was a purely private one. In May the Rhodesian Prime Minister flew to Pietermaritzburg to open the Royal Agricultural Show there. A few weeks later he flew to Cape Town where he held talks with Mr. Vorster. On his return Mr. Smith declined to give details of any talks he had held in South Africa.

RELATIONS WITH PORTUGAL

Like South Africa, Portugal is represented in Rhodesia, both being technically accredited to Her Majesty's Government in London. Also like South Africa, Portugal has refrained from complying with the United Nations' resolutions on mandatory sanctions.

The cement binding the friendship between Rhodesia and Portugal is, of course, the territorial proximity of Portugal's overseas Province of Mozambique in which is situated Rhodesia's chief outlet to the sea, the port of Beira. Mutual interest in containing the guerilla threat to Mozambique makes it reasonable to suppose that the friendship will continue.

At the end of August 1972 the Defence Minister, Mr. J. H. Howman, in an interview with the *Financial Gazette,* said that Rhodesia would be ready to send military assistance to Mozambique if requested.[52] In October the Rhodesian Prime Minister paid a visit to Portugal where he had talks with Portugal's Prime Minister, Dr. Caetano. The talks were believed to have centred around the security position in Tete and the effect this was having on Rhodesia.

According to reports (later denied in Lisbon) Rhodesia's unofficial representative to Portugal was called to the Portuguese Foreign Ministry in early January 1973 shortly after Rhodesia's closing of the posts on the border with Zambia, to be told of Portugal's 'deep concern' over this action. Lisbon was reportedly concerned that the danger posed to the Zambian economy would increase the possibility of a deeper commitment by President Kaunda to the Chinese-financed Tan-Zam railway project and also that the way might be opened to some kind of a Communist bridge-head in the form of air-borne assistance to Zambia. On economic grounds there were also fears for the port of Beira, which would have its annual handling of tonnage reduced by about 50 *per cent*. It was pointed out also that Portugal, despite 'considerable provocation' had never closed the outlets of Beira in Mozambique and Lobito Bay in Angola, which would have caused considerable havoc to the Zambian economy. According to the *Daily Telegraph*'s reporter, Bruce Loudin, the Portuguese had long been 'pre-occupied in extending the reliance of Zambia and other countries of Central Africa on the White-dominated south ... [believing] it is better to talk than present ... short-sighted ultimations.'[53]

In early February the *Daily Telegraph* noted that Sir Alec Douglas-Home would, during a stop-over at Lisbon en route to Nigeria, hold 'short but important discussions' with the Portuguese Foreign Minister, Dr. Rui Patricio. The subject of discussion was reportedly the growing tensions in southern Africa resulting mainly from the border closure for, according to the newspaper's correspondent in Lisbon, 'Portugal is pre-occupied with what it sees as Rhodesia's bungling of affairs with Zambia. There are fears that without some delicate diplomacy there will be dangerous consequences for Portugal.'[54]

RELATIONS WITH THE
UNITED STATES OF AMERICA

In mid-March 1970 the United States broke her last official ties with Rhodesia by closing her consulate-general in Salisbury. It was reported that the U.S. had taken this step in response to 'extraordinary' pressure from Britain for the U.S. had not been over-enthusiastic over the move, primarily because of Rhodesia's importance to the U.S. as a source of chrome.

The U.S.A. had previously stopped importing Rhodesian chrome ore in response to the United Nations' imposition of mandatory sanctions against Rhodesia. Towards the end of 1971, however, with the adoption of the 'Byrd' amendment (which rescinded the American President's authority to ban the import of strategic materials because of American treaty obligations to the United Nations) the U.S. Congress completed its action to lift the ban.

In early 1972, therefore, when the 'Byrd' amendment was implemented some sections of Rhodesian society were agreeably surprised to find that the general licence permitting mineral imports from Rhodesia covered a range of other minerals in addition to chrome ore and ferro-chrome.[55]

During November Rhodesia welcomed the visit of Mr. Clark McGregor, President Nixon's campaign director, for, despite brief and fallacious speculation about possible U.S. recognition of Rhodesia's independence, it was felt that the visit of an influential American, described as a 'Republican moderate', reflected the slowly changing American public attitude towards Rhodesia.

At the end of January 1973 the British Prime Minister paid a two-day visit to President Nixon. It was thought likely that one of the minor topics which would come up for discussion would be the situation in Southern Africa, particularly the danger of an escalation of tension caused by the Rhodesian-Zambian border closure, for both governments were reputedly concerned to keep the situation from becoming worse.

During February the *Herald* Bureau correspondent in Washington discussed the views of diplomats and government officials in the American capital and wrote that doubts that the Rhodesian government was in firm control of the country were being expressed. The disclosure of the collaboration between indigenous tribesmen and infiltrators into the country; the border closure—which was seen as bearing 'the imprint of panic irrationality and ignorance of international factors'; and the question of the extent to which South Africa would be ready to compromise its own interests for the sake of Rhodesia forming the basis of these doubts.[56]

In March the United States abstained, together with Britain, from voting in a second resolution at the United Nations which called for a constitutional conference in Rhodesia and declared that self-determination and independence for the people of Rhodesia was the only solution for the 'grave situation' caused by the border closure.[57]

In May the Rhodesian representative at the Rhodesian Information Office in Washington was called to testify before the U.S. Congress sub-committee on Africa which, under the chairmanship of Mr. Charles Diggs, was holding hearings on the presence and activities of the Rhodesian Information Office.[58] Also in May, following the shooting of Canadian and American tourists at Victoria Falls, it was reported from Washington that the United States was dissatisfied with the official Zambian explanation of the shooting. It was reported that the United States' Ambassador in Lusaka would seek a more satisfactory explanation from the Zambian government.[59]

RELATIONS WITH THE UNITED NATIONS

In February 1972 the Security Council adopted a resolution criticizing the United States for permitting the lifting of the ban on the importation of chrome ore from Rhodesia. It set up a special committee to determine methods of ensuring compliance with the 1968 resolution on mandatory sanctions.

Later in the year Dr. Waldheim addressed the opening session of the ninth Organization for African Unity summit conference in Rabat. He warned 'the white-ruled countries [that] if no progress was made to end racist policies' the only issue would be violence, isolation and ostracism.

In September Dr. Waldheim's categorical statement that Uganda's action in expelling Asians was a domestic affair, and therefore the United Nations was debarred from taking any action, was severely criticized in a number of letters to the editors of various Rhodesian newspapers. The United Nations was seen as an organisation which applied double standards, for Dr. Waldheim had recently been calling for an intensification of the sanctions campaign against Rhodesia in what was seen as domestic issue between Rhodesia and Britain.

Early in December the United Nations' General Assembly voted on three resolutions affecting the 'white-ruled' Southern African states: Britain was called upon to 'take forthwith all effective measures to bring down the rebellious minority regime' in Rhodesia. (A measure adopted by 93 votes to eight, with 23 abstentions); an intensification of sanctions and the extension of these measures to South Africa and Portugal was called for; while the third resolution, reaffirming the Assembly's view that there should be no recognition of Rhodesia's independence before majority rule was enforced, called for a national constitutional conference to be held in Rhodesia.

Following a report on the border closure, by Zambia's chief delegate to the U.N., to a 57-member group of the 'non-aligned nations', it was announced towards the end of January 1973 that Zambia planned to bring the issue before the Security Council. The Zambian delegate later asked the Security Council to condemn the 'wanton aggression, including economic blackmail and military threats, of the illegal regime of Ian Smith against the Republic of Zambia'. He also put forward a 12-point programme of action which he considered the Council ought to take to meet the crisis caused by Rhodesia.[60]

In response to a request from African member-states, the Security Council eventually appointed a special four-man commission to study Zambia's need for international aid. The commission, accompanied by 23 United Nations advisers, arrived in Zambia during the second week in February. Its report to the Security

Council, presented in early March, was accompanied by a list of the Zambian government's requirements to keep its foreign trade flowing. According to this report, the Zambian view was that if the international community aided Zambia effectively it would be very difficult for 'Ian Smith and the rebels to continue for very long.' The commission's report estimated that U.S. $124 million would be needed to enable Zambia to set up new trade links through Malawi and East Africa.[61] The South African news magazine, *To The Point,* commented that the commission had some very 'odd' features. Firstly it was unlikely, since Rhodesia was totally ignored, that it would be able to produce objective figures; secondly, since the reasons for the border closure were essentially political it seemed an exaggeration for the Security Council to treat the situation as though it were an natural disaster—'to be alleviated by voluntary aid to the tune of 124 million dollars.' The magazine felt that the commission was 'spectacularly successful in solving nothing at all.'[62]

Later in March the Security Council approved a resolution calling for immediate technical, financial and material aid for Zambia. A second resolution, calling on Britain to convene a constitutional conference in Rhodesia, was passed by thirteen votes (with two abstentions—Britain and the United States).

In May it was announced that the U.N. Secretary-General would visit Zambia to confer with President Kaunda. The *Herald* was of the opinion that it was right and proper for Dr. Waldheim to discuss the border tension with the Zambian government, for 'the fact that he will get a one-sided account of the situation; that he will get a mendacious report of the recent shootings; and that he will be generally fed unreliable information does not mean he should not listen.' However the newspaper thought that in order to get the full picture 'he should cross the Zambezi and see for himself ... [for] without coming here he will ... inevitably give the U.N. an inaccurate picture.' It also directed attention to the fact that 'no matter what the legal status of our Government in U.N. eyes, Rhodesia's near 6 million people are as entitled as any to "human rights". We are being menaced, have been attacked,' and it asked what Dr. Waldheim proposed to do about it.[63]

While in Zambia Dr. Waldheim was taken on a tour of the border area, in particular to the scenes of the land-mine blasts near Kasengula and of the shootings at Victoria Falls. A Rhodesian government spokesman commented later 'One would have thought that even the Secretary-General of the United Nations would indicate some sort of revulsion at the wanton killings at the Victoria Falls. Instead Dr. Waldheim has misdirected his thoughts and expressed sympathy for Zambia. He is seeing only half the picture, and the wrong half at that.' The *Mail* in its turn commented 'As a former Wehrmacht officer, his [Dr. Waldheim's] inspection of the scene should have been enough to alert him to the physical absurdity of Zambia's fantastic claim [that the murdered girls had been swimming in Zambian waters]. But he swallows the lies, or appears to.'[64]

RELATIONS WITH AUSTRALIA

As early as 1963 the older 'white' Commonwealth countries had expressed their support for Britain over the question of Rhodesia's independence. The Rhodesian view, however, was that—in the words of Rhodesia's Prime Minister at the time, Mr. Winston Field—'The attitude of Commonwealth Governments is likely to be conditioned by doctrinaire considerations or by considerations of national interest which have little or no bearing on the best interests of Rhodesians of all races now or in the future.'[65]

Early in May 1972 an article in the *Herald* speculated on what might be the Australian government's attitude towards Rhodesia if a Labour government replaced the 24 years of Liberal-Country Party rule. Observers were not left long in doubt. Only an hour after the new Australian Prime Minister, Labour Party leader Mr. Gough Whitlam, was sworn in he announced that instructions had been given to Australia's representative at the United Nations to reverse or alter the voting on two resolutions—one to call for stricter enforcement of existing sanctions (which had been opposed by Australia in committee) and the other to call upon Britain to ensure that there would be no independence for Rhodesia until majority rule was established (Australia had previously abstained from this vote). It was also announced that steps would be taken to close down the Rhodesian Information Centre in Sydney. Shortly afterwards the passport of Australian-born Air Vice Marshal H. Hawkins, Rhodesia's accredited diplomatic representative in South Africa, had been cancelled.

These moves were followed by a ban on wheat exports from Australia to Rhodesia. This led the *Sunday Mail* to comment 'there is no denying that Australia's new attitude will tend to make things more awkward for Rhodesia. If not openly friendly, Australia has long followed a line that was almost neutral. Now she is plainly hostile.'[66]

During November 1972 a letter, from Mr. Whitlam to the Premier of New South Wales, Sir Robert Askin, asked for the de-registration of the name Rhodesian Information Centre. The letter was published in the press, as an order to close the Centre, before it reached Sir Robert himself. The affair rapidly became the centre of controversy between the Federal government in Canberra and the State government in New South Wales and a decision on the subject was finally referred to the Supreme Court of New South Wales. The Rhodesian Information Centre was started in 1966 as a public relations office. Controversy about its activities started early in 1972 when the Centre was broken into and several correspondence files stolen, extracts from which were subsequently published.[67]

On the 18th April 1973 it was reported from Sydney that the Australian post office had cut off telephone, telecommunications and mail services from the Centre. The Australian Postmaster-General, who had ordered the withdrawal of these services, was quoted as saying that the decision had been taken following an official investigation of the Centre. The following day an interim injunction by the Australian High Court was granted restraining the government from stopping mail and telephone services to the Centre.[68]

It was also in mid-April that an announcement was made that a party of Australian farmers would be visiting Rhodesian farms as part of a comprehensive African and South American tour. The following month, however, a cable, sent by the organizers of the tour, to Salisbury (via South Africa) was received announcing that the Australian government had forbidden all airlines operating in Australia to issue tickets to Rhodesia. The periodical reporting this informed its readers that behind this prohibition there had been an implied threat from Australian trade unions that their members would refuse to service any airline which did not comply with the government's fiat.[69]

SANCTIONS

The former British Prime Minister, Mr. Harold Wilson, left Rhodesians and their government in no doubt as to the consequences of a unilateral declaration of independence when he said, during his visit to Salisbury in October 1965, 'we have stated the economic, political and constitutional measures Britain would inescapably have to take ... I would not wish anyone to be in doubt about our ability and our will to put through these measures, or to be in any doubt about the decisive consequences that would result from them.' Despite these threats, however, the government issued the proclamation of Rhodesian independence on the 11th November 1965.

BRITISH ACTION

On the day following the proclamation the British government expelled Rhodesia from the sterling area; stopped all aid; banned the export of British capital to Rhodesia and imposed special exchange control restrictions; blocked Rhodesian reserves in London and froze Rhodesian accounts in Britain; revoked all licences for the sale of arms, ammunition and aircraft to Rhodesia; withdrew Commonwealth preference on tobacco and sugar; stopped export credit guarantees; and declared that all Rhodesian passports were to be considered illegal. Closely following this action, on 15th November Britain banned all imports of Rhodesian sugar and tobacco and tabled a motion in the United Nations' Security Council calling upon all countries 'to refrain from any action which would give aid and comfort to the Smith regime.' Later in the same month Britain introduced measures to restrict cash gifts to Rhodesian residents and imposed regulations on currency for British residents travelling to Rhodesia.

Early in December the British government gave directions for controlling financial transactions with Rhodesia. Dividends, interest and pensions were to be paid into blocked accounts in Britain; funds from firms in Britain were prohibited from being sent to their subsidiaries in Rhodesia; the Board of the Reserve Bank of Rhodesia was replaced by a British Board; and British banks were forbidden to finance trade between Rhodesia and a third country and to provide banking facilities for Rhodesian residents or firms.

Shortly afterwards imports of various kinds, (representing about 95 *per cent* of British imports from Rhodesia) were banned. In mid-December sanctions on oil were introduced.

Early 1966 saw a continuation of this policy with the announcement that a British subject importing or exporting certain named commodities from or to Rhodesia would be liable to prosecution. The ban on oil and arms was extended to cover all imports from Rhodesia and there was a progressive extension of a ban on the export of various commodities from Rhodesia.

The British House of Commons in November 1972 debated the motion that the British Order-in-Council on sanctions should be renewed for the forthcoming year. Faced with protest, both from dissidents in the Conservative Party and from the Left, the Foreign Secretary, Sir Alec Douglas-Home, said that it was not Britain's intention to bring Rhodesian people to their knees, for that would be an ignoble and inhuman aim, but while there was a chance of a negotiated settlement it would not be wise to concede the defeat of the sanctions policy. He outlined certain concessions in financial, non-financial and administrative matters, which, as the *Herald*'s reporter in London commented, in economic terms were not of great value but were designed to have a high humanitarian impact. The concessions included a small increase in the value of cash gifts which could be sent from Britain to Rhodesia; travel allowances for elderly British residents to visit relatives in Rhodesia; increases in the amounts Rhodesian residents could draw from blocked funds; changes in the amounts British charities could send to Rhodesia and the transfer of life assurance funds from Britain; the issue of British passports to any Rhodesian resident genuinely seeking specialist medical treatment in Britain and the introduction of an order making valid in British law certain Rhodesian marriages, divorces and adoptions regarded by the British courts heretofore as invalid. According to the *Herald*, Rhodesian reaction to the concessions differed sharply, with the government describing them as valueless and designed to placate dissident back-benchers of the Tory Party; the Centre Party welcoming them as a gesture which would restore the faith of moderate Rhodesians in Britain's traditional sense of fair play; and a spokesman for the A.N.C. who said that the changes in the sanctions regulations amounted to *de facto* recognition of Rhodesia.[70]

In December the *Financial Gazette* considered as 'concrete evidence of the futility of economic sanctions' the fact that the latest batch of economic indicators suggested that the growth rate of the Gross Domestic Product during 1972 would once more be in double figures. Thus in three of the last four years the G.D.P. would have expanded by more than ten *per cent*. [71]

A little later in the month the press forecast an important new move in the question of payment of overdue interest for holders of Southern Rhodesia 6 *per cent* stock following the decision of the Queen's Bench to allow a Petition of Rights to be presented to the Queen. Although the Rhodesian assets were blocked, holders of Rhodesian government stocks living outside the United Kingdom have been paid by the Rhodesian government. With regard to holders living in the United Kingdom, however, the Rhodesian government has taken the attitude that in taking responsibility for Rhodesian affairs and imposing sanctions Britain had also taken upon itself responsibility for these payments. [72]

In February 1973 the *Herald* Bureau in London reported that prospects for payment of overdue interest and capital to more than 1 000 British holders of frozen Southern Rhodesian 6 *per cent* stock, had been brought a stage nearer when the Queen had signed a Petition of Rights presented by a retired member of the old Northern Rhodesian Legislative Assembly, Mr. Harry Franklin. The next step would be to seek a court judgement to be served upon the bank holding the frozen assets. [73]

In mid-April Mr. Franklin was given judgement in the High Court in London on his claim for payment of interest on his bonds. Although the amount which he was claiming was a relatively small one the importance of the judgement lay in the fact that, using this as a test case, many other holders of the stock could proceed with claims for overdue interest, estimated to total about £63 million. In a written answer to a question in the House of Commons, Lord Balniel, Minister of State at the Foreign Office, explained how the problem raised by the existence of large holdings of Rhodesian stock in the United Kingdom would be resolved. This action would, in effect, be carried out by declaring the Rhodesian government bankrupt and ordering the sharing-out of its assets in Britain among stock holders. It was made clear that the only funds which would be available for this purpose would be the holdings of the Reserve Bank of Rhodesia in the United Kingdom. [74]

The Bank of England, which is the registrar of certain Southern Rhodesian stocks, later stated that it would not be possible to part with more than a minimal sum. A spokesman for the bank explained that money of two kinds was held by the bank: interest which, but for the Unilateral Declaration of Independence, would have been paid to the Rhodesian government and a balance of less than £2 000 to various private stockholders; and 'certain assets' for the Reserve Bank of Rhodesia which would not be available for the claims of stockholders. [75] Mr. Franklin was eventually paid a sum of £41 (to meet his claim of £218) overdue interest by the Bank of England which explained that this sum had exhausted 'the moneys of the Government of Southern Rhodesia which the bank have in their possession.' [76]

Following an order for the chief accountant of the bank to appear in the High Court for cross-examination on the assets of the Rhodesian government held by the bank, a writ was issued asking for a declaration that on the true construction of the Colonial Stock Act (upon which Mr. Franklin had based his case) the Reserve Bank of Rhodesia in the United Kingdom could not be regarded as an agent of the government of Southern Rhodesia and did not have in its possession any moneys belonging to that government. At a hearing on the 22nd May the High Court reserved judgement on the case. At a later hearing the Appeal Court ruled, however, that the Bank of England could not be compelled to appear before the Court to be examined on the whereabouts and extent of Rhodesian assets in England and Wales. [77]

In mid-April the *Daily Telegraph*'s reporter Ian Colvin reported that the latest estimates reaching London regarding the amount of exports shipped from Rhodesia (worth £137 million) were providing the Conservative back-bencher pressure group in the House of Commons with the rationale for demanding that Britain 'lift or phase out sanctions in the absence of any sign that Rhodesia's major trading partners are prepared to enforce sanctions.' Major sanctions breakers were alleged to be the United States, West Germany, Japan, France and Holland and it was noted that international dealers had cleared nearly all of Rhodesia's stockpile of tobacco leading to a prediction of increased tobacco planting on Rhodesia's farms during the next season. Rhodesia had also been particularly successful in disposing of chrome ore and it was confidently forecast that Rhodesian exports would soon be boosted by the export of beef, possibly in the newly acquired Boeing 720 airliners.

In its editorial of the same day the *Telegraph* commented that the 'arrival of the Boeings in Salisbury dramatises the continuing farce of sanctions, while the American chrome decision underlines its uselessness ... Britain, almost alone among trading nations, still painstakingly continues to apply sanctions ... France, Italy, West Germany and most of Britain's other allies trade merrily with both Black and White Africa.' The newspaper recommended that it was time for Britain 'to cast off the past and do likewise.'[78]

In mid-year it was reported in Rhodesia that from the beginning of the year the British newspaper the *Daily Mirror* had been conducting an investigation into the origins of European goods reaching Rhodesia despite international sanctions. The newspaper had published names of Dutch and French shipping lines which, it alleged, consigned the goods to Mozambique ports without the knowledge of the consignees. It also gave the names of six British companies said to have sold goods to Rhodesia. The *Daily Mirror* demanded government action to stop what it called 'an international smuggling network.'[79]

It was also in mid-year that the House of Commons was given the latest estimate of the direct cost (up to March 1973) of sanctions against Rhodesia. Lord Balniel said that since November 1965 the cost to the British taxpayer had been £49 million and added that in the last year of normal trading with Rhodesia (i.e. 1965) British exports to Rhodesia had been valued at nearly £31.5 million. [80]

UNITED NATIONS ACTION

Following the Security Council resolution in November 1965, (which received general support from all countries except South Africa and Portugal) the U.S.A. announced support for Britain's imposition of oil sanctions and a ban on chrome ore. In April 1966 the United Nations announced that 66 countries had notified to it their actions in not recognising the 'regime'; in banning the export of arms to Rhodesia; and in endorsing the arms embargo. In late 1966 the Security Council, at Britain's request, ordered mandatory sanctions against Rhodesia and called upon all U.N. members to join in preventing shipment of all named commodities from and to Rhodesia. Non-members of the U.N. were urged to join in carrying out the provisions. (Switzerland had already blocked the Rhodesian Reserve Bank's account in the Swiss National Bank). In May 1968, again at Britain's request, the Security Council passed further mandatory sanctions, calling on all members to ban trade, financial dealings and air services with Rhodesia, together with non-mandatory clauses calling upon members not to recognise Rhodesian passports and to withdraw consular and trade representation in Rhodesia. [81]

In a report written in 1972 for the Africa Bureau in London, the authors say that: 'At their present level of functioning ... sanctions may be said to have achieved a stalemate: the world at large can express its disapproval of the illegal regime in Rhodesia without either exerting itself too much or taking action that will seriously cost it anything; and the Smith regime can continue in uneasy control of Rhodesia, sitting on a racial powder keg, and having to spend more and more of its energies and resources in devising new ways to evade sanctions and, in consequence of them, standing still economically.' [82]

In early February 1973 the Security Council's sanctions committee (set up in 1968 to supervise the application of sanctions against Rhodesia) was reported to be studying a document on world trade which contained detailed statistics showing that some 160 million Rhodesian dollars' worth of Rhodesian goods had reached world markets during 1971. The study added that if the implication drawn from these trade figures was accepted 'it would mean that, during 1969-71, exporters in South Africa and Mozambique were handling merchandise from Rhodesia at a level of more than Rhodesian $125 million annually.' [83]

In April the sanctions committee made various recommendations for the introduction of stringent new procedures to block the import of embargoed items from Rhodesia through South Africa and the Portuguese African territories. Following a meeting of the Security Council to debate the report and recommendations of the sanctions committee, it was reported from New York that the Security Council had approved a resolution (with Britain, France and the U.S. abstaining) endorsing the sanctions committee's recommendations, designed to enforce the embargo against Rhodesia more strictly: to impose a limitation (based on the 1965 trade figures) of imports of various commodities from South

Africa, Mozambique and Angola; to deny landing rights to carriers of countries granting landing rights to Rhodesian aircraft; and to extend the naval blockade of Beira to Lourenco Marques.[84]

UNITED STATES ACTION

In early 1972 the U.S. government lifted the ban on strategic mineral imports from Rhodesia. Rhodesian mining officials were reportedly agreeably surprised by the wide effect of the general licence published by the U.S. Treasury for they had expected that only the import of chrome ore would be allowed. Despite attempts by various organizations within the U.S. to have the ban re-imposed, however, it was reported in June that the Senate had voted to continue with the imports.[85] During April 1973 a bid was made, by several negro members of Congress, to halt the mineral imports from Rhodesia. The Supreme Court, however, ruled on the 16th April that the United States could continue to import Rhodesian minerals despite the U.N. embargo.[86]

Towards the end of May the U.S. representative at the United Nations joined his British colleague in vetoing a Security Council resolution which asked for countries with legislation allowing imports of minerals from Rhodesia to repeal it immediately and also to limit imports of various mineral and other products from South Africa, Mozambique and Angola (who were suspected of allowing Rhodesian exports to pass through their countries) to the levels prevailing in 1965. The U.S. representative, Mr. John Scali, was reported as saying that American imports of chrome ore and nickel from Rhodesia represented less then 5 *per cent* of the projected Rhodesian export earnings for 1972.[87]

RHODESIAN REACTION

In the Rhodesian House of Assembly during 1972 the Minister of Law and Order, Mr. D. W. Lardner-Burke, moving for an extension of the period of the State of Emergency, argued that the emergency regulations were not only for national security but also to 'counter financial restrictions and economic sanctions imposed on Rhodesia.' Mr. Lardner-Burke reminded the House that although 'it may seem to some people unnecessary to maintain a high standard of secrecy in our economic and business dealings when everything seems to be going so well [but] one of the reasons we are succeeding in the sanctions war is by confounding our enemies ... [we] must always be on the watch for leaks in our sanctions breaking security.' He continued by explaining that 'there has been a gradual erosion of sanctions because, in the first place, they are being applied by many countries with little enthusiasm and, secondly our counter measures, supported by the emergency regulations, have been very successful.' Concluding his statement, the Minister warned that 'we cannot afford to reduce our efforts or to dismantle our precautions until it is clear that sanctions are a dead letter and are completely eroded.' [88]

In mid-March 1973 a British South Africa Police Fraud Squad detective gave warning of a by-product of the sanctions policy. He warned, in a speech given to the Salisbury East Rotary Club, that international confidence tricksters were coming into Rhodesia on lightning visits and attempting to swindle Rhodesian businessmen on 'sanction-busting deals'. In its editorial on the following day, the *Herald* commented that 'unfortunately Rhodesia today presents an environment which has many attractions for the confidence trickster' and agreed with the detective that businessmen should be very careful adding that they should 'also be wary of their own greed' for, as the *Herald* stated, 'it is an unfortunate fact that beating sanctions has forced some businessmen to practices which they would in normal circumstances regard as crooked.' The newspaper concluded by saying that the only real hope of improving matters lay in a political settlement which would enable extradition rights to be negotiated with other countries. [89]

In the middle of April the Minister of Transport, Mr. R. T. R. Hawkins, welcomed the arrival a few days previously of three Boeing 720 passenger jets as being 'undoubtedly the biggest hole that has been made in sanctions.' The *Financial Gazette* also considered that the arrival of the jets was a morale booster at a time when the general public needed reassurance that the sanctions campaign remained ineffective. It pointed out that 'one of the most disappointed onlookers must be the British Aircraft Corporation, which had been hoping to sell its BAC 1-11's to Air Rhodesia in the event of a settlement.' The newspaper considered that the presence of the Boeings in Rhodesia 'must demonstrate forcibly to the British Government—once more—the futility of the whole sanctions exercise ... whatever effect sanctions have had, its main victims inside Rhodesia have been the African and outside Rhodesia the British businessman.'[90] The aircraft, the arrival of which took most Salisbury citizens by surprise, had apparently flown from Switzerland. It was later reported that in 1970 they had belonged to Calair Transportflug of Frankfurt and had very recently been sold to a company in Liechtenstein from which they were acquired by Rhodesia.[91]

Later in the year another warning was given to Rhodesian businessmen and industrialists, this time by government security officials, who warned of a recent Security Council's sanctions committee decision to establish a fund out of which special investigators would receive remuneration for reporting on sanctions breaking. Firms were later urged by the Associated Chambers of Commerce to adopt a list of suggested security measures to help to limit the effectiveness of these informers.[92]

NOTES

1 *Rhodesia Government Notice No. 17A of 1973 : Government Gazette Extraordinary* 12 January 1973.
2 *R.H.* 10 January 1973.
3 *The Times* (London) 15 January 1973.
4 *R.H.* 18 January 1973.
5 *The Times* 24 January 1973.
6 As reported in the *Daily Telegraph* (London) 31 January 1973.
7 *The Times* 1 February 1973.
8 *Daily Telegraph* 27 January 1973.
9 *R.H.* 5 February 1973.
10 *R.H.* 9 February 1973.
11 As reported in *R.H.* 12 March 1973.
12 *Daily Telegraph* 20 March 1973.
13 *Daily Telegraph* 9 April 1973.
14 *Daily Telegraph* 10 April 1973.
15 As reported in *R.H.* 25, 28 May 1973.
16 *R.H.* 14 June 1973.
17 *West Africa* No. 2904. 5 February 1973.
18 As reported in *R.H.* 10, 12 January 1973.
19 *R.F.G.* 19 January 1973.
20 *R.H.* 15, 17 January 1973.

21 *R.H.* 20 January 1973.
22 As reported by *R.H.* from Lusaka 31 January 1973.
23 As reported in *R.H.* 30 January 1973.
24 *R.H.* 1, 5 February 1973.
25 *S.M.* 4 February 1973.
26 As quoted in *Africa Research Bulletin:* Vol. 10, No. 2. 15 March 1973: Cols. 2762-3.
27 *S.M.* 11 February; *R.H.* 13 February 1973.
28 *R.H.* 1 May 1973.
29 *Times of Zambia,* 17 February 1973: As quoted in *Africa Research Bulletin,* Vol. 10, No. 2. 15 March 1973.
30 *R.H.* 21 February 1973.
31 *R.H.* 26 February; 3, 5, 7 March 1973.
32 *R.H.* 8 March 1973.
33 *R.H.* 19 May 1973.
34 *Daily Telegraph* 19 May 1973.
35 *The Times* 18 May 1973.
36 *S.M.* 20 May 1973.
37 *R.H.* 21 May; report by Herald Africa News Service in *R.H.* 23 May 1973.
38 *R.H.* 24 May 1973.
39 *R.H.* 26 May 1973.
40 *R.H.* 23, 26 June 1973.
41 *R.H.* 3 March 1972.
42 *R.H.* 27 October 1972.
43 As reported in *R.H.* 11 January 1973: South Africa was reported to be Zambia's second largest trading partner and major supplier of mining machinery for the mining industry from which Zambia derives nearly all her export revenue.
44 *R.H.* 15 January 1973.
45 As reported in *R.H.* 20 January 1973.
   The four principles to which Mr. Vorster referred are that South Africa—does not interfere with the domestic affairs of other countries; does not initiate boycotts or reply to sanctions with counter-boycotts; is unconditionally opposed to terrorism and will render assistance to governments who seek assistance in their fight against terrorism; when directly threatened will at all times take steps to protect the life and property of South Africans and the territorial integrity of South Africa.
46 As reported in *S.M.* 28 January 1973.
47 *R.H.* 30 January 1973.
48 *R.F.G.* 2 February 1973.
49 *R.H.* 12 February 1973.
50 *R.H.* 12 April 1973.
51 *R.F.G.* 19 April 1973.
52 *R.F.G.* 1 September 1972.
53 *Daily Telegraph* 11, 13 January 1973.
   Copper shipments account for about 95% of Zambia's foreign exchange earnings.
54 *Daily Telegraph* 6 February 1973.

55 *R.H.* 27 January 1973.
56 *R.H.* 8 February 1973.
57 As reported in *R.H.* 12 March 1973.
58 As reported from Washington by *R.H.* 16 May 1973.
59 As reported from Washington by *R.H.* 8 June 1973.
60 As reported by *R.H.* 30, 31 January 1973.
61 *R.H.* 10, 12 March 1973.
62 *To The Point:* Vol. 2, No. 6. 24 March 1973.
63 *R.H.* 22 May 1973.
64 *S.M.* 27 May 1973.
65 Quoted in 1970: Gale, W.D.: *Rhodesia 1890-1970: eighty years onwards:* Salisbury: H.C.P. Anderson.
66 *S.M.* 17 September 1972.
67 Reported from Sydney in *R.H.* 16 January 1973.
    The Rhodesian Information Centre is registered in Australia as a private company.
68 *R.H.* 19, 27 April 1973.
69 *Rhodesian Farmer:* Vol. 43, Nos. 45, 49. 20 April, 18 May 1973.
70 *R.H.* 10, 11 November 1972.
71 *R.F.G.* 1 December 1972.
72 *R.H.* 2, 17 November; 6 December 1972.
73 *R.H.* 15 February 1973.
74 *R.H.* 20, 23 February 1973.
75 *Daily Telegraph* 5 May 1973.
76 *R.H.* 7 May 1973.
77 *Daily Telegraph* 30 June 1973.
78 *Daily Telegraph* 18 April 1973.
79 As reported in *R.H.* 8 June 1973.
80 As reported in *R.H.* 27 June 1973.
81 *op. cit.* Gale, 1970.
82 1972: Arnold, Guy: *Sanctions against Rhodesia 1965-1972:* London: The Africa Bureau.
    Also see:
    1972: Arnold, Guy and Alan Baldwin: Rhodesia: *Token Sanctions or Total Economic Warfare:* London: The Africa Bureau.
83 As reported from New York by *R.H.* 10 February 1973.
84 As reported from New York by *R.H.* 23 May 1973.
85 *R.H.* 27 January, 1 June 1973.
86 As reported from Washington by *R.H.* 7 April 1973.
87 As reported from New York by *R.H.* 23 May 1973.
88 *Hansard:* Vol. 81, No. 9. 16 June 1972: Cols. 674-6.
89 *R.H.* 21, 22 March 1973.
90 *R.F.G.* 19 April 1973.
91 *S.M.* 22 April 1973.
92 *R.F.G.* 15 June 1973.

IV

THE POPULATION OF RHODESIA

The latest population figures available are those in the Economic
Survey for 1973 which gives a comparative table of figures from
1963 to 1972 of the estimated *de facto* population by racial categories.[1]

TOTAL POPULATION AT DECEMBER 31, 1972 (THOUSAND)

Year	African	European	Coloured	Asian	Total
1963	4 050	215	11,8	7,7	4 280
1964	4 190	209	12,4	7,9	4 420
1965	4 330	213	13,0	8,2	4 560
1966	4 470	214	13,6	8,4	4 710
1967	4 630	218	14,3	8,7	4 870
1968	4 790	226	15,0	8,9	5 040
1969	4 960	234	15,7	9,1	5 220
1970	5 130	243	16,5	9,2	5 400
1971	5 310	255	17,2	9,4	5 590
1972	5 490	267	17,8	9,6	5 780

The tables also give figures for births and deaths per thousand of population, by racial groups, together with the natural rate of increase per
thousand.

	African	European	Coloured	Asian	Total
Births per annum	52	18	n/a	22	n/a
Deaths per annum	16	7	n/a	5	n/a
Natural increase per annum	36	11	49	17	35

POPULATION CONTROL

With these figures in mind it is not surprising that a number
of points regarding the government's policy on family planning
were brought up during the debate in 1972 on the Revenue Vote

for the Ministry of Health. Mr. E. G. Watungwa, M.P. for Harare, said that in his opinion the reason why family planning was on the decline was because the African people thought that the government was advocating this policy from political expedience. Mr. Watungwa also thought that not enough attention was being given to teaching the people so that they could appreciate the necessity for family planning and for raising their standard of living. Mr. R. T. D. Sadomba, M.P. for Nemakonde, said that Africans were suspicious of the government's intentions for on the one hand they saw the government encouraging immigration of Europeans and on the other speaking of the urgency of family planning for Africans. In his reply the Minister of Health, Mr. I. F. McLean, deprecated the suggestion that the government was bringing politics into family planning and denied that the policy was declining in the African areas. [2]

During September 1972 Mr. C. A. R. Savory, M.P. for Matobo, addressed the Rhodesia National Affairs Association. In his address, entitled *Land, Politics and People,* Mr. Savory made the point that 'as long as the facts of life are denied to Rhodesian blacks in their own country on the grounds of colour alone there will be no population control. In fact the reverse will pertain and there will be every incentive to breed.' He then went on to warn that without a balanced economic growth, land stability and population control there would be no solution to the problems of Rhodesia. [3]

An editorial in the *Herald* attempted to explain the position (which was being considered by a Cabinet committee set up in 1971 by the Prime Minister) by saying that the problem was not one of the rising population alone, but the fact that the country's financial resources were not increasing at a proportionate rate. In October it was announced that the government had increased its grant to the Family Planning Association from $65 000 in 1971 to $135 000 in 1972. According to the Minister of Health the government hoped that a further substantial increase would be made available for this work which, the Minister said, the government had accepted as being the responsibility of a number of Ministries. [4]

According to *Moto*, 'Rhodesia's imbalance is mainly caused by a minority of citizens who control a disproportionate amount of wealth ... while the many are reduced to a state of want ... Rhodesia is still unable to fulfil sufficiently such aspirations [economic, educational and modern status] of the African people in a truly national context. As long as there is no thaw in this respect family planning will be doomed. The poor and oppressed will always retain an effective weapon: children.'[5] John Robertson in his column View-point in the *Herald*'s weekly *Business and Financial Review* put a different point of view. 'It is not hard to see why the African in Rhodesia remains unconvinced by the arguments presented to him. Basically he is asked to believe that the costs of bringing chil-dren into the world will keep him forever poor ... But to the African poverty is having too few children. He knows that in the sense Europeans speak of poverty, he is poor already, and that for this reason the Government has to bear most of the cost of health services and education for his children ... Unless the system is changed to ensure that Africans, like Europeans, feel the direct consequences of their own actions and preferences in terms of money, this state of affairs will continue until the tax-paying capacity of the money economy has been bled to death by population growth.'[6]

MIGRATION

The migration figures given in the *Economic Survey* show another side of the picture:

NET MIGRATION

Period	European	Asian & Coloured	Foreign African Men
1963	− 3 880	+ 96	− 6 100
1964	− 8 410	− 98	− 8 200
1965	+ 3 460	+ 6	− 3 380
1966	− 2 090	− 29	− 16 200
1967	+ 3 320	+ 83	− 4 680
1968	+ 6 210	—	− 2 560
1969	+ 5 040	+ 33	− 2 140
1970	+ 6 340	− 10	− 9 270
1971	+ 9 400	+ 57	− 9 750
1972	+ 8 820	+ 17	− 7 450

The current Immigration Act was passed in 1966. According to the then Minister of Immigration, Mr. J. H. Howman, it was designed to replace the previous Act of 1954 with amendments introduced 'consequent upon the assumption of independence; to permit of a more efficient control of our borders and, in the interests of security.'[7]

In 1971, during the debate on the Revenue Vote for the Ministry of Information, Immigration and Tourism, Mr. R. T. D. Sadomba asked the Minister for a statement on his policy regarding immigration and, as far as it affected the races, queried whether the policy of selective immigration was only 'geared for the white people?' The Minister, Mr. P. K. F. V. van der Byl, in reply said that he was repeating what he had said on many occasions previously that 'the policy of immigration is to bring people to Rhodesia whose presence is in the national interest.' He reminded the House that there were some half a million African immigrants (migrant labourers) in Rhodesia, from Malawi, Zambia and Mozambique.[8]

The National Immigration Board was set up in July 1971. Its prime function according to its chairman, the Secretary for Immigration, was to advise and to make recommendations to the Minister on all aspects of immigration and emigration, on the effects of housing, health, education, transport and employment problems and how the various functions of the government and the world of commerce could be co-ordinated to assist in ways of encouraging the greatest numbers of suitable immigrants.[9]

ASIAN IMMIGRATION

It was also in 1971 that Mr. L. Masenda, M.P. for Mabvazuwa, asked at question time if the Minister would make a statement concerning Asian immigration: to which the Minister replied 'in conformity with the policy of successive Rhodesian Governments we do not encourage Asian immigration.'[10]

Later the same year it was reported that in response to questions asked by the press a Ministry spokesman had said: 'Asiatics, Coloureds and Indians are not admitted to this country. Certain personnel in some specialized posts have been admitted in the past on temporary permits, but this type of exception will not be permitted in future. Parties to a [racially] mixed marriage are similarly not welcome as immigrants.' A delegation from the National Association of Coloured Peoples (N.A.C.P.) later had an interview with the Minister who confirmed that this press report was true. The

N.A.C.P's Secretary was afterwards quoted as saying 'we can now see a rapid acceptance of the South African apartheid system coming into being in Rhodesia. The Government is now going to have to clearly define people's ancestry.'[11]

During the 1972 debate on the Revenue Vote for the Ministry of Information, Immigration and Tourism, Mr. J. A. Newington, M.P. for Hillcrest, said that he was seriously perturbed that the Minister had permitted, during the first six months of 1972, the entry of almost five times the ordinary number of Indian immigrants to the country for permanent residence. He said that he believed it would be wise for Rhodesia 'to accept that there are sound reasons for the total refusal of African states to accept any of those [Asians] presently about to be expelled from Uganda.' He was supported in his views by Mr. D. J. Brink, M.P. for Karoi. In his reply, the Minister said that the figures for Asian immigration were not substantially more than usual and made the point that 'the only immigration which is normally accepted in this regard ... [is] local Indian citizens [who] marry outside the country [and] bring in their wives ... a normal practice in any country.' He then went on to explain that the converse was not allowed, Indian women citizens who married foreign men did not confer the right of domicile on their husbands. He also said that the right of entry was restricted to one wife only.[12]

In September what was described in the press as 'a new and startling proposal' was made by a British M.P. who suggested, at a Conservative Party meeting, that Rhodesia should take in some of the Asians being expelled from Uganda. The idea received some degree of notice in letters to the editor of the local newspapers with an apparent rough equality of numbers being for and against the idea. According to the chairman of the Rhodesia National Party this was in connection with the rumours of British officials visiting Rhodesia to offer a new settlement deal. The new settlement deal had, according to the R.N.P. Chairman, a proviso that Rhodesia should take in a certain number of the expelled Asians to placate world opinion in the event of a settlement. This rumour was later denied by government sources. A government spokesman was quoted as stating the government had no intention of offering to take any Asians from Uganda, whether or not there was a settlement with Britain.[13]

ASSISTED PASSAGES

In November 1971, during consideration of supplementary estimates for the Ministry of Information, Immigration and Tourism,
two African M.P.'s, Mr. R. C. Makaya and Mr. M. M. Bhebe, queried the sum of $105 000 which was to be provided for assisted
passages for immigrants. In reply the Minister said that he felt
that in these questions, there was an element of criticism that the
government was not being selective enough in the admission of
immigrants. He reminded the House that the degree of selectivity
was in fact rigorous. As far as economics were concerned, the Minister said that far from being a drain on the Exchequer, the money
being spent on assisted passages could be described as a finance-
earning industry, for not only do the immigrants bring assets into
the country but 'there is a direct and absolute correlation between
the number of immigrants coming into the country and the rise
in job opportunities and actual, factual African employment.'[14]

The Minister went on to describe the two categories of immigrants who would be eligible to receive assisted passages: those
persons who had a particular or unusual skill which was urgently
needed in the country, and assistance for family passages for the
man who had emigrated to the country of his own volition and
expense and had succeeded in establishing himself in a skilled job
and then wished to send for his family.[15] The Minister added
that the percentage of all immigrants who actually received assisted
passages was sixteen *per cent.*[16]

DEVELOPMENTS DURING 1972-3

In 1972 the figures of net immigration were 8 833 Europeans and
17 Coloureds and Asians.[17] During April 1972 the president of
the African Trades' Union Congress, Mr. P. Sithole, commented
on the recently released Economic Survey for 1971 which showed
a deficit in the balance of payments. According to Mr. Sithole
the reasons given for this in the Survey (international currency
instability, depressed world base metal prices and some recession
in world trade) were not the only reasons for the deficit. He argued
that the country's trading position was being harmed by unskilled
Europeans being brought into the country on subsidized or fully
paid passages, being trained locally and then paid inflated wages.

This had the result of pushing up both production costs and prices.[18]

In the January 1973 issue of *Centrepoint* (one of two special issues for the youth branch of the Centre Party) the government's immigration policy was criticized in an article entitled *We Don't Need These Immigrants*. The article proclaimed that 'We, the young members of the Centre Party, think that the Front Government is failing in its duty to Rhodesia by its interpretation of this [the Immigration] Act.' It went on to illustrate where it considered the failure lay. From pamphlets emanating from the Department of Immigration it was estimated that the total cost of bringing a man, his wife and three children to Rhodesia would be about Rhodesian $1 700 in the form of assisted passages, income tax relief, assisted housing etc. It was argued that if the immigrant was, for example, a doctor, the outlay would be justified in that the amount would represent only a small fraction of the cost of his training. But, 'the bulk of immigrants arriving in this country every month are however families of semi-skilled builders and other artisans, whose main qualification appears to be their claim to European descent'. The article commented that the government was apparently trying to counter-balance the high African birth rate by uncontrolled immigration, but had little chance of succeeding. It ended by stating 'We are being invaded by hordes of illiterate and semi-literate people who have no stake in the country and who, unwittingly, are pushing us nearer the brink of political and economic disaster.'[19]

Throughout the rest of the first six months of 1973 concern was shown in most newspapers about the slowing down of immigration. The figures of net immigration for the first six months of the year (January to June 1973) were 1 940 as compared to 5 370 for the same period in 1972.[20]

EMIGRATION

In July the *Herald*'s editor commented on the reasons why it considered it 'sad that for every two white people who come to live in Rhodesia one who has lived here leaves' and said that there was dissatisfaction over two essentials, housing and jobs. The editorial went on to consider that there was a case for a better briefing of prospective immigrants and queried whether 'immigrants are warned that they will have to do without the many social props characteristic of the sophisticated human environments they are leaving, and learn to make their way in an immature society which values those who can stand on their own feet and help to build a nation?'[21]

In August it was reported that government officers had been analysing, over a period of some months, the reasons why people were leaving the country. A senior official of the Ministry of Immigration was quoted as saying 'of the 14 743 immigrants last year, only 624 left again between July 1971 and May 1972. One person had said the reason was housing difficulties and 59 had cited employment difficulties.' The official went on to explain that the immigration figures included those persons who had initially come to the country temporarily and had then decided to look for a job. Many people who complained of employment difficulties were in this category, he said.[22]

ALIEN AFRICANS

During the same month Harare African Township Advisory Board reported to Salisbury's Health, Housing and African Administration Committee its concern over the number of non-indigenous Africans being allowed into the country. The Board felt that there should be strict control over migrant labour and asked that the government be urged to take action to control the influx of alien Africans.[23] Replying to questions on this topic a spokesman for the Ministry of Internal Affairs gave the information that there were more foreign Africans leaving than entering the country and reminded the Board that the provisions of the Closed Labour Area Order confined foreign African workers to the rural areas except for those workers who had entered the country before certain dates.[24]

According to the *Sunday Mail*, many people directly concerned with immigrants and those actually leaving the country regarded the chief reason for this to be the uncertainty regarding a settlement with Britain; another important reason, however, was thought to be that too many people, particularly the young and the professionally and technically trained, were not finding opportunities in employment. The *Mail* did not consider that the renewal of guerilla activity in the early part of the year or the continuing dispute with Zambia were primary reasons for the drop in net immigration.[25]

NOTES

1 1973: *Economic Survey of Rhodesia for 1972*: Cmd. R.R. 5-1973: Salisbury: Central Statistical Office.
2 *Hansard*: Vol. 81, No. 24. 4 August 1972: Cols. 2094-2103, 2123-4.
3 As reported in *R.H.* 16 September 1972.
   Mr. C. A. R. Savory was formerly a government ecologist and is now a private consultant ecologist as well as being an M.P. and founder member of the Rhodesia Party.
4 *R.H.* 25 October, 27 November 1972.
5 *Moto*: Vol. 14, No. 33. 12 August 1972.
6 *R.H. Business and Financial Review* 29 March, 14 June 1973.
7 Immigration Act No. 43 of 1966.
   Hansard: Vol. 64, 27 July 1966: Cols. 917-27.
8 *Hansard*: Vol. 79, No. 13. 22 July 1972: Cols. 827-30, 834.
9 *R.H.* 7 July 1971.
10 *Hansard*: Vol. 79, No. 13. 22 July 1971: Col. 1635.
11 *S.M.* 5 September, *R.H.* 4 September 1971.
12 *Hansard*: Vol. 82, No. 7. 24 August 1972: Cols. 605-82.
13 *R.H.* 21 September; 1 November 1972.
14 According to the Minister of Information, Immigration and Tourism, from 1965 a total of 73 000 immigrants had declared assets of about R. $52 million.
15 This category of immigrant is allowed to stay on a temporary permit for six months. If he obtains employment he can apply for a residence permit on the grounds that his skill is necessary to the country.
16 *Hansard*: Vol. 80, No. 12. 18 November 1971: Col. 857.
17 *op. cit.* See note 1.
18 As reported in *R.H.* 21 April 1972.
19 *Centrepoint* (Special Issue) Vol. 3, No. 3. January 1973.
20 *Monthly Digest of Statistics*: Salisbury: Central Statistical Office, July 1973.
21 *R.H.* 26 July 1972.
22 *S.M.* 13 August 1972.
23 *R.H.* 24 May 1972.
24 *R.H.* 17, 21 August 1972.
   The dates of entry differ in the various urban areas but generally speaking foreign Africans who can produce reasonable proof that they have lived in Rhodesia for more than four out of the seven years immediately preceding 1 January 1964 are not affected by the order which comes under the Foreign Migratory Labour Act of 1958.
25 *S.M.* 3 June 1973.

V

LEGISLATION DURING 1972-1973[1]

During 1972 Parliament was adjourned, after sitting for one day (29th February) and was not resumed until the 2nd June. This was because, according to the Minister of Justice, the government did not think it advisable to debate the settlement proposals during the period of the Pearce Commission investigations with its attendant disorders.[2] On the 2nd June, after the State Opening of Parliament, the rest of the day was taken up by the President's speech, which outlined legislation planned for the coming session. The *Herald*, in its editorial, commented the following day that 'the President's statement ... gave no obvious indication of a swing to the right and a decision to pursue "hard line" policies ... it would seem that Parliament ... will be busy—and what is more, busy on much work which should be productive.'[3]

In his speech at the opening of Parliament during 1973 the President outlined plans to provide for the registration and identification of all persons resident in the country; proposals for the amendment of the Industrial Conciliation Act, the Tribal Trust Land Development Corporation Act, the Natural Resources Act, Town and Country Planning Acts, Rural Councils Act, and the African Beer Act; and measures to improve safety conditions in the mines with special reference to the Commission of Enquiry into the Wankie Colliery disaster.[4]

THE 1972 BUDGET

For the first few days of its 3rd Session, Parliament during 1972 was occupied with the debate on the Pearce Report and there were first and second readings of various bills. On the 13th July the Minister of Finance, Mr. J. J. Wrathall, read the budget statement.

Reviewing particular aspects of the economy, he said that 'a most satisfying feature of 1971 was the high rate of employment generation for all races. The country was able to absorb the highest net gain of European migrants in 14 years and, in percentage terms, the increase in African employment opportunities exceeded the net increase of the African population. The trend is continuing.'

The Budget proposals, as far as they affected racial groups, were for an increase in the rate of old age pensions to bring them up to a maximum of $50 a month and also to remove the differences in the rates between Europeans, Coloureds and Asians; and the imposition of an excise tax, from January 1973, of one cent per litre on the brewing of opaque African beer.[5]

During the debate on the Budget Mr. M. M. Bhebe, M.P. for Ntshonalanga, asked the Minister of Labour and Social Welfare whether it was not time that Africans were also included in the old age pension scheme. Mr. McLean explained why this was not possible—apart from the administrative difficulties the financial burden would be more than the country could stand in present circumstances.[6]

THE DEPARTURE FROM RHODESIA (CONTROL) AMENDMENT ACT AND THE IMMIGRATION AMENDMENT ACT

On 17th August the Departure from Rhodesia (Control) Amendment Bill was introduced by the Minister of Information, Immigration and Tourism, Mr. P. K. F. V. van der Byl. At its Second Reading the Minister explained that the Bill dealt mainly with bringing the principal Act up to date, but it also had a number of new features. Among these the significant one was the introduction of new provisions enabling the government, if it considered it to be in the public interest, to prevent the legal departure of any person from Rhodesia and make it an offence to refuse the surrender of a passport or other travel documents when required to do so. The Bill also empowered emigration officials at ports of exit to declare foreign travel documents, of persons trying to leave Rhodesia, invalid. At the time the Minister assured the House that 'though we fully recognise that the powers contained in this Bill are considerable, I would undertake that these will be used with the utmost care and discretion and there will certainly be no abuse.'[7] Later, at Committee stage, Mr. van der Byl claimed that the Bill was 'designed specifically and only against people whose journey is not in the interest of Rhodesia.' He denied that it would be used to deter opponents of the government from going abroad and, in answer to a query from an African M.P., stated that the Bill was 'entirely non-racial' and would be applied to anyone who fell into the category of undertaking activities, while abroad, against the interests of Rhodesia.[8]

At the beginning of September, the Minister of Information, Immigration and Tourism introduced the Second Reading of the Immigration Amendment Bill. This Bill was to amend the Immigration Act of 1966. Under its provisions the Minister could take over powers previously held by the President to declare any person an undesirable inhabitant or visitor to Rhodesia. It also changed the situation whereby persons declared (or about to be declared) prohibited immigrants were allowed to remain in the country while appealing against the restriction. The Bill also curtailed the protection given to the wife or child of a prohibited immigrant for they could also be declared prohibited immigrants on economic grounds or 'because of unacceptable standards or habits of life.'[9]

In its leader entitled *Arbitrary Powers* of 5th September, the *Herald* discussed the effect of the two Bills taken together, and concluded that the Minister was being given 'tremendous new powers ... he can stop a Rhodesian citizen from travelling; he can stop any non-citizen from entering (or re-entering); he is appointed arbiter of a citizen's intentions when about to travel. Provision for appeal is meagre. Qualification of citizenship by birth is whittled down. And no reasons need apparently be given for action that can be taken as a result of "sifting various bits of information to get at the truth"—in other words, possibly unconfirmed informer's tales.' The newspaper queried whether Rhodesia's safety really depended upon such measures.[10]

On the day that the Departure from Rhodesia (Control) Act became law the Rev. Canaan Banana was served with orders in terms of the Act to withdraw his Rhodesian passport and any other travel documents in his possession. On the 10th September the *Sunday Mail* reported that Bishop Muzorewa's Rhodesian passport had been cancelled under the Act.

THE CHILDREN'S PROTECTION
AND ADOPTION ACT

The Children's Protection and Adoption Bill received its Second
Reading in August 1972. Among other queries Mr. M. M. Bhebe
asked how the Bill would affect the rights of parents in the context
of customary and tribal law and African custom and was reassured
by the Minister of Social Welfare, Mr. I. F. McLean, that there
was no intention in the Bill of interfering with tribal custom or
tradition and that there were welfare officers for the different racial
groups in the country who would be aware of the standards and
customs of the races with whom they came into contact. At Committee stage Mr. J. M. Khabo asked whether, under the clause
regarding neglect of children, African parents who do not send
their children to school could be forced to do so. The Minister
replied that as schooling for African children was not compulsory
this was not something which was covered by the Bill.[11] When
the Act was gazetted on the 27th October, the *Herald* commented
upon its provisions which 'have modernized and streamlined the
law, bringing it into line with current thinking' and ended by not-
ing that 'the part of the Act covering the protection of infants
now includes African children as well as those of other races.'[12]

THE LAW AND ORDER (MAINTENANCE) ACT

In 1962 under Sections 50 and 51 of the Law and Order (Maintenance) Act the power of restricting persons was conferred upon
the Minister of Law and Order. Section 52 of the Act, however,
limited the power to restrict up to 1st September 1964 unless the
Governor (later the Officer Administering the Government and,
from 1970, the President) had by 'proclamation in the *Gazette*
announced that these powers may be exercised pursuant to a resolution of the House of Assembly.' The order has been renewed each
biennial since 1962 and was due to expire on 31st August 1972.
Introducing the motion to extend the period of the power to
restrict, the Minister of Law and Order, Mr. D. W. Lardner-
Burke, said that in the previous debate on the topic in 1970 it
had appeared that members of the House were under some misapprehension as to the object of the motion. He thought it necessary,
therefore, to explain exactly what the motion meant, and reminded

members that restriction was something different from detention. '...restriction can be used to deal with those persons in respect of whom it is necessary to impose some curtailment of movement. For instance, under a restriction order it is possible to require a person to remain within an area of land surrounding his place of residence; a restriction order can also be employed to require a person to remain outside a defined area in which his presence may lead to a breakdown of law and order ... The restriction system is, therefore, highly flexible, and involves far less interference with the normal life of the individual concerned and his family.' The Minister then went on to say that at the present time no one in Rhodesia was subject, under the Act, to a restriction order.

Asking for a five-year extension instead of the customary two years, Mr. Lardner-Burke pointed out that when the new clause was introduced into the original Act in 1962 there had been no specific reference to any period of years in which the powers of restriction could be exercised. It had only specified that the powers could not be exercised after a date two years after the enactment of the Act without reference to Parliament. As the Minister commented 'presumably at that time the government of the day was of the opinion that the two-year period up to the 1st September 1964 would suffice, and that the organizers of violence would change their tactics and pursue their political objectives by constitutional means. In the event this has proved to be a futile hope.' Mr. Lardner-Burke explained that his reasons for requesting a longer period of extension of the powers to restrict was that 'years have gone by with little or no sign that the subversive political organizations presently based in Zambia, the Organization for African Unity and certain dissident elements within Rhodesia are prepared to work constitutionally towards their political objectives. All these people are pre-occupied with violence as a means of achieving political power.' He went on to say 'there seems little doubt that these extremists are merely opportunists greedy for the spoils of political power which they can convert to their own ends ... That they have overlooked and continue to overlook, however, is that they were not dealing with an overseas government willing to abdicate its responsibilities, but with a locally based government responsible to an electorate which was determined to ensure that government remained in civilized hands and that law and order was maintained. These organizations have, therefore, made no progress; they are entirely dependent on support from the Organization for African Unity and Left-wing elements in the West and communist countries. It cannot be expected that this support will be withdrawn within the foreseeable future. We must, therefore, face the long haul as far as subversion is concerned.' Mr. M. M. Bhebe was the only M.P. to comment upon the Minister's introductory speech for he considered that the powers which the Minister was seeking to extend were 'hitting the Africans the hardest ... it is common knowledge that the African politician, whether he be working within the law or outside the law, will be hard hit.' The Motion was put and agreed to without a division. On the 25th August *Rhodesia Government Notice* No. 783 was issued proclaiming that the period during which the powers conferred on the Minister under sections 50/51 of the Law and Order (Maintenance) Act had been extended to the 31st August 1977.[13]

In June 1972 it was announced in the *Government Gazette* that the Minister of Law and Order had issued an order prohibiting all public gatherings, except those of a non-political nature, in the African Purchase areas. Another order was also issued requiring all public meetings outside the Tribal Trust Lands and African Purchase Areas to be held in halls. Both orders, made in terms of the Law and Order (Maintenance) Act, were to be valid for three months.[14] Following this proclamation a number of persons were charged and sentenced to prison terms (with the option of fines) for holding unauthorized meetings in the Tribal Trust Lands.

DETAINEES

Introducing the motion to extend the powers of restriction under the Law and Order (Maintenance) Act, the Minister of Justice and of Law and Order reminded members of the House of the difference between restriction (see p. 195) and detention—'detention implies the incarceration of the individuals concerned, either in a prison or in a detention camp, with the result that his freedom of movement and his access to the outside world are severely hampered. Detention is, therefore, used to deal with those individuals who are regarded as being a serious threat to the national security and public safety.'[15]

At the end of 1971, in accordance with the agreement for the settlement, 31 detainees were released. Many people considered that these detainees were behind the outbreaks of violence and intimidation which accompanied the start of the Pearce Commission investigation.

In August 1972 Mr. D. M. Namate, M.P. for Tuli, tabled a private member's question asking how many times the case of Joshua Nkomo had been reviewed and upon what date this detainee would be freed. [16] In his reply the Minister said that in compliance with the requirements of the Constitution the Tribunal set up on 10th October 1970 had twice reviewed Mr. Nkomo's case and that he, the Minister, maintained a continuous review of all cases of detainees. With regard to the second part of the question Mr. Lardner-Burke said that he was unable to answer it. [17]

During October it was reported that the London *Times* had published a letter purporting to have been smuggled out of Salisbury and signed by 34 detainees. The letter alleged that the detainees were being held in close confinement and without proper food, clothes and bedding. In answer to this allegation a spokesman for the Ministry of Justice said 'the allegations are so preposterous as to warrant no answer from this Ministry'. He commented 'in case it is not generally known, perhaps it should be pointed out that representatives of the International Red Cross pay regular visits to detainees in Rhodesia.' These representatives are free to see detainees in private, to receive their complaints and to investigate them. [18]

The International Red Cross Society in Geneva refused to comment on the detainees' letter but pointed out that its representatives did in fact visit places of detention in Rhodesia twice a year. The Society said that reports made by their representatives are only made available to the organization's headquarters and the government concerned. The last visit to a detention camp in Rhodesia was by the former general delegate for the Red Cross in Africa, Mr. George Hoffman, who privately met 50 detainees in five camps in April 1972. Another visit was scheduled before the end of the year. [19] Despite the government's rejection of the charges however, Amnesty International, was reported as pressing ahead with arrangements for a High Court law suit in Salisbury to establish the truth of the charges.

In the Report of the Secretary for Law and Order for the year ending 31st December 1972, it was noted that during the year two visits had been made by representatives of the International Committee of the Red Cross and that a satisfactory report had been received on the first of these visits, both on the conditions under which the detainees were held and on their health. (The report on the second visit had not been received at the time the secretary's report was written). The memorandum (or letter) signed by the 34 detainees had apparently initially been received by the Secretary for Law and Order and had only later featured in the British press. The Secretary pointed out that investigations had been made concerning the detainees' allegations and they had been found to be 'without substance'. A finding which had been confirmed by the report from the Red Cross representatives. [20]

At the end of November 1972 a motion was moved by Mr. N. A. Gandanzara, M.P. for Manica, deploring the restriction orders which prevented Bishop Muzorewa and the Rev. C. Banana from entering Tribal Trust Lands and asking that the government remove all restrictions upon other citizens. In reply the Minister of Internal Affairs, Mr. L. B. Smith, explained that there was no one under restriction at the present time. The Bishop had been prohibited from entering Tribal Trust Land during 1970 and, said the Minister, there was no intention of lifting the ban on him for it was considered that the Bishop 'had departed from his duties of the pulpit and entered into politics... There is much more that is damning to the reputation of Bishop Abel Muzorewa ... however I have given a clear indication why it is essential that this sort of influence should not be let loose on the tribal people of this country.' Mr. Gandanzara then moved that the debate be adjourned until he had had time to study the Minister's reply. When the debate was resumed, however, Mr. Gandanzara said that he was withdrawing the motion for he intended to consult the government privately over what appeared to be a personal decision by the Minister. [21]

The Report of the Secretary for Law and Order, presented to Parliament in June 1973, stated that 77 persons had been detained during January 1972, the number had then fallen to 63 in the early part of the year, but had then increased to 90 persons by the 31st December 1972. The Review Tribunal had, during the course of the year, held four sittings during which 140 detention orders had been considered. Twenty-six detainees had, at their own request, appeared in person before the Tribunal while others had submitted representations in writing. The Secretary noted that most detainees had not taken advantage of the invitation to make representations to the Tribunal, although written notice had been given to each detainee that his case was about to be reviewed. The Tribunal had recommended the release of two detainees, subject to certain conditions, and had also recommended that the conditions, applied to the release of a certain class of detainees, should be relaxed to give greater freedom of movement, particularly with regard to employment. It was reported in the press in January 1973 that the Minister of Law and Order had already accepted all the Tribunal's recommendations and had acted upon them. Asked about the detention order on Mr. Garfield Todd, who was confined to his farm, a government spokesman was reported as saying that the matter was under constant consideration. [22]

In February 1973 changes in the detention regulations were published in the *Gazette* as Prisons (Detained Persons) (No. 2) (Amendment) Regulations. The changes prohibit publication about detainees except in the case of proceedings before a court in which the detainee or restrictee has appeared or if the Minister authorizes publication; re-define the definition of a detained person to exclude those whom the Minister has allowed to leave a place of dentention indefinitely; and lay down the conditions under which detainees may receive visitors. It was reported that these changes would be re-inforced by amendments to the Law and Order (Maintenance) Act later in the year. [23]

When the Report of the Secretary for Law and Order was published in June the *Herald* noted with approval that it contained a reference to the system of releasing detainees on parole which had proved satisfactory in most cases. The newspaper commented 'the concept of detention without trial is an unpleasant fact of life ... We do not like it but we accept the reality of the situation. With that proviso we believe that reasonable people will look on the parole system with favour ... If the energies and abilities characteristic of some detainees can be put to constructive use, they and the country will benefit.' [24]

THE EMERGENCY POWERS ACT

During the debate on the Second Reading of the Constitution Bill in October 1969, the Minister of Justice and of Law and Order said that although the power to declare a State of Emergency was contained in the Emergency Powers Act the government considered that this power was of sufficient importance to be provided for in the Constitution itself. The proposed Constitution would declare that an 'emergency exists or, alternatively, that a situation exists, which if it is allowed to continue, may lead to a state of emergency.' The powers given to the President would be subject to confirmation by the House of Assembly as would the renewal of the declaration of a state of emergency, which would only subsist for a maximum of twelve months before a further renewal would have to be obtained. The House would also retain the right to authorize the declaration for a shorter period or to revoke it at any time.

Mr. Lardner-Burke then went on to review the history of circumstances under which states of emergency could be declared and why it had been necessary to amend the Act from time to time. He also referred to the Declaration of Rights which would be amended to bring it into line with existing legislation and foreseeable future requirements. The right to personal liberty was a section which the Minister considered needed special mention, for preventive detention and restriction were more appropriately brought under this heading. The powers of preventive detention and restriction would only be permitted in the interests of national defence, public safety or public order. Safeguards against wrongful detention or restriction were to be strengthened by making provision for an impartial tribunal, headed by a judge 'who is or has been a judge of the High Court', to review each detention or restriction order. The tribunal would review the case of a detainee or a restrictee, at his request, within three months and be obliged to review every case within 12 months and thereafter at intervals of 12 months. A recommendation by the tribunal to release a detainee or restrictee must be followed unless the President orders otherwise and places a notice to that effect in the *Government Gazette*.[25]

Moving that the House pass a resolution authorizing the declaration of a state of emergency for a further twelve months (in terms of section 61 of the Constitution) Mr. Lardner-Burke said that in 1970 when he had addressed the House on a similar resolution he had outlined the reasons why the declaration should not be revoked at that time. He regretted that exactly the same conditions were still present in 1971, thus making the extension of the state of emergency essential for a further year.

The two main reasons, for requesting the extension of the state of emergency, explained the Minister, were the threat of 'terrorist' infiltration from Zambia and the threat posed by United Nations sanctions against the economic survival of Rhodesia. Although there had been no incursions in the previous 12 months the threat of 'terrorist' infiltrations remained a real one for not only were 'terrorists' being trained and held at camps in Tanzania and Zambia but financial and material support for the 'terrorists' had increased. In regard to the fight against sanctions, the Minister assured the House that the powers conferred by the Emergency Powers Regulations had played a vital part in enabling the government to take successful counter measures against them. The Minister also commented that 'the emergency powers which we possess today are in fact used to only a very limited degree. The Government is not exercising the full power available to it for the very good reason that such powers are unnecessary save in isolated cases. The important point is that the powers are there, and our enemies know that they would be quickly and effectively dealt with if they cause trouble ... It is the very fact that the Government has these powers at its disposal which contributes to a large extent to our well-being in both the fields of law and order and economic prosperity.' [26]

In moving a similar motion in 1972 the Minister said that although he had indicated from time to time that the government wished and intended to allow the State of Emergency to lapse as soon as circumstances would permit 'Regrettably and understandably, I think, I have to report once again that that time has not yet arrived. Very similar circumstances affecting the security and economic well-being of Rhodesia exist today as existed 12 months ago ... Moreover the wide-spread disorders which accompanied the visit of the Pearce Commission to this country serve to remind us that emergency powers must be readily available at short notice when the political climate is disturbed by agitators and intimidators.' [27]

In his speech Mr. Lardner-Burke specifically referred to the
A.N.C. to whose ranks, he considered, many dissidents had been
attracted and which had resorted to violence and intimidation.
He charged the A.N.C. with being a potential threat to security
and warned that the government would act without hesitation the
moment the A.N.C. endangered public safety. In reply the A.N.C.
rejected the Minister's accusations and stated that 'We wish to
reiterate that the A.N.C. is not a subversive organization and that
it has not been connected with any disturbance in the country.
Our leaders have worked hard at all our gatherings to see that
people assemble and disperse quietly.'[28]

During 1973 the Deputy Minister of Law and Order, Mr.
J. J. L. de Kock, reminded the House that the State of Emergency
would lapse at midnight on the 25/26th June unless renewed by
Presidential decree pursuant upon a resolution of the House of
Assembly. Mr. de Kock considered that 'it must be obvious to
all Rhodesians who believe in civilized Government that the present state of emergency should be declared for a further twelve
months in order to give the Government the power to deal with
the problems facing the country'. At the present time it was more
than ever necessary to maintain secrecy in Rhodesia's economic
and business dealings, for complacency could not be allowed to
be the cause of a slowing-down of the economy. He recapitulated
the events of the previous three months and reminded his listeners
that murderous attacks had been made on Europeans and 'appalling atrocities [committed] against African citizens.' Only with the
backing of a strong and thriving economy could the security forces
be given the weapons, equipment and manpower to wipe out 'terrorism'. African members spoke against the extension of the state
of emergency and, when the House divided, voted against the
motion. It was carried however by a majority of 21 and the state
of emergency was extended for a further twelve months.[29]

COLD COMFORT FARM

It was the Emergency Powers Act which empowered the police
to make a raid on the multi-racial *kibbutz*-style co-operative Cold
Comfort Farm in late November 1970. One man was arrested at
that time and placed in detention under the Emergency Powers
regulations.[30] Shortly afterwards Cold Comfort Farm Society's

treasurer Mr. Guy Clutton-Brock was served with a notice that the government intended to deprive him of Rhodesian citizenship under the Citizenship of Rhodesia Act which had come into force, with the Constitution Act, on March 2nd 1970. Having refused to appeal against this decision Mr. Clutton-Brock was formally deprived of citizenship on the last day of December 1970. Closely following this action he was declared a prohibited immigrant under the Immigration Act and was given just under a month to leave the country.

In mid-January 1971 Cold Comfort Farm Society was, itself, declared an unlawful organization in terms of the Unlawful Organizations Act.[31] In a proclamation by the President which appeared in the *Government Gazette* it was explained that 'this action has been taken because the President is satisfied that the activities of the Society and some of its members are likely to endanger public safety ... The Government is satisfied that, over a period of years, under the cover of an organization whose aims are ostensibly to promote understanding, friendship and co-operation among people, in reality officials and members of the Society not only sympathize with, but actively support the terrorist cause as a means of overcoming the Constitution and the Government.'[32] Mr. Clutton-Brock was quoted as saying in reply 'All of us were and are still opposed to violence in any form. The allegations are totally unfounded.'

Protests about the government's action came from Labour peers in the British House of Lords, Mr. Bashford, the Centre Party leader, and a number of friends and sympathizers in Rhodesia. The British Foreign Secretary was reported as expressing regret over the decision to close down Cold Comfort Farm and the action over Mr. Clutton-Brock and added that these developments 'underlined the need to establish whether the constitutional dispute could be settled.'[33]

In mid-January 1971 another leading figure of the Cold Comfort Farm Society, Mr. A. Chadzingwa, appeared before the Salisbury Magistrate's Court on various charges under the Law and Order (Maintenance) Act and under the Unlawful Organizations Act. Mr. Chadzingwa was remanded twice until the following month when he appeared before the Salisbury Regional Court. The first and main charge against him alleged that he had continued to be an officer of the Zimbabwe African Peoples' Union (Z.A.P.U.)

which had taken up its headquarters in Lusaka. The two alternative charges alleged that he had in his possession at the Farm 'a letter or programme of activities' relating to Z.A.P.U. and that he also had documents containing details of Z.A.P.U's objectives and purposed subversive activities within Rhodesia. A few days later, at the end of the trial, Mr. Chadzingwa was found guilty of being a member of an unlawful organization and fined $200 (or 4 months) and was also given a suspended sentence of 12 months' hard labour. [34]

Early in March 1971, the Minister of Justice detailed reasons for the government action against the Society when he moved a motion asking for a Presidential proclamation to declare the Society to be an unlawful organization in terms of the Unlawful Organizations Act. [35] The Minister explained (as far as security interests permitted) that the Society had not been declared an unlawful organization nor had Mr. Clutton-Brock been declared a prohibited immigrant for the experiments in inter-racial living which they had organized but for clandestine activities in the field of subversion.

In detailing the history of the Society and Mr. Clutton-Brock's involvement with it, Mr. Lardner-Burke said that the latter had entered Rhodesia in 1949 and during 1951 had become an agriculturalist at St. Faith's Mission in Rusape. 'In the year that followed St. Faith's became noted as a centre which attracted Left-wing elements whose object was to undermine the existing structure of society ... the co-operative farming venture established there by Mr. Clutton-Brock played second fiddle to his political activities ... He became associated with the leaders of the present terrorist organizations now operating in Zambia.'

The Minister then went on to explain that Mr. Clutton-Brock had become involved in the formation of the Southern Rhodesian African National Congress, the activities of which had been the direct cause of a state of emergency being declared in 1959 during which the organization had been banned and Mr. Clutton-Brock had been detained for a short time. Following the reign of terror initiated by the other two nationalist organizations (Z.A.P.U. and Z.A.N.U.) and their subsequent banning in August 1964, the Minister explained that Mr. Clutton-Brock had played a leading part in establishing the Cold Comfort Farm Society which 'later provided a link with external and internal elements for subversive

activity within Rhodesia on behalf of the terrorist organizations.'
The Farm itself had been bought with money from the World
Council of Churches 'whose sympathy with terrorist organizations
has been more fully demonstrated in recent times.'

The Minister continued by describing Mr. Clutton-Brock's involvement with 'people who are at the present time organizing
terrorist attacks on Rhodesia' and commented that it was difficult
to reconcile Mr. Clutton-Brock's public avowals of his opposition
to the use of violence with statements he had made on two occasions
at the University of Rhodesia.

The activities of the chairman of the Society (who had been
detained) and of Mr. Chadzingwa as outlined in his recent trial
were then described. The Minister also gave instances of the con-
nections between the Society and unrest at the University and
also of links between it and persons associated with civil disobedience campaigns, with the leader of the Tangwena tribe, and with
the University lecturer and student who had left the country illegally after becoming involved in subversive activities. He concluded this part of his speech by saying 'the cumulative effect
of all the evidence leads to the only possible inference that the
society was a source of general subversion in the country.'

In the debate which followed some of the African M.P's
expressed similar sentiments to those expressed in the *Herald's*
editorial which had followed the proscription of the Society: 'the
activities of the Society, as described ... are a contravention not
only of the Emergency Regulations, but also of the Law and Order
Maintenance Act and half a dozen other statutes. Indeed they
amount to treason ... Why aren't the members of the Cold Comfort
Farm Society—or at least its leaders—being prosecuted in a court
of law?'[36]

In reply the Minister said that in the first place 'the presentation
of evidence would frequently involve the appearance of sources
of information in court which would obviously be contrary to
security and might well lead to their exposure. In the second place,
evidence of clandestine subversive activity by its very nature is
difficult to obtain and it is hardly likely that associates of the person
being charged, who are in the best position to give evidence, would
do so. One must also remember that the procedure of our courts
demands that the case against the accused must be proved beyond
all reasonable doubt. It is a heavy onus which is cast upon the

state. There are instances where the evidence satisfied the Government ... but either that evidence is not admissable in court procedure or it cannot be produced for security reasons. Is the Government supposed to allow the wrongdoer to continue his activities to the detriment of the community?'[37]

Shortly afterwards the *Herald* commented 'As the Government is sure of the accuracy of its information and of the reality of the threat to the State, it was right to act as it did and ignore any bad impression given outside. But were it to emerge in time that its information was not absolutely accurate, its action will have done great harm to intelligent racial co-operation.'[38]

Later in the year it was rumoured that Mr. Clutton-Brock was in Zambia but Zambian officials would neither confirm or deny the report. In early 1972 it was reported that no decision had yet been made on the disposal of the assets of the Society.[39]

NOTES

1 The Legislation discussed in this section does not include legislation dealt with in other parts of the Survey which deal with specific topics.

2 *Hansard:* Vol. 80, No. 18. 29 February 1972: Col. 1204.

3 *R.H.* 3 June 1972.
A swing to the right and 'hard-line' policies had been widely forecast as a reaction to the negative Pearce Report.

4 *Hansard:* Vol. 84, No. 1. 14 June 1973: Cols. 1-5.

5 *Hansard:* Vol. 81, No. 12. 13 July 1972: Cols. 961-78.

6 *Hansard:* Vol. 81, Nos. 13, 17. 18, 23 July 1972: Cols. 1008, 1451-52.

7 *Hansard:* Vol. 82, No. 5. 22 August 1972: Cols. 389-92.

8 *Hansard:* Vol. 82, No. 6. 23 August 1972: Cols. 496-526.

9 *Hansard:* Vol. 82, No. 12. 1 September 1972: Cols. 1054-60.

10 *R.H.* 5 September 1972.

11 *Hansard:* Vol. 82, Nos. 5, 8. 22, 25 August 1972: Cols: 393-423, 689.

12 *R.H.* 28 October 1972.

13 *Hansard:* Vol. 81, No. 4. 18 August 1972: Cols. 301-9.

14 *R.H.* 30 June 1972.

15 *Hansard:* Vol. 81, No. 4. 18 August 1972: Cols. 301-9.

16 Joshua Nkomo was the President of the banned African nationalist party, Zimbabwe African Peoples' Union (Z.A.P.U.). He has been in detention since 1964.

17 *Hansard:* Vol. 81, No. 24. 4 August 1972: Col. 2072.

18 As reported in *R.H.* 1 November 1972.

19 As reported in *R.H.* 2 November 1972.

20 1973: *Report of the Secretary for Law and Order for the year ending 31 December 1972:* Cmd. R.R. 17-1973. Salisbury: Government Printer.

21 *Hansard:* Vol. 83, Nos. 6, 10. 29 November, 6 December 1972: Cols. 423-79, 829-36.

22 *R.H.* 18 January 1973.

23 *Rhodesia Government Notice No. 160 of 1973:* 16 February 1973. *R.H.* 17 February 1973.

24 *R.H.* 6 June 1973.

25 *Hansard:* Vol. 75. 2 October 1969: Cols. 1067-73.

26 *Hansard:* Vol. 79, No. 8. 10 June 1971: Cols. 458-73.

27 *Hansard:* Vol. 81, No. 9. 16 June 1972: Col. 669.

28 *R.H.* 17 June 1972.

29 *Hansard:* Vol. 84, No. 4. 21 June 1973: Cols. 186-228.

30 *R.H.* 19 November 1970.

31 *R.H.* 16 January 1971.

32 As reported in *R.H.* 27 January 1971.

33 *R.H.* 19, 27 January 1971.

34 *R.H.* 16, 20 February 1972.

35 The Unlawful Organizations Act No. 38 of 1959 was amended four times during the years 1962-3, Section 3 (3) states that a proclamation as laid down in Sections 1 and 2 shall not be subject to any court of law but shall be laid before the House of Assembly as soon as may be after publication in the *Government Gazette* and unless confirmed by resolution of the House shall, within 21 days, elapse and cease to have effect.

36 *R.H.* 16 January 1971.

37 *Hansard:* Vol. 78, No. 17. 4 March 1971: Cols. 1072-1121.

38 *R.H.* 6 March 1971.

39 *R.H.* 29 March 1972.

VI

THE NEWS MEDIA

THE RHODESIAN PRINTING AND PUBLISHING COMPANY

Rhodesia did not have long to wait for a newspaper of her own. According to W. D. Gale, the Argus Printing and Publishing Company (established in 1889 with Cecil Rhodes as a shareholder) had sent Mr. W. E. Fairbridge 'in the wake of the Pioneer Column to represent the company in Salisbury.' Previously a company representative had been sent to explore the possibility of sending plant and machinery for the establishment of a press and had reported adversely on the physical difficulties of getting such articles to Mashonaland. In June 1891 Mr. Fairbridge brought out the mimeographed *Mashonaland Herald and Zambesian Times*.

As an augury for the future, that newspaper almost immediately failed to satisfy its public—the settlers, who considered that the newspaper was an instrument of the British South Africa Company, and the authorities, who considered that the newspaper should not print articles critical of the Company's administration. (It is interesting to learn that Mr. Rhodes himself, when on a visit to Mashonaland, reminded Mr. Fairbridge of the Company's power to deport him).

Following the completion of the telegraph-line connecting Salisbury with the Cape and the flotation of the Beira Railway Company to build a railway line through Portuguese East Africa to Umtali, the Argus company sent the necessary plant and equipment to publish a printed newspaper in Salisbury. Mr Fairbridge was appointed local Managing Director and Editor. The first issue of the *Rhodesia Herald* appeared on 29th October 1892.[1] The *Herald* soon 'became a real forum of public opinion, and public opinion was forthright in its criticism, and condemnation of various policies adopted by the Chartered Company.'

Following the Matabele War and the annexation of Matabeleland the Argus Company invested in a new subsidiary company
to control the *Herald* and commence publication of the *Bulawayo
Chronicle* in 1894 with the same 'independent policy pursued by
its elder sister the *Rhodesia Herald*.' The *Umtali Advertiser* (now
the *Umtali Post*) preceded the *Chronicle* by almost a year and was
absorbed by the Rhodesia Printing and Publishing Company in
1895. [2]

In 1922 a referendum was held to decide the future of Rhodesia.
The choice lay between becoming a fifth province of the Union
of South Africa or responsible government under the British
Crown. By November the majority had opted for responsible government despite the campaign by the two Rhodesian daily newspapers for union with South Africa. However, 'in the public mind
the fact that the two Rhodesian daily newspapers were controlled
by a company domiciled in the Union of South Africa, with strong
Rand mining company associations, was ground for suspicion ...
[that there had been] pressure on the editors by vested interests
in the south who wanted Rhodesia in the Union [of South Africa].'
These suspicions led to talk of forming a subsidiary company which
would acquire the Rhodesian interests of the Argus Company and
in 1927 the present-day Rhodesian Printing and Publishing Company Limited was formed with a large Rhodesian shareholding
and directorship. By 1935 the Company had acquired both Rhodesian Sunday newspapers (the *Sunday News* in Bulawayo and the
Weekly Review in Salisbury, the latter being re-titled the *Sunday
Mail*). [3]

CENSORSHIP

Writing in 1966 the Minister of Justice said 'considerable criticism
has been levied against us because of our censorship regulations
... As far as Rhodesia is concerned, we have only two daily newspapers, both owned by the same group, so that people in Rhodesia
are not able to choose any other papers to obtain an objective
portrayal of the facts, and these newspapers in my opinion appear
to be dedicated to the substitution of the present Rhodesian Government by some other Government, and, further, appear intent
on helping the British Government in their plans. The Rhodesian
public being what it is must be protected from the vicious propa-

ganda that is being put over by the British Government and which would be echoed in the local press.'[4]

Shortly before the Declaration of Independence (U.D.I.) in 1965 new Emergency (Maintenance of Law and Order) Regulations were promulgated in the *Government Gazette*. The section dealing with published matter stated that the 'protecting authority may issue orders for the regulation, control, restriction or prohibition of the printing or publishing of any book, newspaper, magazine, periodical, bill, placard, poster, pamphlet, circular or other written matter within the area or any portion of the area [designated within the regulations].'[5]

The Declaration of Independence was announced by the Prime Minister at midday on the 11th November 1965 and by the following day the *Herald* reported that government censors were already at work at the newspaper offices by invitation in order to avoid the inconveniences and delays of proofs having to be sent to separate censorship offices. The *Herald* pointed out that editors 'are compelled to submit galley-proofs of all editorial material to the censorship offices for approval before publication.'[6] Forthwith the *Herald* editors adopted a policy of leaving blank spaces to draw attention to the censored material and also of printing a front-page box informing readers that the contents of the newspaper had been subject to censorship.

At the first sitting of Parliament, after the adjournment following the Declaration of Independence, on November 25th 1965 a member of the opposition, Dr. Ahrn Palley, criticized the emergency regulations, particularly the powers given to the government over censorship. He pointed out that it was the first time that censorship regulations had been applied—'a complete censorship of anything published.'[7]

In mid-January 1966 an application was made to the High Court by the monthly news-journal, the *Central African Examiner*, which challenged the validity of the Rhodesian Constitution of 1965 (introduced after U.D.I.); the legality of the Rhodesian Government; and also asked that the censorship regulations be revoked in view of a United Kingdom Order-in-Council made on 19th November 1965. The application was eventually dismissed by Mr. Justice Lewis, in a 17-page written judgement in which he said that the action was 'not appropriate' because the Attorney-General would not agree either to the court exercising its discretion or to being bound by any of its decisions. According to the *Herald* Mr. Justice Lewis suggested that the *Examiner* adopt a course of publishing banned articles, or articles not shown to the censor, so that the validity of the censorship regulations could be tested through the resulting prosecution. On both occasions the report in the *Herald* of the application and its result were accompanied by blank spaces for the main editorials of the day. [8]

On the 17th January 1966 the Prime Minister, in a broadcast interview, was asked for his views on censorship. According to the *Herald* editorial on the following day 'the reply he made clearly referred to this newspaper although he did not name it.' The editorial went on to say that many points arose out of the Prime Minister's interview but it did not propose to make use of them for the simple reason that it 'was not in the same happy position of Mr. Smith who can say anything he likes for the public to hear or read, without any inhibition. Whatever we might wish to say in our defence would have to be submitted to persons under the authority of the administration headed by Mr. Smith, who is our accuser ... In these circumstances we hope nobody will hold us in contempt for declining to answer what Mr. Smith has said.' [9]

Early in February the Constitutional Council issued a report stating that although the regulations pertaining to censorship and the dissemination of information contained provisions 'which are, on the face of them, inconsistent with the Declaration of Rights relating to freedom of expression, the Council regards these two instruments as saved through their having been made under the authority of an existing law and during the existence of a period of public emergency.' The regulations were accordingly reported as not being inconsistent with the Declaration of Rights. [10]

At the same time new regulations on censorship were gazetted under the Emergency Powers Act. Section 5 of the Emergency Powers (Control of Publications) Regulations states that no person shall

a) print or cause to be printed any publication so as to indicate whether expressly or by omissions or by blank spaces or otherwise that any material has been omitted because of the actions of a censorship officer or that the publication is subject to censorship or has been censored;

or b) publish or cause to be published any publication which is printed in contravention of the provisions of paragraph (a)

Section 6 states that 'A censorship officer may direct that any material which is to be printed in any publication, including the headlines relating to any material, shall be altered or changed to another page of the publication.'[11] The *Herald* later commented that this latter section made the most significant change but that it was not clear whether the new regulation gave the censor on duty power to direct the way in which material would be altered or merely to direct that it must be altered.[12] In its issue for that day the report on the new regulations was partly blanked out and the main editorial for the day appeared as a blank space.

During this period the House was debating the Supplementary Estimates for 1965/6 and the new censorship regulations came in for comment from a number of M.P's. Mr. J. M. Gondo, M.P. for Ndanga, criticized the spending of £11 000 on Ministry of Information expenditure in connection with censorship. He was supported by Mr. R. H. James, M.P. for Salisbury City, who asked the Deputy Minister for Information to explain the criteria upon which censorship worked. The Deputy Minister, at that time Mr. P. K. F. V. van der Byl, in reply stated that censorship was 'in the opinion of the Government necessary, vitally necessary in the public interest at this particular time.' He added that he did 'not think anyone would dispute that a large number of the newspapers we have in this country are working strongly for the enemy, as we see the enemy, in this country in the context of its present struggle for independence and survival.' Later in the debate he said that he would have thought it unnecessary to have to explain 'that it is not merely the substance of any particular article which can do damage or alternatively do good, but it is the manner in which this is handled. The juxtaposition of certain articles can have a good or bad effect.' Mr. van der Byl then went on to give examples of material and presentation in recent newspaper issues to illustrate his contention.[13]

During the following week the Supplementary Estimates Revenue Vote for the Ministry of Information as a whole was debated in the House. Mr. Fawcett Phillips, M.P. for Hillside (Bulawayo), pointed out that the *Herald* was still leaving blank spaces to indicate where censorship had taken place and queried whether, in view of the recently introduced regulations, this was not flouting the government. He urged the Minister to take over control of the Press. In his reply the Deputy Minister of Information indicated what he considered to be the major reason for censorship. He stated 'if indeed there was to be a separate organ of the Press, as opposed to the present group which owns all of the daily newspapers in this country, then it is highly possible that the bulk of the reasons for censorship would not merely fall away but would never have existed.'[14]

A few days later the South African newspaper, the *Eastern Province Herald*, (owned by a sister company of the Argus Group) commented that for the first time in weeks neither the *Rhodesia Herald* nor the *Bulawayo Chronicle* had had any blank spaces and queried whether the newspapers were winning the censorship war or whether the Rhodesian government was easing its restrictions. It added, however, that the presence of Mr. Selwyn Lloyd in the country might have delayed any action being taken against the newspapers.[15]

On the 18th February in the House, Mr. E. J. Mhlanga, M.P. for Matabeleland South, asked the Minister of Information for details of what his Ministry considered to be unsuitable for publication. The Minister of Information (at that time Mr. J. H. Howman) replied that on general principal it would 'include matter which in the opinion of the censorship officer is a) likely to undermine the actions of the Government; b) might create alarm and despondency; c) might lead to contraventions of the law or a breach of law and order; d) divulge any industrial, commercial or financial dealings or undertakings with other countries which the Government, for obvious reasons, wishes to keep confidential; e) might endanger the security of the state.'[16]

In late June the Leader of the Opposition, Mr. C. M. Chipunza, M.P. for Bindura, asked (during a motion for adjournment of the House) whether reports of parliamentary debates were censored. The Minister of Information replied that he could not accept that reports of proceedings in *Hansard* could be freely reported in the Press. He assured his listeners, however, that 'we do not censor any article or anything said in this House except in what we believe to be the national interests of this House and of the country at large.'[17]

In mid-July 1967 the Censorship and Entertainments Control Bill received its Second Reading in Parliament. The Minister of Internal Affairs (then Mr. W. J. Harper) explained that the Bill was before the House 'for one reason only, because the Government believes implicitly in the right of society to protect itself and because we are tenacious of our inheritance, our customs, our way of life and our power for good.' He further enlightened his listeners by elucidating that the proposed legislation was to control pornography and material prejudicial to security which appeared in magazines, films, plays and broadcast material. He said that as far as control of the Press went this was dealt with by the Ministry of Information and therefore did not come within the scope of the Bill. [18]

The lifting of the emergency regulations regarding censorship was announced by the Prime Minister on the 7th April 1968. The *Herald*, which had kept up its policy of blank spaces and front-page box to indicate that it had been censored, welcomed the news and commented that the conditions for keeping Rhodesians 'properly informed have now returned—it is to be hoped permanently.' It placed on record that it 'and its associate newspapers [had always] sought to operate as though censorship did not exist' and pointed out that 'when full instead of token white spaces were used this was indicative of the importance of the news which was being withheld.' The editorial also drew attention to the fact that the 'need for a degree of self-imposed Press censorship had always been accepted ... [for] Rhodesia's needs must come before Government, party or Press. Matters affecting national security or trading against sanctions have always been carefully examined to discover whether publication would be harmful to the country's interests.' [19]

Towards the end of 1972 the Rhodesian Press was mentioned in the annual report of the Director of the International Press Institute in Switzerland. The report, quoted in the *Herald,* said that 'the feud between the Rhodesian Press and the Government has erupted with new bitterness after a period of neutrality ... the Press maintains that [censorship which] started as a security network ... has broadened to cover incompetence within the Government. The chief target of the Press has been the Ministry of Information ... the Government has counter-attacked, saying the Press is sowing seeds of distrust and suspicion and has accused it of misrepresentation, distortion, lying and working hand-in-glove with the country's "enemies". In an article by Richard Peel, the English-language editor at the International Press Institute, however, the position of the Press in Rhodesia was discussed in a wider context. He wrote that read in isolation 'the report of the Press in Rhodesia may seem grave for the Press. Read in the context of reports of declining press prestige elsewhere in the world, its position in Rhodesia is seen as the almost normal, almost healthy, Press-Government friction which is part of the normal working of democracy.' The writer explains the use of the word 'almost' as being 'because it is clear that under the emergency regulations the threat of renewed censorship or other moves to control the views of the media still remain.' The writer then discussed the reported position of the Press in many other countries and concluded that in Rhodesia 'Press freedom, though restricted here and there, is not lessening, and the position is not deteriorating at the moment.'[20]

In April 1973 a *Sunday Mail* reporter discussed the Annual Congress of the Rhodesian Guild of Journalists and the address by the Guild's president, in which he had mentioned that during the last ten years at least 58 journalists had been declared prohibited immigrants by the government. The Guild's president considered that the basic trouble in Government-Press relations was suspicion and cited the recent trial of Peter Niesewand, which had made most journalists wary. He said that he thought that most journalists recognized the need for 'at least some of the extraordinary powers the Government has given itself in both the security and sanctions fields' but were critical of the way the regulations were implemented.[21]

THE RHODESIAN FRONT AND THE ARGUS PRESS

During the Rhodesian Front Annual Congress in 1972 the R.F. chairman, Mr. D. Frost, called for the nationalization of the press. He was quoted as saying that in his opinion 'few people believe them [the newspapers] when they refer to internal policies—knowing their intention is the downfall of our present Government. With Government control the same lack of belief will continue ... So we will have lost nothing in the process but Rhodesia will have benefited immensely by the fact that liberalism will not be pushed down our throats day after day.'

This led the *Financial Gazette* to comment that this idea was still-born for it was a suggestion bound to be turned down by the government 'as it would do it far more harm internationally than any other move it could possibly make.' Later in the year, at a radio and television press conference, the Prime Minister gave his views on the 'Argus Press' and said that while he did not agree that the press should be nationalized he would like to see some kind of 'watch-dog' association which would ensure the press told 'nothing but the truth'. [22]

Speaking in the debate on the President's speech at the opening of Parliament in June 1973 Mr. J. P. B. Nilson, M.P. for Jameson, argued that the Argus Press had, ever since the R.F. government had first been elected, 'done everything in its power to discredit and depose this Government.' He considered that the editorial policy and the philosophy of the Argus Press did not reflect Rhodesian thinking and that it was 'more aligned to that of the United Nations, the Organization for African Unity and other leftist extreme governments of the world.' He saw the results of the Victoria by-election as proving that the Rhodesian electorate could not be moved or influenced by the Argus Group and asked who this Group was operating against and what the reasons were for 'this continual vindictive vendetta'. Mr. Nilson considered that the situation had deteriorated alarmingly and urged the government 'to take the strongest possible steps before it is too late, the future of Rhodesia is at stake and not the freedom of the press [which is] in our case ... but a parrot cry to cover a sinister anti-Rhodesian movement.' A few days later, during the renewed debate, Mr. J. A. Newington, M.P. for Hillcrest (Bulawayo), came to the defence of Mr. Nilson, who had been criticized for his ideas on the Press by the *Herald,* and appealed to what he called 'the top brass' of the local press to 'help fight Rhodesia's battles rather than attacking ... from the rear.' [23]

THE PRESS AND THE PEARCE COMMISSION

During 1972 the Minister of Internal Affairs, Mr. L. B. Smith, opened the Senate debate on the Pearce Commission report. He said that he and his Ministry had been accused of being out of touch with the African people, particularly those from the rural areas, but he felt that most of the accusations on this score had

come from 'areas hostile to the Government, and more unfortunately still, from political opportunists anxious to use the time that
the Pearce Commission was in the country to advance their own
cause and try and embarrass the Government.' He spoke particularly of the Argus Group of newspapers circulating in Rhodesia
'all of whom did their utmost to create mistrust of Government
in the minds of the African people whilst genuinely, no doubt,
supporting the principles set out in the Settlement Proposals.'[24]
The *Herald*, however, denied the Minister's charges and stated
that it considered that during the Pearce Commission's visit 'we
leant over backwards to present all points of view.'

MOTO

Early in June 1972 the offices of *Moto*, the weekly newspaper published by the Roman Catholic Mambo Press for African readers,
were visited by the police as 'a routine part of investigations for
possible contraventions of the law.' In September the Board of
Censors banned the whole of the edition for the week beginning
August 26. The newspaper's editor, Mr. Justin Nyoka, was quoted
as saying that he knew of no reason for the ban particularly as
the announcement of the banning had appeared in the *Government
Gazette* after all copies of the edition had been sold.[25]

In October it was announced that *Moto's* Managing Editor,
Father A. B. Plannger, would appear in Salisbury's Regional Court
in connection with allegations of contravening the Law and Order
(Maintenance) Act in that he caused to be published a subversive
statement. The alleged subversive passages were contained in an
article by Bishop Donal R. Lamont, the R. C. Bishop of Umtali,
which appeared in the August 5th edition of the newspaper. Father
Plannger was eventually found guilty and sentenced to five months
gaol conditionally suspended for three years.[26]

During late February and March 1973 an appeal by Father
Plannger against his conviction and sentence was heard by Mr.
Justice Macdonald, the Acting Chief Justice, and Mr. Justice
Lewis, the Acting Judge President. The basis of the appeal was
a proviso in the Law and Order (Maintenance) Act which deals
with statements made fairly, temperately and in good faith without
corrupt or improper motives. The appeal was, however, dismissed

by the Appeal Court, both judges confirming the conviction and sentence. [27] Mr. Justice Macdonald was later criticized in an article in the *Sunday Mail* by Henry Maasdorp who quoted the Acting Chief Justice as saying, when commenting upon the alleged subversive article, that what this country was short of 'is not destructive criticisms based on problems which admittedly exist, but concrete and practical proposals for their solution ... To harp on the known problems without offering concrete and practical solutions to them can only exacerbate the situation.' Henry Maasdorp considered that had the Acting Chief Justice 'been enunciating a general principle to be applied at all places and at all times the remarks quoted would clearly have been open to question. If everybody who wanted to protest against a felt wrong were limited by necessity to offer concrete and practical solutions in the same breath, there would be few protests and many wrongs would have to be suffered in silence.' [28]

GOVERNMENT NEWS SHEETS

The Ministry of Information publishes two news sheets, available free to members of the public: *The African Times*, which is mainly directed towards readers in the tribal areas and is printed in English, Shona and Ndebele; and the *Rhodesian Commentary* which is printed in English, Afrikaans, French, German, Italian and Portuguese.

During the Senate debate on the 1973 Presidential speech, Senator Dr. O. H. Robertson spoke of the need 'to use every means at our disposal to publicize to our own African population what Government is doing and what they intend to do for them in the future, and indeed in the near future.' She continued by saying that it was in this field that failure had come for she believed that it was 'tragically true that the massive weight of the local press is used to misrepresent both the motives and aims of Government, ... there is not nearly enough vigorous counter-propaganda.' Senator Lever, later in the debate, also referred to the need for 'disseminating the true information to the masses', which he considered was not being pursued with sufficient intensity. For his part, the Minister of Information found that the speeches of the two Senators caused him 'grievous and deep disappointment', for he found it difficult to understand why such 'eminent and knowledgeable persons' as the two Senators 'should be so ignorant of the efforts which have been made by Government at all times, and most importantly, over the last eight years in keeping the African population informed of all these developments.' He said that he considered that the African population had never before been better served by the news media and went on to say that the *African Times* 'probably enjoys the highest circulation of any paper in southern Africa—almost 400 000 per issue. This newspaper is aimed at providing the African people with factual information and keeps them informed of what Government has done, is doing and intends to do in the future ... The readership is calculated to be in excess of one million per issue. It will be difficult to visualize how much more massive this particular effort could possibly be.'[29]

THE RHODESIA BROADCASTING CORPORATION AND RHODESIA TELEVISION

During 1970 the Minister of Justice, Law and Order stated in the House of Assembly that the Rhodesia Broadcasting Corporation (R.B.C.) is 'subject to censorship and control of what is published.'[30] In May 1973, Mr. C. A. R. Savory (M.P. for Matobo and founder-member of the Rhodesia Party), speaking at a party meeting in a Salisbury suburb, accused the government of misusing T.V. and radio and, in a list of 'musts' for the safety of Rhodesia's future, stipulated that radio and television should be taken out of the hands of party politics and placed in the hands of private enterprise.[31] A few days later it was announced that Mr. Savory had accepted a challenge from the chairman of the Board of Governors of the R.B.C., Mr. J. M. Helliwell, to produce evidence of party political control of the broadcasting media. Mr. Helliwell had rejected Mr. Savory's allegations earlier in a broadcast statement during which he stated that there was no control whatever by any political party. In reply to Mr. Helliwell Mr. Savory said that the only way he could take up Mr. Helliwell's challenge would be 'of course, to call in Parliament for a full and politically impartial commission of enquiry into our national broadcasting service.' At the end of June, Mr. Ken Marshall (chairman of the Highlands North (Salisbury) branch of the Rhodesia Party), in a talk to the Rhodesia National Affairs Association, supported Mr. Savory's call for a public enquiry into the control of radio, television and the press. [32] Rhodesian television, although a private limited company (with the Rhodesian Printing and Publishing Company as a major shareholder) is associated with the R.B.C. in the provision of news services.

THE RHODESIAN FINANCIAL GAZETTE

In early 1970 a South African newspaper publishing group started publication of the *Rhodesian Financial Gazette*. From the beginning the company had said that this venture must eventually be locally owned and controlled and in mid-August 1972 the *Financial Gazette* announced that control of the newspaper had passed into Rhodesian control headed by Senator W. R. Whaley as chairman. It was reported that this move had been at the request 'of several prominent and influential Rhodesians who were perturbed at the way in which the monopolistic Argus Press was going about its job of handling news and influencing opinion.' [33]

DETENTION OF PETER NIESEWAND

In mid-February 1973 it was announced that a Salisbury free-lance journalist, Mr. Peter Niesewand, had been detained under section 16 of the Emergency Powers (Maintenance of Law and Order) Regulations. The *Herald* noted that, as is customary, no reason for his detention had been given other than the widely embracing formula of the detention order. It reminded its readers that, although detention without trial took place in other countries confronted with an emergency, this did not reduce the need to use powers of detention only as a last resort in compelling circumstances. It questioned whether this test had been applied in this particular instance and warned that 'most of the world will look upon the detention as an example of harassment by the Rhodesian Government of its critics.' [34]

Considerable reaction to the detention was reported in the overseas press and protests were received from the Commonwealth Press Union, the International Press Institute, the South African Society of Journalists, the National Union of Journalists and the Institute of Journalists, both of London. Within Rhodesia a delegation of members of the Rhodesian Guild of Journalists had a meeting with the Minister of Justice.

On the 9th March Mr. Niesewand appeared in the Salisbury Regional Court on a charge of contravening Section 3 (a) (ii) or alternatively Section 4 (2) of the Official Secrets Act.[35] He was remanded until later in the month after the Director of Public Prosecutions, Mr. B. Treacy, Q.C., had handed to the court the authority of the Attorney-General authorizing prosecution of the charges and, on behalf of the State, applying for an order (in terms of Section 403A of the Criminal Procedure and Evidence Act) that the trial be held in camera 'in the interests of State security and because of the secret information which is alleged to be involved in this case.'

Mr. Treacy listed other prohibitions which came under Section 403A and reminded the magistrate that if the order were granted it would affect publication of any particulars contained in the indictment. Having decided to grant the order the magistrate summed up his reasons, stating that 'Naturally the Court abhors holding proceedings in camera. But it is quite clear from the schedule that these particulars refer to defence matters ... on the face of it, it does appear that it is in the interests of the defence of the country that the proceedings be held in camera ... and that the whole proceedings, apart from limited exceptions, should not be published.' The *Herald* asked its readers to consider what the Director of Public Prosecutions had said with regard to the importance of State security, for it considered that although 'it is an argument Rhodesians are in a mood to accept, ... we would urge them to ponder over its deeper implications long and earnestly. For while State security is being protected, is not a blow being struck at the security of the individual which rests so importantly on justice that is seen to be done?'[36] Mr. Niesewand, who was also being detained under the Emergency Powers regulations on charges unrelated to those under the Official Secrets Act, had already appealed to the Minister of Justice, as he was entitled to do, for the Minister's personal re-consideration of the detention order and had lodged an appeal to be brought before the Detainees' Review Tribunal.

The trial of charges under the Official Secrets Act, to both of which counts Mr. Niesewand pleaded not guilty, took place on the 19th and 20th March. The Press was not present at any time during the proceedings. Judgement and sentence were eventually delivered on 6th April. The accused was found guilty of the first indictment (under Section 3 (a) (ii)) of the Official Secrets Act and was sentenced to two years' hard labour of which (because he had acted openly and not in secret) 12 months was suspended for three years under certain conditions.[37] An appeal was lodged as soon as the transcript of the trial became available.

Following wide-spread international criticism and protest, especially from Britain, the Ministry of Information issued a statement declining to comment on the merits of such criticism because of the impending appeal which made the case *sub judice*. It pointed out that in Britain and elsewhere proceedings under the Official Secrets Act were frequently held in camera and stated that 'Although by virtue of the order of the Court members of the public were excluded from the trial, Mr. Niesewand and the legal representatives of his choice were in Court for the entire proceedings.'[38] According to an edited version of the judgement in the Regional Court (which was later released by an order of the Appeal Court) the charges were concerned with the contents of three dispatches, intended for publication in overseas newspapers, which related to guerilla operations and also to operations of the Rhodesian military and air forces.

The Appeal was heard on the 27th April before Sir Hugh Beadle, the Chief Justice, Mr. Justice Macdonald, the Judge President, and Mr. Justice Goldin, the Acting Judge of Appeal. When the court opened the public and press were allowed in; the appellant, however, was not present. At the start of the hearing the Chief Justice announced that the Court would release an edited version of the judgement in the lower court. Later in the morning, however, a certificate signed by the Minister of Justice was received. This stated that the Minister considered that it would not be in the public interest for public disclosure of the appeal proceedings except in respect of those matters which the Court and Counsel had agreed could be published. Following receipt of this certificate the hearing continued in closed session.

At the end of the hearing a judgement of several thousand words, dealing exclusively with the legal points involved, was handed down by the Chief Justice, who concluded by stating that the Court was satisfied that it had not been shown that what Niesewand had published was in fact prejudicial to the interests or safety of Rhodesia, and as the appellant had been found not guilty on the alternative charge, the appeal was allowed and the previous verdict and sentence set aside. [39] Following this judgement the Minister of Justice and of Law and Order announced that he would re-examine the question of Mr. Niesewand's continued detention. The following day Mr. Niesewand left for London and the Ministry of Information issued a statement explaining that his detention order had not been revoked for it was still expedient that he should not be released within Rhodesia. His presence outside the country, however, was not considered likely to be detrimental to the interests of the country. According to the Press Mr. Niesewand gave a brief interview on his arrival in London during which he stated that he had been released from detention after signing a document agreeing to leave Rhodesia immediately; not to write or disclose information on Rhodesian military matters; and agreeing to say nothing of his recent trial under the Official Secrets Act other than what could be said inside Rhodesia. [40]

Within Rhodesia, the *Herald* wrote that it was not surprising that Mr. Niesewand had decided to leave Rhodesia and commented that there were 'many disturbing loose ends about the whole affair, not the least of which is the reason for the detention order in the first place.' The *Herald* noted that when releasing Mr. Niesewand the Minister of Justice had maintained that the reasons for not releasing him in Rhodesia were not directly connected with the recent charges under the Official Secrets Act and it asked what these charges actually were. The newspaper concluded that 'the concern caused by the circumstances of the whole case serves to highlight concern for the rights of all.' The *Sunday Mail* considered that the whole affair was 'a sad episode' in Rhodesian history and that 'We can only hope that the consequences of this incident will give the authorities pause for serious thought in future.' *Moto* confined itself to strict reporting on the outcome of the trial but printed a letter from a reader signing himself '*Always in Trouble*'. This letter outlined the reasons why the writer found it amazing that people in Britain had shown so much concern over the Niesewand case when 'there are many Rhodesian Africans lamenting in detentions and prisons without trial.'[41]

NOTES

1 The term *Rhodesia* was not officially recognized by the British Government until 1897. It had, however, first appeared in the *Cape Argus* in 1891 and was in common usage. The Editor of the *Rhodesia Herald,* explaining the use of the term, said that it had been adopted for the newspaper because the term Mashonaland did not properly apply to Manicaland, nor to the low veldt in the west. Neither did it describe the huge new territory to the north of the Zambezi recently come under the B.S.A. Company control. Since Mr. Rhodes had made possible the founding and the rapid development of the country it was 'deemed right and proper to make the title at once more representative and euphonious'.

2 Not to be confused with the present-day Rhodesian Printing and Publishing Company which was founded in 1927.
The *Umtali Post* appears three times a week.

3 1962: Gale, W.D.: *The Rhodesian Press : The history of the Rhodesian Printing and Publishing Company Ltd. :* Salisbury: Rhodesian Printing and Publishing Co. Ltd.

4 1966: Lardner-Burke, D.W.: *Rhodesia : the story of the crisis :* London: Oldbourne.

5 *Rhodesian Government Notice* No. 736, 6 November 1965.
The emergency regulations empowered the Commissioner of Police to appoint 'protecting authorities' to be in charge of specified areas of the country.

6 *R.H.* 12 November 1965.

7 *Hansard : Parliamentary Debates :* Vol. 63, 2 February 1966: Col. 43.

8 As reported in *R.H.* 15, 28 January 1966.

9 *R.H.* 18 January 1966.

10 *R.H.* 5 February 1966.

11 *Rhodesian Government Notice No. 61,* 5 February 1966.

12 *R.H.* 9 February 1966.

13 *Hansard : Parliamentary Debates :* Vol. 63. 4 February 1966: Cols. 223-48.

14 *Hansard : Parliamentary Debates :* Vol. 63. 10 February 1966: Cols. 430-1.

15 *Eastern Province Herald* (Port Elizabeth) 16 February 1966.

16 *Hansard : Parliamentary Debates :* Vol. 63. 18 February 1966: Cols. 717-8.

17 *Hansard: Parliamentary Debates:* Vol. 64. 30 June 1966: Cols. 363-4.
18 *Hansard: Parliamentary Debates:* Vol. 68. 20 July 1967: Cols. 6-34.
19 *R.H.* 8 April 1968.
20 *R.H.* 3 January 1973.
21 *S.M.* 1 April 1973.
22 *R.H.* and *R.F.G.* 22 December 1972.
23 *Hansard:* Vol. 84, Nos. 2, 5. 19, 22 June 1973: Cols. 72-6, 297-301.
24 *Hansard: Senate Debates:* Vol. 3, No. 5. 13 June 1972: Cols. 108-11.
25 *S.M.* 3 September 1972.
26 *R.H.* 16 November 1972.
27 *R.H.* 28 February, 24 March 1973.
28 Henry Maasdorp: *What is the Way to Right a Wrong?* in *S.M.* 1 April 1973.
29 *Hansard: Senate Debates:* Vol. 4, Nos. 2, 3, 5. 19, 20, 28 June 1973: Cols. 19, 53, 134-6.
30 *Hansard:* Vol. 76. 10 February 1970: Col. 2031.
31 As reported in *R.H.* 25 May 1973.
32 *S.M.* 27 May, *R.H.* 30 June 1973.
33 *R.F.G.* 18 August 1972.
34 *R.H.* 21 February 1973.
35 The Official Secrets Act No. 16 of 1970 makes it an offence in *Section 3* for

Any person who for any purpose prejudicial to the safety or interests of Rhodesia:—

    (a) approaches, inspects, passes over or is in the vicinity of or enters any prohibited place;

    (b) obtains, collects, records, publishes or communicates to any person—

        (ii) any model, article, document or other information which is calculated to be or which might or is intended to be useful directly or indirectly to an enemy.

        (An enemy is defined as including a hostile organization).

Section 4 (2) for any person who

    (a) has in his possession or under his control any model, article, document or information which relates to:—

        (i) munitions of war or other military matter: or

        (ii) the preservation of the security of Rhodesia, the maintenance of law and order by the British South Africa Police or any other body or organization appointed by the Government for the purpose of assisting in the preservation of the security of Rhodesia;

and (b) publishes or communicates such model, article, document or information to any person in any manner prejudicial to the safety or interests of Rhodesia.

On the main charge the Act stipulates, on conviction, a prison sentence not exceeding 25 years while on the alternative charge, the stipulation is for a fine, not exceeding $ 20 000 or a prison sentence not exceeding 20 years, or both fine and sentence.

36 *R.H.* 10 March 1973.
37 As reported in *R.H.* 20, 21 March, 7 April 1973.
38 As reported in *R.H.* 10 April 1973.
39 As reported in *R.H.* 2 May 1973.
40 As reported in *R.H.* 5 May 1973.
   Published too late for comment in this Survey—1973 (September):
   Niesewand, Peter: *In Camera : Secret Justice in Rhodesia :* London:
   Weidenfeld and Nicolson.
41 *R.H.* 5 May; *Moto :* Vol. 15, No. 18. 5 May; *S.M.* 6 May 1973.

VII

GUERRILLA WARFARE[1]

The year 1964 in Rhodesia ushered in a struggle between African nationalist political parties accompanied by an intensive campaign of subversion which led to decisive government action to end the lawlessness. It had been claimed previously that the Zimbabwe African Peoples' Union (Z.A.P.U.) had been involved in the infiltration of trained men, arms and ammunition into Rhodesia from its headquarters in Zambia. Z.A.P.U's campaign increased in intensity during the following year, when evidence was found of organized training facilities in Zambia and Ghana with Russian, Chinese, Algerian and Tanzanian instructors. During 1966 there was a further intensification of the campaign, reputedly through the activities of another banned nationalist organization, the Zimbabwe African National Union (Z.A.N.U.) which was sending armed and trained groups of men into Rhodesia on guerrilla assignments.

After a lull early in 1967, activity was again intensified, spurred on by two meetings of the Organization for African Unity (O.A.U.) which, in July, envisaged the sending of three to four thousand guerrillas along four routes aimed at penetration into South Africa. In October the O.A.U. passed a resolution to allocate about half its yearly budget to the support of 'freedom fighters.'

During the first eight months of 1968 it was reported that about 100 guerrillas had been killed and an undisclosed number captured. It was also reported that an arms dump had been destroyed and piles of weapons seized by Rhodesian Security Forces. The *Herald* stated that the aim of the gangs 'which were infiltrating from Zambia ... [was] to ferment a rebellion among the local African population. They are bringing across arms, ammunition and supplies to be hidden and drawn on later when, in theory, enough trained men have crossed over and formed rebel groups around them,

all over the country.' The newspaper added the terse comment
'their record up to date is one of dismal failure.'[2]

At the end of 1968 the Minister of Defence, Mr. J. H. Howman,
reported that since the terrorist incursions from Zambia had
started in 1966 more than 160 terrorists had been killed and a
considerably greater number had surrendered or been captured.
During this period there had been twelve members of the Rhodesian forces killed and thirty wounded.[3]

During 1969 it was reported that there had been no large scale
infiltrations of guerrillas from Zambia. In September it was noted
that Rhodesia had been included, for the first time, in the annual
report of the Institute for Strategic Studies—*The Military Balance*.
The report showed that Rhodesia's spending on defence in 1968/9
was 1.9 *per cent* of the gross national product ... 'Lower than all
but a handful of the 52 nations enumerated.'[4]

In January 1970 the Prime Minister, Mr. Ian Smith, made a
statement in the House on the 'terrorist' incursions from Zambia.
He reminded the House that the government had 'at all times
declared that it has no aggressive intentions towards any other
country.' He instanced as proof of this that Rhodesia had provided
maintenance of essential power and transport services to Zambia
'in spite of that country's provocative behaviour in harbouring
and assisting terrorists.' The Prime Minister said that recently
captured terrorists had provided conclusive evidence that the Zambian authorities were not only well aware of the terrorists' activities
and intentions 'but have actively aided their incursions into Rhodesia.' He continued by stating that 'our policy is to live in amity
and peace with all our neighbours, but I wish to make it clear
that the Rhodesian Government cannot ignore the continuance
of assistance to terrorist incursions into Rhodesia.'[5]

During 1970 there were a number of trials both in regional courts
and in the High Court of guerrillas (two of whom were sentenced
to 18 years' hard labour) and of tribesmen for assisting them.

Early in September the World Council of Churches (W.C.C.)
announced that grants would be made to nineteen organizations,
including the banned Rhodesian African nationalist organizations.
This announcement followed a decision taken in August 1969 to
contribute funds to combat racism. A spokesman for the W.C.C.
stated that it was 'convinced that the $140 000 donated to

oppressed racial groups, including fourteen in Africa, would not be used to buy weapons.'[6]

This action was interpreted variously by different people. The Prime Minister labelled the decision as an attempt by churchmen to overthrow Christianity and substitute paganism in its place —'one cannot help wondering whether the World Council of Churches has given any thought to the violent acts of sheer terrorism perpetrated by those organizations which they choose to call freedom fighters ... Those organizations, they say, are waging war on the racialists of Africa and therefore deserve the support of the Christian Churches. How can they be so blind to the fact that the organizers themselves are the greatest racialists in the world, sworn to drive out or exterminate all races other than their own in Africa?'[7]

The Christian Council of Rhodesia on the other hand, following a meeting attended by about thirty representatives from most of the major denominations, made a statement expressing gratitude for the money which had been given to Rhodesia in the past, for school buildings, relief of the needy and 'extension of Christian work in general'. The statement concluded by saying 'in particular we record our appreciation for the recent gesture of concern for the oppressed people of Rhodesia. We interpret the W.C.C. action as support for the Church's world-wide Christian programme against racism.'[8]

In October it was announced that, at its annual conference, the British Labour Party had unanimously voted to offer 'moral and material' support to the 'liberation' movement in Southern Africa. This statement led the *Herald* to comment that 'nobody should underestimate the fact that the idea of a violent overthrow of white Governments in Southern Africa has been given a kind of political respectability.'[9]

Towards the end of January 1973 the *Herald* correspondent in Geneva reported that the W.C.C's executive committee had made another allocation of U.S. $200 000 to 25 organizations which were 'combating racism on five continents.' The Council stated that slightly more than one half of this money would go to the medical, educational and social service activities of 'liberation movements' in Southern Africa.[10]

At the end of April 1971 three members of the Rhodesian Light Infantry were killed when their vehicle ran over a land-mine while on a routine patrol on the Mozambique-Rhodesian border. The men had crossed into Mozambique for 'friendly contact' with Portuguese forces and had hit the land-mine on their return. This was the first known occasion that Rhodesians had been killed or wounded in a neighbouring territory through guerrilla activity and to assuage public anxiety government sources published a statement explaining that, while Rhodesian and Portuguese authorities co-operate in the exchange of military intelligence, Rhodesian forces were not used on active service in territories outside Rhodesia's border. [11]

In July 1971 three arrests were made when a cache of guerrilla arms and equipment was found stored in a warehouse in Salisbury's light industrial area. According to the subsequent statement of one of the accused at the preliminary hearing in Salisbury Magistrates' Court, he had been contacted by a banned political organization and had received funds to fly to Malawi where a meeting was arranged on the Malawi-Zambian border. There he was asked to assist in the arrangements for road transport of boxes of ammunition from Lusaka. [12]

The following month the press reported dissension within the ranks of Z.A.P.U. and Z.A.N.U. in Lusaka. It was considered that both organizations were racked by tribal rivalry. Earlier in the year the Liberation Committee of the O.A.U. had suspended grants to Z.A.P.U. because of this lack of unity. President Kaunda was reportedly considerably worried about the situation and observers believed that it was the President himself who had recently ordered more than 100 guerrillas to leave Zambia. On the 16th August President Kaunda warned the rival Rhodesian nationalist groups that they would have 'to choose between getting together or defeating Zambia's willingness to accommodate them.' The previous week the Rhodesian Ministry of Information confirmed that a number of Rhodesian Africans from Zambia had been taken into custody by immigration officials at posts on the Zambian-Rhodesian border. [13]

During September the first reported action of Rhodesian troops against Frelimo (Front for the Liberation of Mozambique) guerrillas was announced. Seven members of a band which had crossed the Mozambique border had been killed and one captured. There were more Rhodesian deaths from land-mines on a road in the Tete district and reports of a sharp rise in Frelimo activities in an attempt to halt the building of the Caborra Bassa dam. The following month there was also news of a new anti-Rhodesian guerrilla organization being formed in Lusaka, Frolizi (Front for the Liberation of Zimbabwe), reputedly from a merger of the rival Z.A.P.U., Z.A.N.U. organizations there.[14]

Again during 1971 a number of trials took place and several Africans were sentenced to various terms in jail after being found guilty of offences such as murder, recruitment for guerrilla training and for not reporting the presence of guerrillas in their neighbourhood.

DEVELOPMENTS DURING 1972-73

Early in 1972 another cache of arms was found a few miles from Salisbury. At their trial in the High Court the men who had brought the arms into the country spoke of their training in Tanzania by Chinese instructors and said that they had been briefed by representatives of a banned party to enter Rhodesia to disrupt the work of the Pearce Commission. They had brought the arms over the border by taxi and had later been given a lift by a European woman. The three were sentenced to varying terms of hard labour.[15]

It was reported in May that, according to the Report of the Secretary for Law and Order for 1971, although a number of 'terrorist' agents had crossed into Rhodesia to establish cells for internal subversion, there had been no infiltration of bands of armed 'terrorists' from Zambia. The Secretary, Mr. J. A. C. Fleming, warned, however, that numerous 'terrorists' were undergoing training in Zambia and Tanzania and that there was an increase in 'terrorist' activities in the Tete district of Mozambique together with sabotage of the main road between Rhodesia and Malawi. The Secretary pointed out that this increase in Frelimo activities meant that it would be 'necessary to maintain a watch on the northeastern border—[a] further extension of the areas which require constant supervision.'[16]

On the 16th June, the Minister of Justice and of Law and Order, moved a motion in the House that the State of Emergency be renewed for a further period of twelve months. He gave as his reasons the fact that 'very similar circumstances affecting the security and well-being of Rhodesia exist today as existed 12 months ago,' when he had moved a similar motion. The Minister then went on to say that 'so far as the external threat is concerned, the possibility of infiltration by groups of armed terrorists from across our borders has in no way diminished. Indeed, we know that trained terrorists in considerable numbers are waiting in Zambia. Others are undergoing training elsewhere... There is evidence to suggest that these organizations [the 'terrorist' organizations] have examined the tactics which they have employed in order to find a more efficient means of destroying law and order within Rhodesia. Instead of large bands being sent across the Zambezi it has become the practice to infiltrate intelligence agents and specially selected men with specific instructions ... The pattern now appears to be directed towards stimulating internal subversion with the aid of those dissidents already within the country ... During the year an additional threat to our borders has emerged as a result of increased terrorist activity in the Tete district of Mozambique ... The presence of hostile forces adjacent to our border is a potential threat to the security of this country. This threat is underlined by the statement made by a Frelimo leader in Cairo recently when he stated that Frelimo would be able to assist the Rhodesian terrorist organizations ... The Organization for African Unity appears to have taken on a new lease of life ... Communist aid in the form of arms and money continues to flow via the O.A.U. to the terrorist movements. The World Council of Churches and certain Left-wing organizations in the west and in Scandinavia continue to give moral and financial support.'[17]

A few days later the Minister of Foreign Affairs replied to some of the points raised during the debate on the President's speech. Mr. Howman, who is also Minister of Defence and of Public Service, brought up the question of dialogue with Zambia which had been referred to previously by Mr. W. S. Moraka, M.P. for Matojeni, who considered that 'our first contact should be with Zambia ... we must not be afraid of Zambia. We must go to Zambia and make Zambia understand that the harbouring of the terrorists is not only interference with Rhodesia alone, it is a complete interference with Zambia as well. Let Zambia count their own costs. We get hold of the terrorists. Who are they? Some of them possibly are my brothers. Some of them are men I can talk to. Why don't we go over to Zambia and ask these people to talk to us and finish off this terrorist business? I am getting fed up with it.' The following day Mr. Howman said that he considered Mr. Moraka to be very naive if he imagined that 'Zambia is amenable to reason or to talk or even common decency' when attempts were made to try and persuade them to stop 'acting as a base for those who wish to upset the peaceful development in this country by attempting to kill and maim people. Despite all the assistance and co-operation that has been offered by Rhodesia, the only response we receive from Zambia is the futile and sterile support of terrorism ... any communications addressed to those in authority in Lusaka on matters such as this [the harbouring of "terrorists"] meet with a deafening silence.'[18]

At the end of August a visitor to Mana Pools National Park (which is on the banks of the Zambezi River, the natural boundary between Rhodesia and Zambia) was injured in an explosion. Rhodesian security forces later found this to have been caused by 'a land-mine of a type with which terrorists based in Zambia are known to be equipped.' The Security Force's statement added 'although this represents something new in the field of terrorists' operations against this country, it provides further confirmation that the killing and maiming of civilians is clearly a prime objective.' The government later issued a statement warning Zambia that 'since it is within the scope and the power of the Zambian authorities to prevent terrorists operating from their country, the Rhodesian Government feels it must make it clear beyond all doubt that if the Zambian Government fails to recognize its responsibilities in this matter then the consequences would rest squarely on their shoulders.'[19]

The *Herald*, the next day, considered that this was 'the bluntest warning yet to Zambia' and continued by saying that up to the present time it had 'opposed an escalation of Rhodesia's anti-terrorist campaign and [had] commended the Rhodesian Government for its restraint'. It now had to agree that 'the authorities cannot allow to develop here—and we have no doubt that the Rhodesian Government will not allow—a situation similar to that in Mozambique's Tete Province [for] if that is what the terrorist groups, with Rhodesia as their target, have in mind they are almost certainly in for a rude awakening. Stern and effective action will be demanded; and neither the terrorist groups nor the Zambian Government should have any illusions that Rhodesia will hesitate to take it ... Rhodesia has the means and the resolution to make reprisal painful and effective.'[20]

THE DEFENCE ACT

On the 30th August the Minister of Defence introduced the Second Reading of the Defence Bill and stated that the Bill was to replace and consolidate adapted Federal legislation which was, in certain degrees, no longer applicable and also to incorporate changes proved to be necessary as a result of experience of changed requirements. It transferred the power of 'ordering the employment within or outside of Rhodesia of the whole or any part of the Territorial Force or Reserve' from the President to the Minister of Defence, and also empowered the Minister 'to promote or temporarily appoint officers up to and including the ranks of major and squadron leader, also to place officers on the retired list up to such ranks.' The Bill also gave the Minister power, 'should the need arise', to increase the initial period of continuous training and the total liability for service in the Territorial Force. Mr. M. M. Bhebe, M.P. for Ntshonalanga, found the Bill disappointing as regards Africans, for, as he said, there was only one sentence which indicated that Africans would not be precluded from engaging themselves as volunteers for service in the Defence Force. Mr. Bhebe considered that even though 'there are quite a number of things that may make the white folk uneasy about incorporating Africans into military training ... I think it is time ... that [the government] should start to think seriously about ... conscription of Africans.' The Minister in replying to questions said that military service had never been compulsory for Africans in Rhodesia and that although the African volunteers serving in the African regiments had been a very valuable part of the defence forces it was a matter of conjecture firstly whether people throughout the country, who did not have a tradition of military service, would welcome such a move. Secondly, it would be impossible to undertake the necessary training for 'to introduce compulsory service would dissipate the funds and dissipate the services and would be highly unwise', the Minister concluded, and added that if Mr. Bhebe would like to pursue the subject he would welcome a private discussion with him.[21]

THE UNITED NATIONS

In September the United Nations General Assembly passed (by 66 votes to 27, with 33 abstentions) a motion calling for 'measures to prevent international terrorism which endangers or takes human lives or jeopardizes fundamental freedom.' The *Herald* thought that 'it would be too much to term it [the U.N. Resolution] a victory against extremism. But the decision to debate terrorism in the United Nations General Assembly against the wishes of most African countries does show there is a limit to giving in ... the fact remains that the world body will now have to debate terror tactics in a climate in which there is a growing revulsion against terrorism.'[22] At the end of September the General Assembly's Fourth Committee, which deals with trusteeship and non-self-governing territories, voted to seat members of African 'liberation' movements as observers when the committee dealt with questions on Rhodesia (among other territories). Representation was expected to go to one, or a combination, of the three banned nationalist groups.[23] In November it was reported that the United Nations, (in a report prepared by its Secretariat as a guide on current General Assembly moves to formulate anti-terrorism measures) 'has given the African insurgent movements further assurances that they will be excluded from any measures taken by the U.N. to curb terrorism ... for the report specifically divorces from the terrorism issue the 'legitimate' use of force by any national liberation movement.'[24]

During April 1973 the United Nations held a conference on apartheid in Oslo organized in co-operation with the O.A.U. It was reported that nine organizations (from South Africa, South West Africa, Rhodesia and the Portuguese overseas territories) attended, together with officially accredited ambassadors to the U.N. from many member countries. In accordance with its terms of reference, the meeting was called to look for peaceful ways of ending apartheid and colonialization, but certain African nationalist groups were reported to have made it clear 'both publicly and privately, to nations who supply a good deal of their humanitarian aid, that their most crying need is for arms and logistic support.' The final report, made to the U.N's Secretary-General, backed the call for arms as well as for other support.[25]

RENEWAL OF GUERRILLA ACTIVITY 1972-73

At the beginning of December 1972, following an announcement that the Prime Minister would hold a press interview, it was surmised that this was in response to numerous calls on the government to improve its relations with the press and to give more information to the public. It was also thought likely that the interview would give the Prime Minister the opportunity of informing members of the public of the government's case for introducing legislation which had been considered as apparently in conflict with his appeal, at the recent Rhodesian Front Party congress, for an end to petty racialism. In the event, however, much of the Prime Minister's broadcast was a warning on the dangers of becoming too complacent over the 'terrorist' problem. The next day, in what the *Herald* called 'dramatic emphasis' on the Prime Minister's warning, it was announced that several guerrilla infiltrators had been killed and captured together with a considerable quantity of arms and ammunition of Communist origin. This statement by the Rhodesian Security Force headquarters was the first report of guerrilla activity inside Rhodesia since August 1971 when seven Frelimo guerrillas were killed by Rhodesian troops. The *Herald* considered that 'it was clear that this was no hit and run raid. The terrorists were said to have crossed into Rhodesia to establish bases and arms caches and to preach subversion.' The newspaper added its warning to that of the Prime Minister—'Rhodesians must be prepared for more crossings.'[26]

On the 15th December the Minister of Defence announced that National Service training was to be increased from 245 to 365 days. The Minister had warned about this eventuality when introducing the new Defence Bill in August. It was noted, however, that the area over which the armed forces had to keep watch had increased, for 'until a year or so ago it was, roughly speaking, the Zambezi, but now it is known that there are elements of terrorist organizations in Botswana along our western border and, of course, in the Tete province of Mozambique on our north-eastern border. In other words it is half-way round Rhodesia.'[27]

During Christmas week a group of armed guerrillas attacked a farm and an African trading post in the Mulingura Hills in the Centenary area (65 km. from the Mozambique border and about 240 km. from Salisbury). At the farm the only casualty was an eight-year old girl who received gunshot wounds in the foot. The nearby African trading post was looted and set on fire. Security forces, together with Portuguese forces on the border, later killed two guerrillas. All Army and Air Force leave was cancelled and police reservists in Salisbury were placed on stand-by during the Christmas period.

On the 22nd December guerrillas attacked another farm in Centenary. The owner of the farm, which had been attacked two days previously, had, with his family, taken refuge there and in this new raid he received numerous shrapnel wounds in his legs while his nine-year old daughter received a large gunshot wound in her stomach. During this raid the attackers set fire to six neighbouring African huts, but the occupants escaped without injury. Later, during the morning of 22/23 December a patrolling army vehicle struck a concealed land-mine near the farm and its four occupants were severely injured, one of them, Corporal N. D. R. Moore, dying from his wounds a few days later.[28]

Following these attacks it was announced that the Security forces had killed and captured a number of guerrillas without casualties to themselves and that intensive operations were being conducted on the north-eastern border by a joint operational command of police, army and air force, with African troops taking a full part in the activities.[29]

THE RHODESIAN SECURITY FORCES

Early in the New Year 1973, three more Rhodesian servicemen were slightly wounded in a land-mine explosion. Security Force headquarters reported that during continuing operations further arrests of guerrillas had been effected and that arms and a quantity of offensive material of Communist origin, including mines, had been captured. In an interview with the *Financial Gazette*, the Minister of Defence summed up the situation on the north-east border area. He stressed that the situation was being contained and that there was no evidence that guerrillas were spreading south-westwards into a more populated area. Regarding the attitude of the local African population, Mr. Howman pointed out that 'when there is an armed African terrorist sitting outside the door, there's an initial hesitation. That could happen to anyone. But after that we have had good co-operation.'[30]

In an article in the *Herald*, by Ian Mills, senior security officials were quoted as making it plain that it would be a lengthy operation to clear the north-eastern area. All the signs showed that the guerrillas had adopted a different approach from that used previously. They had two main aims: to subvert the local African population and to avoid direct confrontation with Security Forces. Up to date the guerrilla operations had been well planned, for there were indications that there had been a slow build-up of arms and ammunition and, in the opinion of Security officers, the rocket attacks on the two European farms during the latter part of 1972, which had had little or no strategic value, had been made to impress local Africans. The north-east area from the Zambezi River border consists of an 80 km. wide strip of Tribal Trust Land stretching along a 300 km. front which then gives way to a rugged escarpment (offering countless hiding places for guerrillas) before the first European farm settlements are encountered.[31]

The South African news-magazine *To The Point* summed up the position in mid-January, when it noted that the renewed guerrilla activity followed a two-year build-up and that the Lusaka-based guerrilla organizations appeared to have opened a new front by using Mozambique as a staging point for attacks on Rhodesia. The magazine pointed out that by using Mozambique, which has a more favourable terrain than the Zambezi Valley, the guerrillas would be able to make use of stores and camps established by Frelimo and would also spread the Rhodesian forces as thinly as possible along the entire northern border.[32]

In mid-January Security Force headquarters mounted an operation to clear the Mount Darwin area (to the east of the Centenary area) of guerrillas. After nearly a week fourteen guerrillas were reported to have been killed and an undisclosed number wounded. Large quantities of offensive material and weapons 'almost exclusively of Communist origin' were impounded, in some instances as a result of the 'increasing tendency of local tribesmen to impart information.'[33]

In February, operations moved once again to the Centenary area when a European farm was attacked, resulting in the death of a European woman (see p. 241). Security Force headquarters reported the killing and wounding of a number of guerrillas belonging to the same gang which had been responsible for the attacks on European farms during the preceding two months. The report also stated that information from local tribesmen had resulted in the arrest of 31 guerrillas or people who had assisted the gangs. A few days later headquarters issued another communiqué announcing that members of this gang had been almost all killed or captured together with large quantities of arms and offensive material. One member of the Security Forces was killed and another slightly wounded during these operations.[34] Later in the month a member of the Security Force was killed and six others injured from a land-mine explosion in the Centenary area.

In late March the killing of a young European farmer and an African baby in the Wedza district (see p. 243) precipitated an extensive search for a gang of 4 men. Security Forces killed one of the gang and wounded another. In April, what was described as the heaviest Rhodesian loss in an engagement since the beginning of the guerrilla attacks in late 1972, was reported by Security headquarters. One African and three European soldiers were killed and five European soldiers and an African civilian were seriously wounded in an ambush by guerrillas in the north-eastern border area. During the engagement 3 guerrillas were killed and an undisclosed number captured. The remainder of the guerrilla band slipped back across the border. According to the *Financial Gazette* these incidents, together with an action involving South African police in the Caprivi Strip, suggested 'a new, and potentially dangerous, development in the terrorist campaign in Southern Africa.' The newspaper outlined three factors which it considered underlined the 'serious and changed situation'. The scale of casualties; the change in tactics—'infiltration, with supporting arms, replaced by deliberately provocative hit-and-run raids'; and 'the possibility that the two attacks were co-ordinated by terrorist headquarters in Zambia.' The newspaper considered that the 'enigma in the present situation is why the terrorists have changed their tactics? and what role President Kaunda is playing in the new scheme?' and warned that in such a delicate, changed situation cool heads were demanded.[35]

In early June guerrillas abducted two African policemen on patrol on the north-eastern border, the first time that security force personnel had been abducted (see Guerrilla Attacks on Civilians). Later in June police shot and severely wounded a guerrilla fighter who had fled when an African-owned bus was being searched in Enkeldoorn. A box containing firearms, ammunition, grenades and a mine were also found on the bus. This was the first time, during the current guerrilla activities, that a shooting incident with guerrillas had taken place in an urban area. [36]

SOUTH AFRICAN POLICE ACTION

On the 8th January a land-mine was detonated by a South African police vehicle. Two of its occupants were killed and five were wounded. At the scene of the explosion, close to the Zambezi River border with Zambia at the Victoria Falls, pamphlets were found which, according to the statement from the Security Forces, emanated from a terrorist organization operating from within Zambia. During the remainder of January South African police were involved in an action when guerrillas attacked a police post, and later a patrol on the Zambezi border. Six policemen were wounded. South Africa's deputy Minister of Police, commenting upon this action, said that he believed that this was the first time that guerrillas had attempted an attack on a South African police post. He did not agree that the attack was necessarily an escalation of guerrilla activity but regarded it as a sign that the guerrillas were using new tactics. [37]

Towards the end of April, during the Easter holidays and at the same time that Rhodesian Security Forces suffered their greatest number of casualties since the beginning of the renewed activities, a South African police foot patrol was ambushed in the Caprivi Strip. According to the South African Minister of Police, an ambush was set up by a group of guerrillas from over the Zambian border and when the first 7 members of the police patrol, accompanied by a locally employed tracker, were in the area of ambush they were fired upon with heavy and sub-machine guns. The tracker and four African policemen were killed and subsequently the guerrillas returned across the border. [38] The Zambian Foreign Minister later denied that the 'freedom fighters' had been from Zambia.

GUERRILLA ATTACKS ON CIVILIANS DURING 1973

On the 8th January 1973 a band of guerrillas attacked the village of Mount Darwin, 160 km. north of Salisbury, but succeeded only in damaging a bridge to the south of the village. According to a résumé of guerrilla attacks in the *Herald,* the Rhodesian closure of the common border with Zambia (which took place on the 9th January) was a result of five months of 'hit-and-run raids' accompanied by 'provocative claims by banned organizations installed in Zambia' that they had been responsible for the ensuing deaths and injuries. [39]

A few days later the murder of two government land inspectors and the disappearence of another, Mr. G. Hawkesworth, in the Mount Darwin forest area was announced. Reporting this action, Security Force headquarters stated that an active investigation was being carried out but the possibility of 'terrorist' action could not be ruled out. [40] In early February, the national chairman of the banned Z.A.N.U. party, Herbert Chitepo, was quoted from Arusha (Tanzania) as stating that Mr. Hawkesworth was a 'prisoner-of-war' in the hands of Z.A.N.U. guerrillas in Mozambique. [41] As Mr. Hawkesworth holds a British passport the British Foreign Office took up investigations into his whereabouts and in May it was reported that unsuccessful approaches had been made to the Zambian, Tanzanian and Portuguese governments as it was considered likely that the missing man was being held in one of these territories. [42]

In February another European farm in the Centenary area was attacked by guerrillas who were armed with hand-grenades, small arms and plastic explosives. The farmer, Mr. J. C. Kleynhans, was wounded and his wife was killed, making her the first European civilian to be killed in an attack upon a farm since June 1966. This murder led to more than 100 farmers in the area signing a petition calling upon the government to close down a German Jesuit Mission—St. Albert's Mission, 40 km. north-east of Centenary, on the edge of the Mzarabane Tribal Trust Land—on the grounds that the mission was a threat to security. A guerrilla band had apparently been found close to the mission and local farmers, knowing of the missionaries' fluent knowledge of the local language and close contact with local Africans, found it difficult to believe that the missionaries had not known of guerrilla activities in the area. Father E. Rojek, the Superior, however, denied all knowledge of the guerrilla base, which had not been found on mission land and said that neither the missionaries nor the people who worked, came to school or attended the hospital at the mission were involved nor did they intend to become involved with them.[43]

Shortly afterwards, in an interview with the *Financial Gazette*, the Minister of Justice and of Law and Order was quoted as saying that he had proof that guerrillas were 'operating like the Mau Mau, working on farms in the day and becoming terrorists at night.'[44] Mr. Lardner-Burke, however, later denied that he had said this and, commenting upon the attack on the Kleynhans' farm, said that he considered that the attack had been a show of arrogance, for a police camp was situated only about 2 km. from the farm.

On the 1st February guerrillas attacked an African store on a European farm in the same area with machine guns and grenades. The African escaped unharmed. Later, in the same week, another farm attack was made and the elderly father of the European farm manager (on holiday from Britain) was killed. Towards the end of the month another farmer, driving home from work, had a narrow escape when shrapnel from an exploding grenade smashed against the windscreen of his car. The following morning security men found the dead body of a guerrilla at the scene of the incident.

In early March guerrillas attacked and severely damaged an isolated farmhouse in the Mangula area. As the farmer and his family were away from home at the time of the attack no-one was injured. A short time later an armed guerrilla, wearing camouflage uniform, entered a farm store in the northern border area. The guerrilla stole a quantity of food and other articles and left the store, taking with him the African storekeeper as hostage. Shortly afterwards security forces caught up with the guerrilla and he was killed.

In mid-March a gang hi-jacked a car at Hartley (near Gatooma in the Midlands) and carried out an armed robbery at a petrol station in Gatooma. One member of the gang was arrested. A police spokesman was quoted later as saying that there were indications that a few other members of the gang had made their way into different parts of the country and that further incidents in both rural and urban areas could be expected.[45] At the end of March it was announced that two Coloured men, in possession of automatic pistols, grenades, ammunition and explosives, had been captured in Salisbury. They were linked with the gang which had moved into the central area of Rhodesia and had assisted at the attack on the farmhouse at Mangula. In the same report the murder of a farmer in the south Wedza area was announced. Shortly afterwards two Africans held up a store on the same farm. Warnings were given that this gang of four Africans was armed and dangerous. [46]

Towards the end of April a farm near Shamva (120 km. northeast of Salisbury) came under rifle fire from four armed guerrillas; the owner of the farm kept the guerrillas at bay and finally drove them off. Two weeks later a Centenary farmer came under fire while driving home; his car was damaged but he was not injured. At about the same time guerrillas fired rockets and threw handgrenades into a farmhouse near Sipolilo. The owners of the farm were away and only superficial damage was caused to the house. An African store near the farm was looted and set on fire.

During the second week in May it was reported that guerrillas were operating in the north-east border tribal area. Two African civilians were murdered and two women were severely assaulted, their huts pillaged and their possessions stolen. A day later an African beer-hall attendant was shot twice in the back by guerrillas, who escaped after terrorizing other Africans in the area. In the early hours of the same day an African farmer in a nearby Purchase area was made to burn down his farm outbuildings at gun point and reports were made of a number of thefts from Centenary farm employees. A government spokesman was quoted as saying that the 'terrorists have once again demonstrated their tactics of intimidation and utter callousness towards African victims in the remote tribal areas.' [47] The following week commenced with the murder of an elderly European prospector and the abduction of two Africans by armed guerrillas. On the same day another elderly European was killed and another injured when their car was blown up by a land-mine in the Mana Pools Game Reserve. Towards the end of the month, 21 Africans (12 of them women) were abducted by guerrillas operating in the area north of Centenary. One woman was shot dead and an African farmer and storekeeper were assaulted and robbed by armed men. Two African huts were burnt down. In early June guerrillas gunned down and killed another European farmer in the Mount Darwin area.

RHODESIAN GOVERNMENT ACTION

The Rhodesian government announced the closure of the border with Zambia on the night of 9th January. According to a later assessment of the position 'Rhodesia's decision ... [was] a diplomatic reaction to a provocative situation. It gives Zambia full notice of Rhodesian anger at Zambia's policy of playing host to anti-Rhodesian terrorists. And it contains the danger of terrorists and arms being smuggled into Rhodesia by rail or heavy road transport.' [48]

On the 18th January, in what the *Financial Gazette* called a 'tough speech, clearly aimed at dispelling rumour', the Prime Minister on radio and television warned that guerrillas were co-ordinating action on a wide front and that it would be some time before the situation returned to normal. Mr. Smith spoke of the position on the north-eastern border, where guerrillas had had some success in subverting the local people either at the point of a gun or by bribing local witch doctors, and informed his listeners that tough measures would be taken against anyone found doing this. With regard to the border closure, Mr. Smith made it clear that anything like normal relations would only be restored if the Zambian authorities disassociated themselves from aiding the guerrillas. [49]

The following day new Emergency Powers (Collective Fines) Regulations were published in the *Gazette*. A government spokesman said that these regulations had been passed in response to demands from tribal authorities for appropriate measures to be provided in law, based upon tribal tradition of collective responsibility. The regulations authorized officers such as provincial commissioners and members of the Defence Forces to impose collective fines on the inhabitants of any place or area if they believed that a person living there had committed an offence in terms of the regulations. Offences were defined as murder, arson, malicious damage to property, contravention of certain sections of the Railway Act or any provisions of part of the Law and Order (Maintenance) Act whether or not the person had been convicted of any offence; the harbouring, assisting or concealing of any person who has committed or is about to commit any of the above offences; or failing to render all the assistance necessary to effect the arrest of any person committing such offences. The regulations also contain provision for details of such punishments to be sent, together with any appeal against them, for Presidential review. The President was given the power to confirm, set aside or vary the fines imposed. [50]

In an article in the *Mail*, Henry Maasdorp, pointed out two aspects of the regulations which he considered gave the government '*Power to Bully the Innocent*', as he called his article. Thus an authorized officer was empowered to impound, for a period not exceeding three days, any property in the area involved. Mr. Maasdorp considered that this was unfair both to members of the Defence force who might become involved and rather more unfair to the villagers, for although 'our territorials and regulars are far from being a brutal and licentious soldiery ... they do not have the training in the niceties of police conduct let alone judicial'. Second, in executing a collective fine imposed by a provincial commissioner (the only person empowered to do so) it would not be necessary for the 'authorized officer' to ascertain 'to which particular inhabitant of such place or area such cash, stock or property belongs'; this would ensure that 'any felt obligation to ensure that more is not taken from some individuals than others is waived in advance.' [51]

Later the same month the Minister of Finance announced that a bill would be introduced into Parliament to provide for payment of medical expenses and disability benefits for persons injured or disabled and compensation for damage to property as a direct result of guerrilla activity. The Minister explained that this would in no way replace the Terrorist Victims' Relief Fund which had been launched to provide such assistance on a voluntary basis.

On the last day of January the Prime Minister held a press conference at which newsmen from some of the world's more famous newspapers were represented. Interest was mainly over the border closure but Mr. Smith also alluded to the guerrilla infiltration and said that official estimates were that incursions into the north-east had been going on for some six to seven months previously but there was no evidence to suggest that base camps had been set up. Mr. Smith admitted that there had been a breakdown in security which had aided the incursions and that about two hundred Africans were facing charges for aiding 'terrorists.' [52]

In early February a warning on rumour-mongering was issued by the government. A spokesman for the Ministry of Law and Order said that it was hoped that for those people with Rhodesia's interests at heart the warning would be sufficient but if this was not so ample provision existed under the Law and Order (Maintenance) Act to deal with people who spread false rumours. [53] It was also in early February that all schools and African businesses were closed, for security reasons, in the Chiweshe Tribal Trust Land adjoining the Centenary area. Chief Makope from Chiweshe was also detained 'in connection with a security matter'. Later in February the primary and secondary African schools at St. Albert's Mission were closed and the Chesa African Purchase area near Mount Darwin was sealed off, all schools, shops, beer-halls and grinding mills in the area being closed while Security Forces mounted a search for guerrillas.

These events led the Rev. F. B. Rea, of the Trinity Methodist Church, Salisbury (in an address to the Rotary Club, Salisbury), to call upon the government to assure all Rhodesians that 'the policy adopted in these territories was not a deliberate campaign of counter-terrorism in the implementing of which security forces were used to instil fear into the hearts of the whole population.' The *Herald* urged the government to accord the Rev. Rea the dignity of frank and courteous answers to his queries, for the action in the Chiweshe and Chesa tribal areas was something which was worrying many people. The following day the Minister of Internal Affairs stated that the army was carrying out its difficult task with 'their customary desire to be at harmonious relations with the civil population'. He denied that 'terrorism was being met with terrorism' but stated that 'Stern discipline is being enforced'. [54] By mid-March all the schools, institutions and businesses in these areas were re-opened. The schools at St. Albert's Mission, however, were closed again shortly afterwards.

On the 16th February an amendment to the Emergency Powers (Maintenance of Law and Order) Regulations was published in the *Gazette*. [55] The regulations raised the maximum penalty for aiding 'terrorists' or failing to report their presence from five to 20 years' imprisonment with hard labour. They also increased the powers of magistrates dealing with cases contravening the Act, and clarified the powers of protecting authorities in ordering closure of places for security reasons. It was announced at the same time that a new bill to amend the Law and Order (Maintenance) Act would be introduced into the next session of Parliament to bring the Act into line with the new regulations. Later in February the Ministry of Internal Affairs announced that four new Districts had been created along the north-eastern and eastern highlands area. According to the Minister the new districts would have their own district commissioners and staff and were designed to improve contact between the administration and rural Africans.

At the end of March the Minister of Justice, Mr. Lardner-Burke, moved that the House of Assembly 'take note of the security situation in all its aspects.' Mr. Lardner-Burke said that the renewed terrorist infiltrations should not have come as a surprise to anyone for he had given full warning, in his address to the House when moving the motion for an extension of the period of the State of Emergency in June 1972, of the threats which were to be expected. Recent events had confirmed the prognostications which he had given at that time. The Minister said that subsequent to this warning information, gathered from several sources, had been obtained that Rhodesian guerrillas, co-operating with Frelimo guerrillas who were infiltrating through Mozambique to the Tete area, had joined the Frelimo advances from the Zambian border and had then made their way down the country adjacent to the north-eastern border between Mozambique and Rhodesia from whence came the principal threat. From points along the border groups of guerrillas were able to enter Rhodesia and had had a certain amount of success in subverting the local population 'by fear and the use of spirit-mediums.' [56]

The Minister went on to explain that some spirit-mediums had been abducted forcibly into Mozambique while others had been subverted to the guerrilla cause. Through exploitation of spirit-mediums a spiritual hold over primitive tribesmen was gained and in consequence no information was being volunteered to government agencies. Infiltration had also been facilitated by the fact that the terrain was a difficult one with no natural obstacle (such as the Zambezi River between Zambia and Rhodesia) to impede crossings into the country.

Mr. Lardner-Burke then alluded to the attacks on isolated farmsteads. Expressing deep sympathy for persons who had suffered bereavement, injury or loss of property, he said that 'when one takes cognizance of the amount of subversion which had occurred in the areas concerned, it is amazing that further incidents of this nature have not happened.' He went on to say that there were now indications that tribesmen were beginning to realize that sup-

port for guerrillas would not be in their interests in the long run
and that information had now begun to come in once again. He
warned however that there were still some tribesmen who were
not co-operating with the security forces. This was the reason for
the new regulations for the administration of justice and for the
introduction of collective fines.

Turning to future plans, the Minister outlined proposals to bring
the security forces up to strength; the scheme for allowing con-
scripts to join the police force for their national service; the new
system for financial incentives to servicemen to continue their period of service; and the sub-division of certain administrative districts into four new districts. He drew attention to the fact, however, that he was naturally restricted in what he could say about
the future intentions of the government.

During the ensuing debate, which ranged over five days, the
Minister of Internal Affairs referred to the strengthening of district
administration, and the necessity for imposing collective fines. He
made a plea for Rhodesians to look into their own history for he
considered that 'what we have been going through this year is
nothing to the situation that existed during the closing years of
the Federation' and advised people, when summing up Rhodesia's
security problems, to 'take careful note of conditions existing
beyond our borders. [For] terrorism in some shape or form is ram-
pant throughout the known world and racial friction is growing
in intensity ... There is more terrorism and racial friction in the
United States and now in Britain occurring every day than has
taken place in this country for many years.' The Minister of Transport outlined plans for construction of new roads and outlined
the background to the copper traffic being carried by Rhodesia
Railways to Zambia which had been affected by the Rhodesian-
Zambian border closure and the Prime Minister spoke on the
necessity for a settlement of the constitutional dispute with Britain.

In conclusion, Mr. Lardner-Burke referred to various points
raised during the debate and in particular to the question of the
border closure and guerrilla incursions prior to that action in order
to correct any misunderstandings. He said that prior to the border
closure 'Major terrorist infiltrations both in the east and the west,
on either side of Lake Kariba, were immediately threatened ...
At the same time the attack from Mozambique had already begun'.
The possibility of further major incursions from Zambia while

security forces were involved on the north-eastern border was an unpleasant situation which had to be faced. The outcome of the border closure therefore was that Rhodesian 'security objectives ... have been achieved beyond our expectation.'[57]

Summing up the debate, the *Mail*'s reporter, Henry Maasdorp, wrote that it led to the 'painful conclusion: If one aim of the terrorist incursion had been to divide Rhodesians ...—then that aim is on a fair path to achievement. Very little meeting of minds occurred in the long debate, ... The ruling party wanted to talk about methods and resources to be used against the terrorists, its African opponents about wrongs. Neither gave the other understanding.'[58]

The promised amendment to the Law and Order (Maintenance) Act was given its Second Reading in the House of Assembly on the 8th May. Introducing it the Minister of Law and Order explained that it had three main objectives—to amend the law relating to the publication of subversive statements which had 'become necessary due to the recent practice of certain elements of the Press to highlight subversive statements when they form the subject of criminal trials'; to increase the penalties for certain offences under the principal Act—that is an increase in the maximum penalties for the crimes of assisting or harbouring terrorists or failing to report their presence to the Police; and for raising the jurisdiction of magistrates dealing with offences under the Act. The last two amendments had been made, as interim measures, in the amendment to the Emergency Powers Regulations in February. During the debate African M.P's were described as being 'fiercely critical' of the bill and, in his reply to the debate the Minister accused these M.P's of expressing support for 'terrorism'. He mentioned in particular, Mr. R. T. D. Sadomba, M.P. for Nemakonde, and said that his contribution to the debate was typical of the African National Council of which he was a member. Mr. Lardner-Burke said that it was known that the A.N.C. was supporting the 'terrorists'... 'and doing everything to cause a breakdown of law and order in this country.'[59]

On the 18th May the amendment to the Emergency Powers (Maintenance of Law and Order) Regulations 1970 was gazetted. The 1970 regulations had empowered the Commissioner of Police to exclude persons from any particular area or portion of an area during periods when the police or members of the Defence Forces were conducting operations against persons threatening to endanger public safety or disturbing or interfering with public order. The 1973 Regulations empowered the Commissioner of Police, where persons had been excluded from a particular area, to issue orders for the confiscation, seizure or destruction of any moveable or immoveable property within that area if he was of the opinion that such property may be or would be likely to be used by persons threatening to endanger public safety. Further sections gave legal immunity for the government, the Minister, any police officer or member of the Defence Forces, acting in good faith, against death or injury of any person excluded from the area and gave the Commissioner of Police power to restore confiscated or seized property leaving the decision as to any question of compensation to the Minister. Further amendments gave the Protecting authority power to impose a curfew during the period of operations or to order persons to remain in their houses unless in possession of written authority.

At the same time it was announced that tribesmen living along the northern border were to be evacuated, screened and resettled in another area. A Ministry of Information spokesman was quoted as saying that this action had been taken because a number of tribesmen living in the northern border area were being subjected to such intimidation that they were unable to lead normal lives. He said that the new area in other parts of the Zambezi valley not far from their original villages, was, from the point of view of land and water, far superior to the old area. In an interview the following week the Minister of Internal Affairs gave further details of the re-settlement scheme. He said that the old villages, which had been raided for many months, would be destroyed and the villagers would be able to live in specially prepared camps until arrangements had been completed for their reception in their new homes. They would receive food and medical care while in the camps and an educational centre had already been established. When they were moved to their new homes they would be provided with seed for the new season's planting. [60]

Towards the end of June new regulations were published requiring employers to submit returns showing details of all their male European employees between the ages of 17 and 30 years and requiring every male European between the ages of 17 and 50 years normally resident in Rhodesia for a continuous period of not less than six months to register for national service. The new regulations were described, by a spokesman for the Ministry of Defence, as being for the purpose of assisting the Registrar General to check on the accuracy of his records and for helping to detect anyone who failed to register.[61]

TRIALS FOR CONTRAVENTION OF THE LAW AND ORDER (MAINTENANCE) ACT

During early February three African men appeared in the Salisbury Magistrate's Court for a preparatory examination in connection with allegations of murder arising from the attack on a farm at Centenary and the death of Corporal Moore during December 1972. Following a plea by the prosecutor, the magistrate ordered that the proceedings be held in camera. At the end of the hearing the three men were committed for trial at the High Court. The trial, held in camera with only accredited members of the press present, lasted six days. The men appeared before Mr. Justice Davies and three assessors and were charged with the murder of Corporal Moore and with 'committing acts of terrorism or sabotage' in contravention of the Act, to which they pleaded not guilty. The three men were subsequently found guilty of the first count of murder and sentenced to death. One of the three men was also found guilty on the second count of contravening the Act and was sentenced to death while the other two men, found guilty on a similar charge, were sentenced to 20 and 16 years' hard labour respectively, for they, unlike the first accused had 'not been members of the original terrorist gang, but had assisted it.' Mr. Justice Davies explained that the second and third accused were local tribesmen who had been recruited and trained in the use of arms and that other tribesmen, probably through threats, had also assisted the terror gang by carrying arms and supplies, in providing food and in acquainting the gang with the locality.[62] In May an Appeal against the death sentence was heard by the Chief Justice Sir Hugh Beadle, the Judge President Mr. Justice Macdonald, and the Acting Judge of Appeal Mr. Justice Macauley. They agreed unanimously that the findings of the High Court judge had been justified and dismissed the appeal. The three men were executed in a Salisbury prison on the 21st May.

In mid-March another three African men were tried in the High Court Salisbury. They had pleaded guilty to contravening a section of the Act in that they had had arms of war in their possession, on the north-eastern border during late December 1972, for the purpose of committing acts of terrorism and sabotage. The weapons, which the accused admitted to having had in their possession, were described by Mr. Justice Jarvis as 'an arsenal' and included grenades, land-mines, bazookas, mortars and machine guns. There were also large amounts of ammunition. Mr. Justice Jarvis in sentencing the men to death observed that the provisions of the sections of the Act under which the men had been charged provided for a death sentence or imprisonment for life. In the circumstances where the three accused had left Rhodesia voluntarily to train as 'terrorists' and had entered the country with the firm intention of carrying out attacks but had been prevented from doing so only by their early capture, it was quite clear that they had not been intimidated into acting as they did and therefore the harsher sentence was imposed. The sentences were upheld in June by the Appeal Court Salisbury. [63]

Towards the end of March two African men were sentenced to death in the High Court Bulawayo for entering the country (during 1970) armed with weapons of war. The charge listed 'various arms and materials of communist origin, including 18 rifles, one machine-gun, three pistols, 6 689 rounds of ammunition, 26 hand-grenades and 3,5 kg. of T.N.T.' Commenting upon this trial, the *Citizen* (which describes itself as Rhodesia's only independent national weekly newspaper) commended the Rhodesian Courts, for it was of the opinion that the men had been 'given more than a fair trial and were treated like normal people guilty of an offence.' The paper said that, in their defence, the men had pleaded that they had been trained respectively in Cuba and in Russia and commented that 'One can freeze from fright in imagining what fate would have befallen these two men had they been captured performing terror movements against either of the two countries in which they were trained.' At the end of May an appeal against the sentence was heard; the Chief Justice Sir Hugh Beadle found that there was nothing to show that the death sentence was manifestly excessive and the sentence was upheld. [64] The two men were hanged in a Salisbury prison on the 22nd June.

Also at the end of March the trial took place in the High Court

Salisbury of an African spirit-medium on three charges under the Act: of recruiting four Africans for 'terrorist' training; of guiding 'terrorists' into the country and 'being a spirit-medium by repute' of purporting to protect them by super-natural powers; and of failing to report to a police officer, within 72 hours, the presence of 'terrorists'. The accused pleaded not guilty at his trial, which was held in camera with accredited members of the press being present except during the hearing of evidence by African civilian witnesses. At the end of the 11-day trial the accused was found guilty on all three charges and was sentenced to 25 years' hard labour. [65]

The trial of two Coloured men on two main charges of having in their possession offensive weapons and materials and of endangering the maintenance of law and order in Rhodesia by committing acts of terrorism and sabotage at a farm at Mangula took place on 4-5th June. The two accused men had, earlier in the year, been mentioned in connection with the trials in Salisbury Magistrate's Court of two men on charges of harbouring and assisting them. One, a brother of one of the armed men, had supplied them with food, drink, clothing and accommodation and was given a sentence of six years' hard labour. At the end of June an appeal was made against this sentence and it was reduced to three years. The other man, whose charge was later reduced to one of 'failing to report the presence of two known terrorists' was given a sentence of two years' hard labour suspended conditionally for three years. [66]

During their trial, the two Coloured men described to the court how they had originally served with the Rhodesian armed forces and had later crossed into Zambia where they had undergone terrorist and political indoctrination for a period of about 18 months under the guidance of Frolizi (the Front for the Liberation of Zimbabwe). [67] The heavily armed raiding party to which they had been assigned (a group of Frolizi men) had entered Rhodesia and had made its way through the Zambezi valley. The raiding party had placed a cache of arms at Enkeldoorn and had then set up a camp in a rocky outcrop at Umvuma (almost the centre point of the map of Rhodesia). The two accused, when arrested at Mangula during February, had been found with a large amount of arms in their possession. Mr. Justice Jarvis, in passing sentence, said that although the accused had entered Rhodesia for an unlawful purpose, even assuming that it had only been for recruiting others for training in Zambia, he did not consider that it was a proper case for imposition of the death penalty. However, any sentence imposed must act as a warning and a deterrent to others who might be thinking along the same lines as the accused and he accordingly sentenced the two men to twenty-five years' hard labour each. On the second count, that they committed acts of sabotage by setting fire to a farm at Mangula, the two men were found not guilty because of doubt that they had had fore-knowledge that the farm-house was to be set on fire. [68]

It was also in early June that two Rhodesian African tribesmen were charged in the High Court Salisbury of committing acts of terrorism and sabotage by placing land-mines on roads in the country. Both men pleaded not guilty. In his summing up Mr. Justice Jarvis complimented their defence counsel for his most cogent defence of the two men. The two men were, nevertheless, found guilty on each count for, as Mr. Justice Jarvis said, the Court found it very difficult to agree that each of the accused was acting under coercion at the time the offences were committed. One of the men was sentenced to 18 years' and the other to 15 years' hard labour. A week later three Africans appeared in the High Court Salisbury charged under the Law and Order (Maintenance) Act. Two of the men were sentenced to death for possessing arms of war and for burying three land-mines in Rhodesia. The other man, whose degree of participation was found by the court to be less than that of his colleagues, was given a sentence of 18 years' hard labour. [69]

Throughout the first six months of 1973 various trials were held of persons accused of harbouring and aiding guerrillas. In one case, during the hearing of the appeal, the Chief Justice spoke of the dilemma in which people in the affected areas of Rhodesia found themselves—'terrorists threatening the tribesmen if they made a report to the authorities; and the authorities threatening the tribesmen with punishment if they did not make a report.' In the case in question Sir Hugh Beadle found that the conviction, on a charge of failing to report the presence of 'terrorists' in the neighbourhood, should stand for 'the appellants' clear duty was to the forces of law and order.' The *Herald*, a few days later, commented that there could be no quarrel with this decision for 'those who fail in their duty must expect to be punished.' The newspaper warned, however, that circumstances may differ in cases and that the role of the courts was all important in deciding what bearing these circumstances had on the case.[70]

NOTES

1 An armed Rhodesian African nationalist who invades his own country for the purposes of subversion, intimidation and sabotage is frequently called a 'terrorist' in Rhodesia; a 'freedom fighter' in the country where he is based. Academic and military treatises on this type of activity tend to use the word 'guerrilla' as being a more comprehensive and objective term with a fairly consistent international usage. The use of this latter term has often been criticized in Rhodesia (recently by the Minister of Justice—see *Hansard*: Vol. 83, No. 19. 6 April 1973: Cols. 1356-8—and by the Prime Minister—see *Hansard*: Vol. 85, No. 23. 7 December 1973: Cols. 2214-5) and in South Africa (see the *Star* Johannesburg: 27 October 1973) where the editor of the South African Press Association felt compelled to defend the use of the term by quoting definitions from both the Shorter Oxford English Dictionary and the Encyclopaedia Brittanica which, in his opinion, made it clear that the term 'guerrilla ... aptly describes the bands of armed men who cross the borders of South West Africa, Rhodesia and Mozambique from the north, and their activities.'

The term 'guerrilla' is used in this text, not because it is disputed that the word 'terrorism' accurately describes some of the methods used for the purposes of subversion, but because the word denotes a more comprehensive concept well established in the literature and also indicates not only the techniques but also the underlying political intentions which motivate those who organize and send such armed men into Rhodesia.

2 *R.H.* 6 August 1968.

3 As reported in the *Cape Argus* (Cape Town) 27 December 1968.

4 As reported in *R.H.* 12 September 1969.

5 *Hansard*: Vol. 76. 29 January 1970: Cols. 1608-9.

6 *R.H.* 5 September 1970.

7 As quoted in *R.H.* 2 November 1970.

8 *R.H.* 12 November 1970.

9 *R.H.* 2 October 1970.

10 *R.H.* 23 January 1973.

11 The *Times* (London) 26, 29 April 1971.

12 *R.H.* 24 July 1971.

13 *R.H.* 17 August 1971.

14 *R.H.* 7 September, *S.M.* 3 October 1971.
15 *R.H.* 5, 6 April 1972.
16 *R.H.* 17 May 1972.
17 *Hansard:* Vol. 81, No. 9. 16 June 1972: Cols. 668-76.
18 *Hansard:* Vol. 81, No. 11. 21 June 1972: Cols. 887-92.
19 As reported in *R.H.* 6 September 1972.
20 *R.H.* 7 September 1972.
21 *Hansard:* Vol. 82, No. 10. 30 August 1972: Cols. 851-80.
22 *R.H.* 25 September 1972.
23 *R.H.* 28 September 1972.
24 *R.H.* 10 November 1972.
25 *R.H.* 19 April 1973.
26 *R.H.* 7 December 1972.
27 *R.H.* 16 December 1972.
28 *R.H.* 22, 24 December 1972.
29 *R.H.* 25 December 1972.
30 *R.H.* 5 January, *R.F.G.* 5 January 1973.
31 *R.H.* 12 January 1973.
32 *To The Point* 13 January 1973.
33 As reported in *R.H.* 23, 24, 25 January 1973.
34 *S.M.* 4 February, *R.H.* 9 February 1973.
35 *R.H.* 2, 25 April, *R.F.G.* 27 April 1973.
36 *R.H.* 2, 17 June 1973.
37 As reported from Cape Town by *R.H.* 30 January 1973.
38 As reported from Cape Town by *R.H.* 25 April 1973.
39 *R.H.* 10 January 1973.
40 *R.H.* 13 January 1973.
41 As reported in *R.H.* 6 February 1973.
42 *S.M.* 13 May 1973.
43 *R.H.* 26, 27 January 1973.
44 *R.F.G.* 2 February 1973.
45 *R.H.* 17 March 1973.
46 *R.H.* 31 March 1973.
47 *S.M.* 13 May 1973.
48 *R.F.G.* 12 January 1973.
49 *R.F.G.* 19 January 1973.
50 *Rhodesian Government Notice No. 101 of 1973.*
51 *S.M.* 28 January 1973.
52 *R.H.* 1 February 1973.
53 *S.M.* 4 February 1973.
54 *R.H.* 9, 10 March 1973.
55 *Rhodesian Government Notice No. 183 of 1973.*
56 According to Holleman: 'Tribal life is further characterized by the recognition of a 'tribal spirit or spirits', *Mhondoro* (no plural), usually the spirit of some important ancestor of the chief's lineage, operating through a living medium... the importance attached to these spirits and the attention given to them by the people, is far greater amongst these north-eastern tribes.'
1953: Holleman, J.F.: *Accommodating the Spirit amongst some North-Eastern Shona Tribes:* Rhodes-Livingstone Papers No. 22:

London: Oxford University Press for the Rhodes-Livingstone Institute.

Accounts of the activities of spirit-mediums during historical times and during the Mashona Rebellion in 1896-7 can be found in articles by Abraham, D.P.: *The Roles of 'Chaminuka' and the Mhondoro-cults in Shona Political History.*

Ranger, Terence: *The Role of Ndebele and Shona Religious Authorities in the Rebellions of 1896 and 1897.*

In 1966: Stokes, Eric and Richard Brown (Eds.) *The Zambesian Past: Studies in Central African History:* Manchester: The University Press.

57 *Hansard:* Vol. 83, Nos. 15, 16, 18, 19. 29, 30 March, 4, 5 April 1973: Cols. 1070-83, 1178-1247, 1295-1320, 1335-61.

58 *S.M.* 8 April 1973.

59 *Hansard:* Vol. 83, No. 24. 8 May 1973: Cols. 1728-81.

60 *Rhodesia Government Notice No. 512 of 1973: R.H.* 18, 24 May 1973.

61 *Rhodesian Government Notices Nos. 664 & 700 of 1973.*

62 *R.H.* 8, 13 February, 1, 2, 3, 6, 7, 8 March 1973.

63 *R.H.* 20, 21 March, 14 June 1973.

64 *R.H.* 27 March, 29 May, *The Citizen* 30 March 1973.

65 *R.H.* 27 March 1973.

66 *R.H.* 3, 5, 13 April 1973.

67 It was noted in the press report of the trial that no ban of any kind was placed on the press and that it was the first time that an organization such as Frolizi had been mentioned and allowed for publication in a Rhodesian court.

68 *R.H.* 5, 6 June 1973.

69 *R.H.* 7, 13 June 1973.

70 *R.H.* 29 May, 5 June 1973.

VIII

THE TRIBAL AREAS

According to one authority 'the disastrous inroads upon African land rights during the first years of white pioneering had revealed the vulnerability of indigenous landed interests and moved the Imperial Government to insert protective measures in the Matabeleland Order in Council of 1894.' In later years 'the basic feature of defined areas reserved exclusively for African use and occupation became the sheet anchor of Southern Rhodesian African policy and administration.'[1] This policy was continued after the 1923 Constitution was passed and led to the Land Apportionment Act of 1930.

Until the Amending Act of 1950 land which had been set aside for the African area could be purchased and worked on an individual basis but after this time the area was divided into land for the tribal areas—land which would not be available for individual ownership but under communal tribal ownership—and 'native' purchase areas—where land could be purchased by approved individual African farmers.

Towards the end of 1959 the Southern Rhodesian government approached the United Kingdom with a proposal for the revision of the Constitution with a view to the transfer of powers in the field of 'native' administration still retained by Britain. In late 1960 and early 1961 a Constitutional Conference was convened, under the chairmanship of the then Secretary for Commonwealth Affairs, Mr. Duncan Sandys, which recommended changes eventually approved by the parliaments of both countries. As far as the apportionment of land was concerned further land was transferred to the African area and it became possible, for the first time, for Africans to buy or lease land in designated African townships in the urban areas.

In August 1962 at the opening of the debate in committee on the Land Apportionment Amendment Bill, the Prime Minister,

Sir Edgar Whitehead, declared that 'if we are returned [at the forthcoming general election] we shall certainly repeal the Land Apportionment Act.'[2] At the end of 1962 there were five categories of land—

Tribal Trust Land	40 020 000 acres
Native Purchase Area	4 220 000 acres
Unreserved Land	5 769 600 acres
European Area	35 750 400 acres
Forest and National Parks Area	10 840 000 acres[3]

At the 1962 general election however Sir Edgar Whitehead's United Party lost to the Rhodesian Front and in late 1969 the Land Tenure Act superseded the Land Apportionment Act.

THE LAND TENURE ACT

In terms of the Land Tenure Act No. 55 of 1969, the 96 520 000 acres of land in Rhodesia was divided into 44 950 000 acres each for African and European areas and 6 620 000 acres of National or Unreserved Land. According to the 1969 census Rhodesia had a total population of 5 070 370 people; 4 817 950 Africans and 252 450 Europeans (including Coloureds and Asians).[4]

A later report (using revised figures of the 1969 census and metric measurement) gives the following figures for the African population divided into the areas in which they live:

Tribal Trust Land (163 143 sq. km):	2 911 040 or 60.1%
African Purchase Area (17 047 sq. km):	132 810 or 2.7%
European Rural Area (210 390 sq. km):	998 510 or 20.6%
Urban Areas	891 760 or 16.6%

There were also 362 840 foreign-born Africans in various areas of the country.[5]

Dr. M. I. Hirsch wrote of the relationship between racial problems and legislation dealing with land rights in 1967:—

The right of the various races to possession and domicile in
Southern Africa is basic to the whole race problem... Land more
than any other factor, has always been at the root of the black-
white conflict, with the right of occupation and possession always
in dispute... [The African] claim to possession rests primarily
on the 'African' assertion as a self-evident fact that they alone
are indigenous... [and] rests secondarily on the fact that black
Africans are the racial majority in all States of non-Arab Africa.
In Rhodesia, whites refute the African claim to exclusive racial
rights. They deny African primary right of domicile and possession in approximately 50 *per cent* of Rhodesia. Through the Land
Apportionment Act, white Rhodesians assert the exclusiveness
of white rights in European areas with Africans virtually as
aliens.[6]

When the Minister of Lands and Water Resources, Senator P.
van Heerden, introduced the Second Reading of the Land Tenure
Bill in the House of Assembly on 15th October 1969, he acknowledged that 'the system of land tenure and the security of land
rights have always played a vital role in both the political and
economic fields in Rhodesia'. He went on to trace the history of
the division of land from the early days of European settlement,
when the Chartered Company reserved land for African occupation on a communal basis to prevent alienation of land to whites,
to the Land Apportionment Act, which the present Bill was in
part intended to replace.

The Minister defined the main objectives of the Bill as being
to divide the major portion of land in Rhodesia into two equal
areas 'in one of which the interests of Europeans, and the other
of which the interests of Africans, will be paramount.' There would
also be a National Area where interests of neither race would prevail and a Purchase Area where Africans would be able to purchase
their land (as distinct from the communal ownership in the tribal
areas).[7]

At the end of March 1970 the Roman Catholic Bishops' Conference issued a pamphlet putting forward the Churches' objections
to the Act. These objections had been voiced earlier when the
Bill was first published, before the Referendum on the new Constitution, in June 1969.[8]

In January 1971, discussing the interim report on the 1969
population figures, the *Herald* pointed out that 'The statistics of
Rhodesia's population and apportionment of land between Afri-

cans and other races have frequently been used by critics of this country to show how badly the African is treated. The figures normally used for this purpose are: Half the country is allocated to nearly 5 million Africans, while the other half is for only a quarter of a million Europeans, Asians and Coloureds. As the proportion of Africans to other races is about 20 to one this division of land is grossly unfair. There is another way of looking at it however ... This report confirms the already-known population figures—4 846 930 Africans to 252 414 other races. But it goes on to show where these people live and produces a picture of the occupation of the land areas by the majority race which is very different from that seen by many Rhodesians, let alone the outside critics. It shows that the European area is in fact occupied by just over 2 million people—1 730 000 of them Africans. The African area is occupied by just 3 million people—all but about 3 000 of them being Africans. So the statistical breakdown becomes: Half the land area is occupied by 2 million people and the other half by 3 million people.'[9]

EVICTIONS

At the end of 1971, in the proposals for the settlement, special mention was made of two cases in which the Rhodesian government was considering eviction of Africans from land in the European area—Epworth and Chishawasha Missions. It was noted that the Rhodesian government had given an assurance that steps for the eviction of the occupants of these two areas 'or from other areas in which they are living' would not be taken until after the report of the proposed commission on progress towards ending racial discrimination had been fully considered. In the simplified version of the Settlement Proposals, however, it was stated that 'The Rhodesian Government have said that they may move some Africans living in forest or park areas who should not be there but for the time being they will not move African tenants living in other areas.'[10] During the sitting of the Pearce Commission, therefore, it was not considered to be a contravention of the agreement to proceed with the removal of people from the Stapleford Forest Estate which is a tract of National Land in the eastern highlands of the country. The removal of the Tangwena tribe, which had aroused much controversy over the years, was not proceeded with until after the results of the Pearce Commission had been announced.

THE TANGWENA TRIBE

Shortly after the occupation of Mashonaland, Portugal, who had 'failed to take the elementary and essential precaution of occupying the territories she claimed',[11] began to realise the danger of losing sovereignty over that part of central Portuguese East Africa (as Mozambique was generally known at that time) which would give the British South Africa Company's newly acquired territory of Manicaland a natural outlet to the sea. After various intrigues (on both sides) and a small battle, at a village then known as Macequece (now Vila de Manica), between Company forces and those of the Portuguese, a small buffer zone was created between the Portuguese and B.S.A. Company territories. Characteristically of the colonization of Africa during the 19th century, the boundary took no account of tribal ancestral holdings. It was thus that the Tangwena people became separated by what was to them an unknown line on the map.

In 1902, when Chief Makombe's tribe living to the east of the Tangwena land rebelled against Portuguese rule, the Tangwena Chief Dzeka Chigumira asked and obtained permission from the authorities to bring about 70 Tangwena families from Portuguese territory to join the rest of the tribe on the other side of the border in Manicaland.

A few years later in 1905 the B.S.A. Company sold about 250 000 acres of land in Manicaland to the Anglo-French Matabeleland Company. This land, designated as Unreserved or Crown land, included a major part of the ancestral tribal holdings of the Tangwena people. Since the Anglo-French company did not use the land the Tangwena were unaware that it had been alienated. They were also unaware of the end of B.S.A. Company rule in 1923 and of the passing of the 1931 Land Apportionment Act, which divided the land of Southern Rhodesia between Europeans and Africans. Under this Act the land bought by the Anglo-French company was declared European land, and in effect, the Tangwena living there became squatters. The remainder of the land belonging to the tribe was designated African and subsequently became part of the Holdenby Tribal Trust Land.

In 1944 the Anglo-French Matabeleland Company sold part
of its holding to the Gaeresi Ranch Company and a fence was
erected around its land, which eventually enclosed part of the land
where the Tangwena were living. In 1963, following a report by
agricultural officers on the poor state of the land where the Tangwena 'squatters' were living, the Managing-Director of Gaeresi
Ranch issued several eviction orders to the Tangwena.

Since the death of Dzeka Chigamiri in 1928 the chieftainship
had been in dispute. It was not until 1965 that a younger son
of the old chief, Rekayi Tangwena (who had been working in one
of the urban areas), returned to his tribe to claim the chieftainship.
According to Shona custom, Rekayi's claim had been approved
by the ancestral spirits through a spirit-medium and by the people
of the tribe. Unlike his immediate predecessors Rekayi preferred
to live in the area in which his father, Dzeka, had lived, namely
in that area abutting on to the Gaeresi Ranch. Government
officials, however, informed Rekayi that his chieftainship would
not be officially recognized by the government until those people
who were 'squatting' on European land had gone to live with
the rest of the tribe in the neighbouring tribal trust land. The
official insignia of an officially installed chief was taken from the
tribe.

Following a final notice to quit, the Director of Gaeresi Ranch
took the case to court and the hearing was held at the Inyanga
Magistrate's Court between 5th May and 2nd June 1967. On a
charge of wrongfully and unlawfully occupying land in the European area and thereby contravening the Land Apportionment Act,
Rekayi was found guilty by the magistrate who fined him £30
(or three months' imprisonment with hard labour) and £20 (or
two months' hard labour) to be suspended until 31st July on condition that Rekayi and his people left the ranch by that date. The
magistrate expressed his sympathy for the evicted people at the
time of the judgement. The fines were paid but the people
remained on the disputed land.

Later in 1967 Rekayi was again brought before the court on
a similar charge. On this occasion his legal adviser raised the issue
of Section 93 of the Land Apportionment Act, which permitted
Africans who had lived on Crown land in the European area before
the land had been apportioned under the Act to remain there
unless ordered to leave by Proclamation.

In his judgement the Senior Magistrate at Inyanga found that the land in question had ceased to be Crown land in 1905 when the land had been sold to a European company. He therefore fined Rekayi £30 (or three months). Later, however, an appeal was made to the High Court on the grounds that the Land Apportionment Act could not apply retrospectively and therefore did not apply to the alienation of land which had taken place in 1905. The appeal was heard by the Acting Chief Justice, Sir Vincent Quenet, and two senior judges. In delivering his judgement (in which the two other judges concurred) Sir Vincent found that the Tangwena, as represented by Rekayi, had probably occupied the land before its alienation in 1905 and he therefore quashed the conviction and set aside the sentence. Sir Vincent added that until such time as a Proclamation had been made in terms of the Land Apportionment Act the Tangwena were lawfully residing on their ancestral land. Later in the year Rekayi's previous conviction and sentence was set aside by Mr. Justice Lewis.

The government, however, issued the necessary Proclamation in early 1969 after a census of the Tangwena people and a count of their livestock. The Proclamation ordered 36 listed people, together with their families or other persons living with them, to depart permanently with all their property from the Gaeresi Ranch by 31st August and to go to the nearby Holdenby Tribal Trust Land. As the Minister of Internal Affairs said when he made a statement on the matter in the House in late August 'the essence of the [High Court] judgement was the interpretation of the law ... which was contrary to what the administration believed it to be'. The Minister quoted a case from 1957 as setting a precedent for this belief and went on to outline what he considered to be the relationship between the neighbouring Nyafaru co-operative farming scheme (of which two of the directors were Guy and Molly Clutton-Brock also of Cold Comfort Farm) and the continued resistance of the Tangwena people to eviction. He continued by explaining that there were two reasons why the Tangwena had to move from the ranch. 'Firstly, it is private land in the European area and squatter occupation is contrary to the Land Apportionment policy and, secondly ... the land is entirely unsuitable for African farming.' Mr. Smith informed the House that the government had made available a block of 7 500 acres in the near-by Nyangui forest area which it intended to transfer to the category of tribal trust land for re-settlement of the Tangwena. [12]

On 18th September (over a fortnight after the day fixed by the Proclamation for departure) a convoy of trucks carrying uniformed messengers of the District Commissioner, accompanied by police and a bulldozer, arrived in the district to arrest Rekayi and a head-man named Tsatse. The two men were taken to Machena in the Holdenby Tribal Trust Land and held there under police guard for three days. Meanwhile, while their chief was being arrested the people fled from their homes and the ranch was declared a 'protected area', entry being allowed only by special permit. After re-forming about 160 people marched to the office of the District Commissioner in Inyanga to demand the release of their chief and headman. After an attempt by the police with dogs to disperse them they were all taken into custody and spent the night at the police station.

After their release the tribes-people returned to Gaeresi where they were joined by Rekayi and Tsatse and commenced to rebuild their homes. A number of huts had been burnt down or demolished and a certain amount of property had been destroyed or was miss-ing including, in some cases, cash savings which had been hidden in the thatch of roofs or buried under the floor of huts. Certain men, who had gone to the District Commissioner's Office accom-panied by a police officer to make a statement regarding lost and destroyed property, were put into the police cells for the following ten days. By the end of September several huts had been rebuilt and replanting of crops had started.

On the 1st October Mr. R. H. James, M.P. for Salisbury City, moved a motion for the House to express its regret that the govern-ment had not found a solution to the problem of the settlement of the Tangwena. [13] The following day trucks again drove into the disputed area and Tangwena huts were destroyed as their owners fled into the mountains pursued by police dogs and heli-copters. Rekayi, after visiting Salisbury where he had an interview with the Minister of Internal Affairs, returned to the area and took up residence at Nyafaru Farm. Towards the end of the month the people returned and began to rebuild their huts only to have them burned again by government officials in mid-November. By late December, however, many of them returned in order to plough the land in readiness for planting the next season's crops.

During 1970 further attempts were made to move the people and there were various prosecutions of tribesmen for contravening the Land Tenure Act. A claim, used as a test case, by an evicted person for compensation for his lost and destroyed property was also heard in the courts during May. Having been awarded about 80 *per cent* of his claim a number of other claimants took their cases to court and it was estimated that they received a total of about £2 102.[14] Towards the end of the year another attempt was made to move the Tangwena from Gaeresi Ranch and it was estimated that about a thousand men, women and children had gone into hiding in the inaccessible mountain terrain to evade the police.[15] In mid-December about 200 head of cattle, impounded from the tribe in October, were sold at a public auction in Inyanga.

During February 1971 the Nyafaru Development Company was charged under the Land Tenure Act for allowing Rekayi to occupy land in a European area. At the Umtali Magistrate's Court, however, the charge was dismissed since the Magistrate did not accept that Rekayi was 'occupying' the land in the sense of making it his habitual place of residence. Later in the year an African Director of the Nyafaru Development Company was fined $200 for allowing 16 women (all connected with the Tangwena) to occupy land in contravention of the Act.[16] The following month the Minister of Internal Affairs assured the House that no Tangwena people remained on Gaeresi Ranch. Some of the people had reputedly gone to the area set aside for them in the Nyangui reserve, others had gone to the Holdenby Tribal Trust Land; the whereabouts of the remainder was not known.

In May Rekayi Tangwena appeared in the Salisbury Regional Court after pleading not guilty to four charges and six alternate charges under the Law and Order (Maintenance) Act. The charges arose out of alleged subversive statements he was said to have made during a taped interview for an article in a magazine. In July he was found guilty and given a six months' prison sentence, suspended conditionally for two years, on the main charge and a total of $75 fines on the other three charges.[17]

Towards the end of 1971 a large number of people had reportedly returned to Gaeresi Ranch and were planting crops and rebuilding their destroyed huts. The Minister of Internal Affairs confirmed that people had moved back to the ranch and said that the matter was being investigated.[18]

Early in 1972 Rekayi Tangwena and his people were interviewed by Mr. Colin Rawlings, one of the Pearce Commissioners. After having the settlement proposals explained to them, a 'unanimous "No"' was given to the Commissioner and Rekayi listed the grievances which he wished to have laid before Queen Elizabeth. A number of other letters and petitions which Rekayi had addressed to the British authorities had been answered with expressions of sympathy and with regrets that the British government was unable to intervene in the internal affairs of Rhodesia.

At the end of July the area where the people were living was cordoned off and police, assisted by the Rhodesian Air Force, moved in to evict them. Ten tribesmen were arrested and about 200 men and women together with their leader escaped into the mountains.

It was about this time that the Department of Social Welfare removed 110 Tangwena children, ranging in age from 3 to 10 years, to a temporary place of safety at the Harare Hospital in Salisbury. A department spokesman explained that the children had been left on the nearby Nyafaru Farm four years previously when the Tangwena people had first been moved off the Gaeresi Ranch. According to a signed statement by the African manager of the farm, the children were in need of care and attention, for the farm management had been unable to provide adequate food, clothing and shelter, medical attention or education for them. 'Once contact has been made [with the children's parents] steps will be taken to have them reunited' the spokesman added.[19] It was later reported that on arrival in Salisbury the children were found to be suffering from malnutrition and scabies and some were admitted to hospital.

On the 28th July the Minister of Lands issued a notice in the *Government Gazette* in terms of the Land Tenure Act ordering every African remaining in the disputed area to move by the 1st November. This order came as police were reportedly still hunting for tribesmen in the Eastern Highlands to which inhospitable and barely accessible terrain they had fled.[20]

In December *Moto* wrote of the numerous rumours which were current as to the whereabouts of Rekayi who, with his people, was still hiding in the mountains. The rumours claimed that many people were suffering from lack of food, shelter and medical care and that the relatives of Rekayi (who is over 70 years of age) had not heard from him for over six months. Speculation was also growing that the government would soon make another attempt to try and dislodge the people from their 'primitive but impregnable forts' in the mountains.[21]

The Report of the Secretary for Labour and Social Welfare for 1972 (published in April 1973) referred to the Tangwena children and stated that only six of them had been claimed by their parents. In view of the time that had elapsed since they had been abandoned by their parents, the Secretary thought it unlikely that the remainder would be claimed. In May, however, *Moto* reported that Rekayi Tangwena had sent a letter of protest refuting reports that the children had been abandoned, alleging that the children had been taken away without their parents' knowledge, and demanding their return.[22]

Moto's reporter, Justin Nyoka, forecast earlier from Inyanga that the year 1973 'will mean yet another period of continued resistance for Chief Rekayi Tangwena and his followers who have been roaming the mountains here'. Rekayi himself was quoted as stating that 'We have come a long way in our struggle, and are therefore not prepared to give in. We live on wild fruits like animals, but we shall never surrender. We might as well perish but we will not be violent.' According to reports, constant patrols on Gaeresi Ranch are kept up by government officials which have been re-inforced recently by security forces guarding the border area.[23]

AFRICAN COUNCILS

According to D. J. Murray 'Africans were from the first treated as a distinct governmental sector in Southern Rhodesia. For them was provided a separate system of administration centring initially on those in the rural areas, and there was also a distinct political system through which African interests influenced the exercise of governmental power.' In 1930 the government established Native Boards 'to provide the basis for a future system of elected local government.'[24] The Boards, however, had no direct power and could only make recommendations and were not popular. In 1937 they gave way to elective Councils, which in 1944 were given a limited power of taxation and of passing by-laws.

During the period of the Federation a new African Councils Act was passed (in 1957), but by 1962 it was admitted that 'the native council system had further deteriorated' and would have to be completely rebuilt under the new government policy of community development.[25] The period after 1963 showed a rapid spread of councils which were to be the organs through which the policy of community development was to be channelled.[26]

COMMUNITY DEVELOPMENT

Throughout the history of white settlement in Rhodesia efforts have been made to raise the living and farming standards of the African rural areas. Three commissions of enquiry reported in the early sixties mainly that little regard had been paid to the social effects of planning upon a tradition-bound society and recommended that a communal response must be stimulated if future measures for development were to succeed. In 1962, following the change to a Rhodesian Front government, the policy of community development was intensified, and during the years 1962 to 1969 various phases of the policy were put into practice.

Writing at a later date, Dr. A. K. H. Weinrich defines Community Development as aiming 'at mobilizing local resources through the initiative of the people ... [to] raise their living standards and aspirations'. Dr. Weinrich, however, goes on to say that in Rhodesia the situation is complicated because Rhodesian Africans are ruled by a white minority and when community development first became government policy 'many people, especially missionaries and African nationalists, realized that the emphasis on the development of individual communities would intensify the division between Africans and Europeans. From its inception therefore community development acquired racial overtones. It was seen as the thin end of the wedge of separate development in Rhodesia.'[27]

In 1962 the Department of Native Affairs was abolished and was replaced by the Ministry of Internal Affairs; its specialist functions, such as criminal jurisdiction, native agriculture and native lands were transferred to the Ministries of Justice, Agriculture and Lands and Natural Resources. The necessary amendments to the African Affairs Act were also made.

In 1963 the decision was taken that responsibility for primary education in the tribal areas was to be handed over to African Councils. A programme for training community development agents was put into practice and a team was set up to delineate communities in the African rural areas. The next year a number of community boards were constituted; provision was made for funds to be allocated for the encouragement of community projects and the Domboshawa School was converted into an Institute for Training in Community Development and Local Government.

In 1965 the Prime Minister published his *Directive on Local Government and Community Development : the role of the ministries and co-ordination* which laid down the lines for the co-ordination and integration of ministerial services for the purpose of organizing and developing 'responsible, self-reliant and coherent communities within a comprehensive multi-purpose framework of local government.' In 1966 primary education and preventive health functions were handed over to the African Councils. During 1967 the task of defining the functions of various Ministries and determining the rates of assistance to be given by the central government was continued and the Tribal Trust Land Authorities Act was passed. This Act gave 'the tribal chief and his traditional advisers ... the right which he had formerly held of determining the allocation of land and questions pertaining to tribally-occupied territory.' Further legislation was contemplated in the form of a Tribal Courts Act, (which came into existence in 1969 as the African Law and Tribal Courts Act) 'to restore to the tribal authorities' their recognized powers in the field of criminal jurisprudence.

The emphasis during 1968 was on the training of officials and other personnel attached to African Councils and a branch of Community Development Training was created within the Division of African Education, a division of the Ministry of Education.

In 1969, with the focus on development at Local Government level, came the establishment of 12 new African Councils (leading to a total of 94) and the African Law and Tribal Courts Act was passed investing statutory powers in the chiefs and their traditional assessors to handle judicial matters. Tribal Courts were to enforce local by-laws made by the Councils and the Tribal Land Authorities.[28]

During the debate on the motion for an address in reply to the Presidential speech at the opening of Parliament in 1970, the

Minister of Internal Affairs, took the opportunity of emphasizing that 'despite criticisms and remarks as to the deterioration in the Tribal Trust Land—and of course we are very conscious of the problems that face us— ... development is proceeding at a pace and on a scale unprecedented in the history of this country ... there is co-ordination between the tribesmen, the tribal authorities and the Ministries concerned. It is a splendid example of practical community development in operation ... There is tremendous progress taking place in the establishment of African councils as these are being recognized as the most satisfactory vehicle to give expression to the objects of community development ... It needs little imagination to see the future where provincial governments can be managed at a level where many of the amenities and social services and local infrastructure can be supplied and controlled by the people who, in the main, will make use of them, leaving the national affairs to be administered by central Government.'[29]

At the beginning of September 1971 an amending bill to the African Councils Act was given its Second Reading in the House of Assembly. The African Councils Board, which had been composed of a number of officials, including the Secretary for Internal Affairs and officers from the Treasury and the Ministry of Local Government and Housing, was to be abolished and warrant given for a council to provide special fiscal and executive services for the chiefs and headmen, their tribal land authorities and tribal courts. In outlining the points which were to be amended the Minister of Internal Affairs said that the proposed changes would not only bring the Act up-to-date but also ensure 'the continued co-operation between traditional and elected leaders which is so necessary for the future development of the African areas of this country.'[30]

In mid-June 1972 *Moto*'s editorial was concerned with the chief's attitude towards African Councils in their area. It quoted from Senator Chief Sigola's speech in the Senate debate on the Pearce Report—which 'seems to sound all chiefs' general attitude'—that the chiefs had been placed in a dilemma because the Councils were usurping their authority. The editorial discussed the traditional authority of the tribal chief *vis-a-vis* the democratic authority of the elected councils and recommended that chiefs should not be leaders of councils but be given the status of 'something like that of a non-executive president of a country ...'[31]

By the end of 1972 there were 153 African councils (as compared with 55 in 1962). In 1971 these councils had maintained 810 primary schools, 485 dip tanks, 97 clinics, 8 052 km. of roads as well as other services. At the end of 1972 there were 243 community boards in active existence (nearly one half of which had been in active operation for over two years) which had completed 'hundreds of weirs, dams, bridges, access roads, clinics, school buildings, community halls and other projects.'[32]

PROVINCIALIZATION

The annual congress of the Rhodesian Front in October 1971 provided the Minister of Internal Affairs with an opportunity to outline the introduction and growth of the African Councils' system and the government's plans on the full implementation of provincialization. The Minister said that in pursuit of its policy the government was to introduce regional authorities to cover, in the first instance, the African areas. These would increasingly involve the African people in the development of their own areas, both economically and through the provision of social services and communications.[33]

Commenting on this in June 1972, the *Herald*'s political reporter wrote that provincialization was once again the byword in Rhodesian Front politics and in answering his own query on what was meant by provincialization he stated: 'Basically it is a system of separate government for Africans and Europeans at provincial level. Under Rhodesian Front plans African and European provincial parliaments would be set up to govern basic affairs in their respective areas. National matters, such as defence, foreign affairs, and the fiscus would be handled by the national parliament. Provincialization is a major extension of the community development concept.'[34]

In an interview in mid-July the Minister of Internal Affairs disclosed details of the provincialization plans, which he hoped would be started towards the end of 1972. He envisaged the creation of two provincial councils, one for Mashonaland and one for Matabeleland. Details of the system would not be finalized until current discussions with the chiefs had been completed, but Mr. L. B. Smith summed up the system as a 'two-tier form of local government in the African tribal areas, the lower tier being the African councils'.

The councils would be elected, probably through electoral colleges which would be constituted differently from colleges to elect tribal M.P.'s to the House of Assembly. The chiefs would have a greater influence in both councils although they would not form the total membership. The councils would initially have limited powers and would deal with such things as secondary and junior education and other matters on a regional basis. [35]

The *Herald*'s political reporter commented that the plan outlined by the Minister differed from the original Rhodesian Front ideas in that they 'do not cater for a European provincial council ... [and] there is no provision for phasing out Africans from the Central Government.' He referred to the R.F. newspaper the *Rhodesian Forum,* which had in its July issue given what was regarded as the party's interpretation of provincialization. This compared the system with the cantons and federal government in Switzerland. The reporter, Ian Mills, forecast that the subject of provincialization would feature prominently in discussions at the next annual R.F. Party congress. [36]

During the debate on the Revenue Vote for Internal Affairs, a number of M.P.'s shared the misgivings of Mr. C. A. R. Savory, M.P. for Matobo, who said he would sound a word of warning for 'if [provincialization] is an extension of local government and further decentralization there is a lot of merit in this.' However, he had been asked 'is this not pseudo-apartheid, is this not a pseudo-Bantustan type of thing that you are bringing in?' He said he would like the Minister to ensure, while the matter was still in its early stages, that this would not develop. Mr. M. M. Bhebe, M.P. for Ntshonalanga, said that many people were talking about provincialization, but always in relation to African groupings, and they think of it as another name for apartheid. He asked 'if provincialization is a good thing, why should it be spoken of only in connection with the African instead of it being spoken of in connection with all the communities of Rhodesia, both black and white?'

In his reply, the Minister said that there would be ample opportunity for a later debate when all details of the programme had been considered. But he would reiterate, as he had said in public many times 'that this in no way envisages a move towards Bantustans or any other form of government that might exist in other countries of the world. It is entirely a Rhodesian concept built up on a Rhodesian approach to Government and suited to Rhodesian conditions.'[37]

At the Rhodesian Front congress in September the Prime Minister outlined the party's policies and led the *Financial Gazette*'s reporter to comment 'provincialization and decentralization are ... no longer talking points. The R.F. has firmly set its eyes on achieving both. Talk can and will now only be about the most effective way of implementing both.'[38]

In November, in what he described as a vital step forward in the country's constitutional history, the Minister of Internal Affairs introduced the Second Reading of the Regional Authorities' Bill. Explaining the Bill's provisions, he said that communities would be given the opportunity to participate in a wide range of functions at a level between that of central government and the local authorities at present established. Mr. D. J. Brink, M.P. for Karoi, referred to the power to raise taxes and said he was pleased to note that the Bill made provision for this. Mr. A.T. Mungate, M.P. for Zambezi, queried whether and in what way the regional authority would differ from African councils and how the money was to be raised to pay the rates levied by the African councils, the regional authorities and the central government.

The following day the Minister replied that he had every intention of seeing that the chiefs played a dominant role in the regional authorities—for they were the natural leaders of the African people—but he had taken steps to ensure that the councils did not become centres for political intrigue. As far as revenue was concerned, the Minister described the wealth in cattle in the Tribal Trust Lands—half the national herd—and another 'tremendous' asset in goats which at present were only allowed to wander around the lands causing devastation instead of being used to supply the demand for goat-meat both at home and abroad. 'These are but two of the sources of income which are available to the African ... income is the only way that one can ... achieve the social services and amenities which modern civilization requires and which I believe the African people deserve and are demanding.'

Mr. L. B. Smith then continued by answering the question about the difference between African councils and regional authorities. 'The Regional Authorities will be a sort of two-tier or upper tier of the local authority of the African councils which are paro-

chial in extent and possibly deal with matters that are within ...
the little parochial area in which they live. The regional authorities
will have to take on the broader responsibilities of the wider developments that are essential in the service of the African people.'

Turning to what Mr. E. G. Watungwa, M.P. for Harare, had
said earlier, that the government's plans seemed only to have Africans in mind (which had led him to think that 'separatism' was
what the government was aiming at), the Minister said that there
were two different 'set-ups' in the country—the African area—
which is 'not quite half the country, devoted to a tribal system
of cultivation and living' and that this area of land had been
reserved in perpetuity for the African people. If the government
did not believe that this was the right thing to do the position
would have to be faced when private enterprise would swallow
up these areas and the people would have no land unless they
were able to compete successfully with highly capitalized European enterprise. [39]

In its later editorial the *Herald* commented 'because more or
less any devolution of authority, any decentralization of government, is to be welcomed—and because the Government's ordinary
revenue cannot cope with the problems caused by the soaring African birthrate without full development of the T.T.L.—we hope
the tribal Africans will do their best to make the new scheme work.
This support naturally implies that real authority will be devolved
and that the Authorities are not cast for the role of screens between
a Government that should provide services for all its people but
does not, and the deprived section.' [40]

Following a debate in the Senate, during which Senator S. E.
Morris detailed his 'very grave reservations' the Bill was finally
gazetted on 19th January 1973, as the Regional Authorities Act
No. 50 of 1972.

At the end of March a spokesman for the Ministry of Internal
Affairs announced that two new African administrative bodies
were being formed to take over most of the running of the country's
African areas. Regional Authorities would be formed, one in Mashonaland and one in Matabeleland, which would have powers of
taxation and responsibility for health, education and the development of their regions. Members of the Regional Authorities would
be chosen by the chairmen of African Councils in both tribal trust
and African purchase areas and would be guided by provincial and

district commissioners. After selection it was intended that members of the Regional Authorities would attend courses at Domboshawa Training College.[41]

DEVELOPMENT IN THE TRIBAL TRUST LANDS

In early October 1968, the Minister of Internal Affairs, Mr. L. B. Smith, introduced the Second Reading of the Tribal Trust Land Development Corporation Act to provide for 'the establishment of a corporation to plan, promote, assist and carry out the development in Tribal Trust Land of its natural resources and of industries for the benefit of the inhabitants of these areas.'

In his introductory speech the Minister said 'I must make it clear that government sees the establishment of a Tribal Trust Land Development Corporation as only part of the overall scheme and its work must go hand in hand with the other important facets which include community development and local government.' He went on to say that in the initial stages the major development would be in agriculture because this offered a very wide field of 'remunerative activity' and probably held the highest potential for employment. As an example of what could be done through irrigation development, the Minister cited the Chisumbanje Scheme, a company operated through the direction and management of the Sabi-Limpopo Authority. The scheme had started in 1966 and had already injected £40 000 cash in wages paid to Africans employed in construction works and a further £38 000 paid to Africans concerned in the production and reaping of wheat and cotton crops in the area. He went on to say that 'There is no reason, other than capital requirements, why this type of economic activity cannot be emulated in many of the tribal areas of Rhodesia.'

Finance would be derived from the government and the private sector and it was hoped that in time the private sector investment would come from the African people themselves. A board of directors would be appointed by the Minister of Internal Affairs where the shares were not owned by private investors; where shares were held by both government and private investors the government representatives would outnumber directors appointed by private shareholders in order that government control of the Corporation would be ensured. As government-held shares could only be sold after parliamentary approval, only an Act of Parliament would enable government to relinquish authority in the Corporation. African M.P.'s at the time mostly welcomed the Bill, despite the fact (as Mr. C. M. Chipunza, M.P. for Bindura, put it) that the Bill 'entrenched separate development.'[42]

THE TRIBAL TRUST LAND DEVELOPMENT CORPORATION LIMITED (TILCOR)

The Corporation, known as TILCOR, was officially formed in January 1969. By mid-1970 its chairman, Mr. W. A. Bailey, reported that the Corporation's efforts during the year June 1969 to June 1970 had been directed towards assessing the problems and priorities of development in the tribal areas. Mr. Bailey went on to say 'Tilcor is very much aware of its duty to create employment outlets for the emergent African at all levels in Agriculture, Commerce, Industry and Mining and the coming year sees us on the threshold of developments which may well transcend current economic restrictions. The prospects therefore are bright.' In reporting upon agricultural development the corporation's report for 1969/70 stated that 'in our evaluation of the agricultural potential of the tribal areas, it has become obvious that this sector is by far the least attractive ... the unattractiveness of agricultural employment must ... be emphasized and viewed realistically because ... until and unless the current disincentives are removed, the full agricultural potential ... cannot be maximised. The disincentives ... stem basically from poor utilisation of available land, resulting in poor yields, lack of communications and inadequate marketing facilities, all of which are compounded by the high leisure preference of the tribal African.'

Consequently the Corporation felt justified in making development of the commercial and industrial sector its primary objective. The Report concluded that 'unless considerable industrial development is diverted into the tribal areas as soon as possible, the long term future of our country will be in doubt.'

The Corporation's report provided details of the industrial complexes already surveyed and planned in the Seki (near Salisbury), Zimunya (near Umtali) and the Ntabazinduna (near Bulawayo)

Tribal Trust Lands; of the Kariba freight and ferry service to provide a regular transport service for tribesmen on the south shore of the lake; and of the establishment of a small research and exploration unit to initiate work in connection with pegging and securing potential mineral wealth in the tribal areas. [43]

In the report for the year ending 30 June 1971, the Chairman reported that during the year Tilcor had been engaged in a consolidation exercise and had adopted a 'growth-point policy'.

During 1970/71 agricultural pursuits had concentrated upon the programmed development of the Katiyo Tea Estate, situated in the Holdenby Tribal Trust Land (near Umtali), where 88 acres had been planted on irrigated land and an airstrip constructed for light aircraft. Tilcor had also taken over the Chisumbanje Irrigation Scheme, [44] where the current cotton crop was thought likely to yield over 8 million lbs with an expected average yield of 3 400 lbs per acre.

Future plans envisaged the establishment of an Agricultural Training scheme to train 100 tribal Africans annually to a sufficiently high level of proficiency to enable them to be employed as qualified irrigation farmers when they would be given the opportunity to manage and develop 2- to 4-acre plots on an individual basis; the development of grazing schemes; the growing of tobacco; and the development and commercial exploitation of the masau berry. [45]

With regard to mining activities, the Corporation reported that 'the emphasis has been changed from random prospecting ... to a consolidated effort in a specific area [Silobela Tribal Trust Land near Gwelo] using ant-heap sampling as a prospecting tool.'

Progress in the industrial complexes was noted. In Seki, roads had been built, a purification plant installed and electrical reticulation was constructed to serve existing industries and to house a telecommunications terminal carrier system. In the adjoining African township 141 three- to four-roomed houses and a hostel for 128 bachelors had been built, together with accompanying sewerage and piping for water. In Seki also, the re-location of a factory and a large brewery, together with staff housing, had been completed.

In the Zimunya complex, the re-location of a factory for processing skins and hides and production of high quality leather goods had been completed together with tarring of internal roads, fencing, water reticulation and all essential services. In the near-by township 65 three- to four-roomed houses, 20 single-room bachelor quarters and a sewage disposal system had been completed. In the Ntabazinduna complex a feasibility study had been carried out and plans for the re-location of a textile factory completed.

The report estimated that during the thirty-one months of its existence Tilcor had provided new employment opportunity for over 5 900 Africans and supplementary income opportunity for some 2 300 African families throughout the Tribal Trust Lands. [46]

In his report for 1971/72 Tilcor's Chairman, Mr. W. A. Bailey, took an 'objective look at results' and reported that 'despite difficulties, shortages and the inevitable frustrations of breaking new ground' some solid achievements had been made. Both agricultural and industrial projects had made steady progress during the year and they had proved to be a healthy boost to local tribal economy.

The Chairman felt that the steady implementation of Tilcor's Growth Point Policy, had, more than any other aspect, proved to be a particularly important step in the right direction. The objectives of the policy, as Mr. Bailey reminded his readers, 'were to create tribal area growth points in selected advantage situations remote from present day main centres.' Such growth points were to be profitable in concept and above all 'must offer job availability for all sectors of the community including opportunities commensurate with education and ability.'

Mr. Bailey also spoke of the new agricultural pilot scheme at Tuli in south-west Matabeleland. Here initial effort would involve investigation into the economic production of about a dozen different crops under overhead irrigation. A project which 'is expected to provide the quickest answer to south-west Matabeleland's biggest problem—a paucity of exploitable natural resources and a dire need for development.'

At Chisumbanje the land under cultivation was substantially increased and as a result the company achieved its highest ever annual cropping figures of winter wheat and summer cotton.

A tenant farming scheme was to be started to teach basic aspects of agriculture in general, and flood irrigation techniques in particular, to an annual intake of 100 African students, initially to provide for the needs of the Chisumbanje Development Company but eventually to provide trained personnel for other Tilcor agricultural projects.

In the Holdenby Tribal Trust Lands the basis for the growth point was the agricultural development, under overhead irrigation, of an area in the extreme north-east where the Katiyo tea estate had been established. This had had a satisfactory year of progress. Phase three of the development plan, to plant further land with tea, and a pilot scheme for crop diversification, were reported as being under way.

In the Seki industrial complex eight factories have already been established employing nearly 600 African workers who have been housed with their families in the adjoining township. The report noted that 'much of the success of the Seki development is due to the initiative of Chief Seki and his leadership of the tribesmen. Employees in the complex are administered according to tribal tradition. Indications are that cultural security and the benefit of modern amenities may well prove to be key factors in the employment of the African in an industrial environment.'

Work on developing the two other industrial complexes at Zimunya and Ntabazinduna was proceeding well and some twenty other industrial projects around the country are currently being investigated.

The mining sector continued with drilling and a geophysical survey of five prospecting sites. The ant-heap method of sampling is continuing and a blanket prospecting survey is being undertaken in the south-western tribal areas. [47]

TILTRADE LTD.

In April 1972 a new company was formed under the aegis of Tilcor. Four of Rhodesia's large firms, Rhodesia Breweries Ltd., David Whitehead & Sons (Rhodesia) Ltd., Neficrho Acceptances Ltd., and Heinrich's Chibuku Breweries (1968) Ltd., joined forces with the Chisumbanje Development Company to form the new company, to be known as Tiltrade Ltd., with a nominal capital of $250 000.

The company plans to build a chain of modern supermarkets in the Tribal Trust areas where Tilcor has planned large-scale development. The first supermarket complex with a shopping area, restaurant and bar was recently completed at the growing Chisumbanje irrigation scheme in the lower Sabi area, 241 km. south of Umtali, where more than 10 000 people have already settled around the estate.

According to a spokesman for Tiltrade: 'Chisumbanje provides the classic example for the future pattern of development in the Tribal Trust Lands. Already there are 140 tenants and up to 3 000 labourers working on the first phase of the scheme which last year produced a net profit of $260 000 ... By taking the city lights to the rural African we believe a general reaction can be set off where-by industrialists will be attracted to set up manufacturing units near these points of demand.' It was announced at the same time that Tilcor would hold Tiltrade shares worth $35 000 for disposal to African shareholders. [48]

A second supermarket is nearing completion at Mutema, north of the Greater Sabi Estates and a third one is planned for Seki Tribal Trust Land near Salisbury.

Criticism has come largely from African and the few European businessmen in the areas, who charge that the Tiltrade operations undercut prices and that government-sponsored big business is pushing them out. Tilcor's chairman explained that there were no African directors or shareholders in Tiltrade at the present time because earlier when African chiefs and traders were invited to join in the planning stages they had refused to do so. However, Tilcor had set aside 10 000 extra shares to offer to Africans at par ($1 a share). If sufficient African money was involved, said Mr. Bailey, an equitable directorship would naturally follow. It was hoped that the whole scheme would eventually be a wholesale and not a retail scheme and if African businessmen supported the scheme this would happen sooner. [49]

TRADE FAIRS IN THE TRIBAL AREAS

Also during April 1972 it was announced that a group of Salis-bury industrialists had formed an association to organize mini-trade fairs in the Tribal Trust Lands, with the support of the Ministry for Internal Affairs and Tilcor. The chairman of the new Rhodesian African Show Society was quoted as saying 'our aim is to take our products to the Tribal Trust Lands and demonstrate them to the widest possible audience. In this way, we hope to open up vast new markets, which are virtually untapped and to benefit the economy by stimulating the tribal areas' entry into the cash economy.'[50]

The first trade fair was held over a two-day period at Dendera in the Urungwe Tribal Trust Land, about 20 miles west of Karoi. It drew a total of about 17 000 spectators. The Society's vice-chairman said that the show had been a great success and the 20 stands with a range of products such as seed maize, solar heaters, fertilizers, textiles, sugar and flour had created a tremendous impression. Altogether five shows were held in the Tribal Trust Lands during 1972. During the early months of 1973 it was reported that the Show Society appeared to be well off the ground. It planned to hold 19 Shows all over Rhodesia (excluding Matabeleland) throughout 1973.[51]

During May Salisbury businessmen went on a tour, organized by the Associated Chambers of Commerce of Rhodesia (ACCOR), of Musana Tribal Trust Land about 60 km north-east of Salisbury. Before leaving Salisbury the businessmen had been informed of the almost complete lack of employment opportunity in the Tribal Trust Lands and the problem of bringing tribesmen into the cash economy. The tour was reported as giving them a clearer understanding of 'the rapid advances that could be made with expert advice and guidance, the success of self-help projects, and the Africans' enthusiasm for modern agricultural methods once their value had been demonstrated.'[52]

Later in the month the Prime Minister opened the annual conference of the Local Government Association and in his speech said that the government must use every opportunity to bring about a more equitable spread of the wealth of the country. Mr. Smith said that the bulk of African earnings was being spent in —and being poured into—the European sector of the economy and that this had created an unhealthy lop-sided position. Giving figures of about 400 000 employed Africans in the European urban areas with an annual spending power of about $150 million, with a prospect of doubling these figures during the next decade, Mr. Smith said that more and more of this spending power must be gradually diverted and channelled back into the African areas.[53]

DECENTRALIZATION

At the end of August 1972 the Parliamentary Select Committee on Decentralization tabled its report in the House of Assembly, calling upon the government to start a decentralization and economic development programme without delay and recommending that this should be done under a newly created Ministry of Planning and Economic Development.

In commenting upon the Commission the *Financial Gazette* said that such a commission was nothing new to Rhodesians, for such committees had been established by both the Federal and Southern Rhodesian parliaments in the 1950's. The present committee therefore did not argue the case for decentralization—'for the problem is now more acute than it was 15 years ago'—but confined itself to finding ways and means of implementing this policy.

Following a summary of the Commission's report, the *Financial Gazette* continued by saying that 'on the crucial issue of development of the Tribal areas, the Select Committee recognizes the merits of perimeter development (border industries) but stresses that development in African areas should *not* be limited to the borders of the T.T.L.'s' for if a planned balanced economy was to be developed it would require concurrent development in the Tribal Trust areas.[54]

Another newspaper, the *Herald,* commented upon the Committee's concept of perimeter development, which was a familiar concept in South Africa. The Committee's definition of the term was that it describes development under which an industrial complex is sited on the border of a European area, the African labour for which is housed over the border in the tribal area and added that the main purpose in 'promoting perimeter development in the Rhodesian context is to bring overall prosperity to the Tribal Trust Lands.' The Committee had recommended that a 'buffer area' should be set up between the industrial complex in the European area and the residential area in the Tribal Trust Lands to prevent encroachment one upon the other, with the object of protecting the African entrepreneur in the African shopping area.[55]

The chairman of the Decentralization Committee, Mr. E. Broomberg, M.P. for Bulawayo East, moved the motion that the House of Assembly take note of the Commission's report. He drew attention to the recommendation that a single new Ministry of

Planning should be set up, to which should be attached the Sabi-Limpopo Authority, the Agricultural Development Corporation and Board, the Agricultural Land Settlement Board and the Tribal Trust Land Development Corporation for, said Mr. Broomberg, there was a lot of duplication of expertise in these statutory bodies at the present time. He stressed that, although the Committee had not been able to set a time table, decentralization was an urgent matter. [56]

Later in the debate Mr. R. T. D. Sadomba, M.P. for Nemakonde, welcomed the recommendation for a separate Ministry, especially if it were to take over the development of the Tribal Trust Lands or the work of Tilcor. For, as Mr. Sadomba said, the present situation, in which this matter came under the Ministry of Internal Affairs, was unsatisfactory in so far as that Ministry was a purely administrative one and could not be expected to cope with the duty of developing 50 *per cent* of the country's land as well as with about 90 *per cent* of the population. Mr. Sadomba agreed that the recommendations in the report should be implemented without delay but put forward his own recommendation that the Tribal Trust Lands should be developed first so that it could then carry with it the development of the rest of the country. [57]

THE CHIEFS

In the early days of European settlement, particularly after the suppression of the Matabele and Mashona Rebellions, tribal leadership was made subservient to the European district commissioners and its main sources of traditional power and authority—power to allocate land and to control tribal courts—came under European dominated administrative control. In the early sixties, however, with the threat from African nationalist forces, the government turned to the chiefs for their help and advice. At a five-day conference in May 1961 government representatives met with the chiefs to discuss mutual major problems.

At this conference the chiefs elected 21 of their number to form an interim Council of Chiefs which before the end of the year became legislatively recognized by the Chief's Council and Provincial Assemblies of Chiefs Act No. 58 of 1961. From the first it was considered that the government was trying to turn the chiefs into an organized political force 'closely dependent upon, and therefore allied with, the white government against African nationalism and its fervent ambitions.'

Although the government denied these charges the chiefs were subsequently 'drawn to the very centre of the political arena through the sheer force of political development.' The first major move took place at the Domboshawa *Indaba*[58] in 1964. According to Holleman this was held to satisfy the British demand (before agreeing to recognize Rhodesian independence under the 1961 Constitution) that independence on such terms was acceptable to the majority of the people of Rhodesia as a whole.[59]

The support given to the government by the tribal authorities at this *indaba* 'obviously imposed the obligation by Government to redeem its promises' and this involved granting additional powers to the chiefs.[60] From mid-1966, with the passing of an amendment to the African Affairs Act, this trend has continued. Starting with the 1969 Constitution, which established an Upper House—the Senate—for the first time in Rhodesian history, the Council of Chiefs elect ten of their number to sit in the Senate, while in the Lower House of Assembly, eight of the sixteen African M.P.'s are elected through tribal electoral colleges consisting of chiefs, headmen and councillors of the Tribal Trust Lands in the two Provinces of Mashonaland and Matabeleland.

In November 1970 an Act 'handing back certain judicial powers to African chiefs' was gazetted. Introducing the Second Reading of the African Law and Tribal Courts Bill in early 1969, the Minister of Internal Affairs had said that it was 'one of the most important, far-reaching and interesting bills concerning the traditional lives of the African people of this country which had come before the House.' In opening the debate the Minister said he was making a 'fundamental declaration that this Bill is founded on respect for and goodwill towards indigenous African law ... and recognition of the value of African customary law, ... the African's good qualities and their capacity for communal harmonious living.' The Minister continued by saying that through the Bill the government was building up the power and status of chiefs and headmen as part of the more vital goal of building up a judicial institution.[61]

Before the sitting of the Pearce Commission much thought was given by its members to the question as to how far the chiefs and other tribal leaders could be said to voice the opinions of their followers. The Commission decided that the opinion expressed by the Secretary for Native Affairs and Chief Native Commissioner in 1961 that 'in the political field chiefs should be able to express their views and government should attach as much importance to those views as it does to any other responsible and organized representative group such as the Chamber of Mines or Commerce, but in no way substitute for or exclude normal political expression and other representative African thinking'[62] was the most suitable for their purpose.

In March 1972 the Minister of Internal Affairs, speaking at a conservation course for chiefs at Fort Victoria, referred to the breakdown of law and order in the country during the visit of the Pearce Commission. He said that in some areas chiefs and their senior followers had capitulated to a mob of youths and to the intimidation of people acting under influences alien to the tribe. He urged the chiefs to put their houses in order and advised them to 'regain and hold the confidence of your people and when these intruders threaten your territory, deal with them ... the law stands behind you to help.'[63]

LEGISLATION

In November 1972 a further amending Bill to the African Affairs Act had its Second Reading in the House of Assembly. In introducing the Bill the Minister of Internal Affairs said that the amendment was to allow for the better administration of the tribal areas, to up-date the Act and to remove some anomalies. The Bill contained three new clauses. These provided for the appointment of Assistant District Commissioners with the same powers as District Commissioners in the absence of the latter; for the appointment by Provincial Commissioners of acting chiefs for a limited period of 90 days (to allow for the legal hiatus caused by the death or the removal of a chief from office); and gave the chiefs the authority to appoint heads of kraals in order to end disputes over these appointments.[64]

A week later an amendment to the African Law and Tribal Courts Act was given its Second Reading. According to the Minister of Internal Affairs it was being introduced so as to give more powers to the tribal courts. Under the existing Act, if a tribal court decided that a person should be removed from the area of its jurisdiction it first had to provide alternative land similar to that from which he was to be removed and pay compensation for any improvements he may have made. According to the Minister this made the Act virtually impossible to implement and therefore the amendment, by removing these two requirements, would make it easier for a person to be removed from a tribal area when it was in the interests of tribal harmony. As a safeguard the district commissioner could, when reviewing a removal order, return the order to the tribal court for further consideration as to compensation where necessary. During the debate, however, seven of the African M.P.'s took the view that giving the chiefs this additional power was not in accordance with African tradition. These seven M.P.'s voted against the Bill: nevertheless, with less than ten members opposing, the Bill was read a second time and was gazetted on the 19th January 1973. [65]

On the same day as the amendment to the African Law and Tribal Courts Bill received its Second Reading a further amendment to the African Affairs Act was also given a Second Reading. Entitled African Affairs Amendment (No. 2) the Bill was introduced, according to the Minister of Internal Affairs, to amend those sections of the Act dealing with control of entry into, and the prohibition of meetings in, the Tribal Trust Lands. The Minister explained that under the existing Act the chief and the district commissioner could exercise control over meetings in the Tribal Trust Land or other tribal area but not over the whole of the African area in the district concerned. The Minister said he wished to standardize procedure and vest the powers of prohibition from entering or remaining in a tribal area with the Secretary for Internal Affairs. In effect this would mean that control of public meetings would apply to the whole of the African area as defined in the Land Tenure Act.

Another amendment would require any person employed at a mission station within a tribal area to apply for permission to enter or be in such an area from a district or provincial commissioner or the Secretary for Internal Affairs. The Bill also amended the wording, but not the provisions, of the main Act by allowing the Secretary for Internal Affairs to ban anyone from entering or remaining in any tribal area if he believed, after enquiry, that that person's presence would be against the public interest or against the interests of Africans living in the area.

In replying to criticisms by African Members the Minister gave an assurance that the missions would not be hampered in the continuance of their work but that the legislation had become necessary because of missionaries who were closely associated with church organizations which 'support and encourage acts of terrorism amounting to nothing more or less than murder.'

Regarding the power to control meetings, the Minister gave an assurance that this would not be used to victimize people who criticized the government, but would only be used to control 'those people who attempt to undermine the authority of a chief acting in the best interests of his people in consultation with the administration of the country.'[66]

Following representations by the churches, who saw the legislation as questioning the integrity of all mission workers, representatives of the Roman Catholic and of the Denominational churches met the Minister in early December and it was agreed that there would be advantages to be gained both by the Ministry and by the churches if further discussions should take place to resolve mutual problems.[67]

In mid-December the President announced to Senate that the Senate Legal Committee had submitted an 'adverse report' on two clauses of the Bill.[68] The two clauses objected to were, first, the one requiring district commissioners to give permission for meetings attended by more than 12 persons in the tribal areas; the second giving district commissioners power to ban individuals from holding or addressing meetings in an African area.[69]

Moving the motion that Senate agreed with the report of its legal committee, Senator J. Pincus said that he considered that the report needed little by way of explanation or elaboration, for the provisions of the amending bill had been found to be inconsistent with the Declaration of Rights. The next day the Minister of Internal Affairs moved that the Senate resolve that, although the two clauses were inconsistent with the Declaration of Rights, the clauses under consideration were nevertheless necessary in the national interest.[70] He explained that the principal legislation had been applicable in the Tribal Trust Lands for many years before the present Constitution was passed and asked whether 'the protection which has existed for the African people [should now be allowed] to be undermined by failure to extend this provision to the remaining small area.' After a short debate the motion was agreed and the Bill was subsequently gazetted on the 26th January 1973.[71]

THE FINGO LOCATION BILL

On the 22nd November 1972, the Minister of Lands and Natural Resources presented the Fingo Location Bill to the House of Assembly. However, the Speaker of the House, Mr. A. R. W. Stumbles, informed the House that he had reached the conclusion that the Bill was a hybrid one as defined in the Parliamentary Standing Order No. 127 and must be referred to the Examiners of Petitions for Private Bills in terms of Standing Order No. 128.[72]

The Bill had been introduced to bring the administration of the Fingo Location in line with that in the Tribal Trust Lands for, according to the *Herald*, the numbers of the Fingo people had grown so much that the land over which they held title deeds was too small and tighter control was needed on its occupation and use.[73]

According to a *Herald* reporter land issues have been the cause of dispute between the Fingo people and the government from the time when the British South Africa Company administered the country. The Fingoes at that time were African tribesmen from the Eastern Cape Province (a few of whom accompanied the Pioneer Column from South Africa to Mashonaland in 1890) and other tribesmen who were invited later by the country's founder, Cecil John Rhodes, to settle around Bulawayo in 1898 in order to counter any hostile movements of the Matabele. They were eventually given rights to land in Bembesi for their services in the Matabele War and Rebellion.

A government spokesman was quoted as saying there were probably about 3 000 Fingoes presently in the area, which comprises some 10 000 ha of Battlefields Block, 40 km north of Bulawayo on the main Salisbury road. Strictly speaking, the spokesman said, the Bill was not aimed at removing the tribesmen's land rights but at transferring individual rights to the tribe as a whole, for part of the land was communal grazing land for which no-one was legally responsible and which at present was being used by illegal occupants.

Under the proposed legislation the location would still be Purchase land but title would be held by the Fingo chief, being administered through him by a Fingo Location Land Authority. The only people who would be allowed to live in the location would be people recognized by the chief as belonging to the community. Fingos affected by the proposed law would be paid compensation to cover loss of title, loss of land improvements and the cost of moving (if this arose).

In early December a group of 22 Fingoes staged a silent placard-carrying protest outside the House of Assembly. A spokesman for the protesters was reported as saying that the Fingoes wanted their land rights left undisturbed. [74]

In early January 1973 it was announced in the *Gazette* that after the Bill was introduced to Parliament a Select Committee would be set up to hear evidence for and against the Bill's provisions. [75] In mid-March land title holders in the Location received a Parliamentary Notice advising them that an application was to be made to the House of Assembly for an Act to provide for the extinguishing of land rights in that area and asking them to indicate whether they assented to or dissented from the proposed Bill.

On the 28th March, in answer to a question by Mr. L. A. Ndhlovu, M.P. for Insukamini in Matabeleland, the Minister of Lands informed the House that he intended to present a bill to vest title of the Fingo Location in the name of the Chief of the Fingoes and that when the bill was presented an opportunity would be available then for a full and detailed discussion. [76]

NOTES

1 1969: Holleman, J.F.: *Chief, Council and Commissioner: some problems of government in Rhodesia:* Leiden: Royal Van Gorkum for Afrika Studiecentrum London: Oxford University Press.

2 *Hansard: Legislative Assembly Debates:* Vol. 51. 8 August 1962: Col. 1468.

3 *Report of the Secretary for Internal Affairs and the Chief Native Commissioner for the year 1962:* CSR 27-1963 Salisbury: Government Printer.

4 Figures are as given in the Central Statistical Office Report on the 1969 Census.
5 1972: Kay, George: *Distribution and Density of the African Population in Rhodesia:* Hull: University Geography Department Misc. Series No. 12. Figures used by kind permission of the author.
6 1967: Hirsch, M.I.: *For Whom the Land?* Salisbury: Bardwell & Co.
7 *Hansard:* Vol. 75, 15 October 1969: Cols. 1473-1500.
8 The Roman Catholic Bishops' Conference comprises the five Roman Catholic Bishops of Rhodesia.
   1970: *The Land Tenure Act and the Church:* Salisbury: Mambo Press.
9 *R.H.* 25 January 1971.
10 1972: *Settlement Proposals: an explanation:* Salisbury: The British Commission on Rhodesian Opinion.
11 1970: Nutting, Anthony: *Scramble for Africa: the Great Trek to the Boer War:* London: Constable & Co.
12 *Hansard:* Vol. 75, 26 August 1969: Cols. 147-61.
13 *Hansard:* Vol. 75, 1 October 1969: Cols. 996-1037.
14 *R.H.* 28 May 1970.
15 *R.H.* 28 November 1970.
16 *R.H.* 10, 17 February, 28 September 1971.
17 *R.H.* 7 May, 3 July 1971.
18 *R.H.* 20 December 1971.
19 *R.H.* 28 July 1972.
20 *Rhodesia Government Notice No. 1158,* 28 July 1972.
   R.H. 29 July 1972.
21 *Moto:* Vol. 15, No. 2. 13 January 1973.
22 *Report of the Secretary for Labour and Social Welfare for the year ended 31 December 1972:* Cmd. R.R. 10-1973: Salisbury: Government Printer.
   As reported in *R.H.* 6 April, *Moto:* Vol. 15, No. 18. 5 May 1973.
23 *Moto:* Vol. 15, No. 2. 13 January 1973.
24 1970: Murray, D.J.: *The Governmental System in Southern Rhodesia:* Oxford: Clarendon Press.
25 For background information of Community Development see:
   1971: Passmore, Gloria C.: *The National Policy of Community Development in Rhodesia: with special reference to local government in the African rural areas:* Salisbury: University of Rhodesia.
26 The Chief Native Commissioner's Report for 1930 as quoted in:
   1971: Weinrich, A.K.H.: *Chiefs and Councils in Rhodesia: transition from patriarchal to bureaucratic power:* London: Heinemann.
27 *op. cit.* Weinrich, 1971.
28 *op. cit.* Passmore, 1971.
29 *Hansard:* Vol. 77, 12 June 1970: Cols. 517, 538.
30 *Hansard:* Vol. 80, No. 8. 3 September 1971: Cols. 580-9.
31 *Hansard: Senate Debates:* Vol. 3, No. 6. 14 June 1972: Cols. 156-160. *Moto:* Vol. 14, No. 26. 24 June 1972.
32 Passmore, Gloria: Evolution of C.D. in Rhodesia in *The Rhodesian Community Development Review:* Vol. 3, No. 4. June 1973.
   Community boards are informal. They were set up to plan and

implement projects and were encouraged to make use of every possible local resource before turning to the government for assistance. Government assistance is forthcoming in the form of professional and technical advice and in material aid such as tools, machinery, cement, etc. No cash grants are made although staff such as teachers and medical orderlies might have their salaries paid by government.

33 As reported in *R.H.* 8 October 1971.
34 *R.H.* 16 June 1972.
35 *R.H.* 13 July 1972.
36 *R.H.* 14 July 1972.
37 *Hansard:* Vol. 81, Nos. 19, 21. 27 July, 1 August 1972: Cols. 1594-1690, 1785-1864.
38 *R.F.G.* 19 September 1972.
39 *Hansard:* Vol. 83, No. 7. 30 November 1972: Cols. 566-94.
40 *R.H.* 4 December 1972.
41 As reported in *R.H.* 27 March 1973.
42 *Hansard:* Vol. 73. 1 October 1968: Cols. 24-48.
43 *Tribal Trust Land Development Corporation Ltd.* (TILCOR) *Annual Report 1969/70.*
44 Taken over as a going concern from the Sabi-Limpopo Authority.
45 According to the Report the masau berry is the fruit of the *Ziziphus Mauritiana* tree which has been used by the indigenous people for many years. It has a wide variety of uses and forms the basis of an alcoholic beverage being marketed as *Masawi Kachasu,* a soft drink and an edible food.
46 *TILCOR Annual Report for 1970/71.*
47 *TILCOR Annual Report for 1971/72.*
    See also: 1972: Wark, J.: *The Chisumbanje Story:* Salisbury: TILCOR.
48 *R.H.* 27 April 1972.
49 *S.M.* 24 December 1972.
50 *R.H.* 13 April 1972.
51 *R.F.G.* 28 July 1972.
52 *R.H.* 11 May 1972.
53 As reported in *R.H.* 23 May 1972.
54 *R.F.G.* 1 September 1972.
55 *R.H.* 1 September 1972.
56 *Hansard:* Vol. 82, No. 15. 7 September 1972: Cols. 1326-75.
57 *Hansard:* Vol. 82, No. 18. 15 November 1972: Cols. 1574-84.
58 *Indaba* is a Sindebele word meaning 'affair' or 'dispute'. For a discussion of tribal democratic machinery see pp. 40-42 of *The Demand for Independence in Rhodesia. Consultation with the African Tribesmen through their Chiefs and Headmen: The Domboshawa Indaba.* Salisbury: The Government Printer.
59 At the Domboshawa *Indaba* unanimous support for independence under the 1961 Constitution was given.
60 Information and quotations from Chapter 9. The Re-discovery of the Chiefs. *op. cit.* Holleman, 1969.
61 *Hansard:* Vol. 73. 28 January 1969: Cols. 617-34.
62 As reported in the *Pearce Report,* Chapter 9.

63 As reported in *R.H.* 28 March 1972.
64 *Hansard:* Vol. 82, No. 19. 16 November 1972: Cols. 1609-18.
65 *Hansard:* Vol. 83, No. 4. 24 November 1972: Cols. 268-91.
66 *Hansard:* Vol. 83, No. 4. 24 November 1972: Cols. 250-67.
67 *R.H.* 6 December 1972.
68 i.e. that the two clauses were inconsistent with the Declaration of Rights, Clause 9.
69 *Hansard: Senate Debates:* Vol. 3, No. 33. 13 December 1972: Col. 1167.
70 Section 44 (3) of the Constitution Act 54/1969 reads:—If the Senate resolves that a provision of a Bill would, if enacted, be inconsistent with the Declaration of Rights the Senate shall not pass the Bill containing that provision or, as the case may be, agree to that provision unless the Senate has further resolved that the enactment of that provision is necessary in the national interest.
71 *Hansard: Senate Debates:* Vol. 3, Nos. 34, 35. 14, 15 December 1972: Cols. 1218-35, 1296-1306.
72 *Hansard:* Vol. 83, No. 2. 22 November 1972: Cols 111-112. A 'hybrid' bill is a public bill which affects private interests.
73 *R.H.* 7 December 1972.
74 *R.H.* 21, 7 December 1972.
75 *R.H.* 6 January, *R.F.G.* 11 May 1973.
76 *Hansard:* Vol. 83, No. 14. 28 March 1973: Cols. 1035-6.

IX

THE URBAN AREAS

According to T. R. M. Creighton, writing of the Federal era and Southern Rhodesia's role in it, the Land Husbandry Act[1] was 'causing landless Africans to try and change to an urban industrial life [while] the Land Apportionment Act [was] making it impossible for them to do so with any dignity or ease.' He saw the Land Apportionment Act and other legislation, such as the Natives (Urban Areas) Act, as ensuring the complete segregation of Africans in all towns in Southern Rhodesia, for they could 'only live, or occupy any sort of business or professional premises, in areas designated by the European town councils as African locations.'[2]

Writing at a later period, Claire Palley described the Land Tenure Act of 1969 as re-enacting 'with many modifications the segregatory provisions of the Land Apportionment Act ... certain provisions of the African Land Husbandry Act ... and other similar legislation'.[3]

In his introduction to the Second Reading of the Land Tenure Bill the Minister of Lands, Senator P. van Heerden, took the opportunity of replying to critics of the apportionment of land between the races, for he regarded these critics as ignoring the economic facts of the position that 'some 650 000 Africans live in the European area, mostly with their families, and enjoy a far higher standard of living than most Africans living in the African area.'

AFRICAN TOWNSHIPS

Senator van Heerden then described the circumstances, according to the proposed Land Tenure Bill, under which persons of one race could own land in an area set aside for persons of the other race. He explained that the circumstances 'are strictly circum-

scribed and are limited... to the acquisition of residential accommodation in a non-racial residential area, or in a township specially
set aside for Europeans in the African area and for Africans in
the European area.'[4]

In July 1972 new regulations on African townships were gazetted. In terms of the Local Government Act these lay down the
conditions under which Africans are allowed to take up residence
in certain townships throughout the country.[5] Each township must
be under the control of a superintendent appointed by the relevant
local town or city council who, with his assistants, is responsible
for the township's administration and for the enforcement of regulations.

His powers are similar to those of any landlord or landlord's
agent in respect of any large housing estate. The regulations as
regards public gatherings and visitors to the township, however,
are probably more stringent than in other countries. The Superintendent must be notified, not less than 10 days previously, of any
gathering other than for weddings, baptisms, funerals and for
attendance at a church, cinema or for sporting events and such
like. He may forbid or order the dispersal of other types of public
meetings. As regards visitors, no person can occupy premises or
reside in the township for more than 48 hours unless he is a registered tenant or lodger, a dependent of a tenant or owner,[6] or has
a valid permit authorizing him to visit a tenant or owner.

African townships in other parts of the country have developed
roughly along similar lines. Salisbury has the largest number and
variety of townships and their development is perhaps more mature
than elsewhere. It is for these reasons therefore that townships
in Salisbury are described below.

HARARE

Harare, south of the Salisbury central business district and separate
from it only by the railway line, is also probably the oldest of
the townships. It was established in 1907 on the site of the original
'native location' set aside, as was customary, from the earliest days
of European settlement.

In 1972 the population of Harare was estimated at just under
34 000; of which just over two-thirds are single men accommodated in four large hostels.[7] Houses for married persons to rent

are of six types, ranging from two-roomed flats to six-roomed semi-
detached houses for which rentals are based according to income,
from a minimum of $5 up to a maximum of $18,50 per month.
For people in a higher income bracket, home-ownership schemes
were started in 1963 with either freehold or 99-year leasehold
tenure. There are blocks of flats for single men and women which
provide their tenants with 'comfortable and private accommodation at economic rentals.' A hostel caters for visitors, with accommodation varying in price from 35 cents to 75 cents a night
'depending upon the degree of privacy required.'[8] During October
it was announced that Salisbury City Council was to spend about
$765 000 over the next four years in replacing all the communal
ablution blocks and lavatories with water supply and lavatories
to individual houses.[9]

Harare has a shopping centre with shops ranging from small
retail to large supermarkets and a large market for the sale of
poultry, fresh fruit and vegetables. Public buildings include a
Magistrate's Court, a large hospital and various clinics, a post office
and police station, numerous churches and a mosque. There are
also beer-halls and gardens, restaurants (for both European and
African-type food), schools and youth centres, cinemas (plans are
in hand for two more luxury cinemas in the near future), sports
fields, facilities for numerous sports and the largest soccer stadium
in Southern Africa, built eventually to seat 50 000 spectators. Harare is also the site of the Rhodesia Broadcasting African Service
studio. Home industries and craft centres have been established
and large numbers of girls are employed at the Harare Weaving
Centre which produces high quality garments for export. For boys
there is the Harare Vocational Training Centre which runs two-
year courses in various trades and issues certificates of proficiency.
The township is served by numerous bus services both into the
city and for long-distance travel.

A new bus terminal was opened at Harare in 1973, on the 19th
anniversary of the starting of a bus service in the township. The
new terminal was to be used exclusively for local services operating
between African townships in Salisbury. The adjacent long-distance terminal was also scheduled for reconstruction at a cost of
about $28 000.[10]

In May, in what the *Financial Gazette* called 'a change of policy
by Salisbury City Council', the door was opened to African

businessmen to develop and run their own hotels in the townships. The African Affairs Committee decided to invite tenders from Africans to build a licensed hotel on a 2-acre site in Harare. This reversed an earlier decision which had recommended that the Council should build the hotels itself and lease them on a short or long-term basis to African businessmen.[11]

HOME-OWNERSHIP SCHEMES

KAMBUZUMA

Although Harare is of a similar type to other townships run by European local councils there are other, more modern, townships which have been built around home-ownership and other schemes. Kambuzuma, which is less than 5 miles from the centre of Salisbury, is such a township and was started about 1964. The report of the Secretary for Local Government and Housing for the year ending 31st December 1963, had reported on the increasing shortage of housing to cope with the African population 'explosion'. It was understood that the government was investigating ways and means of reducing building costs and had decided to experiment with both 'site and service'[12] and 'buy and extend' schemes. It was decided therefore to develop the 620 acres at Kambuzuma along the lines of the latter scheme with the object of providing a home-ownership scheme for the African middle income group.

The scheme, as it was developed at Kambuzuma, was to build the nucleus of a house on a plot of 2 800 sq. ft., consisting of a living room, kitchen, water closet and shower with a metred water supply and water borne sewerage (electricity to be installed by the purchaser) for a purchase price of £275. Re-payment to be made, after an initial deposit of £10, over a maximum of 30 years. When full re-payment had been made free-hold title would be given provided that the original building had been extended, within a period of 10 years, by a minimum of 2 rooms. If the extensions had not been carried out during this period the agreement would be cancelled, the amounts of monthly repayments being regarded as rent and the house transferred to another purchaser. Would-be purchasers were required to be in receipt of a minimum wage of £16 per month.[13]

By the end of 1966 Kambuzuma was fully developed with a total of 2 365 houses. In 1971 it was noted, in a newspaper article by the deputy director of the Rhodesia Council of Social Service, that out of the total number of houses only 22 had been re-possessed during the previous 3 years, the number of householders extending their houses having increased from 105 in December 1966 to 1 190 at the end of October 1971. The deputy director commented 'further evidence of the settled and contented nature of the community is provided by the crime rate, which, at an average of only one common law crime a month per 1 150 people, is believed to be the lowest of any urban African community in Rhodesia.'[14]

During February 1973 it was reported that the first phase of a new luxury hotel at Kambuzuma had been completed and was in operation. The new proprietor and licensee, Mr. P. W. T. Chipudhla, said that the hotel, which then comprised 12 double bedrooms, a cocktail and public bar, dining room and residents' lounge, would eventually have between 36 and 48 bedrooms, a new cocktail bar and a functions hall which would eventually hold 500 people.[15]

GLEN NORAH

Another type of township was developed at Glen Norah near Salisbury. In the 1971 report of the director of African Administration for the City of Salisbury it was noted that the total number of Africans in known accommodation was about 249 000, an increase of 11 000 over the previous year.[16] The provision of housing on such a scale can be understood, therefore, to be a formidable one. In an attempt to overcome some of the financial problems the government evolved a scheme whereby the larger employers of labour could lease houses for their African employees. The plan envisaged building about 6 000 houses in a township to be known as Glen Norah, with infrastructure being provided from government sources. It was hoped that this scheme would not only have the effect of releasing houses in other, overcrowded townships to waiting tenants but would also release government finance for building additional houses. In reply to critics that this would represent government involvement in 'tied-housing' schemes, a government spokesman said that tied housing was not uncommon in Rhodesia. He instanced the mining corporations, the railways and large industrial corporations which had operated such schemes for many years.

The first houses at Glen Norah became available early in 1971: by 1972 the Minister of Local Government and Housing was speaking of the government's disappointment at the poor response on the part of employers to the scheme. Employers responded by explaining that the reasons for the lack of support were largely due to what they considered to be the government's inflexible attitude in allowing only married persons to occupy the houses and to the fact that building societies were precluded from providing loans for them.

In May 1973, in what was described as a final effort to promote the financial and other advantages to be gained by those who lease houses in the Glen Norah scheme, tours around the township were jointly organized by the Ministry of Local Government and Housing and the Salisbury Chamber of Industries. It was noted that not more than 1 000 of the 4 500 houses already built had been leased by industrialists. The vacant houses had therefore been handed over to the Salisbury City Council to assist it to provide leased accommodation for the large number of Africans who had their names on the Council's waiting lists for accommodation. [17]

MARIMBA PARK

Marimba Park is a 766-acre high class African township about 10 miles west of the centre of Salisbury. It was established in 1961 to cater for the demand for low-density, high-cost housing by Africans in the higher income brackets. In its early days only 2-acre plots were available but this was followed by a scheme for one-acre plots with a building clause of $10 000 and later by smaller plots, all with building clauses. The houses in Marimba Park are as well-built, spacious and well-kept as houses in the better class European suburbs of Salisbury. As Marimba Park is a proclaimed African township the land is available for freehold tenure. Bulawayo's Luveve Township is reputedly becoming a second Marimba Park.

The African attitude towards home ownership was ably put by Mr. R. T. D. Sadomba, M.P. for Nemakonde, during a debate in the House of Assembly in August 1972: 'home ownership ...

develops ... individualism, responsibility and independence. These are the places where you can see responsible Africans proud ... I am sure if at any particular time ... something happened which would bring down the destruction of Marimba Park, the residents in that place would stand to defend it because it is their property. They feel they have a sense of possession, but if anything happened to destroy some of those places that are not owned, like Mpopoma and Harare, people would just pack up and go, and let them be destroyed.'[18]

Other townships in Salisbury have home-ownership schemes. At Highfield, a former government township, there is a similar scheme to the one at Kambuzuma but designed for a lower-income group, while at Dzivaresekwa there are site and service stands available where people are provided with plots and building materials against monthly repayments to build their own accommodation.

In July 1972, Mr. N. A. Watungwa, M.P. for Manica, put a private member's question to the Minister for Local Government and Housing on home ownership schemes for Africans. The Minister, Mr. M. H. H. Partridge, replied that there were in all 32 home-ownership schemes operated by local authorities throughout the country. The total number of plots available for purchase was 734. Mr. Partridge then tabled particulars of the scheme.[19] The debate on the Revenue Vote for the Ministry of Local Government and Housing also took place during July. During the debate Mr. R. G. S. Simmonds, M.P. for Mtoko, and Mr. M. M. Bhebe, M.P. for Ntshonalanga, asked the Minister for details of his policy regarding home-ownership schemes in African townships. Mr. Partridge replied that he did not favour any alienation of land for the provision of low-cost housing in the townships. The problem, as he saw it, was that as the African people were increasingly demanding better standards of housing, the re-acquisition of land could be a lengthy and expensive business and, with rising land costs, the end cost of houses then re-built would be very high. He favoured the provision of better housing and the alienation of land for this purpose. The Minister then said that he considered that it was not a healthy state of affairs when African housing had to be provided either by the local or central government and that one of his main aims was to endeavour to involve the private sector in the problem so that finance could more readily be obtained.[20]

On the 23rd May 1973 the Prime Minister announced certain changes in the Cabinet. Mr. Mark Partridge was moved over to become Minister of Lands and Natural Resources and his place as Minister of Local Government and Housing was taken by Mr. W. M. Irvine, M.P. for Marlborough.

At the end of May John Robertson of the *Herald*, in his weekly column, discussed what he called 'disturbing evidence' which had come to the attention of municipal authorities that future plans to establish home-ownership schemes for Africans would not receive the blessing of the government. Mr. Robertson considered that one implication of this was that all housing built for Africans in the urban areas would have to be paid for by the tax payer; another was that the government did not intend to allow any more Africans to invest in urban property. Mr. Robertson came to the conclusion that 'Clearly there is a fundamental error in Government policy.'[21]

ACCOMMODATION FOR DOMESTIC SERVANTS

According to the 1969 Census Report the number of African domestic servants living in the European areas of Salisbury exceeds the number of Europeans in those areas. What is true of Rhodesia's capital city is no less true for the other urban centres. Under the Africans (Urban Areas) Accommodation and Registration Act employers of these servants have either to make suitable arrangements for their accommodation on the property where they are employed[22] or on council-owned land in the townships. On private property, however, the Act forbids the accommodation of any dependents or of any person not directly employed by the owner of the property and makes it his responsibility to see that this requirement is adhered to. In effect this means that even if both man and wife are employed and accommodated on European premises their children cannot live with them.

SITING OF AFRICAN TOWNSHIPS

Over the years since European settlement the sprawling low-density European suburbs have tended progressively to envelop the older established African townships, which were once at a 'tolerable' distance from the European town. During 1972 it was noted in the *Herald*'s editorial that the provision and siting of townships for Africans working in European areas had become a major issue. In April the Minister of Local Government had spoken of the backlog of some 28 300 African housing units throughout the country and had explained the reasons why proposals for siting African townships in tribal areas could not be implemented at the present time.

The question of siting African townships in Tribal Trust Lands adjoining the towns and cities had been under consideration for a number of years. From the earliest days of white settlement the close proximity of large numbers of Africans had been considered as a threat to European security (memories of the Matabele and Mashona rebellions died hard), while at the same time cheap and readily available labour was a necessity. In 1971, during the debate on the Revenue Vote for Local Government and Housing, Dr. C. E. Barlow, M.P. for Avondale (Salisbury), took the opportunity of drawing the attention of the Minister of Local Government and Housing to the issue. Referring to Salisbury, Dr. Barlow pointed out that when townships such as Harare had been constructed they had been on the outskirts of the City, but at the present time they were near the centre of the business area. He then went on to urge the Minister to give a lead and see that some of the development of African townships was pushed further out into the adjoining Tribal Trust Lands.

In reply, the Minister referred to the question of transport which had been investigated, in the case of a railway branch line to Seki (the Tribal Trust Land nearest to Salisbury), four years previously and found not to be practicable. He said that he had established an agreement with the Minister of Transport that representatives from both Ministries would discuss the whole matter of transportation with representatives of the Salisbury City Council and the Rhodesia Railways. [23]

The question was considered to be such an important one that some days later Mr. G. R. Hayman, M.P. for Mazoe, brought it to the Prime Minister's notice. Mr. Hayman said that it had become apparent during the debate that the problems of siting African townships 'was more than one Minister could assume, that it was a matter of co-ordination between several Ministries.

In fact, it was a matter of a lead being given by the Prime Minister and the Cabinet.'

In reply the Prime Minister said that he had 'no hesitation in saying that this whole question of African influx, the tremendous build-up of the African population and allied to that the siting of African townships, is something that is receiving attention at the moment, and maybe it is receiving more attention than some of the other mundane subjects ... when I or any of my Ministers are in a position to say anything to assist ... we will come forward with our constructive suggestions.'[24]

Shortly afterwards the *Herald* reported on the Prime Minister's speech at the opening of the Tribal Trust Land Development Corporation's new industrial complex at Seki, which it considered to be relevant to the debate on the siting of townships. Mr. Smith had spoken of the economic imbalance between the European areas and the Tribal Trust Lands. At this time there were about 400 000 Africans employed in the European urban areas with an annual spending power of about $150 million which would double in 10 years unless recent trends changed. This spending power, which was being poured back into the European sector economy, further aggravated the imbalance and, said Mr. Smith, 'I think that gradually we must face up to the problem and see if it is not possible to divert this spending power and channel it into the Tribal Trust Lands by the development of townships for these people.'[25]

In October 1971 the Salisbury City Council adopted a motion calling for a ban on the buying or allocation of any more land for African housing within the city boundaries, and for the 'disestablishment' of Harare and Rugare townships.[26] As the chairman of Salisbury City Council's Health, Housing and African Administration committee explained, 'We now have the situation where there are eight large African townships ringing Salisbury. What would happen if the residents become politically motivated? Salisbury could be caught in a stranglehold of strikes and mob violence.'[27]

In May 1972 it was reported that delegates to the annual conference of the Local Government Association were divided over the possible siting of new African townships and that the Minister of Local Government had told the conference that it was government policy to site new townships in the tribal areas only if this was practicable and would help development there.[28]

During the debate on the Revenue Vote for Local Government and Housing in 1972; the Minister was strongly critical of those who had taken part—'Hon. members have made much play on the question as to the location of African townships... [they] are now suggesting quite seriously that we should build a tree from the leaves down; that we should start with a leaf—the question of a place where an African township should be—and then, from that, build down to the whole question of infrastructure, communications, etc. I find this a most surprising way of thinking... the plain facts of the matter are that their suggestions make economic nonsense in most instances.' Mr. Partridge added that it was government policy to encourage African townships in the Tribal Trust Lands where it was practicable and, in the African townships in the European areas, to encourage Africans to conduct their own businesses. [29]

Early in January 1973 the *Mail* announced that the Salisbury City Council was to examine new plans to replace the existing African townships with a major satellite city in the Seki Tribal Trust Land for housing about two hundred thousand Africans. A few months later it was reported that City Council representatives had been holding discussions with Ministry of Internal Affairs representatives and that an investigation of the feasibility of such a satellite city at Seki was being carried out by Tilcor (The Tribal Trust Land Development Corporation) in association with the Ministry. [30]

In mid-May the Minister of Local Government and Housing, in an address to the annual congress of the Local Government Association, announced revolutionary new policies for regional planning. These envisaged the division of the country into ten regions for planning purposes and the creation of regional planning councils. Mr. Partridge spoke of the call for housing African workers in the tribal areas and said that the government had accepted that where this was practicable it could be done but he stressed that the test of practicability must be related to all the services such an arrangement would necessitate. He did say, however, that the solution to the problem 'is surely better found in the regional concept of urban growth than in adopting uneconomic expediences. I see, therefore, the regions as including both the European and Tribal Trust areas, and development on the basis of a regional plan of complete satellite towns in both the Tribal Trust areas and the European areas.' [31]

LOCAL GOVERNMENT

Urban local authorities in the European areas (which include Coloured and Asian people) operate on broadly similar lines to local authorities in other countries influenced by British customs and traditions. Hitherto, Asians and Coloureds have not in practice been members of the larger municipal councils; in July 1971, however, it was announced that for the first time in its civic history Bulawayo had two non-European candidates for its municipal elections. Not until 1972, however, was the first Asian actually elected to Bulawayo City Council. At the same time, also for the first time, an Asian candidate was elected to Salisbury City Council.

Until 1969 the African townships situated in the vicinity of all Rhodesian towns were the responsibility of either the central government or of the local authorities of the nearest European urban centre. In recent years the larger townships have had Advisory Boards, elected by qualified residents, but as the name indicates these have been strictly advisory. In Salisbury, for instance, there were a number of townships, Mufakose, Mabvuku, Harare and Tafara, which were the responsibility of the Salisbury Municipality's African Administration Department. On the other hand there were Kambuzuma, Highfield, St. Mary's, Dzivaresekwa and Glen Norah which were under the control and management of the government.

In early 1971 an amendment to the Municipal Act was tabled in the House. Explaining its features, the Minister of Local Government referred specifically to African townships, for the Bill contained new provisions directly affecting them. The Minister stated that, although it was government policy to disengage from the operation of African townships and progressively to hand over its existing townships to the local authorities, it would nevertheless retain an over-all national responsibility for standards of administration, services and accommodation and for social policy. These standards would also be extended to established townships currently administered by local authority.

The Minister explained that under the Constitution it was provided that in European areas no African could have a local government vote except in African townships established there. It was government policy therefore 'to encourage African participation in the local government of the African residential areas and to

seek an evolving form of local government in the African townships.' In pursuit of this policy, the Minister said that, as it was
considered that local authorties were more competent to discharge
the responsibilities of day-to-day administration and planning than
the central government, the government's townships would gradually be transferred to the appropriate municipalities.[32]

Shortly after the Second Reading of the Municipal Amendment
Bill, a Ministry spokesman announced that Rhodesia's first urban
African local authority would come into being in June (subject
to the passing of the Bill) at St. Mary's Township, about 12 miles
south of Salisbury and near to the border of Seki Tribal Trust
Land. The spokesman described this as 'a significant development
in urban African self-government' and went on to outline the
procedure and arrangements being made.

St. Mary's Township Board would have 12 members elected
by a secret ballot by the township's residents and three members
nominated by the government (this was later changed to four
members, two to be nominated by the government and two by
the Salisbury City Council). The initial function of the Board
would be the management of primary schools in its area but there
would be a gradual extension of responsibilities in the fields of
preventive health facilities, welfare and amenities, recreation and
entertainment and the operation of markets. The Board would
also consider and report on any by-laws and regulations which
the Salisbury City Council proposed to make for the Township,
and on any matter referred to it by the Minister of Local Government or the City Council. Additionally it would undertake such
other responsibilities and functions as might be assigned to it by
the Minister on the recommendation of the City Council. Revenue
would come from tax levies and from government grants.[33]

Previous to the election it was announced that St. Mary's
Township had a population of 17 584, of which about 3 500 were
qualified to vote.[34] Of those people qualified to vote 64,5 *per cent*
had registered for the coming election. There would be forty-four
candidates contesting the election.

The election was held on the 13th June 1971, and twelve
members were elected in a 60 *per cent* poll. The nominated
members were Councillor T. Tanser, chairman of the City Council's Health, Housing and Administration Committee and Mr.
R. C. Briggs, director of the Council's African Administration

Department; the government's nominated members were Mr. E. Roper, the senior Community Development Officer and Mr. B. Jones, an assistant secretary of finance.[35] The Minister of Local Government commented later that the results of the election augured well for the future and that similar plans were in hand for other townships where local authorities did not exist at that time.

During 1972 Harare and Mabvuku held elections for their respective Advisory Boards and Mufakose held its first election for its newly established Advisory Board. In March the Minister of Local Government described future plans for the establishment of local authorities (which would replace the old Advisory Boards) in African townships in an address to the Associated Chambers of Commerce of Rhodesia. Mr. Partridge considered that this move was necessary because of the increased flow of Africans to the urban areas. The African population, he said, had increased 50 times in the last 100 years, 'consequently their ordened social system could not function in urban areas where large numbers of Africans now lived.'[36]

In September a departmental draft of the Urban Councils' Bill was gazetted. It was designed to take the place of the Municipal Town Management and Local Government Acts and to clear the way for a new system of local government. With regard to African townships, changes were to be made in their administration and financial control and all revenue was to be administered by a council.[37] The Bill also provided for ownership of land in an African township and for the erection of residential accommodation for Africans by employers and others; it also empowered councils to sell residential and business accommodation in the townships to Africans.

In early November it was reported that the Salisbury City Council was challenging large sections of the Bill on the grounds that it gave the Minister power to make radical changes without prior consent of Parliament. With specific reference to the African townships, the *Financial Gazette*'s reporter, Bernard Miller, commented that 'Mr. Partridge envisages African townships running their own affairs and paying their own way to an increasing extent. They would become autonomous, answerable only to his Ministry. The City Council obviously sees this as another threat to its powers, with African township councils eventually representing and controlling more people and more revenue than the City authority itself.'[38] Later in November it was announced that the City Council was supported, in its criticism of the Urban Councils Bill and in its opposition to the powers proposed to be vested in the Minister, by the Salisbury Municipal Employees' Association and the Local Government Association of Rhodesia.[39]

Shortly after the publication of the draft Urban Councils Bill it was reported that Salisbury City Council had told the Ministry of Local Government some four months previously that it was opposed to the allocation of additional functions to St. Mary's Township Board before the settlement of the question of future local government of African townships in European areas. The Ministry had apparently suggested that the constitution of St. Mary's Board be extended to permit it to undertake the administration of market stalls and to permit it to be responsible for the provision and maintenance of welfare and recreational facilities.[40]

Early in 1973 a spokesman from the Ministry of Local Government stated that the powers of St. Mary's Township Board had been extended despite strong opposition from the Salisbury City Council. The Ministry had already set up commissions of residents to consider the establishment of township boards in the former government townships of Dzivaresekwa and Kambuzuma with a view to extending the same powers to the boards of these townships. Later in the year Mr. E. G. Watungwa, M.P. for Harare, asked the Minister when he proposed to establish local boards at the townships of Highfield, Mufakose, Harare and Mabvuku. He considered that the people of these townships, particularly Highfield and Harare, would be more able to run their own board than a newly established township such as St. Mary's. Mr. Partridge replied that he could give no firm date for this for the whole question was under discussion with the Salisbury City Council.[41]

Towards the end of March the Urban Councils Bill was published in the *Government Gazette*. In the debate in the House, which followed in early May, the Minister explained that in order to cover the intended repeal of the Municipal, Local Government and Town Management Act it was necessary to introduce provisions for African township administration into the Bill. Establishment and development of African townships, fixing of rents and service charges, the replacement of the African revenue account by an African Affairs account designed to meet only expenditure generated from within a township, and provision for the right of an African to own land in an African township were all provided for in the Bill. The measure which the Minister regarded as being of primary importance was that relating to the promotion of local government for Africans. By this, Mr. Partridge said, he did not intend that local authorities should be divested of their responsibility to provide and maintain houses and major engineering services but that 'Africans should be encouraged to participate progressively in the operation of their own social, recreational, welfare and other service functions in their own way.' Commenting later, on the passage of the Bill through Parliament, Mr. Partridge was quoted as saying that only two of its 272 clauses had caused much debate. These two clauses related to the question of adding fluoride to the water supply and to the question of whether M.P's would be allowed to be members of local authorities. [42] The Bill was eventually gazetted as the Urban Councils Act No. 12 of 1973.

URBAN INFLUX

The intention behind the Africans (Urban Areas) Accommodation and Registration Act is not only to ensure that African employees, both in the private and the commercial sector, are housed in adequate, properly serviced accommodation. It is also an attempt to curb large numbers of unemployed people and their families from flooding the urban areas, a wide-spread problem in Africa.

Another Act concerned with curbing urban influx is the Africans (Registration and Identification) Act, which, when it was first passed, barred alien Africans from taking up employment in urban areas and provided for the registration of Africans above the age of 16. During November 1972 an amending bill was introduced into the House designed to change this Act in several ways. It makes it obligatory for an African to carry his registration papers on his person at all times and, in regard to alien Africans, makes it possible for them to be ordered back to their countries of origin.

The Bill caused much controversy and churches, political parties, members of Parliament and private individuals all voiced their objections to it. [43] In a special interview with the *Financial Gazette* the Minister of Internal Affairs, Mr. L. B. Smith, was quoted as saying that the Bill's primary purpose was not in connection with influx control although, by supplying an effective means of identification, it could facilitate such control. In reply to criticism that the Bill could be thought of as discriminatory, the Minister said that the reason why other groups in the country were not required to carry identity documents was, in the main, the expense of a general registration and the fact that members of other races were more readily identifiable.[44]

The Africans (Registration and Identification) Act No. 48 of 1972 was gazetted on the 26th January 1973. The *Herald* commented that 'Africans now face stiff penalties for not carrying identity documents': contravention carries a fine of up to $100 or imprisonment of up to six months or both.[45] In February amendments to the Act were published in the *Government Gazette*. Exemptions from carrying identity documents for certain categories of Africans (Rhodesian citizens arriving at a designated point of entry with a valid passport; tribesmen residing within Tribal Trust Land—with the exception of certain areas in the north-east of the country; members of the police, prison services, army and air force, and district assistants employed by the Ministry of Internal Affairs in uniform; African owners or lessees of farms in the Purchase areas and employees on farms and mines while on the employer's property) were brought into force.[46]

At the opening of Parliament in mid-June 1973 the President announced that a bill to provide for the registration and identification of all persons would be brought before the House in the next session. While welcoming this announcement, the *Herald* commented that support for such a bill would have to await publication of its details. It warned, however, that a demand by the authorities for too much information—such as 'would turn the exercise into a racial inquisition or a list of a man's convictions or changes of employment—would rightly arouse opposition.'[47]

Following the Registration and Identification Bill, the Vagrancy Amendment Bill had its Second Reading on the 1st December 1972. In introducing the Bill, the Minister of Internal Affairs spoke of the need to give the authorities power to remove undesirable elements from the urban areas. According to the Minister repeated prosecutions had had little effect on the problem of 'the loafer, the idle person who is living off his wits, the man who is prepared to sponge off his relatives and fellow men for

indefinite periods for his own ends and the detriment of the standard of living of the whole community that lives in the urban
areas.'

Replying to a question as to where these persons would be sent
the Minister said that in some ways the African was better off
than the European because he could always return to the tribal
areas. He reminded his questioner that in the tribal areas undesir-
ables could be barred from a particular area by their own chiefs
and the tribal courts but this did not preclude them from all tribal
areas. If they were unable to find residence and employment in
the tribal areas, however, they would be entitled to seek work in
any rural area of the country, including the African Purchase areas,
where there were many opportunities for employment. The Minister added that there was no need for anyone in Rhodesia to be
unemployed. On the other hand, the Minister said, 'the average
European who loafs ... is found as a vagrant in the urban areas
of our country has no country home to go to; he has to find his
own remedy for the problems which he creates for himself ... the
method of dealing with European vagrants is laid down in the
principal Act.'[48]

On the 7th December the Minister of Internal Affairs moved
that the Vagrancy Amendment Bill be read for the third time.
Mr. E. G. Watungwa, however, stood to register his objection to
the passing of the bill and asked that it be suspended for six months
to give the Minister more time to study the points raised during
the debate. He felt that the Minister had not heeded the fears
expressed by other African M.P.'s about the amendment. Mr.
Watungwa said that the amendment 'indirectly forces the African
people to go and seek jobs on the farms and elsewhere in the Tribal
Trust Lands.'[49] After a division, however, the Bill was read for
the Third Time. It was gazetted on the 26 January 1973 as the
Vagrancy Amendment Act No. 51 of 1972.

SQUATTERS

After a number of years during which repeated attempts had been
made to stop the continuing increase in the number of illegal shanties
being built, particularly around Harare Township, the Salisbury
City Council announced, in January 1972, that it had passed a

resolution to ask for the aid of the B.S.A. Police to remove squatters from areas in Harare Township.[50]

In March new by-laws were approved (which had to be promulgated by the government) to enable the Director of African Administration to demolish unauthorized structures in areas next to African townships. Shortly afterwards the Director issued a statement that all residents in a shanty town known as Old Bricks, Harare, would soon be informed that their continued presence was illegal and that those people who were unemployed should return with their dependents to their homelands. According to the *Herald* this was the first phase in the removal of some 5 000 squatters in the area.[51]

In an editorial on the problem the *Herald* commented that the shanties were going up quicker than the municipality could deal with them and queried whether, even with the most rigorous policing under the new by-laws, it would make much difference to the 'overcrowding' that must be reflected by 18 000 unsatisfied applicants for married accommodation.[52]

By the end of the first week in April 1 000 shanties had been demolished and a rehabilitation team, consisting of staff from the Ministries of Internal Affairs and Labour and Social Welfare and from the City Health and African Administration Departments, moved in to offer assistance to the people affected. It was reported that many residents of Harare Township had expressed relief and pleasure at the demolition for they regarded the squatter's camp as a threat to their well-being in respect of vice, crime and health.[53]

In its editorial on the subject, the *Sunday Mail* considered that the destruction of the shanty town had 'quite apart from the obvious ones ... served one good purpose: it has drawn public attention to the problem that affects most of Rhodesia's towns and cities.' The *Mail* queried whether the municipality had its priorities right—'there is much talk of influx control. This is another way of saying that the problem should be swept under the carpet. The problem is not how to stop Africans flooding into the towns, but how to stop them wanting to.'[54]

This appeared to be an opinion also held by the Minister of Local Government and Housing. In his address to the annual conference of the Local Government Association, later in the year, he said 'intensive and rapid development of the Tribal Trust Lands, coupled with more attractive conditions for agricultural employees in European farming areas, are pre-requisites to the success of any measures to control the influx of Africans to major centres in the country.'[55]

In October the Prime Minister took the opportunity of referring to the same problem. He warned that it could prove to be a double-edged sword 'not only by creating problems of over-population in the big urban centres but by creating problems of under-population in vast areas of our country which are already today under-populated.'[56]

In mid-February 1973 a three-day symposium on influx and urbanization problems in Salisbury was held at the University of Rhodesia. The main paper, presented by Councillor E. R. Langley, gave the figures of population density in Salisbury as 2 230 to the square mile but pointed out that Harare, with an area of two square miles, had a density of 34 000 to the square mile. Discussing these figures Councillor Langley said 'Fundamentally, the need is to curb the influx into Salisbury from the rural areas; and more desirable still is to induce many already living in Salisbury to return to the rural areas. It is, of course, the African with whom we are concerned.' The symposium, attended by government ministers, city councillors, sociologists and economists, discussed a number of ways in which the problem could be dealt with, in particular the necessity of developing the tribal areas to provide a higher standard of living and more attractive conditions. It appeared to be accepted by all, however, that a great deal more research was needed on a problem which was not, by any means, merely confined to Rhodesian cities. [57]

HOUSING FOR THE COLOURED AND ASIAN COMMUNITIES

In 1967 the Secretary for Local Government and Housing stated in his annual report—'the majority of Asian and Coloured families are either living in leased private properties or own their own houses. In the larger centres, however, government and local authorities have made an important contribution for these communities in the form of home ownership or letting schemes.'[58]

The Constitution classifies all people other than Africans as 'Europeans'; its accompanying Act, the Land Tenure Act, therefore, does not preclude members of the Asian and Coloured groups from living in any of the European areas defined by the Act. In practice, however, only a small minority of the wealthier members of these groups have actually bought houses in the European suburbs. Housing estates have been developed by local authorities in the larger urban centres of the country both for letting at economic rentals for the lower income groups and for home ownership schemes.

In 1968 the government introduced a scheme whereby it guaranteed 90 *per cent* of the cost of building new houses in the recognized areas for Europeans, Coloureds and Asians and for African townships. Government policy encourages the building of low-cost housing and thus loans under the scheme are restricted to $8 000 in Salisbury, Bulawayo, Umtali and Gwelo and to $8 550 in the smaller centres. By May 1971 it was noted that, since the scheme had been introduced, a total of 1 059 guarantees had been granted for the construction of new private dwellings, a figure which was considered to be very low, probably because the scheme had not been sufficiently publicized. [59]

WESTWOOD

Apart from suburbs almost exclusively populated by separate racial groups, there is a non-racial township in Salisbury known as Westwood. It lies about seven miles west of the city centre and comprises about 310 acres.

Westwood began life as a European residential area, but when Kambuzuma African Township was established on its borders most Europeans moved away and the government decided to purchase the area and develop it as a non-racial township. During 1970 a government spokesman gave the information that the total number of plots already sold in the township was 31 and that applications were continual.

Although there was a continuous demand for plots in the township the government has a selective policy in granting property rights in the area. All applications are considered on their merits and sales are confined to persons who have a genuine reason for wanting to live in the area. The spokesman gave as an example of a genuine reason persons who had entered into a racially mixed marriage.

Plots varying from a quarter to one acre in size are available and at present (1973) prices range from $350 to $1 250 depending upon plot size. Building regulations stipulate that properties built on the land must be of the minimum value of $2 000 on the quarter-acre, $2 500 on the half-acre and $5 000 on the one-acre plots.[60]

THE RESIDENTIAL PROPERTY OWNERS (PROTECTION) BILL

In 1970 the draft of the Residential Property Owners (Protection) Bill (P.O.P. Bill) was published. The government had announced as far back as 1967 that such legislation would be introduced and had produced nine drafts of the bill in the intervening three years. At a press conference held to introduce the 1970 draft bill, the Minister of Local Government and Housing said that the government was firmly of the opinion that, with the Coloured and Asian population amounting to 10 *per cent* of the European population, it was essential, in order to preserve racial harmony and to deal with problems affecting property valuations when the influx of one race into the area of another occurred, that legislation of this description should be introduced.

The Minister referred to the fact that residential segregation had been the custom for many years but that it had only the partial support of the law. The practical effects of this had meant that the housing problems of Asians and Coloureds had gone by default, resulting in overcrowded conditions and the impoverishment of whole areas. 'The problems were inherently due to differences of culture and custom, distinguished generally by race and no other practical criteria' added the Minister.

The draft bill was described as being designed to operate in European areas that were predominently residential in character. It was concerned with the occupation and ownership of residential land by the main non-African races. In terms of the Bill, the President could (subject to the stated procedures) declare a residential area to be an 'exclusive area' within which persons of the 'excluded' race or denomination could not occupy or own land.

In reply to a suggestion that the bill was a Rhodesian version of the South African Group Areas Act, Mr. Partridge said that study would show that Rhodesia's approach to the problem was 'quite dissimilar'; there were many differences between the two measures. The *Herald* in its editorial on the same day commented that 'distaste for the Bill's purpose need not blind one to the fairness of some of its provisions. We have a feeling that both the R.F. and leaders of the Asian and Coloured communities had expected something much tougher.'[61]

At the beginning of 1971 *Herald* reporter Ian Mills said that the Bill was in danger of running aground for it had been 'the target of almost constant criticism and condemnation ... Asian and Coloured organizations and church groups led the fight against it. Now local authorities are attacking its financial provisions and their obligations under them.' A few days later the Prime Minister was reported as saying at a press interview: 'our minds are still open. We are always prepared to think—and re-think—and this must apply particularly to controversial legislation such as this Bill. If anybody can tell us how to improve this Bill then we will improve it. At this stage nothing is final.'[62]

The Bill did not feature in the President's speech at the opening of parliament in June 1972. When asked later about this omission and whether the government still planned to introduce it, the Prime Minister answered that certain legislation, which had been contemplated, had been suspended during the period of the test of acceptability but was now being re-examined. The P.O.P. Bill, he explained, represented a problem, for 'these were racial problems and the Government would try to deal with them in an honest way and to the best advantage of all Rhodesians.'[63]

In November, however, it was reported that the government was considering amendments to existing legislation designed to protect property values. The report added that it was understood that the government had decided not to introduce new legislation in terms of the P.O.P. Bill but to achieve its aims by amending current laws involving the application of restrictive clauses in residential property title deeds.[64] The new legislation, contained in the General Laws Amendment Bill, was tabled in the House by the Acting Minister of Justice, Mr. J. H. Howman, on the 8th December. The specific amendment, to the Deeds Registries Act, would allow property owners, intending to establish a township or to sub-divide land, to apply for registration of restrictive conditions of title. Questioned by reporters after the House was adjourned, Mr. Howman said that this amendment was not a substitute for the Property Owners' Bill for this was still under consideration by the government. He explained that where a restrictive condition had been registered a land owner could subsequently apply for the eviction of anyone thereafter occupying the property in contravention of the restrictive clause. The definition of owner did not include the State, a local government authority or any other authority. [65]

AFRICAN BEER

Until 1963 the sale of 'western-type' liquor to Africans was prohibited (with the exception, since 1959, of bona fide residents of hotels). The brewing and sale of traditional African or opaque beer [66] for commercial purposes (as distinct from the brewing of beer for social and ritual purposes in the tribal areas) has been subject to legislation since an Ordinance of 1911 which regulated production and sales and designated that profits therefrom should be used solely for African welfare.

Latterly the brewing and sale of this beer has become big business and the virtual monopoly of the various municipalities throughout the country. The combined turnover of the 48 selling outlets operated by the Greater Salisbury Liquor Undertaking Department for the year July 1971 to 1972, for instance, reached $6 171 842. Profits are entirely ploughed back into sporting, recreational, social, health and cultural services for Africans living in the municipal area.

In the 1972 Budget the Minister of Finance, Mr. J. J. Wrathall, gave notice that he was going to introduce a tax of one cent per litre on African beer brewed and sold for commercial purposes. He estimated that he expected this tax to yield about $670 000 in the 1972/3 financial year and about $1 600 000 in a full year.

Following his announcement about the tax the Minister went on to say that, in diverting part of the profits from the sale of African beer, he had in mind the recommendation of the Select Committee on Liquor Licensing which had recommended that part of the beer profits should be spent in the Tribal Trust Lands, but he felt that the tax should not be designated for any specific purpose but allocated on a priority basis and would therefore be paid into the Consolidated Revenue Fund. [67]

Protests followed from various municipalities and talks between Treasury officials and representatives of the city councils of Salisbury, Bulawayo, Umtali and Gwelo followed. In October the Minister announced that he had agreed to halve the amount of the tax until 1975 when the position would have to be reviewed.

In choosing whether to pass the cost of the tax on to the consumer or to reduce health and welfare services, Bulawayo City Council decided to raise the price of beer while Salisbury City Council decided upon extensive cuts in its programme for welfare facilities in the African townships.

In the report of the general manager of the Salisbury Liquor Undertaking Department for the year 1971/2 it was noted that the consumption of Western-type beer by Africans, sold throughout the municipality's beer-halls, had more than doubled during the period. The general manager attributed this as partly due to consumer resistance to the increase in the cost of African beer. In estimating the profit for the next year the manager said that it should be in excess of $2 million.[68]

In his speech at the State Opening of Parliament in June 1973 the President stated that the African Beer Act would very likely be amended during the following session in order to strengthen the position of local authorities and to simplify the procedures.[69]

THE LAND TENURE ACT

LICENCED PREMISES

On the 26th July 1972, in answer to an African M.P's question on the effect of consumption of alcohol on the incidence of crime, the Minister of Justice, Mr. D. W. Lardner-Burke, took the opportunity of announcing that the government was considering action where 'there is evidence that excessive consumption of alcohol is leading to crimes of violence, public nuisance and immorality.'[70]

At the end of the week the *Gazette* published Government Notice No. 717 setting forth the Land Tenure (Licenced Premises) (Prescription of Occupation) Regulations 1972, which defined attendance at licenced premises for the purpose of consuming or purchasing liquor, liquid refreshment, food or any other commodity, or using any of the facilities provided at such premises as

constituting 'occupation' for the purposes of the Land Tenure
Act.

The effect of the regulations (which were to come into force
on the 1st November) was to compel owners of licenced premises
in both European and African areas to apply for permits to enable
them to serve customers of a race other than the one whose 'interests were paramount in that area'. As the *Financial Gazette* commented, these regulations would ensure that African beer-halls and
bars in white areas would soon be a thing of the past. It was reported
that hoteliers and licensees were seeking legal opinion over the
new regulations.

A government spokesman was quoted as saying that 'experience
had shown that there had been an undesirable increase in sexual
offences and violent crimes associated with drinking and intoxicat-
ing liquors. This had led to friction and interference with the
amenities surrounding many licensed premises. The purpose of
these regulations is to control the use of liquor.'[71]

During October the government, in response to a request from
the Hotels Association of Rhodesia, issued a statement clarifying
the regulations. This statement made it clear that Africans would
not be allowed to drink in European area bars (and *vice versa*) after
7 p.m. on weekdays, 1 p.m. on Saturdays and not at all on Sundays.
The *Sunday Mail* considered that 'nothing could be more calculated to create unpleasantness and bitterness.'

From a financial point of view it was calculated that in the Salisbury area alone hoteliers and bar owners stood to lose more than
a million dollars *per annum*. According to the *Financial Gazette*,
however, it was not the actual cash loss to the industry which
was upsetting the trade 'but the Government's alleged manipula-
tion of the Land Tenure Act against private enterprise ... [and]
the Government's insistence on including multi-racial hotels in
the 'occupation' limitations.'[72]

On the 2nd November it was announced that the new regulations
were to be challenged in the High Court. The applicants, the
Federal and Queen's Hotels and Mr. Justin Nyoka, a Salisbury
journalist, were reported to be seeking an order asking the court
to declare the regulations null and void. Respondents were named
as the Minister of Lands, Senator P. van Heerden; the Minister
of Local Government and Housing, Mr. M. H. H. Partridge; the
Municipality of Salisbury; and the Attorney-General Mr. E. A. T.

Smith, Q.C. At the hearing no evidence was given but legal argument was presented by counsel based mainly on the interpretation of words and meaning in the Land Tenure Act from which the regulations had been drawn.

On the 16th November, in a judgement of several thousand words, Mr. Justice Goldin said that 'I am of the view that the Land Tenure (Licensed Premises) (Prescription of Occupation) Regulations 1972 published in Rhodesia Government Notice 717 of 1972 are *ultra vires* the Land Tenure Act [No. 55 of 1969] and are of no force or effect.'

The *Herald*, in an editorial comment in the same issue as its report on the court's ruling, considered that the judgement was most interesting 'not so much because it upholds the protests of those who had opposed the Government's decision but because it emphasizes how careful Governments must be in drafting legislation and how important the courts are as a watchdog of the public right when Parliament is not precise in its intention and its meaning … The judgement does not allow the Minister even the consolation of arguing that his reason for introducing the regulation was a good one. The given reason was to avoid a situation where friction might arise between the races. Praiseworthy as that may be, said the Judge, Parliament had not endowed the Minister with unlimited power to separate the races every time he was of the opinion that friction might arise.'[73] The next day the government announced its intention of appealing against the judgement and warned that licensees should continue to observe the new hours in the meantime.

The government's appeal was heard in the Appeal Court Salisbury on 28th November before the Chief Justice Sir Hugh Beadle, the Judge President Mr. Justice Macdonald and the Judge of Appeal Mr. Justice Lewis. The Appeal was dismissed on the 15th December by a two-to-one majority with the Chief Justice dissenting; before the judgement of the Appeal Court was given, however, the Minister of Lands moved the Second Reading of an amendment to the principal Land Tenure Act. This amendment was originally intended to change the regulations covering the ownership and leasing of land by *bona fide* religious, educational and charitable organizations but at the Second Reading the Minister informed the House that he would, in view of the recent High Court ruling, introduce a further amendment at Committee stage to clarify the government's intentions with regard to the definition of the word 'occupation' in the Act. [74]

The amending Bill was read a third time with the approval of the constitutional two-thirds' majority in the House of Assembly on the 8th December and in the Senate on 15th December. It was gazetted on the 29th December as the Land Tenure Amendment Act No. 53 of 1972.

Criticism was summed up by Henry Maasdorp, the *Sunday Mail* reporter, in an article entitled *Life in a Sort of Political Hell*. Regarding the Minister of Lands as the main offender he wrote 'more than a week before the appeal judges gave their verdict; notwithstanding that he himself had asked them to give one; that the matter was still in the strict sense *sub judice* ... he began a parliamentary process to alter the very section the judges were to pronounce upon. He inserted the words "Notwithstanding the provisions of any other law ..." and substituted "presence" for "attendance". He got this amendment through its final stage in Parliament on the very day the Appelate Division delivered its judgement, which was virtually nullified before it was delivered.' [75]

The new regulations for re-imposing the 7 p.m. closing time for African bars in European areas and vice versa from February 2nd 1973 were published in mid-January replacing the regulations which the High Court had declared *ultra vires* in November 1972. A government statement issued at the time stated that permits already issued would remain valid and in force (these had been given to hotels and night clubs allowing Africans to be served with liquor outside the set hours in certain circumstances). The statement also referred to hotels outside municipal areas, which would be allowed to apply for permits to serve liquor during hours laid down by the Liquor Act (i.e. at the hours in force before the new regulations). [76]

SWIMMING POOLS

On the 29th September 1972, the *Gazette* published a notice to the effect that the Minister of Lands had issued new regulations to be read with section 70 of the Land Tenure Act. These were the Land Tenure (Swimming Baths) (Prescription of Occupation) Regulations 1972. They stated that attendance at swimming baths to which members of the public were admitted would constitute 'occupation' for the purposes of the Act. This, taken in conjunction with the Land Tenure Amendment Act 53/72, (see above) made it clear that public swimming baths were regarded as important as public bars in terms of the Act. As a spokesman for the Ministry of Lands was quoted as saying 'the decision to classify attendance at public swimming baths as being "occupation" in terms of the Land Tenure Act now makes attendance subject to control by permit ... the new regulations will apply equally in European and African areas.'[77]

According to the manager of the Salisbury Municipal Amenities Department the new regulations would not affect many people, for African attendance at public swimming pools outside the African townships was negligible. The president of the Rhodesia Amateur Swimming Association was quoted as saying that he saw 'no difficulty for competitive swimming unless the government becomes difficult about issuing permits. Competitive swimming in Rhodesia is multi-racial from the national to the club level and there is no racially discriminating legislation in any swimming body's constitution.' The *Herald* noted that public pools had been multi-racial since a successful court action in 1961 which had challenged the 'Europeans only' notices at Council swimming pools.

The High Court ruling on the licensed premises regulations under the Land Tenure Act also applied to the regulations, issued in September 1972, applicable to swimming baths. Consequently the amendment to the Act, regarding the use of the term 'occupation' also necessitated the re-issue of regulations concerning public swimming baths. These came into force on 2nd February 1973. Under these regulations Africans wishing to swim at public swimming baths in European areas are allowed to do so only if the person in control of the swimming bath has obtained government permission. The same conditions apply to public pools in African areas where Europeans, Asians and Coloureds might wish to swim.[78]

NOTES

1 The Land Husbandry Act of 1951 provides for the allocation of farming and grazing rights for individual Africans in the Tribal Trust Lands.

2 1960: Creighton, T.R.M.: *Anatomy of Partnership: Southern Rhodesia and the Federation of Rhodesia and Nyasaland:* London: Faber.

3 Palley, Claire: Law and the Unequal Society: *Race:* Vol. XII, No. 1: 1970.

4 'An African may own, lease or occupy land in an African township in the European area and a European may own, lease or occupy land in a European township in an African area. But a European may not own or lease land in an African township in a European area and an African may not own or lease land in a European township in an African area except with the authority of the appropriate Minister and subject to such terms and conditions as he may impose.'
Hansard: Vol. 75. 15 October 1969: Cols. 1476-85.

5 *Rhodesia Government Notice No. 657 of 1972.*

6 The regulations define a dependent as the wife of a tenant or owner; a child under 19 years of age of a tenant or owner or who is enrolled at an attending school or other training institution in the area of the Council's jurisdiction; any aged or infirm ascendent, descendent or collateral relative of a tenant or owner or his wife. An owner is defined as a person who is acquiring or has acquired premises in a part of a township set aside for a home-ownership scheme or for trading purposes and includes a caretaker.

7 These men are those who have left wives and families in the tribal areas either through preference or from necessity. Many are awaiting allocation of married accommodation.

8 *R.H.* 19 October 1972.

9 *R.H.* 9 October 1972.

10 *R.H.* 2 February, 10 May 1973.

11 *R.F.G.* 13 April 1973.

12 'Site and Service' schemes vary in detail but usually they are schemes whereby the local authority supplies a site with water and sewage facilities and lays out roads. Approved persons can then build their own accommodation with materials supplied by the council for a small outlay which can then be repaid over a period of time.

13 *Annual Report of the Secretary for Local Government and Housing. Year ended 31 December 1963:* CSR 20-1964: Salisbury Government Printer.
Measurements and currency units are as in the report which was written in pre-decimalization days.

14 Article entitled *Sylvia Chunga—Mother of Kambuzuma* by Joan Matthewman, Deputy Director, Rhodesia Council of Social Service in *R.H.* 26 November 1971.

15 *R.H.* 15 February 1973.

16 *Annual Report of the Director of African Administration for the City of Salisbury. Year ended 30 June 1971:* Salisbury: Government Printer.

17 *R.H.* 10 May 1973.

18 *Hansard:* Vol. 81, No. 23. 3 August 1972: Col. 2026.

19 *Hansard:* Vol. 81, No. 16. 21 July 1972: Cols. 1278-80.

20 *Hansard:* Vol. 81, No. 20, 28 July 1972: Cols. 1694-1773.

21 *R.H. Business and Financial Review* 31 May 1973.

22 This accommodation, known colloquially as a *kia*, is in the grounds of nearly every European house. It usually consists of a bedroom for each servant (which may or may not be furnished with more than a bed) and a separate area for cooking. The *kias* have their own lavatories and sometimes showers.

23 *Hansard:* Vol. 79, No. 25. 12 August 1971: Cols. 1762-3, 1790.

24 *Hansard:* Vol. 80, No. 1. 24 August 1971: Cols. 20, 46-7.

25 *R.H.* 23 August 1971.

26 *S.M.* 31 October 1971.

27 As reported in *R.H.* 27 April 1972.

28 *R.H.* 23 May 1972.

29 *Hansard:* Vol. 81, No. 23. 3 August 1972: Col. 2004.

30 *S.M.* 7 January, 9 April 1973.

31 As reported in *R.F.G.* 18 May 1973.

32 *Hansard:* Vol. 78, No. 22. 12 March 1971: Cols. 1317-8.

33 *R.H.* 24 March 1971.

34 Voting rights are held by registered tenants and lodgers.

35 *R.H.* 14, 17 June 1971.

36 *R.H.* 14 March 1972.

37 *R.H.* 16 September 1972.

38 *R.F.G.* 10 November 1972.

39 *R.H.* 27 November 1972.

40 *R.H.* 13 November 1972.

41 *R.H.* 24 January 1973.
   Hansard: Vol. 83, No. 18. 4 April 1973: Cols. 1291-2.

42 *Government Gazette* Vol. LI, No. 14. 23 March 1973: Salisbury: Government Printer.
   Hansard: Vol. 83, No. 22. 3 May 1973: Cols. 1528-1627.

43 African registration/identity cards (or papers) are known as *situpas.* Hence the Bill became known as the *Situpa* Bill.

44 *R.F.G.* 1 December 1972.

45 *R.H.* 27 January 1973.

46 *Rhodesia Government Notices Nos. 216, 217.* 23 February 1973.

47 *Hansard:* Vol. 84, No. 1. 14 June 1973: Col. 4.
   R.H. 16 June 1973.

48 The Vagrancy Act No. 40 of 1960 is the principal Act. It lays down the regulations by which vagrants can be sent, on magisterial order, to reception centres by the Department of Social Welfare.
   Hansard: Vol. 83, Nos. 8, 9, 10. 1, 5, 6 December 1972: Cols. 653-70, 726-49, 780-804.

49 *Hansard:* Vol. 83, No. 11. 7 December 1972: Cols. 856-7.

50 *R.H.* 28 January 1972.

51 *R.H.* 30 March 1972.
52 *R.H.* 31 March 1972.
53 *R.H.* 7 April 1972.
54 *S.M.* 9 April 1972.
55 *R.H.* 24 May 1972.
56 *R.H.* 21 October 1972.
57 *R.H.* 20, 21, 22 February, *R.F.G.* 23 February 1973.
58 *Annual Report of the Secretary for Local Government and Housing for the year ended 31 December 1967:* Salisbury: Government Printer.
59 *R.H.* 7 May 1971.
60 *R.H.* 23 March 1970.
61 *R.H.* 27 November 1970.
62 *R.H.* 13, 19 February 1971.
63 *R.H.* 10 June 1972.
64 *R.H.* 25 November 1972.
65 *Hansard:* Vol. 83, No. 11. 7 December 1972: Cols. 852-3.
   R.H. 8 December 1972.
66 African or opaque beer is described by Reader and May as: 'The traditional beer of the African people as brewed from a fermentation of millet, maize or other cereals such as kaffir corn *(Sorghum vulgare).* The result is a cloudy or sediment-laden beer typically containing about 2 to 4 *per cent* of pure alcohol.'
   Quotation used by kind permission of the authors.
   1971: Reader, D.H. and Joan May: *Drinking Patterns in Rhodesia: Highfield African Township:* Salisbury: University of Rhodesia, Department of Sociology. Occasional Paper No. 5.
67 *Hansard:* Vol. 79, No. 8. 10 June 1971: Cols. 458-73.
68 As reported by *R.F.G.* 30 March 1973.
69 *Hansard:* Vol. 84, No. 1. 14 June 1973: Col. 5.
70 *Hansard:* Vol. 81, No. 18. 26 July 1972: Cols. 1481-2.
71 *R.H.* 28 July 1972.
72 *R.F.G.* 27 October 1972.
73 *R.H.* 17 November 1972.
74 *Hansard:* Vol. 83, No. 11. 6 December 1972: Cols. 764-8.
75 *S.M.* 31 December 1972.
76 *Rhodesia Government Notice No. 19.* 12 January 1973.
   R.H. 12 January 1973.
77 *R.H.* 30 September 1972.
78 *Rhodesia Government Notice No. 18.* 12 January 1973.

X

CRIME

The latest figures of crime available at the time of writing are in the reports of the Secretary for Law and Order and of the British South Africa Police for the year ended 31st December 1972.[1]

During that year 228 preparatory examinations were submitted to the Attorney General. As a result 285 persons were charged with a total of 311 criminal offences varying from petty theft to culpable homicide and murder. Broken down into racial categories this figure means that 260 Africans, 18 Europeans and 7 Coloureds were accused of criminal offences during 1972.

A comparison of the three preceding years gives the following tables:

	1969	1970	1971	1972
Preparatory Examinations	372	318	285	228
Crimes	546	583	522	311

ACCUSED PERSONS BY RACE

	1969	1970	1971	1972
African	402	372	341	260
European	12	14	15	18
Coloured	1	2	1	7
Asian	0	0	0	0

The incidence of *serious* crime is also compared with the same three preceding years:

	1969	1970	1971	1972
Arson	5	1	5	3
Culpable Homicide	27	5	3	3
Under Exchange Control Act	—	—	140	20
Housebreaking and Theft	43	28	10	12
Under Law & Order (Maintenance) Act.	7	13	18	12
Murder	173	209	178	141
Attempted Murder	19	29	9	9
Theft	35	98	62	13

The annual report of the British South Africa Police (B.S.A.P.) gives the figures of:[2]

Cases Reported		Cases Cleared	
1971	250 123	1971	215 427
1972	224 338	1972	178 073

It stated that the overall decrease in reported cases occurred in most categories of crime. In particular, crimes against the person and property decreased by 4 698, miscellaneous and statutory offences decreased by 13 993 and offences under the Roads and Road Traffic Act and Regulations decreased by 8 136; crimes of violence, common law, liquor and security offences on the other hand, increased by 337, 358, 445 and 239 respectively. The racial grouping of persons involved in the cleared cases was:

Africans	139 778
Europeans	35 358
Coloureds	2 051
Asians	686
Total	177 873

'CHARACTERISTIC' CRIME

Statistics such as these give a picture of the overall incidence of crime in the country but can give no indication of the particular aspects of crime which can be said to be 'characteristic' of Rhodesia in the meaning given by one social scientist:[3]

> ... criminal behaviour and the nature of social conditions are always intimately related. Certain kinds of society produce certain kinds of crime which appear to be characteristic.

Taking the crime reports of one year's issue of the local daily newspapers, it can be said that during 1972 there was roughly five main types of crime, resulting in prosecution, originating in the kind of society found in Rhodesia. These types may be described as:

a) political crime arising from attempts by guerrillas entering the country to perform acts of terrorism: prosecutions under the Emergency Powers and the Law and Order (Maintenance) Acts arising from the troubled political condition of the country;[4]

b) criminal behaviour by people in rural areas (and in some urban areas) who have primitive beliefs in the power of sorcery and witchcraft;

c) crime arising from the breakdown of tribal law and custom which sometimes accompanies rapid urbanization of large numbers of people;

d) crime in defiance of little understood authoritarian regulations;

and e) criminal behaviour originating in feelings of superiority towards another racial group.

WITCHCRAFT AND SORCERY

In Rhodesia belief in witchcraft and sorcery is, as in other parts of Africa, prevalent among the indigenous population. From the earliest days of European settlement attempts have been made to curb the more undesirable manifestations of this belief. The first regulations were passed in 1895 and were followed a few years later, in 1899, by the Witchcraft Suppression Act (of which Chapter 50 is usually referred to in criminal trials).

The Shona have two different terms to describe the different attributes of the practitioners of witchcraft—*muroyi*—a witch or wizard, a person who deals in black (harmful) magic and *n'anga*—a

diviner or herbalist who deals in 'white' magic. [5] The *n'anga* dealing
with traditional herbs and medicines usually receives esteem and
respect and has a kind of professional standing. The *n'angas* have
formed themselves into an Association (African Nganga Association) which has its own constitution incorporating a code of professional conduct. [5]

Murders associated with witchcraft are not uncommon in Rhodesia and during 1972 there were a number of trials illustrating
varying ramifications of this type of crime.

Towards the end of 1971 and early in 1972 the trial took place
of four men for the alleged murder of a 21-month-old baby girl
at the Chikadze kraal in the Chikwakwa Tribal Trust Land, north-
east of Salisbury. Two of the accused were alleged to have kid-
napped the child on instructions of a witchdoctor *(muroyi)* and
together with him had killed the child. Thereafter they had cut
away certain parts of the body to be used in the making of the
muti (medicine) which the witchdoctor had assured a local African
businessman would ensure the profitability of his business enterprise. All four men were sentenced to death but on appeal the
businessman had his conviction and sentence set aside on the
grounds that the State had failed to establish the case against him
beyond reasonable doubt. The other three men were executed
during September. [6]

In another trial at the High Court Salisbury in April 1972 two
cousins, an African man and woman, were accused of murdering
a woman whom they suspected of being a witch responsible for
the illness of a close relative of them both. The two accused, having
been found guilty, were sentenced to 13 and 10 years' hard labour
respectively. The Court had found extenuating circumstances in
the fact that the two accused firmly believed in the power of witchcraft. They had removed what they believed to be an evil threat
to their relative and to the well being of their community. [7]

Moto's correspondent from Lupane reported in October that
a young man had been sentenced to a total of 24 months' imprisonment on a charge under the Witchcraft Suppression Act (Chapter
50) for calling his brother a wizard and assaulting him. The accused
had attended a beer party with his brother and as they were drinking had accused the brother of being the cause of the deaths of
his two children by witchcraft. Later he had followed the brother
and assaulted him with a knobkerrie. [8]

In November an African *n'anga* was tried in Bulawayo and found guilty of culpable homicide because a seven-year old patient had died after being treated by him for the removal of an evil spirit. The *n'anga* was fined $40 (or 40 days) for, as the magistrate said at the trial, his moral blameworthiness was slight as he had not intended to harm the child.[9]

It was also in November that a 20-year old man severely assaulted his father, who subsequently died. At the young man's trial, at which he pleaded guilty to a charge of culpable homicide, it was explained that he had believed for years that his father, by failing to hold the necessary ceremonies at his grandmother's death, was thereafter responsible for the deaths of three infant members of the family and for the fatal illness of another. He was sentenced to four years' hard labour.[10]

BREAKDOWN OF TRIBAL LAW AND ORDER

In February an African man was tried in the High Court Salisbury, for the alleged murder of his two teenage nieces in the Chilimanzi Tribal Trust Land in the Midlands. He was alleged to have tied them to a stake, beaten them and then burned them with grass. In his defence the uncle said that the girls had been left in his care while their father was away and he had become angry with the girls when they had stayed away from home all night and had returned bringing with them two youths. He was later found guilty of murder with constructive intent and sentenced to 9 years' hard labour.[11]

In April it was reported that the vice-chairman of one of Bulawayo's African Township Advisory Boards had spoken of the increase in crime and hooliganism by youths in the townships. He claimed that the graded system of African education and unemployment had created thousands of idle hands which had turned to crime. His views were supported by an African headmaster of a local primary school who added that the breakdown of traditional family life had resulted in the lack of control over youth.[12]

DEFIANCE OF AUTHORITY

In 1960 the American government, in response to an appeal for technical assistance in community development, placed at Rhodesia's disposal the services of Dr. James Green, a senior adviser on community development, who stayed in Rhodesia for four years. In his first quarterly report he noted that:

> The desire among Africans for material and social progress is more wide-spread than is often recognized... because so many of the programs for his development have been either forced upon him (for his own good, of course) or given to him with benevolent paternalism. In either case, his own values and his social structure of mutual rights and obligations and community have been neglected, by-passed or attacked. In frustration at this too high and unnecessary price of progress the community has often mobilised and struck back at the destroyer (as it sees it) of so much that the people hold dear by refusing to dip cattle.[13]

In early May 1972 it was reported that a number of arrests had been made in the Ndanga Tribal Trust Land (near Fort Victoria) in connection with damage to dip tanks and the associated murder of an African police constable who had been guarding the tanks. At the subsequent trial of five men in the Salisbury High Court it was alleged that the plan to destroy the dip tank had been decided upon at a political meeting in response to an announcement that fees for dipping cattle were to be raised. All the accused were found guilty, but with extenuating circumstances, and were given sentences ranging from nine to fifteen years.[14]

'RACIAL' CRIME

The fifth category (which may conveniently be called 'racial' crime) concerns behaviour by a person of one race towards another which between persons of the same race would hardly qualify as a criminal act, or would not take place between persons of the same race, either because the perpetrators would not think of so behaving or would be too frightened to do so. An example of such a 'racial' crime was a trial which resulted in three European men each being sentenced to two years in gaol (18 months of two of the sentences and 16 months of the third were suspended for three years). They had pleaded guilty to assault with intent to do grievous bodily harm following what the Bulawayo provincial magistrate described as 'cowardly attacks' on African pedestrians. One witness, an African girl, described walking along the road, hearing the noise of a car behind her and suddenly receiving a blow on the back of the head. She fell unconscious and had to be taken to hospital where she received seven stitches for the gash in her head. Two African men were also hit by large stones thrown from a passing car, one of them having his arm broken.[15]

In a similar case two months later, two European youths received sentences (one of $120 or two months and twenty days gaol plus two months conditionally suspended for three years and the other of $50 or 25 days) on charges of assault. They had been driving past two African men at whom they shouted abuse; they then stopped the car and one European held one of the Africans while the other European beat him. The other African ran away. They had then become aware that their actions were being witnessed by a European who happened to be in the vicinity and leaving the African the two youths returned to their car. The African who had fled when his friend had been held by the two Europeans returned to the road to pick up his shoe which had come off in his flight. Moments later he had to jump to avoid the Europeans' car which was driving at speed towards him. The Magistrate who heard the case commented that this behaviour could easily lead to racial friction.[16]

In October a European man was fined $50 (or three weeks) on a charge of *crimen injuria*. He had called out to an African woman and made an obscene gesture to her. When she had told her husband who had gone to the European man to remonstrate with him the European had produced a revolver and threatened to kill the husband.[17]

JUVENILE DELINQUENCY

According to the Report of the Secretary for Labour and Social Welfare for the year ended 31 December 1972 there was a rise of 73 cases of juvenile delinquency dealt with by probation officers over the figures for 1971. The figures for the racial categories showed that the sharpest increase had been in respect of European cases which increased from 197 to 235 (19.3%); African cases had increased from 1 531 to 1 588 (3.8%); and Coloured cases had decreased from 99 to 77. Offences against property (without violence) again accounted for the majority of offences but the sharpest increase was in respect of offences against the State which increased from 10 in 1971 to 103 in 1972. Offences under the Dangerous Drugs Act increased from 132 in 1971 to 151 in 1972.[18]

NOTES

1 *Report of the Secretary for Law and Order for the year ended 31 December 1972.* Cmd. R.R. 17-1973: Salisbury: Government Printer. *British South Africa Police Annual Report 1972 :* Cmd. R.R. 25-1973: Salisbury: B.S.A. Police Printing Department.
2 These totals do not relate to the aggregate of cases reported as one person may have been arrested for more than one offence or, alternatively, a single case may have involved several people.
3 1963: Mays, John B.: *Crime and the Social Structure :* London: Faber & Faber.
4 See chapter on Guerrilla Warfare.
5 Sorcery and witchcraft are defined by R. J. Crawford in his book on the subject 'witchcraft is essentially a psychic act and is, objectively speaking, impossible, while sorcery, which involves the use of spells, medicines and ritual to harm others, while no doubt effective in achieving its object, can be attempted by anyone.'
1967: Crawford, J. R.: *Witchcraft and Sorcery in Rhodesia :* London: O.U.P.
Gelfand says in his book that 'the *nganga*'s treatment consists in finding out whether a witch or a spirit has caused the illness, in advising his patients on the procedure necessary to propitiate whichever is the cause, and in prescribing the right herbal remedy to cure the physical damage already sustained by the patient. The *nganga*'s medical practice is therefore part spiritual and part homeopathic.'
With regard to the *muroyi* he says–'The Mashona look upon the *murovi,* or witch, as a person endowed with the power to manipulate the forces of Nature to the detriment of mankind'.
1964: Gelfand, Michael: *Witch Doctor : Traditional Medicine Man of Rhodesia :* London: Harvill Press.
Although the spelling is given as *Nganga* in the 1961 edition of M. Hannen's *Standard Shona Dictionary* (London: Macmillan) I am informed by members of the African Languages Department of the University of Rhodesia that the correct spelling is *n'anga.* The Association (and Dr. Gelfand), however, retain the older-fashioned spelling.
6 *R.H.* 16, 17 December 1971: 13, 19 January 1972.

7 *R.H.* 12, 14 April 1972.
8 *Moto :* Vol. 14, No. 42. 14 October 1972.
   A *knobkerrie* is a club.
9 *R.H.* 10 November 1972.
10 *R.H.* 31 January 1973.
11 *R.H.* 3, 4 February 1972.
12 *R.H.* 10 April 1972.
13 As quoted in :
   1972: Passmore, Gloria C.: *The National Policy of Community De-*
      velopment in Rhodesia : Salisbury: University of Rhodesia.
14 *S.M.* 7 May, *R.H.* 1-19 August 1972.
15 *R.H.* 31 March 1972.
16 *R.H.* 5 May 1972.
17 *R.H.* 20, 21 October 1972.
18 *Report of the Secretary for Labour and Social Welfare for the year*
   ended 31 December 1972 : (un-numbered) Salisbury: Government
   Printer.

XI

SPORT

Sport in Rhodesia has suffered little legal intervention with its activities. If there is a split along racial lines, it is largely because African interest has centred essentially around such sports as soccer, boxing and athletics. Other sports such as motor racing, horse racing and yachting have remained as spectator sports for Africans, primarily because of the expense involved. Nevertheless, as a prominent African sportsman, Mr. Morrison Sifelani, said when outlining his ideas on how the International Football Federation could be approached to waive their suspension of Rhodesia: 'The situation is this. The world knows our soccer on the field is multi-racial... They also know that off the field there is a colour-bar for players and officials in clubhouses, changing rooms and hotels on the road.'[1]

Politically, sport is affected by the Land Tenure Act in that some venues may not be used for multi-racial gatherings without special permission (which is not always forthcoming) and by the government policy of no enforced integration, a policy which led to the ruling by the Minister of Education that multi-racial sport in government schools could only take place after application for permission had been made to the Minister.

ATHLETICS

At the close of December 1971 a two-man team consisting of middle-distance runners Bernard Dzoma and Aaron Gumbo represented Rhodesia at the international San Silvestre meeting in Luanda, Angola. Bernard Dzoma, a designated member of the abortive 1968 Mexico City Olympic Games, joined a twelve-member mixed racial team later in December 1971 at an international athletics meeting in Lourenço Marques where he beat top

335

South African Springbok Andries Krogman in the 5 000 and 10 000 metres races.

In April 1973 Bernard Dzoma, described as Rhodesia's leading middle-distance runner, was dropped by the Rhodesian Amateur Athletic Union from the team due to compete in the South African Games at Pretoria. The convenor of the Rhodesian selectors said that Dzoma had been left out of the team because of his performance at the South African Bantu Championships in March when he had been well outside the qualifying times. The *Herald*'s sports writer considered that the decision was an unfortunate one, for Dzoma had a personal invitation to take part in the Games. His fellow mine-worker, Adon Treva, however, became the first Rhodesian athlete to win a medal at the South African Games when he came second in the 400 metres race. [2]

THE 1972 OLYMPIC GAMES

At a meeting of the International Olympic Committees in September 1971 it was decided to allow Rhodesia to compete in the 1972 Games subject to certain conditions. Great interest was taken locally in the composition of the team to go to Munich.

Of the eight sports selected, only the Athletics team had African representation, six out of its ten members being Africans. (One of the ten officials chosen to accompany the Rhodesian contingent was also an African, Mr. 'Stuttie' Dhlamini). Selection of teams was strictly on merit, finance being provided largely from sporting organizations and from members of the public. Sporting organizations nominated team members and final selection was by voting at a meeting of the national Olympic committee also attended by representatives of the sports concerned. [3]

Within the country public disquiet began over the team's final acceptance when Dr. Ludwig Huber, vice-president of the Olympics organization committee, reiterated the decision of December 1971, which was to allow Rhodesia to compete providing her team used the same flag (the Union Jack) and the same anthem (the British national anthem) as it had done at the Tokyo Olympic meeting in 1964. [4]

Shortly afterwards it was learnt that Britain had formally protested to the West German government about Rhodesian sportsmen being allowed to compete at the Games. It was reported that this action had placed Bonn in a dilemma. On the one hand the West German government had committed itself to admit sportsmen of every nation invited to the Games (and all members of the national Olympic committees had been invited to partici-pate).[5] On the other hand the West German government pledges itself to uphold U.N. sanctions against Rhodesia. As the *Herald* commented 'the worry now is how many other countries will be inspired by Britain's lead to join in a late attempt to stampede West Germany into emulating Mexico's inglorious example of 1968.'[6]

In August Britain's objection was followed by a request from the Organization for African Unity (O.A.U.) for the West German government to bar Rhodesian athletes from the Munich Games. The O.A.U. was reported to have spoken of the 'disagreeable con-sequences' which might result from Rhodesian participation in the Games.[7]

Also in August the South African news-magazine, *To the Point*, commented 'if Rhodesia had not practised racially mixed sport at all levels and if the selection of its teams had not been solely on merit, in terms of government instructions, this action might have been understandable... These efforts to prevent Rhodesia's participation have nothing to do with inter-racial sport in Rhode-sia, but everything to do with Rhodesia's constitutional struggle. It is another clear-cut example of political interference in sport.'

The periodical concluded its article by asking the world to remember 'that many governments in Asia, Latin America and Africa came to power by unconstitutional means, including rebel-lion, murder, *coup d'état* and civil war. This, rightly, has never been used as a reason to bar their athletes from the Olympic Games.'[8]

On the 12th August a statement was issued by the O.A.U. stating that African teams and those teams of friendly countries wishing to stand by Africa should withdraw from the Games if Rhodesia's participation was confirmed. An appeal was also made to the West German authorities not to issue entry visas to the Rhodesian athletes.[9]

By the time the Rhodesian athletes had settled into their quarters at the Olympic village it was reported that the prospects of a large-scale boycott of the Games by the 41 African countries belonging to the O.A.U. was fading insofar as only two countries—Tanzania and Sierra Leone—had decided to withdraw their teams. A British newspaper, the *Sunday Times,* was reported as saying that 'by agreeing that their athletes should observe all the protocol—flag, national anthem and so on—which applied to the pre-U.D.I., colonial Rhodesia, the Smithites are emphasizing not their self-proclaimed independence but the lack of it: the non-recognition of the outside world of U.D.I. and its supposed attributes. No wonder that angry murmers are now reported coming from some quarters in Salisbury.'[10]

The 'angry murmers' were expressed by the *Financial Gazette* which stated 'we wish we could unequivocally say that we will be proud when Rhodesia marches into the Munich stadium, but it would be less than honest to make such a statement. But to see the country which courageously declared itself independent and has faced the world successfully since then marching under any other flag but its own is a little too much.'[11] The *Herald* pointed out, however, that 'it is easy to be wise after the event. It is easy to accuse the Rhodesian Olympics Committee of hypocrisy. But in accepting the conditions in September they had a very simple objective—to allow young Rhodesians to compete in the world's greatest sporting festival. Their motives were not dishonourable... But whatever Mr. Ossie Plaskett [the Rhodesian *chef de mission*] may say on the record, we do hope that he and his fellow officials are seriously considering now whether it is worth pressing on. The situation at Munich has become thoroughly undignified. It is disgusting. Sport has been abandoned for the worst kind of political infighting.'[12]

Later in August the full session of the International Olympic Committee voted (36 to 31) to exclude Rhodesia from participation in all the events at Munich. It was considered that this action had been taken after threats from 42 nations, including the Communist *bloc,* which had threatened official boycotts to wreck the Games.[13]

Combined with a natural disappointment and a feeling of regret that political forces had destroyed the Olympic ideal, Rhodesian reaction was also one of bitterness for, as the *Herald* asked, 'what more could Rhodesian athletes have done to prove their worthiness to take the Olympic oath? They were told to choose their best team; they did—as they all along intended. They were asked to eat political crow in public at the march-past and on the winner's stand; they agreed to do so. They were asked to associate with blood-stained regimes such as those of Burundi, Haiti, Sudan and Zanzibar; they agreed, refusing to blame athletes for the sins of governments. They met all conditions laid down; and they have been rejected by the very people who laid the conditions down.'[14] (If Rhodesians and other sportsmen throughout the world felt a strong sense of grievance that the Olympic ideal had been sacrificed to political manœuvering, it was with shock and horror that the news was received of the politically-motivated criminal assassination of the Israeli athletes at the Games).

In January 1973 representatives of the International Olympic Committee (I.O.C.) attended the second All-African Games in Nigeria. It was reported that the president of the committee, Lord Killanin, met General Gowon who spoke on the question of Rhodesia's participation in international sports competitions. General Gowon was quoted as saying that if Rhodesia conducted its sporting activities 'irrespective of race, colour or religious affiliations of her sportsmen and women' and ample evidence of this was forthcoming, then Nigeria would not oppose Rhodesia's participation. The following month it was reported from Lausanne, where the executive board of the I.O.C. was meeting, that the question of sending a commission of enquiry to investigate sport in Rhodesia would not be decided until the next meeting of the committee scheduled for June.[15]

BOXING

Boxing has a large African following and all the current Rhodesian professional boxing champions are Africans. Spectators are racially mixed, but matches between black and white boxers have not been common. In early January 1972 it was reported that the Bulawayo City Council had refused to sanction a proposed boxing tournament in the City Hall because all the boxers would be Africans. (The leasing regulations stipulate that the Hall must only be available for Europeans, Asians and Coloureds). The following month in Salisbury, however, it was announced that an African boxing promoter had organized a multi-racial bill to be held at Glamis Stadium at the Salisbury showgrounds. The main bouts were to be between South African white boxers and Rhodesian African champions.[16] The 7th May, the day on which the contest took place, was described by the *Herald* Sports reporter as the 'day when Rhodesian professional boxing came of age' for the Rhodesian boxers beat all four of the South Africans.[17]

ASSOCIATION FOOTBALL

Soccer, together with boxing, are perhaps the most popular sports among Africans. The siting and building of the vast new stadium at Harare Township, which was completed in July 1972, was partly in recognition of this fact (it was paid for by profits from African beer sales which must be spent on African welfare and recreational facilities). Providing seating for 22 000 and standing room for another 14 000, the drainage system alone was reputed to have cost $38 000. The stadium is the home ground for the Rufaro Rovers and Sables teams.

The Rhodesia National Football League (R.F.N.L.) was formed in 1962 and is completely inter-racial as far as actual play is concerned. The majority of players are African but teams are mainly composed of mixed racial groups with players being chosen on merit; there is only one all-European team. All teams play against each other with racially mixed spectators and there are numerous soccer trophies which provide keen competition matches throughout the season. Referees sit the same examinations as in other countries and are also racially mixed.

As Soccer and Athletics are considered as the truly multi-racial sports in Rhodesia both players and followers of the game were despondent about the suspension of the Football Association of Rhodesia (F.A.R.) from the International Football Federation (F.I.F.A.) at its congress in Mexico City in 1970. In June 1972, F.I.F.A. refused permission for the Rhodesian Association to play an international soccer match against a neighbouring country in aid of the Wankie Disaster Fund. As F.A.R. secretary Mr. George Kerr put it 'It seems queer that on the one hand you have the British Government making a donation to the disaster fund and on the other the world soccer body refusing to lift a suspension for one match to assist a national disaster fund which costs them nothing.'[18]

By August hopes were running high that Rhodesian membership of F.I.F.A. would be reinstated at the forthcoming 38th Congress in Paris. At the Congress however, where the executive committee of F.I.F.A. and the Scottish Football Association were to have presented proposals to have the Rhodesian suspension waived, a motion, on behalf of the African Football Association, calling on the Congress to refuse all debate on Rhodesia, while confirming the suspension decision taken at Mexico, was passed by 62 votes to 18. The result, of course, meant that the Rhodesian delegation was given no chance to present its case and much disappointment was felt by all followers of the sport that politics, as in the Olympic Games decision, had taken control. [19]

During October there were a number of unconfirmed reports that the Special Branch was investigating the operation of soccer teams because of fears that African nationalists might be using the sport as a medium to disseminate political views. Both the Football Association and the Special Branch, however, strongly denied these reports. [20]

Towards the end of 1972 *Herald* reporter John Kelley's column *Sports Profile* featured Dynamos' club chairman, Mr. Morrison Sifelani, who outlined his ideas on the new approach to have Rhodesia reinstated in the international soccer organization. Mr. Sifelani suggested that African players should attend international soccer games to talk to the opposition to try and make them understand that only by outside teams playing within the country could there be any strong influence brought to bear to bring about change in Rhodesia. [21]

In May 1973 it was reported that the Special Branch was investigating the circumstances which had led to wide-spread disturbances in Salisbury and Gwelo following soccer matches and a boxing bout. In Salisbury two separate disturbances started within twenty minutes of each other, one at the end of a soccer match at Gwanzura Stadium in Highfield African Township, the other at a boxing match near the Rufaro Stadium in Harare Township. The Gwanzura Stadium crowd, reputedly displeased with a last-minute equalizer goal in a match between the Dynamos and the Arcadia teams, started throwing stones within the stadium and in the car park. According to a police spokesman, however, the crowd quickly calmed down. The disturbances in Harare were apparently sparked off when, as the spectators left the boxing match, a pedestrian was knocked down by a bus. For nearly two hours hundreds of Africans hurled bricks and stones at vehicles in the streets. A riot squad was called in but 24 buses were stoned and private vehicles had their windscreens smashed. Five shop windows on the outskirts of the Salisbury central business district were broken. Twenty-seven people were later admitted to hospital and several arrests were made for violence and looting. In Gwelo the disturbances also started after a soccer match. Rival team supporters clashed and the Riot Squad had to be called out. Several people were admitted to hospital and a number of others were arrested.

According to a police spokesman no evidence was found to link the stone-throwing mobs with any political inspiration. Popular speculation, however, was over the fact that the three incidents had occurred more or less simultaneously at a time when emotions had been aroused by the Victoria and Matojeni by-elections. In June three young African adults and three African youths appeared at the Harare Magistrate's Court charged with public violence. [22]

During 1973 friction between the Rhodesia National Football League and the Football Association of Rhodesia on administrative matters came to a head over the arrangements for the matches with the touring English soccer coaches. The dispute between the two organizations was considered to be one of the main reasons why no headway was made, during the early months of 1973, in having Rhodesia's suspension from the Federation of International Football lifted.

GOLF

In April it was reported that a plan for a championship golf course at Salisbury's Glen Norah African Township had been turned down by the City's African Administration Department on the grounds that the sporting amenities in the townships were allotted according to certain priorities, such as boxing and soccer as the most popular African sports. The present African-controlled Gleneagles Golf Club had put forward proposals for administering the new course as the lease on its own course would run out in five years time and the land would be needed for other development purposes. [23] In September the Australian government announced that it would refuse entry to two Rhodesian European golfers scheduled to take part in the World Cup golf series to be held in Melbourne. [24]

Early in 1973 a report on African sport during 1972, by Misheck Mbewe in the *Herald*, noted that 'Golf struggled to gain recognition, with leading African players failing to get a chance to compete in major events.'[25]

HOCKEY

Two coloured women who play for their province in Rhodesian inter-provincial games were not considered for the national team on racial grounds, the *Herald* reported in May. The national team was to be selected to play in the South African inter-provincial tournament in July and, as the president of the Rhodesian Women's Hockey Association remarked: 'We are affiliated to the South African Women's Hockey Association and although there is nothing in their constitution debarring anybody on racial grounds, we must abide by the South African laws when we are in South Africa... if a Rhodesian team was chosen to play in Rhodesia all players would be eligible.'[26]

SWIMMING

During November *Herald* reporter Reuben Nhandara wrote about the growing popularity of swimming among Africans at Salisbury's African townships. The three main townships of Harare, Mufakose and Highfield all have swimming pool complexes, the main pool at Mufakose being constructed to Olympic competition standards. Mr. Nhandara explained that mixed bathing was against African custom and until fairly recently swimming had been regarded as an activity for children. However, total attendance figures for the three pools now showed that adult admission figures were increasing. At present the only competitive swimming is at school level and some of the secondary schools were scheduled to compete in the Mashonaland Inter-Schools swimming gala in October.[27]

Earlier in the year the International Swimming Federation (F.I.N.A.) announced that during 1973 it would send a commission of enquiry to Rhodesia and South Africa to investigate charges of racial discrimination in the sport. This decision had been taken following calls by Russia, backed by East Germany and the African countries, for the expulsion of both countries 'because of the policy of racial discrimination practised in these countries' at the F.I.N.A. Congress in Munich.[28]

In early January 1973 the Rhodesia Amateur Swimming Association decided to sever its links with the South African Swimming Association. It was considered that Rhodesian swimming standards had reached a stage when competition against South Africa could be considered and this action would mean Rhodesians could form their own swimming teams.

During March 1973 the expected commission from F.I.N.A. began its investigations. The three-man commission to investigate allegations of racial discrimination in Rhodesian swimming arrived in Salisbury on the 21st March. Its chairman, Mr. Javier Ostos M. of Mexico, a former president of F.I.N.A., explained that the commission did not have the power to make recommendations to the executive committee but only to report facts. The report would be considered later in the year before the world swimming championships due to be held in Yugoslavia.

In a timely article in the *Herald,* reporter Brian Streak outlined the development of African interest in swimming which, according to him, was just moving into its first generation, for it had only been in the last seven years that Africans had taken up the challenge of competitive swimming. According to the chairman of the Mashonaland Amateur Swimming Board, however, it was as far back as 1963 that officials of that Board had approached or been approached by both African and Coloured schools for assistance in coaching and technical advice. According to the article it was at the mission schools that the trend for African swimming contests started, the first African secondary school gala being held at the Marist College, Kutama, during 1967. In February 1973 at the invitation of the Rhodesia and the Mashonaland Amateur Swimming Associations, 10 African secondary schools in Mashonaland were affiliated as members of the national body. Plans were for staging age group competitions at African schools, which would mean Africans competing at their own venues until their standards warranted inclusion in the National Age Group Championships.

Members of the commission of enquiry were guests at a multiracial swimming gala held at St. Ignatius College, Chishawasha, on the 24th March. This was the first gala to be granted a permit for mixed competitive swimming under the terms of the Land

Tenure Act. The competition included European swimmers in all age groups from the four provincial boards and African swimmers from the newly-formed African Schools Swimming Association. It was reported that the commission had heard evidence, the previous day, from a wide range of people connected with all aspects of swimming at national, provincial, school and club levels. The commission also, it was later reported, closely scrutinized the provisions of the Land Tenure Act that affected public swimming in Rhodesia. At one stage they asked for the Attorney-General's help in clarifying certain points in the Act. [29]

JUDO

In October the president of the Rhodesian Judo Association (R.J.A.) outlined plans to give active encouragement to African participation in the sport. The president said that there was nothing racialistic in the Association's constitution; there were just not enough Africans interested in judo. This move was reported as being in connection with the R.J.A's application to gain membership of the African Judo Union which would lead to affiliation with the International Judo Union. [30]

In June 1973 the Rhodesia Judo Association sent two delegates to the International Judo Union (I.J.U.) congress in Lausanne to present Rhodesia's case for affiliation. The R.J.A. secretary, Mr. Brian Warren, was quoted as outlining his thinking on multiracial judo and his plans for developing the sport in Rhodesia. He said that at present there were about 600 registered judokas in Rhodesia among which there were about 60 Africans. It was later announced that the I.J.U. had rejected the proposal for admitting Rhodesia without her first joining the African Judo Union. [31]

CRICKET

The game of cricket has, in Rhodesia, aroused little interest among Africans; its players and spectators are mainly Europeans and Asians. In November 1972 it was reported that Mr. Kantilal Kanjee would stand as the first Asian umpire in a Currie Cup match between Rhodesia and Natal. [32]

SCHOOL SPORT

When the White Paper on the Settlement Proposals was published a number of people wrote to the papers expressing the hope that the proposed commission to enquire into racial discrimination would act upon the Ministerial ruling against mixed sport in government schools. It was also recommended that this was a field in which the government could act to demonstrate its good faith to the African population.

The restriction on sport between schoolchildren inspired Mr. Denis Robinson, a Rhodesian Rugby Selector, to organize a series of rugby games between European and African boys in one of the African townships (Highfield) during vacations. Although the European boy's team lost all four of the games they played it was reported that the games had been thoroughly enjoyed by all. [33]

In May Mr. K. Mew of Ranche House College put forward the view that to debar children from engaging in multi-racial sport was to limit the effectiveness of their education for he considered that 'to deprive them of this side of their social training on educational grounds is bad enough, but to deprive them on political grounds is iniquitous.' Mr. Mew then went on to relate that, during the sitting of the Pearce Commission, the People Against Racial Discrimination (P.A.R.D.) had sent circulars to about 200 schools enclosing a letter addressed to the Minister of Education pleading for the reinstatement of multi-racial sport in schools, which had been stopped about five years previously. Mr. Mew said that the response had been very poor and he was now hoping to discuss, with representatives of various parent-teacher associations, the reasons for the reluctance of many parents to allow their children to take part in multi-racial sport.

As Mr. Mew said at the time 'no matter how much we talk about the removal of racial discrimination, if we are not going to allow children to play games together, then it is unlikely that we will ever get down to the much more serious problems of this nature.' [34]

In August during the debate on the Revenue Vote on Education Mr. L. Masenda, M.P. for Mabvazuwa, asked the Minister whether it was government policy to force politics into schools by preventing mixed racial teams from private schools competing against teams at government schools. The Minister of Education confirmed that it was indeed government policy to prevent multi-racial sport in the grounds of European government schools. He concluded by saying 'we are opposed to compulsory integration. There is nothing to stop multi-racial games taking place but they must take place either on an independent ground or on the grounds of one of the private schools.'[35] The reason behind this policy is that schooling is compulsory for European (Coloured and Asian) children and if multi-racial sport were allowed to take place in government schools parents would be deprived of their right to choose whether to allow their children to participate. In other words it would mean 'enforced integration'.

NOTES

1 *R.H.* 22 December 1972.
2 *R.H.* 3, 7 April 1973.
3 *R.H.* 5 June 1972.
4 *R.H.* 7 July 1972.
5 Rhodesia has always been a member of the International Olympic Committee and was invited during March 1971 to participate in the 1972 Games.
6 *R.H.* 21 July 1972.
7 *S.M.* 6 August 1972.
8 *To The Point* 12 August 1972.
9 As reported in *S.M.* 13 August 1972.
   The West German Foreign Minister had stated that the Olympic identity cards issued to competing athletes were valid for entry into West Germany.
10 *R.H.* 14 August, *S.M.* 3 August 1972.
11 *R.F.G.* 18 August 1972.
12 *R.H.* 22 August 1972.
13 *R.H.* 23 August 1972.
14 *R.H.* 24 August 1972.
15 As reported in *S.M.* 14 January, 4 February 1973.
16 *R.H.* 25 February 1972.
17 *R.H.* 8 May 1972.
18 As reported in *R.H.* 14 June 1972.
19 *R.H.* 23 September 1972.
20 *R.F.G.* 13, 20 October 1972.
21 *R.H.* 22 December 1972.

22 *R.H.* 21, 22 May, 1 June; *R.F.G.* 25 May 1973.
23 *R.H.* 26 April 1972.
24 *R.H.* 7 September 1972.
25 *S.M.* 7 January 1973.
26 *R.H.* 23 May 1972.
27 *R.H.* 8 November 1972.
28 *R.H.* 8 September 1972.
29 *R.H.* 22, 23, 24 March 1973.
30 *R.H.* 27 October 1972.
31 *S.M.* 17 June; *R.H.* 21 June 1973.
32 *R.H.* 10 November 1972.
33 *R.H.* 10 May 1972.
34 *R.H.* 11 May 1972.
35 *Hansard:* Vol. 82, No. 6. 23 August 1972: Cols. 542, 564.

XII

THE CHURCHES

THE MISSIONS

In 1859 the London Missionary Society sent four missionaries and their wives, headed by J.S. Moffat, to establish a mission among the Matabele. The mission station which they established at Inyati in that year was the first white settlement in what was to become, about forty years later, the country of Rhodesia.[1]

The early missionaries, who had settled in Lobengula's country, were prevented by him from extending their activities to other parts of the country under his control and it was not until after 1890, and the occupation by the British South Africa Company, that missionary enterprise was extended to Mashonaland.

From the beginning there was of necessity a close association between the Church and the B.S.A. Company. To encourage missions to settle in Mashonaland large grants of land in the rural areas were given by the Company to ten different denominations and numbers of plots were made available in the African 'locations' which were being established in what were to become the larger urban centres. As Oliver and Fage put it:—'at the start of the colonial period missionaries were frequently more numerous, and in many ways more influential, than the representatives of the colonial governments.'

In the very early days no funds were available to the colonial administration for the education of the indigenous people: since missionaries 'were finding all over pagan Africa [that] the school was by far the most effective means of Christian evangelism', they established a dominance in the field of African education.[2]

POLITICS AND LEGISLATION

During a later period the churches also began to enter the field of politics. As one writer of the Federal period put it: 'we are here encountering one of the wellsprings of political action in British Central Africa today. There has been deep and valuable missionary influence in many other parts of colonial Africa, of course... But it is noteworthy how the Christian Church has been forced to assume a political role in South Africa and the Rhodesias... It is not altogether an accident that the leaders of African nationalist movements in southern—white man's—Africa tend to be religious men... This mission influence has motivated white African reformers as well as black.'[3]

Following Rhodesia's unilateral declaration of independence (U.D.I.) on 11th November 1965, the Catholic Bishops of Rhodesia[4] issued a Pastoral Instruction, entitled *A Plea for Peace*. The Bishops emphasized that the Instruction was of a pastoral nature and not to be construed otherwise. It declared that there was no intention of intruding into the field of party politics but pointed out that 'the complicated problem of racial harmony in this country is one, not simply of social adjustment, but of social justice. It is essentially a moral problem and this is why we, the Bishops, have a right and a duty to speak about it, in season and out of season.'

The Bishops considered that one thing, among others, was quite clear: 'vast numbers of the people of Rhodesia are bitterly opposed to the unilateral declaration of independence made recently. They are particularly angered that it should be stated publicly that this action was taken in the name of preserving Christian civilization in this country. It is simply quite untrue to say they have consented by their silence. Their silence is the silence of fear, of disappointment, of hopelessness. It is a dangerous silence'.

In the Instruction the functions of the Church were defined as apolitical; the functions of the State, as the administrative arm of the nation, were described as 'to serve all the people, without favouring one group more than another, working to achieve that complex of conditions in which all men, irrespective of race, religion or political affiliation, can live as fully accepted members of society, having access to all those things which promote their full development.'

It was pointed out that 'much is said about our rights but little about our responsibilities as a supposedly Christian people... there is plenty of opportunity about us for practising practical charity in Rhodesia. [For]... in spite of undoubted progress in many fields of social endeavour during recent years, in spite of vast sums spent on education, medical services, housing, agriculture and the rest, there is still much left to be done.' The Bishops pleaded for people to 'look at the inequitable distribution of land... the scandal of those working conditions in which normal family life is made impossible; the often inadequate wages paid to servants; the humiliations of discriminatory legislation; the inequalities of opportunity in education.'

A word of warning was sounded, however, for the Bishops considered it to be part of their duty to 'enunciate moral principles; to denounce all use of violence; and to do all in their power to promote and preserve public order—[which] is such a great good that people must be prepared even to suffer the diminution of their rights for a time in order that it might be preserved' and they exhorted, 'with all the authority which we command', 'our long-suffering and patient people to resist... the blandishments of those who would urge them to anarchy, only to enslave them thereafter to such barbarism as they have never known or thought possible.'[5]

THE 1969 CONSTITUTION

During 1969, when the new Constitution Bill was being discussed, most of the Christian churches in Rhodesia pleaded with the public to reject it and to condemn publicly those aspects of the Bill which were completely contrary to Christian teaching. In their Pastoral Message, entitled *A Call to Christians* (June 1969) the Catholic Bishops outlined the general feeling of the churches when they stated that particular concern was felt with regard to 'the powers to be conceded to the Administration... [for] in virtue of such powers discriminatory executive and administrative acts would be excluded from the Declaration of Rights... [and] would be the equivalent of signing a blank cheque for government by bureaucratic dictatorship.'

It was the Bishops' opinion that in the proposed constitution 'basic human rights are not described clearly and unequivocally and are declared to be non-justiciable... The guardianship of the

Declaration would be taken away from the Constitutional Council and exercised by Senate, an organ of government, which is not immune to political pressure... [this] would pave the way for the encroachment of government on the rights of the individual.'

The endangered rights of individuals were listed as: freedom of expression, which would be limited; the non-provision of adequate elected representation for all sections of the population; advancement on merit, which was set aside 'in favour of government by group, a man's worth and responsibility being estimated according to his wealth.'[6]

The Bishops concluded that the proposals for the Land Tenure Act were wholly unacceptable and said that the proposals for the new Constitution favoured 'the perpetuation and indeed the increase of tribalism... and militate against the possibility of ever building a single Rhodesian nation.'[7]

THE LAND TENURE ACT

The Constitution having been accepted in the Referendum of June 1969, the church leaders appealed to the government not to press ahead with certain aspects of the Land Tenure Bill. In particular they mentioned Clause 83 'which indicated the Government's intention to abolish the rights of Mission lands, which had hitherto been safe-guarded in the Land Apportionment Act.'

In October 1969 interdenominational church leaders had two interviews with the Minister of Lands, Senator P. van Heerden. A Methodist minister reported that 'under pressure the Senator made one concession: he accorded to ecclesiastical bodies the constitutional right to own church property in both European and African areas, a right he had hitherto proposed to withdraw. However, he was adamant concerning the use of such property and refused to entrench any constitutional right of use. In future this must be subject to the granting of permits by either ministerial or local authority.'[8]

The Land Tenure Act was promulgated in March 1970, after being amended at committee stage to empower the Minister 'to authorize statutory bodies and voluntary organizations[9] to own or lease land... in the European or African areas irrespective of the race of the members thereof.' For, as the Minister said during the debate, 'voluntary associations such as the churches, the Boy

Scouts, the Girl Guides, charitable organizations and trade unions, may have a membership which is multi-racial but which may vary from time to time with a resulting change in the controlling interest. It would not be practicable to require the voluntary association to dispose of its properties in either the European or African area every time its racial composition changed.'[10]

The Anglican point to view was put by the Rt. Rev. K. Skelton, Bishop of Matabeleland, in his sermon at the inaugural service for the incoming president of the Christian Council of Rhodesia on the 4th March 1970. The Bishop said that the Church and the government were 'in total disagreement in principle and practice', the Church being in a particularly difficult position as there was 'an attempt to identify political policy with Christianity.' Earlier, at the annual meeting of the Council, the Bishop had proposed a resolution in which the heads of churches were asked to take immediate action 'to assert and uphold the Christian principles which this nation claims to observe.' The resolution, which was passed unanimously, stated that the Council had 'noted particularly the acceptance by the electorate of an admittedly racialist Constitution, condemned by most Church leaders as in many respects completely contradictory to Christian teachings; the introduction of a Land Tenure Act based upon racial separate development which not only is incompatible with Christian commitment to non-racial free development but also permits interference with the free worship and witness of the Church.'[11]

The Roman Catholics expressed their views in a pamphlet prepared for the Roman Catholic Bishops' Conference on the 29th March 1970. Entitled *The Land Tenure Act and the Church*, the pamphlet itemized ways in which the Church felt particularly restricted by the Act and commented: 'a non-racial church is forbidden to own land in the African or European areas (by definition in the Act, 'land' includes any building or structure on the land...) unless it applies for a certificate to become a Voluntary Association within the meaning of the Act. The Minister may, *at any time*, after giving notice to the Voluntary Association concerned and affording it an opportunity of being heard, *cancel such a certificate*.'[12]

During April 1970 church leaders, including heads, as well as representatives, of all the major Catholic and Protestant Churches in Rhodesia, met together and agreed to issue a combined state-

ment appealing to the government to make it possible for them
to continue with their work. They stated their refusal to register
as voluntary associations in terms of the Act. The statement added
that the churches 'nevertheless intended to carry on their work
in the African and European areas. People of either race would
occupy those areas as the Churches' work required.'[13]

At the end of April the five Roman Catholic Bishops made a
statement in which they outlined their reasons for objecting to
the Act. They described it as being 'wholly unacceptable to us.
Not only does it violate conscience; it grievously restricts the practice of religion [and will] bring to an end the work being done
in our institutions throughout Rhodesia. We refer to our schools,
hospitals, orphanages and homes for the aged etc... We ask those
responsible urgently to consider this plea that the church be not
reduced to the condition of existing merely by permission of the
State.'[14]

In reply to the statement by the interdenominational church
leaders and the later one by the Roman Catholic Bishops, Senator
van Heerden said that at earlier meetings with church leaders he
had made it clear that the churches should feel free to approach
him if they had further problems arising from the Act. 'It is surprising therefore that they did not ask to see me again before affirming
publicly that they would not register as voluntary organizations
and, in one case, before threatening to close all their institutions.'[15]

In early June it was announced that a new attempt to solve
the Church-State dispute would be made when the Prime Minister
met a delegation of seven Rhodesian churchmen (representing
almost all the major churches in the country). Earlier the Prime
Minister had held separate meetings with Roman Catholic and
Anglican bishops but this was to be the first meeting with an inter-
church delegation.[16] Following the meeting, a brief statement described the talks as 'cordial and constructive'. It was reported,
however, that the outcome of the talks was regarded only as a move
forward in the negotiations, for the Prime Minister had undertaken
to communicate further with the delegation in due course.

In August, with just over two weeks to go until the date on which
registration as voluntary associations had to be completed, the
Prime Minister held talks with a delegation of representatives of
the same churches that had been represented at the June talks.
The delegates described the talks as 'friendly and constructive'

but refused to comment further as the Prime Minister had
announced that he would make a statement later in the week on
what he proposed to do to meet the churches' main objections to
the Act.[17]

At the end of August 1970 the Prime Minister made his statement in the House of Assembly. He prefaced his remarks by
observing that he considered that there was a better understanding
by both parties of the other's problems. He went on to say:
'although Government has given very careful consideration to the
possibility of amending the Land Tenure Act in the manner
requested by church leaders, I regret that we are unable to do
this, save in one regard. In this case we are prepared to seek the
approval of Parliament for an amendment which I believe will
assist in removing whatever causes of friction there may have been
between the Churches and Government. In order to eliminate the
need for churches to apply for these permits, [enabling them to
carry on their existing work on mission land] it is our intention
to propose an amendment whereby permits will be deemed to have
been issued in these cases. Government will retain the right to
cancel any such permit should it find it necessary to do so.'

The Prime Minister then informed the House that the period
for application of permits would be extended for a further six
months and concluded his statement by saying: 'Although, as I
have already indicated, these proposals fall short of what the
churches have asked for, they are, I believe, an earnest of the Government's intention to assist the churches in continuing their work
and I trust that the churches will receive them in the spirit in
which they are made.'[18]

In September the Acting Minister of Lands, Mr. L. B. Smith
(Minister of Internal Affairs), introducing the Second Reading
of the Land Tenure Amendment Bill, assured the House that
although the amendment implemented the Prime Minister's offer
'it in no way alters the principles of the Land Tenure Act and
it is in line with the Government's stated intention not to interfere
with the traditional work of the churches in Rhodesia.'

The feelings of African M.P.'s were voiced by Mr. E. G.
Watungwa, M.P. for Harare, who said 'unfortunately, the debate
is just confined to the sections which are to be amended and it
does not give us much room to express our dissatisfaction over
the whole piece of legislation.'[19]

According to the *Sunday Mail* early in 1971, 'another round may be approaching in the long-standing Church-State dispute over the Land Tenure Act and the Constitution.' The *Mail* considered that the editorial in the January issue of the Roman Catholic periodical *Shield* had cleared the decks for action. The magazine's editor, Mr. (now Dr.) T. McLoughlin,[20] was quoted as saying that the Church had achieved very little by the amendment to the Act. He listed four outstanding differences which, in his opinion, remained: 'Churches can still be segregated by Ministerial declaration. There is still no appeal beyond the appropriate Minister's decision. There has been no declared policy by Government on admitting African pupils or patients to predominantly European schools and hospitals in European areas. There is no security of tenure in that all permits can be cancelled at any time—this applies even to agreements already reached.'[21]

By March 1971 it was reported that 39 church groups, including various Roman Catholic orders, had sent the Minister of Lands details of the land which they owned or leased in accordance with the provisions of the Act.[22]

According to the Act all predominantly European and Asian and Coloured independent private schools had to apply for permission to accept African pupils by 2nd March 1971. As these schools mostly belonged to the churches, they voiced their objections to the conditions which were to be imposed. (See also chapter on Education).

In late November 1972 it was reported that church leaders were to seek clarification of proposed new government controls on missionary activities in the tribal trust lands, as envisaged in the African Affairs Amendment Act (No. 2) Bill, and of the implications of the amendment to the Land Tenure Act then before Parliament. This latter amendment provided for religious, educational or charitable institutions to own or lease land anywhere irrespective of race but made these bodies responsible for obtaining permits for African priests, teachers or other employees to occupy an institution's premises in a European area or European priests, teachers or other employees in an African area.

The Roman Catholic Bishops' Conference initiated an inquiry among clergy and laity in the Church's five dioceses into the effect of this amending legislation and, in June 1973, passed a resolution condemning the legislation as unacceptable on the grounds that it contained 'provisions contrary to basic human freedom.' The Bishops particularly resented the provision on the issue of permits for people of one race to enter or occupy the area of another race and the resolution forbidding any application for these permits to be made without the express approval of the church leaders. The Bishops announced that together with representatives of other churches they had made an appeal to the government to repeal the 'offensive' provisions of the legislation. [23]

Among leaders of other churches who opposed the new legislation were the Anglican Bishop of Matabeleland, who was quoted as saying that he hoped 'the Government would not force this issue, since an open breach between Church and State cannot be beneficial to Rhodesia at this critical time. If, however, the Government forces me to choose between obeying my conscience and our apartheid laws, I shall have to obey my conscience.'; the Rev. R. A. Rabey, Methodist Minister in charge of the Wesley circuit, who said that his church had associated itself with the request for the repeal of the legislation; and the Rev. A. M. Ndhlela, Superintendent of the Methodist (U.K.) Church, who said that his church would not accept the legislation. On the other hand, the Presbyterian and Baptist churches did not join with other churches in their protest and the Rev. Arthur Lewis, Anglican Rector of Rusape, said that he would deplore a Church-State confrontation since legitimate grievances should be solved by negotiation. [24]

Early in 1973 Salisbury's City Council's African Affairs Committee recommended the Council to inform the Minister of Local Government and Housing that it was opposed to the issue of a permit under the Act to allow African nuns to occupy a house belonging to the Roman Catholic Church in a European area. The African sisters, members of the order of the Little Children of Our Blessed Lady, were needed to take over domestic duties at the Archbishop's house and another house in the grounds of the Cathedral in central Salisbury to replace European sisters of the Dominican Order who were required for work in other areas. The *Herald* commented, in its editorial entitled *A Ridiculous Idea,* that it was 'ridiculous to think that the presence of African nuns in a house in a European area threatens racial friction, interferes with the rights of the European group or prejudices the principle of paramountcy of European interests in a white area.' It went on

to say that it believed that 'this recommendation is another example
of doctrinaire thinking which has stamped some members of the
Council as unrealistic and unyielding in their attitude to racial
matters.'

At a meeting later in March the Council, by 14 votes to 12,
refused to agree to recommend refusal of the necessary permit
and the question was referred back to the African Affairs Committee. Having re-considered the matter the African Affairs Committee re-submitted its recommendation on the grounds that it would
be contrary to the intentions of the Land Tenure Act and, although
it was reported to have been sharply divided over the issue, the
Council agreed (by 17 votes to 11) to recommend that the application for the permit to allow the nuns to live in a European residential area be refused. [25]

THE FUTURE OF THE MISSIONS

In October 1971 it was announced that the heads of religious denominations would hold discussions upon the future of missions in
European-zoned areas. The *Herald* explained that the missions
fell into two different categories: 'those which are predominantly
schools with agriculture as a subject [and]... those missions which
have tenant farmers in addition to their schools.' It gave as examples Cyrene Mission at Westacre, Bulawayo, which fell into the
first category and Hope Fountain Mission also near Bulawayo
which fell into the second group, having more than 130 tenant
families. [26]

The meeting, as announced, took place in Salisbury from the
19th to 21st October 1971. It was attended by 17 heads of churches
representing 12 denominations. Major churches not represented
included the Presbyterian, the Dutch Reformed and the Greek
Orthodox.

In a statement issued after the meeting, three recommendations
were made to the churches: 'That the churches assure registered
tenants of full support in retaining their rights of occupation as
against the Land Tenure Act'; that the churches would not assist
the government in its 'unjust attempts to evict registered tenants';
that the churches would 'oppose the Government and support
the registered tenants in any attempt at compulsory removal.' [27]
The following day the Ministry of Information confirmed that
about 3 500 Africans living at the Epworth Methodist Mission

near Salisbury were to be re-settled either in the urban African townships or in the tribal areas.

Two days after the announcement regarding the removal of Epworth tenants the General Superintendent of the Methodist Church in Rhodesia, the Rev. Andrew Ndhlela, said that the church authorities would seek an early interview with the Prime Minister to try and work out the future of Epworth Mission. The Church would not co-operate with the proposed eviction of the tenants, said Mr. Ndhlela, for the Christian African community at Epworth had existed since the time when the B.S.A. Company had granted the original 2 700 acres to the Methodist Church in 1892.

The announcement regarding the Epworth tenants gave rise to anxiety about the future of other missions sited in European areas. On the 26th October it was reported that Roman Catholic authorities had received a letter from the Minister of Lands advising that the government was considering ending the rights of occupation of African tenant farmers at Chishawasha Mission also near Salisbury. [28]

The following month, however, it was announced that a settlement had been reached with Britain. The Rhodesian government, it was announced, had given an assurance to the British government that no move would be made to evict tenants from Epworth and Chishawasha and from other missions in European areas until after the proposed commission on racial discrimination had reported and its findings had been considered. [29]

During 1972 Mr. J. M. Khabo, M.P. for Pagati, asked the Minister whether tenants from Epworth were to be evicted and whether he would make a statement on the subject. The Minister of Local Government (answering on behalf of the Minister of Lands) reminded his questioner of the assurance given to the British government under the Settlement terms [30] and said: 'members are aware that the British Government has got itself into a position from which it feels unable to implement its side of the settlement agreement, and consequently the Rhodesian Government considers that it is now free to resume the investigations [into the desirability of removing the Epworth tenants]. The answer to the hon. member's question is, therefore, that the future of the tenants at Epworth Mission will depend upon the outcome of those investigations.' [31]

The resolution, passed by the Roman Catholic Bishops' Conference in June 1973, condemning amendments to the Land Tenure Act, also condemned amendments to the African Affairs Act. One amendment to this latter Act was to require any person employed at a mission station within a tribal area to apply for permission to enter the area from the district or provincial commissioner or from the Secretary for Internal Affairs. Another amendment gave the Secretary for Internal Affairs the power to ban anyone from entering or remaining in a tribal area if he believed that that person's presence in the area would be against the public interest or against the interests of Africans living in the area.

According to Henry Maasdorp, writing in the *Mail*, the Bishop of Mashonaland, the Rt. Rev. Paul Burrough, had written to the Secretary for Internal Affairs in February expressing the view that the legislation would have the effect that 'nobody from a bishop to a catechist could sleep overnight or carry on his normal work in land of the "other race" without a special permit every time.' In reply the Secretary said that it was not envisaged that a special permit would have to be obtained each time for it was anticipated that a blanket permit would be issued automatically for all whose church work took them into tribal areas. He pointed out that unless 'someone transgresses he has absolutely nothing to fear from this legislation.' This was in reference to what the Minister of Internal Affairs had said during the debate on the amending bill in the House. The Minister had described the churches as doing a wonderful job, but had pointed out that in some instances missionaries had supported and encouraged acts of 'terrorism' and that people like this were not really suitable to be closely associated with African affairs. The purpose of the amendment would be to ensure that such people were carefully scrutinized and screened before they could carry out subversive work under the guise of a missionary cloak. [32]

THE RESIDENTIAL PROPERTY OWNERS' (PROTECTION) BILL

During 1967 the Roman Catholic Bishops' Conference criticized the proposed P.O.P. Bill (as it is popularly known) as a piece of legislation which would bring dishonour to the country. In 1971 thirteen heads of major churches in Rhodesia issued a joint statement condemning the proposed Bill as 'a racial segregation Bill, designed ultimately to enforce the complete exclusion of persons of Asian or Coloured descent from areas of predominantly European occupation.' The churchmen criticized specific points of the Bill and concluded by stating that 'this is a principle abhorrent to the traditions of this country and in light of the tragic consequences of its use elsewhere, we most strenuously oppose legislation that necessitates its introduction.'[33]

RELATIONS WITH THE WORLD COUNCIL OF CHURCHES

In 1969 the World Council of Churches (W.C.C.) announced that it had decided to intensify the struggle against racism throughout the world. In September 1970 it further announced that finance was available for this programme and a grant of $120 000 would be made from the Special Fund to Combat Racism to the 'liberation' movements in Southern Africa.

According to the Director of the Programme to Combat Racism, Dr. Baldwin Sjollema, 'grants from the Special Fund... do not constitute an unqualified endorsement of specific tactics employed by the recipient organizations [but] they do represent general support from the W.C.C. for the long-term goals towards which their organizations are working. They also imply that anti-racist organizations which believe they have no other option but to resort to violence are no longer to be automatically excluded from the possibility of moral and practical support from the W.C.C. [The 'liberation' movements] have given the assurance that the funds allocated to them will be used for their social welfare, health, educational and legal aid programmes and not for military purposes.'[34]

Early reaction to the decision came from the Rt. Rev. Paul Burrough, Bishop of Mashonaland, who, in delivering his address to the 39th session of the Synod of the Diocese of Mashonaland, said he believed that the conscience of many Christians had been outraged by the decision to give money to African guerrilla fighters, adding that the outrage arose because the W.C.C. had said, in effect, that the violence which was inherent in apartheid must, in the name of Christ, be answered by violence.[35]

Although the Roman Catholic Church is not a member of the World Council of Churches the editorial in its magazine, *Shield*, for October stated that: 'Not only is the decision of the Council bad theologically, it is bad politics. To take the Council decision at its best, it supports terrorism because it believes that the order brought by terrorists would be more just, more Christian than what we have. This belief is totally untenable...' [36]

The Prime Minister put the Rhodesian government point of view when he cabled the *Sunday Express* in London. He questioned whether the W.C.C. had given any thought to the 'violent acts of sheer terrorism by those organizations which they choose to call freedom fighters?' and how the Council could blind itself to the fact that 'the organizers themselves are the greatest racialists in the world, sworn to drive out or exterminate all races other than their own in Africa?' [37]

The W.C.C.'s decisions were followed, at the end of October 1970, by publication of a report entitled *Violence in Southern Africa* by the International Affairs Department of the British Council of Churches. In an article in Salisbury's Sunday newspaper, this report was criticized by Mr. Ken Mew, principal of Ranche House College in Salisbury. Mr. Mew considered that 'if the published extracts are anything to go by, seldom has Christianity been afflicted by a more ill-considered document... Violence is its key-note.' [38]

In early November 1970 the Christian Council of Rhodesia (C.C.R.) held a day-long meeting in Salisbury at which about 30 representatives of the main denominations attended. Following the meeting a statement was issued expressing appreciation of grants (exceeding about $1 million) which the W.C.C. had made to individual churches in Rhodesia. The grants had been used for school buildings, relief of the needy, and 'extension of Christian work in general.' The statement then went on to record appreciation for the 'recent gesture of concern and compassion for the oppressed people of Rhodesia.' The representatives at the meeting said that they interpreted the W.C.C.'s action as support for the churches' world-wide Christian programme against racism.' [39]

Almost immediately a number of churchmen made statements strongly disagreeing with the C.C.R. The Anglican and Presbyterian churches disassociated themselves from the resolution. The Moderator of the Central African Synod of the Presbyterian Church condemned the action of the W.C.C. and took the opportunity of querying whether the people attending the C.C.R.'s meeting 'took into account the fact that they could hold their meeting, undisturbed, in Salisbury because other people's sons are finding hardships and danger to protect them from the very terrorists to which the W.C.C. is giving moral support backed by support in cash.'

The Rev. Fred Rea of the Trinity Methodist Church made what he announced was a personal comment on the action of the C.C.R.: 'The Council found itself confronted by two separate questions: one, does it support the W.C.C.'s condemnation of the trend of Rhodesia's racial politics?; and, two, does it regard the resort to violent revolution as contrary to the way of Christ in Rhodesia?' Mr. Rea said that he sympathized with those African members of the C.C.R. who felt that any criticism of the W.C.C. would imply tacit support of the *status quo*.[40]

In early 1971 the newly formed Anglican Consultative Council held a meeting in Limuru, Kenya, consisting of some 50 bishops, clergy and laity. The meeting adopted a resolution (opposed by the Bishop of Mashonaland and the Archbishop of Cape Town) approving the W.C.C. grants of aid to African nationalist movements in Southern Africa.[41] Bishop Paul Burrough, who later walked out of the meeting in protest, was quoted as saying: 'Speaking for Rhodesia only, I am asked to encourage the two dioceses to give moral and financial support to organizations pledged to violence against people of that country, especially violence towards Africans. Secondly, I am asked to encourage the Churches of Rhodesia to organize espionage of military, political and industrial structures and to report them to the World Council of Churches.'[42]

At the end of March the W.C.C. headquarters in Geneva issued an announcement that a full-scale campaign was to be launched in the near future aimed at the isolation of Southern Africa. Member churches around the world were to be instructed to press for a ban on arms sales and a stop to white immigration. The Council's Commission for the Programme to Combat Racism also called for 'freedom fighters' to be treated as prisoners of war.

In its editorial commenting upon this announcement, the *Herald* considered that 'when the W.C.C. resolves to instruct its 200 member Churches in 83 countries to discourage white immigration to South Africa and tourism to a wider area... it is becoming embroiled in a punitive political campaign that goes far beyond normal Church issues... the W.C.C. must not be surprised if member Churches in Southern Africa begin withdrawing their support and finally their membership.'

The concluding sentence in this comment, no doubt, referred to a report in the same issue of the newspaper to the effect that the Presbyterian Church had suspended payments to the W.C.C. and, according to a statement by the Moderator of the Presbytery of Mashonaland, that although the Church had decided to remain a member of the W.C.C. it was only 'because it is felt to be of great importance to have a voice on it to express our point of view.' The Moderator added, however, that the Presbyterian Church would consider terminating its membership if 'the W.C.C. continues to dictate unrealistic policies... and fails to give credit to the effort of Churches in Southern Africa to combat racism.'[43]

Later in the year the Anglican Diocese of Matabeleland discussed a motion to sever relations with the W.C.C. and the C.C.R. Bishop Mark Wood explained that membership of the W.C.C. was, as far as both the Rhodesian dioceses was concerned, an indirect one. It was the Anglican Province of Central Africa which was a member (which makes all Anglican churches in the Province members automatically) and only the Provincial Synod could debate such a motion.[44]

In September the Synod of the Mashonaland Diocese asked for an explanation of the connection between the Anglican Church and the C.C.R. in view of the latter's association with the W.C.C. In his reply Bishop Paul Burrough explained why he considered that the Anglican church should continue to be represented on the C.C.R. Among other reasons, he said, 'the Christian Council of Rhodesia is one of the few organizations of Rhodesian church life which tries to bring together the divided churches.'[45]

A few days later both the Anglican bishops issued a statement disassociating the Anglican Church in Rhodesia from the grant made by the W.C.C. to what it called 'black liberation movements'. The Bishops stated: 'For the settlement of doubt we would like to say publicly that no member of the Anglican Church throughout Rhodesia has at any time or place been known to speak or vote for the Church in favour of violent action or intimidation against the present Government. Secondly, that not one cent has ever been given by the Anglican Church in Rhodesia to support the World Council of Churches' programme against racism.'[46]

In early January 1972 it was reported that the Christian Council of Rhodesia had, at an earlier meeting, voted 25 to nine to reject the Settlement proposals. [47] During the following month it was reported that a group of Anglican churchmen had formed an organization 'to counter attempts to use the Church and church bodies as instruments of revolutionary policy.' The Rector of Rusape who announced the formation of the new group—the Rhodesia Christian Group (R.C.G.)—was quoted as saying that 'we are second to none in our enthusiasm for African progress and African participation in the affairs of our country. But we repudiate the World Council of Churches' condoning of terrorism as morally outrageous and practically disastrous, and deplore the tendency of the Christian Council of Rhodesia to follow its parent body.' [48]

In April 1972 the 7th Synod of the Anglican Province of Central Africa was held in Lusaka. [49] On his return from the Synod, the Rev. A. J. Gardiner, vice-chairman of the Rhodesia Christian Group, criticized the Archbishop, the Most Rev. Donald Arden, for refusing to allow, at the Synod, a discussion of a resolution which he had put forward. The resolution read: 'That this Province reduce its annual subscription to the World Council of Churches to a nominal one dollar until it has been satisfied that no further assistance is being given to terrorist organizations' [50].

The Rev. Gardiner was later criticized by both the Rt. Rev. Mark Wood, Bishop of Matabeleland and by an African Anglican church leader, Mr. Percy M'kudu (a former Member of Parliament) who took the opportunity of warning that there could be a split along racial lines in the Anglican church, for as Mr. M'Kudu said African delegates would have voted the resolution down over the objections of most of the Europeans present. [51] Explaining his action in vetoing the motion by the Rev. Gardiner, the Archbishop later wrote in the Mashonaland Diocese newspaper, *Link,* stating that the Standing Committee reviewing the agenda had 'felt that only bitterness would be engendered by debating a motion which would certainly be rejected.' [52]

During the first week in June 1972 new regulations, under the Emergency Powers Act, were published in the *Government Gazette.* These regulations empowered the Minister of Law and Order to declare any trust, organization or person, which had given him reason to believe had assisted or would be likely to assist any unlawful organization or 'terrorist' movement, as specific, so that any money or goods received in Rhodesia from such a specified source could be confiscated by the government. This led to speculation that the W.C.C. would be among one of the first organizations to be so 'specified'.

In August the World Council of Churches voted to increase its special fund to combat racism and also to sell its shares in companies with interests in Southern Africa and in Portuguese territories in West Africa.

The chairman of the R.C.G., Father Arthur Lewis, writing in the Group's newsletter in November considered that 'the support of the W.C.C. for those who seek the over-throw of society by violence and bloodshed and our own Churches' involvement with the W.C.C. are issues of prime concern.' He advised the use of all legitimate means for the withdrawal of Rhodesian churches from the W.C.C. and the formation of a separate Anglican Province of Rhodesia. [53]

Early in January 1973 it was reported that the two Anglican Bishops had protested to the W.C.C. for its continued support of movements employing 'naked terrorism'. The Bishops cited recent guerrilla attacks on farms in the Centenary area of Rhodesia in which two children had been wounded and houses of local Africans burned. The following day it was announced that other church leaders had agreed with what the Anglican Bishops had written to the president of the W.C.C. Among them were the heads of the Roman Catholic Church and of the United Methodist Church, Bishop Abel Muzorewa, who was quoted as saying that he thought it necessary 'first to condemn the cause of terrorism and then condemn terrorism itself.' In his capacity as leader of the A.N.C., Bishop Muzorewa said that the A.N.C. had frequently made known its opposition to the use of violence. [54]

In mid-February the Anglican Bishop of Mashonaland caused a statement to be read from all pulpits in Mashonaland which read 'Having waited in vain for an acknowledgement from the World Council of Churches to a protest made by the Bishop of Matabeleland and myself at their support of groups bringing death and destruction to Rhodesians, black and white alike, I have now instructed the Diocesan Secretary to withold from our Provincial assessment the proportion which Mashonaland pays of the Province's membership of the W.C.C.' The Bishop added in his statement that he commended to all Anglican members of the diocese that the proper work of the church was to combat racism and injustice by Christian means.

Also in mid-February the Christian Council of Rhodesia decided to invite representatives of the W.C.C. to talk to Rhodesian Christians preferably by visiting Rhodesia. In its resolution it stated that, as a Council, it would suspend judgement on W.C.C. grants for welfare and propaganda until such dialogue had taken place. The W.C.C. in Geneva was reported to have said that it would be glad to send a delegation to Rhodesia providing that no conditions would be attached to travel and meeting people. The chairman of the Rhodesia Christian Group, however, considered that any such visit should be handled by the heads of churches in Rhodesia and not by the Christian Council. The *Herald* echoed this opinion in its editorial the following day, stating that the C.C.R. 'clearly... needs reminding that it is made up of Christianity in Rhodesia... the responsibility of ensuring that it [the W.C.C.] hears all shades of opinion is too great to leave to a body... such as the C.C.R.'[55]

It was reported in April that Dr. H. R. Weber, director of Biblical studies for the W.C.C., and the Rev. E. Kendall, of the secretariat of the Conference of the British Missionary Society, had visited Rhodesia towards the end of March. Salisbury churchmen, described as being 'reluctant to discuss' the visits, were largely reported as saying that the two men had visited Rhodesia in their private capacities.[56]

NOTES

1 1953: Jones, Neville: *Rhodesian Genesis:* Bulawayo; Rhodesia Pioneers and Early Settlers Society. See also
1945: Wallis, J. P. R. (Ed.): *The Matabele Mission, a selection from the correspondence of John and Emily Moffat, David Livingstone and others:* London: Chatto and Windus; Oppenheimer Series.
1969: Murphree, Marshall, W.: *Christianity and the Shona:* London: Athlone Press.
2 1962: Oliver, Roland and J. D. Fage: *A Short History of Africa:* Harmondsworth: Penguin.

3 1963: Keatley, Patrick: *The Politics of Partnership: the Federation of Rhodesia and Nyasaland:* Harmondsworth: Penguin.

4 The Catholic Bishops were:
   Francis W. Markall, S. J., Archbishop of Salisbury
   Aloysius Haene, S. M. B., Bishop of Gwelo
   Adolphus G. Schmitt. C. N. M., Bishop of Bulawayo
   Donal R. Lamont, O. Carm., Bishop of Umtali
   Ignatius Prieto, S. M. I., Bishop of Wankie

5 *A Plea for Peace:* Special Supplement to *Shield:* No. 240. December 1965.

6 A reference to the fact that African voting powers are vested in the amount of income tax they pay.

7 Special edition of *Shield,* June 1969. The same five Catholic Bishops as at note 4 signed the Pastoral Message.

8 Article entitled *A Choice to be Made between Church and State* by the Rev. F. B. Rea in *R.H.* 26 March 1970.

9 The Act's definition of a voluntary organization includes a 'religious order or sect'.

10 *Hansard:* Vol. 76, 6 November 1969: Col. 1162.

11 As reported in *R.H.* 3 March 1970.

12 1970: *The Land Tenure Act and the Church:* Salisbury: Mambo Press for the R.C. Bishops' Conference. Italics are in the original.

13 According to *R.H.* 25 April 1970, the signatories to the statement included the five R.C. Bishops, the two Anglican Bishops, representatives of the Methodist (U.K.) Church, the United Methodist Church, the Presbyterian Church, the African Reformed Church in Rhodesia (an independent 'daughter church' of the Dutch Reformed Church), the Salvation Army, the Evangelical Lutheran Church, the United Congregational Church, the Baptist Mission of Rhodesia, the United Church of Christ and the Church of Christ (N.Z.).

14 As reported in *R.H.* 30 April 1970.

15 As reported in *R.H.* 1 May 1970.

16 *R.H.* 4 June 1970.

17 As reported in *R.H.* 25 August 1970. The seven churchmen were:
   The Bishop of Mashonaland, the Rt. Rev. Paul Burrough
   The vice-President of the Roman Catholic Bishops' Conference, the Rt. Rev. Alois Haene
   The Moderator of the Central African Synod of the Presbyterian Church, the Rev. A.G. Leask
   The General Superintendent of the Methodist Church (U.K.), the Rev. Andrew Ndhlela
   The head of the United Methodist Church, the Rt. Rev. Abel Muzorewa
   The Moderator of the African Reformed Church in Rhodesia, the Rev. Christopher Chikasha
   The secretary of the Roman Catholic Bishops' Conference, the Rev. Fr. Richard Randolph, S.J.

18 *Hansard:* Vol. 78, No. 2. 26 August 1970: Col. 98-9.

19 *Hansard:* Vol. 78, No. 7. 3 September 1970: Cols. 221-4.

20 Mr. T. McLoughlin and Mr. A. Chennells, the deputy editor of *Shield*, later resigned from the periodical in protest.
21 As reported in *S.M.* 3 January 1971.
22 *R.H.* 8 March 1971.
23 As reported in *R.H.* 18 June 1973.
24 As reported in *R.H.* 19 June 1973.
25 *R.H.* 7, 8 March; 21 May 1973.
26 *R.H.* 20 October 1971.
27 As reported in *R.H.* 22 October 1971.
   Epworth Mission is run by the Methodist (U.K.) Church. At the Mission settlement are three farms: Epworth Farm, the land of which was given by the British South Africa Company to the Methodist Church in 1892, and the Glenwood and Adelaide Farms, of which 6 000 acres have been bought by the tenants.
28 *R.H.* 25, 26 October 1971.
29 Chishawasha Mission, run by the Roman Catholic Church, comprises some 13 000 acres which was given to the Church by the British South Africa Company in 1891. There are about 1 000 registered tenant farmers and their families.
30 White Paper. Cmd. R.R. 46-1971: *Proposals for a Settlement: Presented to Parliament by the Prime Minister on 25 November 1971.*
31 *Hansard:* Vol. 81, No. 9. 16 June 1972: Col. 667.
32 *S.M.* 24 June 1973.
   Hansard: Vol. 83, No. 4. 24 November 1972: Cols. 263-4.
33 *R.H.* 10 February 1971.
34 As quoted in an article entitled *Christians Condoning the Evils of Racialism* by Peter L. Baka. *S.M.* 29 November 1970.
35 As reported in *R.H.* 19 September 1970.
36 *Shield* No. 299, October 1970.
37 As reported in *R.H.* 2 November 1970.
38 *S.M.* 15 November 1970.
39 The Christian Council of Rhodesia was formed in July 1964 at a meeting attended by many church leaders and laity. Its Constitution outlines its aims as being to bring together for discussion, conference and joint action Christian denominations of different traditions; to foster closer unity of the church; to co-ordinate interdenominational work; and to encourage re-union of the denominations. Neither the Roman Catholic or Dutch Reformed Churches belong to the Council. It was later reported that the churchmen present at the meeting voted as individuals and not on behalf of their churches.
   R.H. 12 November 1970.
40 *R.H.* 13 November 1970.
41 *The Times* (London) 4 March 1971.
42 *R.H.* 4 March 1971.
43 *R.H.* 1 April 1971.
44 *R.H.* 8 May 1971.
45 *R.H.* 5 September 1971.
46 *R.H.* 11 September 1971.

47 *R.H.* 2 January 1972 (See also chapter on the Churches and the Settlement).
48 *R.H.* 16 February 1972: It was reported that the foundation members of the Rhodesian Christian Group were:
    Rev. B. French, Rector of Umvukwes
    Rev. A. Lewis, Rector of Rusape
    Rev. A. J. Gardiner, principal of the College of Christ the King, Daramombe
    Rev. D. Grant, Rector of Hartley
    Rev. G. Kirk, Rector of Lomagundi
    Rev. J. Knight, administrator, African Education, Diocese of Mashonaland.
According to the R.C.G.'s founder, African priests were not invited to join because of fears they might be intimidated by persons antagonistic to the R.C.G.'s aims.
49 The Anglican Province of Central Africa is composed of the Diocese of Mashonaland, Matabeleland (including Botswana), Malawi and Zambia.
50 *R.H.* 28 April 1972.
51 *S.M.* 30 April 1972.
52 *Link,* June 1972.
53 As reported in *R.H.* 5 December 1972.
54 *R.H.* 3, 4 January 1973.
55 As reported in *R.H.* 16, 17, 21, 22 February 1973.
56 *R.H.* 18 April 1973.

XIII

EDUCATION

AFRICAN

Prior to the general settlement of Europeans in Rhodesia missionaries were solely responsible for starting schools for the indigenous people at their mission stations. In response to Dr. David Livingstone's report (in 1857), on the need for missionary endeavour in the area, the London Missionary Society sent out a band of missionaries to Matabeleland. Led by Mr. J. S. Moffat, they first settled in the Inyati valley in 1859 and then started a second mission station in 1870 about fifty miles from the original settlement. This station was the Hope Fountain Mission which is on the outskirts of the present day Bulawayo. The Catholic Fathers of the Society of Jesus followed in 1879 when their station was built on the site of Old Bulawayo.

Following the arrival and establishment of the Pioneer Column at Fort Salisbury in 1890 a further two missions were established; one by the Dutch Reformed Church at Morgenster near Fort Victoria in 1891 and another by the American Board of Foreign Missions at Mount Selinda in the eastern district in 1893. Subsequently the British South Africa Company made grants of land to all these missions when it took over the administration of the country.[1]

The first education ordinance was enacted in 1899 which, although concerned mainly with European education, provided for assistance to the mission schools subject to certain conditions which caused African education to develop along agricultural and technical lines.

In 1924 a commission was appointed to investigate the whole problem of African education. Resulting from its recommendations a separate Department of Native Education was formed in 1925, which in 1929 was absorbed into the new Department of Native Development.

In 1935 the Department of Native Education was revived and because of the larger numbers of Africans coming into the towns and a change in attitudes towards education by African parents more emphasis was placed on academic subjects.

During the Federal period (1953-1963) European education (including that for Asian and Coloured children in separate schools) and higher education for Africans was the responsibility of the Federal government while primary and secondary education for Africans was the obligation of the individual territorial governments. Following the break-up of the Federation, both African and European education were brought together into separate and independent departments under the one Ministry of Education.[2]

During the Second Reading of the Education Bill in 1972 (which was intended to update the Education Act of 1956) the Minister of Education, Mr. A. P. Smith, explained why there was a need for two separate Acts to cover the education for the two racial groups. 'Each of the present Acts has been so drafted so as to take care of quite different situations. On the one hand the Education Act provides for the compulsory education of the European, Asian and Coloured children, the majority of whom are catered for in government schools and only 14 *per cent* attend independent schools. On the other hand the African Education Act, provides for a voluntary system of education for African schoolchildren, and the majority, some 80 *per cent*, attend schools which are not run by the government. At this stage in the country's economic development it would be quite impossible to provide a system of compulsory education for Africans... This is the main reason why two separate Acts are necessary.'[3]

In 1966 a new ten-year plan for African education was announced. It provided for a full primary education for 7 years for all African children able to reach a school;[4] the establishment of post-primary education in the form of about 300 junior secondary schools to provide 2 years of 'vocational preparation' for those children not qualified to enter the more 'academic' senior schools; an increase in the numbers of senior schools; and the rationalization, co-ordination and modernizing of teacher training institutions.

To enable the government to meet the costs of this expansion, it was hoped that the costs of primary education would partly be borne by local government, for the Department of African Education was to function within the government's policy for Community Development.

In so far as its effect on education went, the policy of community development was summed up by Gloria Passmore in her book on the subject, as providing for:—

1. New schools or new segments or streams added to existing schools would in future be eligible for the salary subsidy only if they were run under council auspices.
2. The salary subsidy already granted to missions in respect of existing classes and streams in mission schools would continue.
3. Missions would be able to obtain assistance in respect of new schools, new segments of schools or new streams, only on a private school-aid basis (18 *per cent* of the annual recurrent cost to the state of educating a pupil in African primary schools operated by the Government in urban areas).
4. Aid on the private school formula would be subject to the recommendation of the African council or in the absence of a council, the chief for the area. [5]

When this plan was outlined the African education vote was pegged at 2 *per cent* of the Gross National Product which, according to one report, made the plan 'more static than dynamic.'[6] However, as the Minister of Education said in the debate on the Revenue Vote for African education in August 1969, 'The [ten-year education] plan was based on the 1962 census; it is possible that when the new census is finally issued there may be a difference in figures which may possibly affect the plan.'[7]

In November 1971 during a debate on a motion that the House deplore the system of African education and calling upon the government to redress the system, the Minister of Education said that several of the African M.P.'s who supported the motion were really suggesting that the education of all Rhodesians should be on an equal basis—'In other words we should provide a duplicate of the European, Asian and Coloured educational system.' Mr. Smith went on to explain that this proposition was financially impossible. Basing relevant figures on the 1969 census and costs from the Estimates of Expenditure and the *Monthly Digest of Statistics* he said that it could be ascertained 'that the cost for the present year would be in the region of 380 million dollars. This figure is almost twice as much as the whole of the statutory appropriations, so if we closed all the European, Asian and Coloured schools, both Technical Colleges and the University, and all the other ministries ceased to function, we would still have to double the present level of taxation in order to pay for African education alone.'[8]

In early 1972 it was reported that a total of 2 403 out of 2 477 Africans had passed the Cambridge School Certificate held in November 1971. A spokesman for the Division of African Education commented that this was a 97.01 *per cent* pass rate compared with a 94.9 *per cent* pass rate in 1970. The spokesman also said that 69 candidates had obtained G.C.E. certificates while only five had failed to obtain anything.[9]

The Report of the Secretary for African Education for the year ended 31st December 1972 showed that enrolments in the 3 219 African primary schools during 1972 totalled 692 432 compared with 639 043 in 1971; in the 140 African secondary schools there were 29 012 enrolments during 1972 as compared to 26 077 in 1971. Figures of expenditure on African education during the same two years were $19 912 435 for 1971/2 and $17 341 244 for 1970/1. Estimated expenditure for 1972/3 was $22 470 000. Early in 1973 a spokesman for the Division of African Education announced that 28 040 extra places in African schools (25 500 in primary schools) had been provided from the beginning of the year.[10]

In February 1973 the United Nations Educational, Scientific and Cultural Organization (U.N.E.S.C.O.) in its report at the 29th session of the Commission on Human Rights, claimed that the Rhodesian government was purposefully denying Africans the right to a proper education. Comparing African education to that of white Rhodesians the report stated that 'African education... is geared to providing the semi-skilled labour necessary for industrial development, but not to training to compete with White Rhodesians for top-level posts.' A government spokesman later denied that these reports were true and said that the educational targets recommended by U.N.E.S.C.O., at its 1961 conference in Addis Ababa (at which Rhodesia was represented) were being exceeded in Rhodesia. He added that during the past ten years the enrolment of African pupils in secondary schools had increased by more than 300 *per cent* and there had also been an increase in primary school enrolment. He also pointed out that about 40 *per cent* of students at the University of Rhodesia were African. 'A high standard is maintained in all African schools and pupils who display the ability to progress enjoy opportunities identical with their European colleagues.' he was quoted as saying. [11]

In mid-1973 Mr. R. C. Makaya, M.P. for Lowveld, moved in the House a resolution asking for a review of African education. Commenting upon the ensuing debate, the *Herald* considered that particular attention should be paid to the questions asked and the points raised by African M.P.'s during the debate. It pointed out that 'one theme seemed paramount—the belief that because the general system of African education was different from that in European, Asian and Coloured schools, it was thus necessarily inferior and unsuitable.' [12] Most of the African Members spoke of specific points which, in the words of Mr. Makaya in his introductory remarks, represented 'African parents' grievances.' These were the 'grading' system; the difficulties of moving pupils from one provincial school to another; the division of the Junior Certificate course into two parts; the pegging of finance for African schooling at 2 *per cent* of the gross national product; the imbalance in the dual system of education (which provided for 22 270 African secondary school pupils and 26 844 European counterparts in 1971), when related to the overall population distribution by race; and the difficulties in obtaining trade, craft and technical training and even apprenticeships for Africans. A number of African M.P.'s spoke of education available in other countries and queried why Rhodesia could not follow their example. Replying to the debate, the Minister of Education said that the Rhodesian educational system had always been under constant review and that his Ministry would consider what alternative methods could be employed to answer some of the specific complaints. He questioned, however, whether critics had given proper consideration to the various factors involved and asked them to consider the gross national income, which in Rhodesia averaged, per head of population, between $201 to $400. He pointed out that 'the limitations placed upon us by our human and economic resources must be recognized. We simply cannot have instant compulsory education to a high standard overnight... [for] while we can, and do, have high standards, we cannot expand the system beyond our capacity to pay for such expansion.' The Minister asserted that a worrying aspect was the fact that at the present time there were 4 000 and 1 600 places vacant in the African primary and secondary schools respectively. [13]

EUROPEAN

Although Asian and Coloured education comes under the same Division of Education in the Ministry, European children attend different schools to the ones attended by children of the Asian and Coloured groups. The figures of enrolments of European children are given in the Report of the Secretary for Education for the year ended 30th June 1972. In the 162 government schools for Europeans there were 52 197 enrolments. A further 7 334 European pupils attended the 38 predominantly European Independent schools. [14]

ASIAN AND COLOURED

In 1903, when the country's second Education Act was passed, it was noted that the government was 'to provide schools for Coloured children when necessary'. In 1908 the Report of the Education Commission stated that one witness had referred to the large and growing number of half caste children and the importance of making educational provision for them. A central school was suggested, but the Committee did not feel that it was competent to make specific recommendations 'for dealing with this somewhat difficult class' but believed that the government's attention should be drawn to the problem and recommended to give it further consideration. [15] Since 1928, when numbers justified it, the education of Coloured and Asian children has been included in the terms of Education Acts for Europeans although separate schools have been provided.

During 1944-5 there was a commission of enquiry into the social welfare of the Coloured community. The report of this commission (popularly known as the Tait Commission) estimated that there were at that time about 5 000 Coloured persons living in Rhodesia, basing its figures upon the 1941 Census which had given a number of 3 974. The Commission also took pains to work out a definition of a coloured person (for different legislation had different definitions). In recommending that the government should attempt a recognized decision the Commission said that all it could do was to make a suggestion 'for the term is not capable of a precise definition'. The phrase they suggested was—'Any person other than an asiatic or native who has the blood of an asiatic or native.'[16]

The Commission noted that in 1933 primary schools for Coloured children existed in the main centres and, although some 'asiatic' children also attended these schools there were some schools which had been established for Indian children also. In 1938 education became compulsory for all Coloured and Asian children living within a radius of three miles from a suitable school but at this time there were no post-primary schools and suitable Coloured pupils were sent, with government aid, to the Union of South Africa for secondary schooling. This, it was noted, was to be a temporary expedient until numbers justified the erection of a secondary school. The Commission recommended that the curriculum should not be identical with that for Europeans, for the education of Coloureds and Asians should be on 'modern' rather than on 'academic' lines.

Primary and secondary schools remained segregated and by 1959 primary schools for Asians and Coloureds were available in most centres throughout the country. However the provision of secondary schools lagged behind the provision of school for European children for there were 38 government secondary schools for Europeans and only two for Asians and Coloureds.

The Education Act No. 54 of 1972 (which came into force on the 12th January 1973) was intended to consolidate and to update the Education Act of 1956 with its numerous amendments. It was designed to cover European, Coloured and Asian Education and, like the 1956 Act, gives the Minister powers 'to set aside schools or other educational institutions or school hostels for such class or classes of pupils as he may specify and, in classifying pupils for the purpose of this subsection, the Minister may classify them by race, colour or otherwise as he thinks fit.'[17]

Figures of enrolments for the year ended 30th June 1972 for Coloured and Asian children were 7 553 at the 20 government schools and 1 688 at Independent schools. Expenditure on both European and Asian and Coloured education from the revenue votes of the Ministry of Education and from the Ministry of Works (for school buildings) amounted to $21 388 451.[18]

THE INDEPENDENT PRIVATE SCHOOLS

In 1962 the Education Act was amended to permit African pupils to attend the predominantly European or Coloured and Asian independent, fee-paying private schools and until 1965 no permit was needed for the admission of these pupils.[19] After 1965, however, permission of the Ministry of Education had to be obtained before these schools could admit African pupils. In 1969 the Land Tenure Act made this authorization the business of the appropriate Minister in terms of the Act.

During the Second Reading of the Land Tenure Bill in 1969 the Minister of Lands, Senator P. van Heerden, referred to what he called the fundamental principle of the Land Tenure Bill— 'that the interests of Europeans are paramount in the European area and the interests of Africans are paramount in the African area.' He went on to say 'it is recognized, however, that each race cannot be self-sufficient in its own area, and that it is necessary for persons of one race to own, lease and occupy land in the area of the other race, subject to strict control on a fully reciprocal basis.' Senator van Heerden then continued by outlining the difficulties of the precise meaning of the term 'occupation' and said that although

> attendance at a place to which the public are admitted does not normally constitute "occupation" … in some cases admission to a place of this sort may have to be controlled if racial friction is to be avoided, and it is proposed that the Minister shall have power to prescribe that attendance for a specified purpose at a specified place or classes of place … shall constitute occupation for the purposes of the Act. Furthermore, the Bill makes it clear that a person who attends at a school or other educational institution, whether as a teacher or a pupil … shall be regarded for the purposes of the Act as occupying the land on which the institution is situated.[20]

When the Land Tenure Act eventually came into force, therefore, it became a legal requirement that by March 1971 all predominantly European, Asian and Coloured private schools must apply for permission to accept any African pupil in their school on the grounds that his attendance was regarded as 'occupation' of land designated for another race.

In early 1970, after objections to the implications of the Act from the various churches the Ministry of Education made a statement about which the *Herald's* political reporter commented that it was seen as a warning that 'although Africans will be allowed admission to independent schools in the immediate future, the position will not be allowed to get out of hand and that independent schools will remain predominantly European'. In the past the intake into the private schools had been subject to the approval of the Ministry of Education only. It would now be handled by three ministries (Local Government, Lands and Internal Affairs) under the Land Tenure Act. [21]

In the same issue of the *Herald* the Education Secretary of the Roman Catholic Bishops' Conference outlined, in order to clarify the position, the principal conditions under which, it was understood, permits to admit African pupils would be granted: in schools predominantly European, the enrolment of African pupils must not be more than 6 *per cent* of the whole, all other entrance requirements to be the same as for other pupils. In schools where pupils were predominantly Asian and Coloured, the same conditions for entry would prevail except that the percentage of African pupils must not exceed 15 *per cent* of the total. No private school which had not in the past taken African pupils would be allowed to do so. [22]

A month later the Bishops' Conference stated that with regard to the registration of African pupils at Catholic private schools the Church would accept the requirements under the Land Tenure Act but only under protest. The Bishops made it clear that they did not accept the ideological principle behind the government's conditions and that they did not concede the moral right of the government to impose such conditions. They also stated that they 'do not accept the percentage condition imposed by the Government as anything more than a temporary arrangement' and that they 'totally reject any suggestion that the few independent schools which have not yet taken African pupils will not be allowed to do so in the future.' [23]

Towards the end of the year, however, the Bishops announced that after constant review and having had an opportunity of consultation with their people they had come to the conclusion that 'the implementation of the Government's discriminatory policies, particularly under the Land Tenure Act since then, has made it clear that Government's ideology is so incompatible with the

Church's teaching that further negotiation would serve no useful purpose. They have accordingly instructed the schools that the temporary arrangement is now at an end.'[24] At the same time the two Anglican Bishops called upon Boards governing Anglican private schools to consider the government's requirement that African pupils attend on a percentage basis. It was explained that Anglican private schools were, unlike the Roman Catholic schools, not under the direct control of the Bishops.[25]

The Catholic Bishops followed their announcement with an instruction to their schools that pupils to Roman Catholic schools should now be admitted on one criterion only—that of merit. The Education Secretary of the Bishops' Conference explained that at present although the numbers of Africans at predominantly European schools did not exceed 6 *per cent* the Bishops were taking a 'stand on a matter of principle;... the right of parents to send their children to the school of their choice, the right of private schools to accept what pupils they will, and the right of the Church to serve freely all the people of God, irrespective of race.'[26]

In early November 1972 the Rev. John Brogan, S. J. (Rector of St. George's College, Salisbury) explained in the church magazine the importance independent schools have for Rhodesia. Firstly he referred to the generally accepted fact that all parents have an inalienable right to make decisions about their children's education. The existence of independent schools was mainly to ensure that religious education was in conformity with parents' beliefs and wishes. He spoke of the experience which had been gained at his school of Asians, Africans and Coloureds being accepted on their own merits without any form of indoctrination or 'forced integration' and went on to say that 'we accept that perhaps the contribution being made to better race relations in the country at large by the multi-racial independent schools is marginal at present... [But] if multi-racialism is to succeed (as ultimately it must in this country) then there is great need for an educational outlook which is not narrow and restrictive in racial attitudes, but which encourages toleration and acceptance.'[27] The article was later published in the *Herald* where it reached a larger reading public.

Later in November the new Education Bill was introduced in the House of Assembly. When examined in detail it was found to have omitted a clause which had been introduced into the previous Act at the request of the Churches.[28] Roman Catholic clergy, in particular, felt that the omission of this clause meant that a 'fundamental' right and protection had been scrapped and they protested to the government. [29] On the following Tuesday while introducing the Second Reading of the Bill the Minister of Education referred to 'recent unfavourable press reports' and reassured M.P.'s that 'the provisions governing independent schools remain substantially unchanged... there is nothing in this Bill to preclude the admission of Africans to independent schools, nor is there anything in the Bill to allow the Minister any discretionary powers.'

On the following day in answer to M.P.'s questions the Minister said that he had already pointed out that 'there is nothing in the Bill which precludes African pupils from being admitted to independent schools... [it] clearly envisages the attendance of Africans at independent schools.' He went on to define the term 'independent school' as 'any school which is not a Government school' and said that these schools may be of two kinds, those which do not take any African pupils and those at which pupils who are not Africans preponderate. In the case of the latter schools 'Africans may be admitted until such time as they preponderate. If that did happen, then the school would be regarded as an African school and would have to seek registration under the African Education Act.' The Minister went on to say that African pupils were in the same position as Europeans, Coloureds or Asians 'and nowhere in the old Act or in this Bill is provision made for the rights of these races to attend independent schools. I believe the rights of all four races are the same in so far as this Bill is concerned, and I see no reason for any clause specifically referring to the rights of Africans.'

The Minister continued his speech by saying that before the 1962 amendment to the old Act had been made Africans did not have the right to enter independent schools, but the present Bill had been drafted 'on the assumption that Africans could be admitted to independent schools in terms of this Bill... [which] has been worded accordingly.' [30]

The report of the Secretary for Education, presented to Parliament during 1973, gave the number of Independent schools as 44 and enrolment figures as totalling 9 422 divided by race into 7 334 Europeans, 359 Asians, 1 339 Coloureds and 400 Africans on the registers on 30th June 1972. [31]

TEACHERS

On the 2nd September 1969, the Minister of Internal Affairs, Mr. L. B. Smith, made a statement in the House of Assembly concerning African Education. The Minister explained that he was making the statement instead of the Minister of Education because it had been agreed that it would affect the everyday life of Africans and particularly those Africans living in the tribal areas which came under the portfolio of Internal Affairs. The Minister went on to say that at the present time 70 *per cent* of the African Education Vote was channelled into the primary schools and that this left too little for secondary education. The government had therefore decided to give extra grants to African Councils to enable local communities to take over the responsibility of paying a proportion of primary teachers' salaries. From January 1971 therefore the government would only provide 95 *per cent* of aided primary school teachers' salaries, the remaining 5 *per cent* would be paid by the Councils. [32] As the Minister of Education explained later during the Second Reading of the African Education Amendment Bill in 1970, 'the aim is to allocate a larger proportion of the funds available to post-primary education than has been the case in the past.' [33]

The churches, which during 1970 administered 2 871 primary African mission schools employing nearly 14 000 teachers, were informed in a circular issued by the Secretary for African Education that they could either continue to run the schools as they wished, while making up the 5 *per cent* of teachers' salaries not covered by the government grant or they could relinquish control and the Ministry would organize local committees to run the schools. [34] By early 1971 it was estimated that the bulk of the African primary schools, which had up to the end of 1970 been under the control of church organizations, were now being run by local African Councils or had fallen into the category of sponsored schools (where no African Councils existed). [35]

In June 1971 a statement on the new salary scales for teachers was issued. These made a distinction between the salaries of standard qualified teachers in the Public Service (the schools directly operated by government which are nearly all for Europeans) and those in the government-aided schools, the Unified African Teaching Service. As most teachers in government schools are Europeans, and would therefore get higher salaries than their counterparts in the non-government (state-aided) schools, the new scales were seen as a departure from the government policy of equal pay for equal qualifications and equal work. [36] A spokesman for the Division of African Education was quoted as saying 'The choice was between granting the African standard qualified teachers the same increases as the European teachers employed in the Public Service, or granting the largest percentage increases to the lowest paid teachers who form the bulk of the African teaching service.' [37]

During July two African M.P.'s, Mr. J. M. Khabo and Mr. N. A. Gandanzara, questioned the Minister about the new salary scales. In reply the Minister said that 'there is no justification whatsoever for the claim that the pay review discriminates unfairly and unjustly against the African teacher. Personnel employed in a professional capacity as members of the Public Service of Rhodesia... holding the same qualifications and having the same responsibilities are on the same salary scales whether they be African or European. European teachers employed by missions or other responsible authorities and African teachers in the Unified African Teaching Service holding standard qualifications and carrying the same responsibilities are on the same rate of pay. The true argument, therefore, is not one of racial "discrimination"—which does not exist—but that members of the Unified African Teaching Service should receive the same rates of pay as are applicable to members of the Public Service.' [38]

Figures of teaching staff can be found in the Reports of the Secretaries for Education and for African Education. On the 30th June 1972, there were in government schools (i.e. for Europeans, Asians and Coloureds) 2 744 teachers both graduates and non-graduates. Of these 2 523 were Europeans and 221 Coloureds and Asians; in the independent schools the total number of teachers was 586, comprising 578 Europeans and 8 Asian and Coloured. In the African schools (figures for the period ending 31st December 1972) a total of 18 538 teachers were employed in all African schools. These included 375 African headmasters, and 17 680 African and 483 European teachers. In his report the Secretary for African Education noted that there had been an increase of 689 teachers over the 1971 figures and that there had been a decrease in the number of untrained primary school teachers which 'category now represented 1.42 *per cent* of the total teaching force compared with 9.5 *per cent* five years ago and 27.87 *per cent* a decade ago.' [39]

FURTHER EDUCATION

A brief historical survey of the development of further education for Africans appears in *Racial Themes in Southern Rhodesia* by Rogers and Frantz. This states that the first African training school operated at Hope Fountain Mission from 1898 to 1909. Another was started at Morgenster in 1902.

> As early as 1892, a Jesuit Mission near Salisbury began the first systematic training of Africans in agricultural and technical skills. By 1915 this Order had established three other schools which provided similar opportunities, but its emphasis on industrial training declined with the replacement of German and French by English priests. Some Protestant denominations also gave practical or technical training to Africans... Generally, however, the Protestants stressed literary education more than did the Catholics. The Dutch Reformed Church generally opposed the training of African artisans.

By 1924, seven missions provided training opportunities with the aid of government subsidies. In 1958 there were thirty-three teacher training institutions in Southern Rhodesia, all but one operated by missions. Altogether, forty-seven teacher training courses were being offered in 1959.[40]

A Commission of Enquiry into Native Affairs in 1910 recommended that the government should itself establish industrial and agricultural schools in the Native Reserves. Because of wide-spread opposition by Europeans, who saw the fragmentation of skilled jobs by cheap labour as a threat, it was not until 1919-21 that the government built two technical schools for Africans. During the ensuing years, and particularly during the Depression years, resistance to the training of Africans increased.

In 1950 the government of the Union of South Africa issued a statement that owing to the requirements of its own population it would, after the 2nd November 1950, no longer admit 'native' students from other territories to its primary, secondary and higher institutions of education.[41] The following year, however, the Union government decided to postpone this regulation until 1953 in order to allow time for the governments concerned to provide their own facilities.

Provision of secondary schools and higher education facilities for Coloureds, Asians and Africans in Rhodesia therefore became urgent and a Commission was set up to examine the problem.

The Report of the Commission on Higher Education for Africans in Central Africa in 1953 (the Carr-Saunders Commission) noted that 'consideration for the need for higher education on a Central African basis ante-dates the current discussions of a particular plan for the federation of the three territories of Southern Rhodesia, Northern Rhodesia and Nyasaland.' This referred to the mention in the report of the Asquith Commission on Higher Education in the Colonies (May 1945) that the Inter-University Council would be able to advise on the problems of specific proposals for higher education in Central Africa.

The Carr-Saunders Commission sat for almost a month, spent time in all three territories, reported on aspects of secondary and technical education, and discussed the feasibility of a university in Central Africa. With regard to technical training, the Commission reported that 'there is a strong and praiseworthy emphasis in the education systems of all three territories on technical and industrial training both in the primary schools and at the post-standard VI level.' In considering Southern Rhodesia in particular, the Report stated that for Africans there were 'two government centres, Domboshawa and Mzingwane, [which] provide post-standard VI vocational training courses in building, in carpentry, and in agriculture, and at Mzingwane in leather-work, and at Domboshawa for health workers. Post-standard VI vocational training is also provided at six mission centres—Waddilove (agriculture), Chikore (the Alvord School of Agriculture), Mount Selinda (building and carpentry), Empandeni (building and carpentry), Tegwani (building) and Inyati (carpentry).'

The Commission noted that the Kerr Commission [42] had earlier recommended that courses at these trade schools should be of three years' duration, that courses for plumbers and garage hands should be instituted and day trades schools established for the training of fitters and turners, electricians and sheet metal workers. The Commission also commented that 'technical training of Africans to a standard higher than that of the trades school scarcely exists', concluding that 'this serious gap results partly from the racial situation.'

On technical education, the Commission considered that expansion and strengthening of the upper parts of the academic school system should be instituted immediately, for 'paradoxical though it may seem,' its Report read, 'an improvement in general education is urgently needed if technical education is to be developed.'[43]

In 1962 the Report of the Southern Rhodesian Education Commission stated that 'adult education has been much neglected in the Territory: it needs clearer vision concerning its purpose; it demands a fairly long-sighted policy to co-ordinate its aims.' The Commission (known as the Judges Commission after the name of its chairman) advised that 'additional facilities for higher education will have to be provided, in the very near future, to accommodate substantially larger numbers of African students, in the years to come, who are preparing to take degrees.'[44]

Towards the end of the decade (and after the end of the Federation) the Secretary for African Education wrote that the National Council for Adult Education was 'working efficiently to co-ordinate various groups interested in the development of Adult Education but unfortunately all the work tends to be directed towards the acquisition of academic skills.'[45]

Towards the end of 1969 it was announced that the polytechnics would not take Africans for O and A level courses any more. The Secretary for Education said later that these classes would, in future, be provided by the Division of African Education; Africans would however still be admitted to all technical and commercial courses at the polytechnics.[46] According to a number of reports over the next few months, however, the efforts of the Division of African Education to start evening classes did not receive much encouragement. It was considered that the poor response was largely due to the prospective students' inability to pay the required fees.[47]

In August 1971 the director of Salisbury Municipality's Department of African Administration, Mr. R. C. Briggs, reported that forty-three out of fifty-one African school-leavers who had undergone a two-year training course in welding and woodwork at the Harare Vocational Training Centre had passed their final examinations. The Vocational Centre was started in Harare with the express purpose of preparing school-leavers for a career or for self-employment. Mr. Briggs said that when the students received their certificates (which had been approved by the Ministry of Education) it would be the first time that certificates in welding and woodwork had been issued by a municipality in Rhodesia.[48]

RANCHE HOUSE COLLEGE

Among private colleges perhaps the best known is Ranche House College in Salisbury, which has been described as the only centre for non-racial education of its kind in Southern Africa. It was established by the Beit and Dulverton Trusts and is financed mainly by trusts and other benefactors and controlled by a voluntary Board of Governors. Its aim is to provide adult education for persons of all races.

In May 1971 the Principal of the College, Mr. Ken Mew, said in his annual report that during 1970 more than 3 000 people (roughly half of them being Europeans) had used the College. He estimated that since the College had been established, some ten years ago, about '14 000 men and women of all races had used the College for residential courses, day studies, evening classes and seminars, ninety *per cent* of the fees being paid by participants.'

The College was used by government departments, African trade unions, leaders of women's clubs, the Rhodesian Institute of Management, the Rhodesian Teachers' Association. 'It was also used by the Asian community, the Hebrew congregation, by clergy of all denominations, by doctors, teachers, soldiers, policemen, unemployed and highly skilled; by adults from every sector and from all parts of the country,' Mr. Mew reported.[49]

During May 1973 the Principal of Ranche House College visited Britain in search of extra funds for the College. Although the two trusts provided regular grants for the College, further financial help was needed to maintain the quality of its services. Mr. Mew stated that the need had been intensified by the fact that support from overseas was often withheld because potential donor institutions were afraid of repercussions elsewhere in Africa if Rhodesian educational establishments were not clearly identifiable as 'African'. 'All too often the notion of a non-racial society is paid only lip service by those who hold the purse strings of international charitable funds' Mr. Mew was quoted as saying.[50]

COMMUNITY DEVELOPMENT TRAINING

During March 1972 the Minister of Immigration, Information and Tourism, Mr. P. van der Byl, visited the Domboshawa Training Centre. He said that 'this is where African advancement lies—

where their ambitions and aspirations can be fulfilled.' Domboshawa, built in 1920, was formerly an African boys' school; in 1964 it became a national adult training centre for Africans. The college caters for 300 students at a time. Its main courses are the training of Council secretaries and treasurers; the training of health assistants and of community advisers; and the maintenance and development of its farm for use by the Department of Conservation and Extension. Long and short courses are also run by the various ministries involved in the Community Development scheme. In the report of the Director of the Community Development Training Branch (contained in the report of the Secretary for African Education) it was announced that Domboshawa had, during the year ended 31st December 1972, provided 149 courses in which 3 071 people had participated.

The Director explained that the three main training areas covered by his Branch are in the conceptual field—explaining the principles and techniques of community development; training in local government; and leadership and organizational training for voluntary groups. Apart from Domboshawa, the Branch has training centres in the provinces of Manicaland, Matabeleland, Mashonaland and the Victoria-Midlands area. The formal training courses at these centres are followed up in the field by Mobile Training Units in Manicaland, Matabeleland and Victoria-Midlands provinces. During 1972 courses given at the training centres (excluding Domboshawa) numbered 480, with 10 047 participants. The mobile units held 443 training sessions with 150 235 participants.

In September 1972 the building of a new training centre for Matabeleland was announced. The centre, at Esigodini, was being built on land given by the Esigodini Agricultural College and it was anticipated that when it was ready for use in late 1973 there would be close liaison between the centre and the agricultural college.[51]

TECHNICAL TRAINING

In August 1972 African M.P.'s made a plea in the House for more technical training for Africans. The Minister answered by drawing attention to the establishment of a technical institute for Africans in the rural areas which was to come into use in the near future.

He also spoke of the need for provision of more technical subjects in schools, which was the reason that junior secondary schools had been started. He added that the courses in these schools would soon be increased from two to four years. [52]

In July 1973 African M.P.'s returned to the topic during the debate on the Revenue Vote. Mr. R. T. D. Sadomba, M.P. for Nemakonde, asked specifically whether the numbers of Africans studying at technical schools and colleges were increasing, while Mr. J. M. Khabo requested specific figures of Africans enrolled at the Salisbury Polytechnic and the Bulawayo Technical College and for details of the courses they attended. In reply the Minister stated that at the Salisbury Polytechnic, where the numbers of African students were increasing, there was a total of 184 Africans (out of a total enrolment of 3 338 students) of which 67 were in the commerce department; nine in civil engineering; 18 in the building trade; one in the electrical technical course; two in the electrical craft course; five in the mechanical craft classes; 16 in the motor industry classes; and 64 in mathematics and science. At the Bulawayo Technical College there were 113 Africans (out of a total of 2 870 students), of which 21 were in mathematics and science; five in electrical engineering; 42 in catering; 11 in mechanical engineering; 14 in building and 20 in commerce.

Mr. Khabo considered that the figures which the Minister had given showed that there were very few Africans getting technical education and asked, in view of the very great need for development in the tribal areas and for utilization of Africans in industry, how the Minister intended to increase the number. Mr. Smith agreed that there were comparatively few Africans attending the two colleges and referred to experimental training which was being carried out at an agricultural college at Mlezu (near Que Que), where about 300 students were enrolled for various courses. A working party was studying this. If the experiment proved successful and if the output was suitable for the development of the tribal areas and would be used for such a purpose, the Minister said that he intended to try to develop first one college for each province and afterwards to develop further colleges if there was sufficient demand. [53]

THE UNIVERSITY OF RHODESIA

The Carr-Saunders Commission was set up to consider, among other things, the proposals for the establishment and siting of a university college. The Commission stated that it believed that 'the time has come when this step forward should be considered, and our belief is shared by others who have had a long and intimate acquaintance with the conditions and problems of Central Africa.' It noted that the need for such a College was evidenced by the movement for the establishment of a University for Europeans in Southern Rhodesia. Not only had a group of citizens raised an Endowment Fund but, in 1952, the Legislative Assembly had passed the University Charter and Inaugural Board (Private) Act which, it was hoped, would lead to the establishment of a university.

In its report the Commission commented that three clauses in the Act were of special importance—'Conditions of entrance to the University are to be laid down in the statutes; no test of religious or political belief is to be imposed as a condition of becoming a member of the staff or a student; the [University] Council may establish constituent colleges.'

The Commission also noted that the City Council of Salisbury had granted 250 acres of land in Mount Pleasant suburb to the proposed College. In commenting upon this action the Commission said 'since the site of a college is of fundamental importance, this gift, if retained by the Board, will do much to shape its future.'

In considering the question as to whether a university in Central Africa was justified, the Commission stated 'the impression left upon our minds is clear; the factor limiting the number of potential African university students is not the lack of openings for university-educated Africans but the absence of university facilities.' The Commission went on to discuss the conditions essential for setting up a university institution; this would have to be a true university, for 'no greater disservice could be rendered to Central Africa than to set up an inferior institution and call it a university.' It added that 'it is contrary to university tradition to have regard to race, religion or class when selecting candidates for admission.'

During this period discussions were being held between the interested parties for the forthcoming federation of the two Rhodesias and Nyasaland. With the probability of the federation in mind therefore, the Commission decided to consider four alternative lines of action that had been suggested. These were to set up two institutions, in or near Salisbury, one for Africans and one for Europeans, with a working arrangement for co-operation in certain activities; to set up two (one for each race) independent institutions; to transform the College projected by the Act of 1952 (see above) into an interracial university college; to select another site altogether for an interracial university college.

The first proposal was discussed with the Mount Pleasant site and a site at Highfield (the African township near Salisbury) in mind. The Commission, however, did not consider the Highfield site to be suitable and said that in any case the proposal itself was unacceptable for various reasons, not the least important being that 'the proposal that there should be two co-operating colleges in Salisbury is clearly intended to produce racial segregation; if this were not so, the plan to have two institutions would be irrational.'

Regarding the second suggestion the Commission considered that no advantage would be derived from this for 'whatever might be the nominal situation in respect of admission of students, Europeans would frequent one of them and Africans the other. This would emphasize and tend to confirm racial segregation in a sphere of life where, more than any other, the door to racial co-operation should not be closed.'

The third alternative of using the Mount Pleasant site as an interracial university (for all three territories) was discussed at length. The consensus of opinion appeared to be that the site itself, situated in a built-up area, would allow no room for development. A further disadvantage would be that as 'an interracial institution would be an experiment in Central Africa... to try it out in a European residential area would not give it the best chance of success.'

The Commission ended its consideration by stating its preference for the fourth alternative for if 'the plans for the Rhodesian University [were] not appropriately modified' a centre other than Salisbury should be chosen. After visiting and reporting on possible sites in all three territories the Commission indicated its preference for Lusaka in Northern Rhodesia (now Zambia). [54]

The decision was finally made to have one multiracial university college for the three territories and to take advantage of the offer of the Mount Pleasant site in Salisbury. The University College of Rhodesia and Nyasaland (U.C.R.N.) was established by Royal

Charter on the 10th February 1955. Article IV of its Charter states:
'No test of religious belief or profession, or of race, nationality
or class shall be imposed upon or required of any person in order
to entitle him to be admitted as a member, professor, teacher or
student.' The first full-time students were admitted in 1957.

In 1960 in his book, described on the dust jacket as an analysis
of Rhodesian culture and its relation to the problems of the Federation as a whole, T. R. M. Creighton expressed doubt whether
professions of 'implementing partnership' (which was the slogan
during Federal days) could be taken seriously. He cited the University College as a case in point describing it as 'a lamp of liberal
enlightenment' but doubted whether its beams would be 'strong
enough to pierce the surrounding darkness.' In his chapter entitled
Education for Partnership he says that the College is 'attempting
to do something that has never been done before—to create a
genuinely interracial university ... To have got so far so soon, and
to have established so much harmony within the College, is a
great achievement.' He concludes that it 'would be hard to exagger-
ate the compromises demanded of a liberal academic
administration in starting such a college and the difficulties it has
had to face regarding the theory and practice of interracial life.
It is not the College that deserves criticism but the society which
finances it and which it serves.'[55]

Following the dissolution of the Federation in 1963 a conference
of representatives of both the British and the Southern Rhodesian
governments was held to decide upon the future of the University
College. At its close a joint statement was issued (April 1964) to
the effect that 'the Southern Rhodesian Government... [would]
now assume responsibility for the maintenance and development
of the College as an independent institution of learning open to
all races.'

Later in 1964 a Commission was set up under Sir Charles Morris
to advise upon the future development of the University College
now that it had to meet the needs of Southern Rhodesia alone.
The Commission's report, presented to the Legislative Assembly
during 1965, briefly discussed the College's history and commented that 'the years since 1957, when the University College
of Rhodesia and Nyasaland first welcomed its initial intake of full-
time students, have seen impressive developments in the field of
higher education in Southern Rhodesia notwithstanding the era

of political turbulence through which the country, in common with most of the continent of Africa, has been passing.'

The report went on to say that the College, (which in 1964 had 551 full-time students, 23 'mature' students studying for 'A' level to qualify them for entrance, and 92 part-time students) 'has fulfilled, and continues to fulfil, this purpose [that of providing a university for students of all races from the three Central African territories and beyond] although its very existence was threatened with the passing of the Federal Government (its principal benefactor) and the withdrawal of support from Northern Rhodesia and Malawi... in the final analysis, the major share of the cost of maintaining the College and continuing with its development will have to be borne by the Government and people of Southern Rhodesia.' The Commission concluded by recommending, among other things, that the College should sever its relationship with the University of London and take a suitable occasion to seek the full status of an independent university. [56]

The beginning of the academic year in March 1966 brought the University College of Rhodesia (as it now became known) face to face with its greatest crisis. On Wednesday 16th March a demonstration lasting about five hours and involving some 70 students, mainly African, took place on the campus. The students had been attending an 'unofficial' Students' Union meeting and had decided to lay before the Principal, Dr. W. Adams, grievances they felt should be brought to the attention of the college authorities. When the Principal informed the students that he was unable to see them that day the demonstrators reportedly became more aggressive and a telephone call was made for police assistance. Following the Principal's agreement to meet student representatives in the late evening, however, the request for a police presence on the campus was retracted.

The Principal, together with five senior members of staff, met six student representatives at 10 p.m. that evening. The students explained that the demonstrators wished to raise three points. They wished the College to issue a public statement condemning the declaration of independence made towards the end of the previous year; to issue a public statement condemning restriction orders recently served on two students and two recently graduated ex-students; and to withdraw a number of new disciplinary rules which African students considered to discriminate against them. After

Dr. Adams had agreed to a request for a meeting with the students the next day to discuss these issues, the demonstrators withdrew from the grounds surrounding the Principal's house. According to later reports, however, they then held a further meeting at which they decided to boycott lectures and classes on the following day. [57]

The following morning five members of staff refused to lecture [58] and in the early afternoon further demonstrations occurred and activities in both the Faculties of Arts and Social Studies came to a standstill as boycotts of lectures led to further members of staff ceasing to give lectures. Following a three-hour meeting of members of both faculties a statement was issued and read to the waiting students by the Dean of the Faculty of Social Studies. This statement made it clear that the overwhelming majority of staff members in both faculties (numbering about 35) were in sympathy with the students' views and placed on record that they deeply deplored the restriction orders placed on students and ex-students; that they 're-affirmed their non-recognition of Mr. Smith's administration and their rejection of the illegal Declaration of Independence and its consequences'; and that they believed that recent failures in communication within the College had led the authorities to 'pass rules relating to discipline which are totally unacceptable.'

During the afternoon the Senior Assistant Commissioner of Police, Mr. R. S. C. Bellamy, as the Protecting Authority (in terms of the Emergency Powers [Maintenance of Law and Order] Act 1966) met the Principal and informed him that unless the situation on the campus was brought under control it would be necessary to send police to reinforce law and order and to safeguard lives and University property. The Principal informed Mr. Bellamy that he had arranged to meet the students later in the evening and that in his opinion police intervention was unnecessary.

Following increasing reports of possible counter-demonstrations by mainly European students; reports of boycotting of lectures and intimidation of other students to do likewise; the disruption of college activities in parts of the campus not affected by the demonstration (namely in the Faculties of Science and Medicine); and the receipt of complaints from various sources expressing concern over the disorders and fears for the safety of students; a small number of European and African police were sent to the campus. Later that evening, following the Principal's meeting with the students, a senior police officer served an Order, in terms of the Emergency Powers Act, on the Principal (which had been shown to him earlier but had been deferred until after his meeting with the students) prohibiting all gatherings on the campus, except for normal lectures and activities, without the specific permission of the Protecting Authority. [59]

On the Friday morning what was described later as a more serious disturbance took place. Numerous African students picketed the entrances to the Science buildings to prevent other students from attending classes and stones were thrown. After the Principal had shown the students the Order prohibiting meetings, however, the demonstrators dispersed. During the course of the morning twenty-three members of staff (including those who had previously refused to lecture) decided not to lecture during the period that the police were on the campus. In the afternoon the Principal addressed a meeting of the academic staff, but half an hour later 18 members of the staff (out of 120 attending the meeting), joined later by five others, walked out in protest because, as they said later in a prepared statement: 'we feel our freedom has been infringed upon and the university's charter violated by the imposition of police control.' The statement also informed the authorities that these staff members 'refuse to lecture or give any services, or even to negotiate, before this order on the college has been lifted.' The *Herald* noted that there were 'signs that tension is mounting between European and African students, with the Europeans becoming more vociferous in their condemnation of the political activity at the college and the interruption of lectures.' [60]

The next day, having arranged for the Vice-Principal and the Faculty Deans to act as a joint committee on matters of discipline and public relations and to enquire into the events of the preceding days, the Principal left for London where he was scheduled to hold week-long talks on the financial future of the University College with representatives of both London and Birmingham Universities. Prior to his departure Dr. Adams issued a statement informing students that any breaches of college rules concerning behaviour and attendance at compulsory lectures and classes would result in disciplinary action (normally immediate suspension from the college) and instructing staff that all teaching duties must be continued. [61]

Previously the Students' Representative Council and the Presi--

dent of the Students' Union had asked for strong disciplinary action to be taken against the demonstrators and for a resumption of lectures and action to be taken against members of staff who failed to co-operate. They had also handed a statement to the college authorities giving the names of seven students who, in their opinion, were mainly responsible for the demonstrations. These seven students were summoned to appear before the joint committee on the afternoon of the Principal's departure. Only three of the students appeared and these, having been interviewed individually, were found guilty of misbehaviour. Disciplinary proceedings were deferred.

Throughout the week-end all was quiet and normal religious and sporting activities were permitted. On the following Monday the Senior Assistant Commissioner of Police visited the campus and found that conditions had calmed down sufficiently for him to amend the original Order prohibiting gatherings without his express permission to one permitting all normal functions to take place. Boycotts of lectures by some students, however, continued and it was reported that the number of striking lecturers had risen to 28 and that one lecturer had resigned and several others had threatened to do so if action were taken against their striking colleagues. The Students' Union issued a further statement charging the striking staff with abusing their powers in denying students the right to education unless they accepted specific political opinions—'thereby setting at nought the concept of academic freedom'; stressing that its opposition to certain students who participated in demonstrations was confined strictly to the sphere of discipline; and protesting 'vehemently' against the government's arbitrary imposition of the police on the campus without reference to the Principal. The dissident lecturers also issued a statement explaining their reasons for withdrawing their teaching services and for staging the walk-out during the meeting with the Principal.[62]

During the next few days, while reduced numbers of police patrolled the campus, some students continued their boycott of classes and some members of staff continued their strike. The Executive Committee of the College Council held a meeting to discuss ways of ending the current crisis 'with justice to all'. On the 24th March the vice-Principal issued a statement on the executive committee's decisions. These were to appoint 'as a matter of urgency' an independent commissioner who would investigate and report on the causes of the recent disturbances; study the machinery for liaison between administration, staff and students and make suggestions for improvements; and investigate and report on the machinery for dealing with grievances, and upon the machinery of student government. The committee representing the students boycotting lectures announced that although the student grievances had not been considered they were calling off the boycott. At the request of the college authorities and on the understanding that good order would be maintained, the police commissioner agreed to cancel the Order made under the Emergency Powers Act and to withdraw police still on the campus. Twenty-three of the twenty-eight striking lecturers signed a statement to the effect that, the Order and the police having been withdrawn, they would resume teaching at once, while reserving 'the right to take any action we think fit in the light of subsequent events.'[63]

On the 28th March the vice-Principal announced that Dr. Robert Birley, a former headmaster of Eton (at that time a visiting professor at the University of the Witwatersrand in Johannesburg) had accepted an invitation to act as an independent commissioner. It was noted that several prominent people had been considered but that Dr. Birley had been the first choice because it was felt that his appointment would meet with the approval of all factions in the dispute. As Dr. Birley did not expect to be free to commence his investigations until mid-April, persons wishing to give evidence were requested to submit written memoranda for his consideration.[64]

Shortly before Dr. Birley's arrival in Salisbury further disturbances took place on the college campus when a speaker at a debate in the Students' Union was pelted with eggs and the debate had to be adjourned. The following night African students again caused chaos in the Students' Union when they sang, chanted and stamped their feet and pelted the committee members of the Students' Representative Council (S.R.C.) with wet bread, eggs and tomatoes. Despite this confusion, however, the committee passed (by a majority of mostly European votes) a resolution calling for a vote of confidence in the S.R.C.'s constitution and criticizing political activities of both staff and students. At the same time the Principal, Dr. Adams, offered to resign his position and several other members of staff followed suit.

Dr. Birley arrived in Salisbury on Sunday the 17th April. It was reported that he had already received some 40 documents relating to the March disturbances and would be available to anyone able to assist his enquiry. [65]

The investigation continued throughout the next ten days (during which time Dr. Birley interviewed about 100 people and studied 60 reports) and culminated in the publication of a 47-page report on the 2nd May. In the introduction to his report, Dr. Birley outlined its structure and stated that he would first deal with two matters which, in his opinion, should be considered before it was possible to deal with such questions as the machinery for liaison between administration, staff and students, the regulations for dealing with grievances and the system of student government. These two matters were 'the position of the College today against the background of the Rhodesian society in which it is situated', in considering which he examined the College as a multiracial institution, and the problem of Academic Freedom in a state controlled by Emergency Powers; and the events between March 16th, when the first student demonstration took place, and March 24th, when the boycott of lectures and the staff strike was called off.

Considering the position of the College, Dr. Birley pointed out that political events, particularly since the end of the previous year, had led to a marked polarization of Rhodesian society and commented that the College could not expect to be unaffected by this but was in fact 'not only... more isolated in the midst of Rhodesian society than it was before, but... [was] itself more divided.' In his opinion a multiracial College such as the U.C.R.N.—'out of line with the society in which it is situated'—would be continually faced with almost insoluble problems except for the fact that one element of over-riding importance was present; the fact that any university or, for that matter, any educational institution 'is not concerned so much with the present as with the future.' He said that he did not see how anyone could support the College 'as the multiracial institution it is now' who did not believe that Rhodesia should move towards the creation of a multiracial society; and if he did believe this then he must surely see the College as 'an institution of the very greatest significance, one which can make possible—and perhaps can alone make possible—a harmonious society in Rhodesia.'

Turning to Academic Freedom Dr. Birley said that it was essential that a University institution should make up its mind what freedom it must defend and retain if it was to fulfil its duty. He stated that he could not hope to provide a better definition of Academic Freedom than that which could be found in the Public Statement made by the Council of the University College on December 10th 1965,[66] and had come to the conclusion that it was 'doubts as to the determination of the College to preserve its freedom' which were the 'main factors which have led to the unfortunate divisions in the staff of the College at the moment.'

Following an account of events leading to his investigation, Dr. Birley then assessed the underlying causes of the dispute. One suggestion, which he did not find tenable, was that the underlying aim of the demonstrations was to force the closure of the College in order to embarrass the government. While he did not doubt that this had been in the minds of some of those who had led the demonstrations he was convinced that these were very few and that the essential purpose of the demonstrators had been to put pressure on the authorities for redressing what they considered to be their just grievances. These were, in essence, that African students were not only a minority in the Students' Union, but a minority 'which could not expect fair or reasonable treatment from the majority'; and the fact that they felt the College had not shown proper concern at the fate of students and ex-students who had been restricted. As far as the actions of the staff were concerned, Dr. Birley considered that it was only to be expected that many of the staff, particularly the younger elements, would be distressed at the recent political developments in Rhodesia and 'to ask that the staff of this College should simply accept the social and political trends of Rhodesian society in the recent past and the present is to ask that they should not be the kind of persons who ought to be on the staff of a multiracial University institution.' He did, however, consider that the College authorities had not retained the confidence of the staff as regards academic freedom and recommended that an opportunity should be sought to clarify the position and to take steps to ensure that the academic staff remained in no doubt in the future as to the attitude of the authorities. He added that if the College authorities took the staff fully into their confidence then it would have the right to demand the confidence of the staff and if some people did not feel able to give this confidence then they ought not to remain in the service of the College.

Having made a number of recommendations, Dr. Birley put in a personal plea for the Indian students at the College whom he believed had an important role. In his conclusion he expressed 'as soberly and realistically' as he could, his belief in the need to preserve the University College, for there was a very fair chance 'that within a year or two it will be felt that this College has the future of Rhodesia largely in its hands.'[67]

Following publication of the Birley Report the College Council announced that it had just concluded a three-day meeting to discuss it and stated that it had asked all members of the college to implement 'urgently' its recommendations which included the setting up of machinery to provide students with assistance and advice on legal and related problems; the setting-up of a disciplinary committee; the appointment of a student adviser; and the appointment of an experienced university administrator to conduct a survey on the administration of the College. The Council also decided not to take disciplinary action against students and staff connected with the disturbances. Dr. Birley's suggestion that the government should be approached for an agreement under which restricted students could be restricted to the campus was also accepted and a vote of confidence in the Principal was passed, followed by the withdrawal of his offer of resignation. The *Herald*'s editorial for the following day concluded its comment upon the Report by saying that 'If Rhodesia is to keep to her chosen path of evolution, of advancement by merit, the multiracial U.C.R.N. must survive. It is clear from Dr. Birley's investigations that it needs firmer and more expert care than it has had: it may also be presumed that it will now become the target for attack by those, black or white, who oppose the ideal of a multiracial Rhodesia.'[68]

Certain members of the staff later produced a 40-page memorandum (described as a 'supplement' to the Birley Report and as having the support of 54 members of staff) which gave the backgrounds to the events of March and May as seen by these staff members. In its concluding chapter the memorandum considered the future of the college and explained that although its authors knew of no plan by the government to close the college, or to control its internal administration and programmes of teaching and research, or to limit its freedom to appoint such staff and admit such students as it considered fit, they did consider that there was a danger 'of the College having its rights eroded away by single *ad hoc* acts.' They cited: censorship of publications; restriction of students without trial; refusal to allow some students to remain in Rhodesia; searching of staff offices and houses; and the imposition of police emergency orders; as being particular acts 'symptomatic of a mentality which either does not understand, or is hostile to, the idea of a University such as has grown up in the West.' [69]

In June the Minister of Finance announced, in an address to the annual general meeting of the Associated Chambers of Commerce (at which seven Cabinet Ministers were present) that the government would make £2 550 000 available to the University College over the next three years. [70]

Early in July four members of the team of British officials, which had been in Rhodesia for about four weeks for a second round of preliminary talks and discussions regarding the constitutional dispute, were involved in an incident at the college when about 40 African students carrying placards and shouting slogans filled the entrance to one of the Halls of Residence (where the British officials were dinner guests). On the 17th July some 56 students (including three Europeans and three Asians) staged a demonstration at the College's annual graduation ceremony, making it impossible for two of the main speakers at the ceremony, Lord Malvern (perhaps better known as Sir Godfrey Huggins, former Prime Minister of Southern Rhodesia) and Dr. J. P. Duminy, Principal and Vice-Chancellor of the University of Capetown, to be heard by the 600 people present. Police were called on to the scene to enable the ceremony to continue. It was later reported that the main purpose of the demonstration (apart from protesting about the presence of Dr. Duminy) was to protest the presence of two Cabinet Ministers, which was interpreted as intended to display the College's first official public recognition of the Rhodesian government.

The newly constituted disciplinary committee (formed in accordance with Dr. Birley's recommendation) took up investigations into the disturbance but before they had concluded their discussion the Acting Principal (in the absence of Dr. Adams who had left for London on college business two days after the graduation ceremony) announced that 31 students had been suspended until mid-September and had until noon to leave the campus. It was understood that among the suspended students were two or three Europeans and a similar number of Asians. The suspended students had been sent letters explaining that they would be able to register for the November examinations and could return to the College on the 18th September provided that they signed a declaration accepting the Principal's authority on disciplinary matters. The Students' Representative Council deplored the way in which the matter had been handled. Later in the year the 31 students were informed by the Ministry of Education that their government scholarships for the forthcoming year would not be renewed. [71]

On the 28th July the Minister of Law and Order made a statement in the House explaining his reasons for having detention and deportation orders served upon eight lecturers; for the arrest and imprisonment of nine lecturers and one student (Asian); and for the serving of restriction orders upon nine students. Mr. Lardner-Burke told the assembled M.P's that the government had, for a very long time, 'exercised great forbearance because of the delicate situation with which the college authorities have been faced' and continued by explaining that the government knew that certain persons at the College 'had over the last few years been connected with banned organizations and some of them have had strong communistic leanings ... certain lecturers among those persons have used their unique position to influence students into joining them in furthering their aims ... activities which affect the general security of our country.' [72] That same afternoon a notice was distributed throughout the College announcing that it would be closed forthwith and asking students to leave as soon as possible. The notice also said that the arrest of staff and students had affected the college in that the disciplinary procedures arising out of the recent demonstrations had been disrupted and in some cases nullified; that in a number of departments adequate teaching was no longer available; and that an atmosphere had been created in which teaching could not be carried on. The College would remain closed and would probably re-open in mid-September, when the new third term was due to commence, if conditions were such as to enable it to do so.

In its accompanying editorial the *Herald* criticized the Principal—for once more being away at a time of stress, and also the staff—for not tightening discipline. It also questioned why the government, if it had expected the disorders to spread to the rest of the country and if it knew of the 'clandestine activities' being carried on by some of the people at the college, had not taken action earlier. The editor felt that it was inevitable that the government should take action—albeit with a sledgehammer—when the actions of a few people 'misguided, evil, idealist, boorish, call them what you will' were jeopardizing the careers of the many but commented that, while the over-riding emotion aroused was sadness, 'the over-riding effect will be bitterness' against the 'agitators', against 'Africans' and against government. [73]

At the beginning of August it was reported that one of the arrested lecturers, a Rhodesian citizen who had not been served with a deportation order, had been released from prison and was to leave the country to take up an appointment at a British university to which he had been appointed prior to the disturbances. The following day the remaining eight lecturers were allowed to leave prison for a short time to pack their personal belongings in readiness for their enforced departure the next day. The arrested student was released and left the country. On the 3rd August the remaining eight were released and left the country. Their wives and families were allowed to remain to wind up private affairs. [74]

On the 4th August, after a five-hour meeting of the Academic Board, it was announced that a decision had been made to recommend the re-opening of the College on the 5th September. This was two weeks earlier than the original commencement of the third term. It was also recommended that the third term should end one week late to make up for the three weeks which had been lost by the early closure of the previous term. Examinations were to be deferred until a week later than originally planned. The Board's statement referred to detentions and restrictions, without trial, of staff and students and stated that the Board still could not accept that the future of the College was assured while these conditions were still in effect. On the 11th August the Executive Committee of the College Council, after consideration of a report from the academic board on the long-term future of the College, announced that it affirmed its determination to keep the College in existence under its Charter as a multiracial institution. [75]

On the 17th August, in response to a question from Mr. C. Hlabangana, M.P. for Mpopoma (Bulawayo), the Minister of Immigration (at that time Mr. J. H. Howman) made a statement in the House on the reasons for the arrest and deportation of the staff members of the College. He charged the lecturers with being actively engaged in subversion; with misleading students and others from the African townships; with being in contact with and acting as couriers for banned African nationalist organizations; with inciting students to engage in subversion; and with making broadcasts from foreign radio stations against the interests of the country. Mr. Howman said that the Birley Report had proved conclusively that the government had 'shown the greatest forbearance in its dealings with the affairs of the University' and that it had 'never attempted to interfere with academic freedom.' However, he said that he considered that the time had arrived when 'academic freedom was being interpreted by some lecturers as complete license to engineer a breakdown of law and order' and said that some of the lecturers were open about their communistic ideologies and that their plan had been 'to create conditions which would lead to the closure of the university and result in a state of affairs which might, in their minds, justify intervention by Britain.'

The next day's editorial in the *Herald* found it difficult to understand why the government had gone through the whole procedure of detention and deportation and asked why the lecturers had been deported instead of being brought before a Court where the Minister's 'ample and conclusive' proof could have been publicly demonstrated. It pointed out that Mr. Howman had offered no public proof of his assertions, whereas convictions for criminal offences would be a different matter and would also have given the individuals involved a chance to rebut the accusations.[76]

On 5th September an assistant lecturer at the College, together with another man, appeared at the Salisbury Magistrate's Court for a preparatory examination on allegations of contravening Sections 36 and 37 of the Law and Order (Maintenance) Act, or alternatively of conspiring to commit murder. The alleged offence was that the accused lecturer, with others at the College, had been members of a group responsible for the reception, storage and eventual distribution of offensive materials for use against the European community and against their property and homes. It was also alleged that this group was responsible for maintaining contact with infiltrated guerrillas. Warrants of arrest were also issued for a lecturer who had been among the group deported and for another lecturer who had left the country to take up a post at the University of Zambia.[77] In early October both men were committed to stand trial on charges under the Law and Order (Maintenance) and the Unlawful Organizations Acts. The College lecturer was eventually found guilty and sentenced to 20 years' imprisonment.[78]

The Morris Report was debated, in what had by then become the House of Assembly, in early November 1967. The motion, to give consideration to the development of the University College, was moved by Mr. W. M. Irvine, M.P. for Marlborough (Salisbury). He complained that although the Rhodesian tax-payer was now wholly responsible for financing the University College it had 'virtually no say in the management or control of this institution.' He went on to say that he would support any plea for an increase in revenue for the college as he thought there was a good case for this, but firstly he would have to be convinced that the money would be spent in meeting the national requirements of the country. He regretted that nothing had been done, either by the government or the university to implement the Morris Commission's recommendations. The debate lasted for three days with private members as well as three Ministers taking part. It was generally agreed that the new Principal should be allowed time to take over the reins before proceeding with the severance of the relationship with the University of London.[79]

In March 1970 it was announced that a letter had been received from Her Majesty the Queen Mother resigning her presidency of the University College. At about the same time, for reasons mainly connected with the regulations for the new teaching hospital, the University of Birmingham decided to sever its special relationship with the College's medical school.[80]

Later in 1970 the Principal of the University College, the Rev. Professor Robert Craig, revealed that he had in November 1969 written to the Minister of Lands, Senator P. van Heerden, proposing an amendment to the Land Tenure Bill. The amendment would have given the College an indefinite permit to admit Africans, as students, research workers and staff, which could only be revoked by an Act of Parliament. Professor Craig stated that the Minister had refused to agree to the proposed amendment.[81]

In May 1970 it was announced that new statutes had been passed by the College Council which, after ratification at a second Council meeting in June, would confer independent status on the University College. It was noted that the amendments to the statutes were being made in terms of the College's Royal Charter and that as the University of Rhodesia it would continue to operate under this Charter, which, among other things, forbids racial discrimination in the selection of staff or students. On 12th March 1971, the University began its first academic year as a wholly autonomous institution.

At the beginning of the 1972 academic year it was announced that provisional enrolment figures were almost identical with those for 1971: 1 266 students registered, 967 full-time and 299 part-time students. Of the full-time students 517 were Europeans and 384 Africans. [82]

Later in the year it was reported that there were 1 886 Rhodesians attending South African universities of which 827 received grants from the Rhodesian Ministry of Education. Speaking of this in the House of Assembly, Mr. W. M. Irvine referred to the debt of gratitude which was owed to South Africa for 'this tremendous contribution' and warned that 'It is not reasonable that we should expect this to continue.' The Prime Minister of South Africa, Mr. B. J. Vorster, had recently made a statement to the effect that legislation would be introduced during 1973 that foreign students would only be admitted to South African universities in the future with the consent of the Minister of National Education. Mr. Irvine considered that there was a lack of racial balance at the University of Rhodesia and that provision would soon have to be made to accommodate those students (mostly European) who would not be admitted to the South African universities. [83]

On Saturday 13th May the University's graduation ceremony was, according to the Principal and Vice-Chancellor, 'a great occasion in the history of the University and a milestone in Rhodesia's history' for it was the first time the University was conferring its own degrees. The following month the University launched an appeal for $1 million to establish a Faculty of Engineering. [84] In mid-June 1973 it was announced that Dr. L. M. Muggleton had been appointed to the Inaugural Chair of Engineering.

In mid-July 1972 Professor Craig, in an article in the *Financial Gazette,* summed up the University's achievements in its first year of independence. He spoke of the difficult period since the break-up of the Federation, especially in relations with the outside world. 'The University has had, and still has, to navigate a difficult course between Scylla and Charybdis. On the one hand, there is the danger of becoming in fact what some ill-informed indivi-

duals abroad have often alleged we are: an academic captive of
the Rhodesian Government, not truly independent and therefore
not a true university. On the other hand, there is the danger of
being what a large section of the Rhodesian public once thought
we were: an alien body representing hostile interests ...'

With regard to the danger of subservience to the government,
Professor Craig said 'we are almost entirely dependent on the Government financially, but we must not, and do not, allow that fact
to deter us from speaking our mind responsibly and openly on
matters which concern our existence as a university of national
and international standing ... The University is as free to fulfil
its proper functions as are other universities throughout the world.'

Speaking of academic development, Professor Craig stated that
an important aspect of this was the increased flexibility which the
assumption of independent status had given to the University in
the choice of courses and syllabuses. He then referred to the University's acceptance as a full member of the Association of Commonwealth Universities, a decision taken at the Association's
General Meeting in 1971.[85]

In August, speaking in the debate on the Revenue Vote for the
University of Rhodesia, Mr. W. M. Irvine questioned the Minister
of Education on policy regarding the students' hall of residence.
He said that he had heard that there had been some difficulty
about racial mixing within residences. The Minister in reply
quoted the introductory remarks in the report of the Triennial
Grants Review Committee[86] which had been sitting during the
earlier months of the year: 'At the outset of this report we wish
to state that in the course of our deliberations we have constantly
borne in mind the need for maintaining the University of Rhodesia
as a non-racial institution ... and for ensuring, as far as it is possible
to do so, that a balance in the number of students from the two
main racial groups is maintained ... In regard to the question of
student enrolment at the university, we have noted with some
regret that although over-all numbers of students have increased
perceptibly over the years, the proportion of European students
to those of other races has diminished to the extent that they now
represent little more than 50 *per cent* of the total student enrolment.
Coupled with this is the somewhat disquieting fact that, whereas
more than 90 *per cent* of the African student body lives in residence,
nearly half of the European student population choose not to do

so ... As a result of this imbalance there exist in the hostels 128 empty places. In our opinion, it is essential from the point of view of student unit costs, but more importantly perhaps from a general aspect of campus life, community spirit and student well-being, that the imbalance should be corrected with all possible speed.' The Minister then stated that he honestly believed that 'in spite of the fact that the University has to admit all races ... the halls of residence should be segregated.'[87]

In reaction to Mr. Irvine's query and the Minister's reply, Professor Craig, the vice-Chancellor, issued a statement to the press declaring that residence policy at the university was the ultimate responsibility of the University Council and that any change in policy would be subject to Council's consideration and decision. He added that a committee had already been set up to consider and report on residences following the recommendations of the Triennial Grants Review Committee which had just visited the University.[88]

According to a *Herald* reporter, segregation in the student residences had been the rule in the early years of the university's history and it was the student body itself that had initiated the first moves towards integration. He commented 'Most European students live out of residence for voluntary personal reasons. Most Africans live in residence out of necessity.' He also pointed out that living on campus was more expensive than living outside.[89]

Early in January 1973 the first move was made in the campaign to procure the withdrawal of invitations to the universities of South Africa and Rhodesia to send delegates to the 11th Congress of the Association of Commonwealth Universities (A.C.U.) in August. The National Organization of Labour Students issued its statement through the Labour Party headquarters in London. Asked to comment University of Rhodesia authorities stated that there were no plans to withdraw from the Congress and announced the names of the three delegates which it would be sending: Professor Robert Craig, vice-Chancellor and Principal; Mr. D. M. K. Sagonda, the Principal of Nyatsime College and member of the University Council; and Dr. George Scott, Reader in Botany and a former Dean.[90]

In March the *Daily Telegraph* reported on legal steps being taken by the University of Edinburgh officials to remove the student-elected Rector of that University from his position as theoretical chairman of the University Court, the supreme governing body. The dispute between the Rector and the Principal of Edinburgh University was reported as having come to a head over the issue of invitations to the A.C.U's Congress. Mr. Brown, the Rector, had written to the Ministers of Education of 26 A.C.U. member countries asking what their attitude would be if Rhodesian and South African university delegates attended the Congress and also what their attitude would be if Rhodesia was not expelled from the Association. Apparently some recipients of this letter had believed that this was an official attempt by the University of Edinburgh to dissuade them from sending representatives to the Congress. [91]

The National Union of Students (N.U.S.) was also reported to be asking the A.C.U. to withdraw its invitation. A spokesman for the N.U.S. was quoted as saying that 'It has always been our view that South African and Rhodesian institutions should be isolated while the present Governments exist. It is also our opinion that the universities in both countries (probably because they are forced to) implement the Government policies. They are therefore not multiracial institutions.' The attitude of the A.C.U., on the other hand, was that influence by isolation would not be advantageous. It considered that withdrawing 'moral support for vice-chancellors and students who are fighting apartheid would be wrong. By attending A.C.U. conferences they are given support in their fight.'

The calls for cancellation of the invitations continued throughout the next few months and by the last days of June it was reported that the universities of 8 African countries—Mauritius, Zambia, Kenya, Uganda, Tanzania, Ghana, Nigeria and Sierra Leone—would boycott the Congress if the invitation to the South African and Rhodesian universities was not withdrawn. It was further considered highly probable that universities in the West Indies, India, Sri Lanka and Malaysia would do likewise. Although the A.C.U. holds such purely academic congresses every five years to exchange ideas of mutual interest and benefit and to engender a community feeling among the universities of the Commonwealth, British politicians (16 members of the Labour Party) and trade unionists (the Scottish T.U.C., the Edinburgh Trades Council and the Scottish region of the National Union of Mineworkers) were reported to be assisting the N.U.S. in its campaign. The

United Nations Special Committee on Apartheid congratulated the N.U.S. on its stand.[92]

At the end of June it was reported that three University of Rhodesia students: Mr. Witness Mangwende, president of the Students' Union, Mr. Herbert Makoni and Mr. Arthur Munzara had withdrawn a letter which they had previously sent to two British newspapers, to the secretary-general of the A.C.U. and to Miss Judith Todd in London, asking the A.C.U. not to reject the University of Rhodesia from its Congress as this would be 'tantamount to recognizing the illegal regime.' The letter also pointed out that the numbers of African students at the University were growing steadily and that halls of residence were multiracial 'against the wishes of the Smith regime.' The three students explained that they had changed their minds on the issue because it had been pointed out to them that the campaign for withdrawal of the invitation was not directed at the University but at the Rhodesian government and its supporters. The telegram which they had sent repudiating the original letter of support stated that 'at least 85 per cent of the African student body supported the case for withdrawal of the University's invitation.'[93]

In March 1973 student registration figures were given by the Academic Registrar, who emphasized that the figures were not final ones for the late release of the Cambridge Higher School Certificate results meant that some students were still in the process of registering while others were awaiting the outcome of decisions on bursaries. The figures showed that new entrants numbered 489, divided racially as 280 Europeans, 174 Africans and 35 others. Returning students numbered 507 of which 300 were Europeans, 201 Africans and 38 others. With 102 students studying for higher degrees and 341 part-time students the total student body numbered 1 439.[94]

In April the spearhead of what was to become later a more serious verbal attack upon the University appeared in the monthly periodical *Property and Finance*. In an article, claimed to be based on an interview with a member of the University, claims of filth in the student residences, of 'wide-spread' theft of funds of student organizations and of a subversive African student body were made against what the periodical called 'the African-dominated University.'[95]

In May it was announced that 354 graduands would be presented to the Chancellor at the graduation ceremony. Among these students was Mr. Ephrim Mandivenga whose thesis entitled '*An Examination of the Theistic Philosophy of Lord Herbert of Cherbury (1583-1648)* had earned him the first Master of Philosophy degree to be awarded by the University since it attained its independence. In his speech at the graduation ceremony the Vice-Chancellor, Professor Craig, referred to opponents both within Rhodesia and abroad who opposed the multiracial character of the University. He said that it was on the issue of the multiracial character of the University that extremes of the political Right and Left came together: an all-white or an all-black university would equally serve both. What apparently infuriated both was 'the modest and fragile success which we so far have achieved...'[96]

NOTES

1 See: 1945: Wallis, J. P. R. (ed.) *The Matabele Mission: a selection from the correspondence of John and Emily Moffat, David Livingstone and others 1858-1878:* Oppenheimer Series: London: Chatto and Windus.
   1953: Jones, Neville: *Rhodesian Genesis:* Bulawayo: Rhodesian Pioneers and Early Settlers Society.
   1970: Thomas, T. M.: *Eleven Years in Central South Africa:* Bulawayo: Books of Rhodesia (Facsimile of the 1873 edition published in London by John Snow & Co.)
2 1970: Taylor, J. R. *African Education: the historical development and organization of the system:* Salisbury: Ministry of Information.
3 *Hansard:* Vol. 83, No. 3. 23 November 1972: Col. 202.
4 Calculated at that time to be about 80 *per cent* of all African children.
5 1972: Passmore, Gloria, C.: '*The National Policy of Community Development in Rhodesia:* Salisbury: University of Rhodesia.
6 1972: Grant, G. C.: *The African's Predicament in Rhodesia:* London: Minority Rights Group.
7 *Hansard:* Vol. 75. 21 August 1969: Col. 45.
8 *Hansard:* Vol. 80, No. 11. 17 November 1971: Col. 778.
9 As reported in *R.H.* 23 February 1972.
10 *Report of the Secretary for African Education for the year ended* 31 December 1972: Cmd. R.R. 7-1973: Salisbury: Government Printer: *R.H.* 27 January 1973.
11 As reported in *R.H.* 27 February, 1 March 1973.

12 *R.H.* 11 May 1973.
13 *Hansard:* Vol. 83, Nos. 25, 26. 9, 10 May 1973: Cols. 1950-2006, 2167-86.
14 *Report of the Secretary for Education for the year ended 31 December 1972:* Cmd. R.R. 9-1973: Salisbury: Government Printer.
15 1908: *Report of the Education Commission:* Salisbury: Argus Printing & Publishing Company: A5-1908.
16 1945: *Report on a Commission of Enquiry regarding the Social Welfare of the Coloured Community:* Salisbury: Government Stationery Office.
17 The Education Act No. 54 of 1972: Part 1, Section 4 (2).
18 *op cit.* See note 14.
19 Up to 1965 the total admission of African pupils to private schools was 59.
20 *Hansard:* Vol. 75, 15 October 1971: Cols. 1483, 1486-7.
21 *R.H.* 16 January 1971.
22 This clause exempted St. Martin's Roman Catholic School in Arcadia (a Coloured township in Salisbury) which was allowed to have as many African pupils as it wished.
23 As reported in *R.H.* 18 February 1971.
24 *R.H.* 7 November 1971.
25 *R.H.* 9 November 1971.
26 *R.H.* 7 December 1971.
27 *Shield:* No. 324. November 1972.
28 The amending clause read: 'Nothing in this Act shall preclude the admission into and attendance and instruction at registered private schools of persons who are Africans.'
29 *S.M.* 19 November 1972.
30 *Hansard:* Vol. 83, Nos. 1, 2. 21, 22 November 1972: Cols. 95, 179-80.
31 *op cit.* See note 14.
32 *Hansard:* Vol. 75. 2 September 1969: Cols. 531-2.
33 *Hansard:* Vol. 78, No. 7. 3 September 1970: Col. 421.
34 *R.H.* 1 January 1970.
    (For the Churches' response see Chapter on Churches).
35 *R.H.* 4 February 1971.
36 It should be noted that women in government service receive lower salaries than their male counterparts.
37 According to the report of the *Southern Rhodesia Education Commission of 1962* the Unified African Teaching Service was established by the Native Education Act of 1959 and 'it has created conditions of equal service, a disciplinary code for professional behaviour, and (by statutory legislation) identical salaries for teachers in Government and aided schools... and ability to transfer without prejudice from one system to the other.' Chapter 1, Section 21 of *The Report of the Southern Rhodesian Education Commission 1962.* C.S.R. 37-1963.
38 *Hansard:* Vol. 79, No. 11. 23 July 1971: Cols. 848-50.
    R.H. 26 June 1971.
39 *op cit.* See Notes 10 and 14.

40 1962: Rogers, Cyril and C. Frantz: *Racial Themes in Southern Rhodesia : the attitudes and behaviour of the white population :* New Haven & London: Yale University Press.
41 The government of the Union of South Africa also agreed to substitute the term 'non-European' for 'native' students.
42 The Kerr Commission was the Commission of Enquiry into Native Education in Southern Rhodesia, 1951. Report—C.S.R. 6-1952.
43 1953: *Report of the Commission of Enquiry on Higher Education for Central Africa :* Salisbury: Central African Council.
44 1962: *Report of the Southern Rhodesia Education Commission :* C.S.R. 37-1963.
45 *Report of the Secretary for African Education for the year ended 31 December 1969 :* Cmd. R.R. 5-1970: Salisbury: Government Printer.
46 *R.H.* 21 January 1970.
47 *R.H.* 15 July 1970.
48 *R.H.* 2 August 1971.
49 *R.H.* 6 May 1971.
50 As reported in *R.H.* 16 May 1973.
51 *op. cit.* See note 10.
52 *Hansard :* Vol. 82, Nos. 6, 7. 23, 24 August 1972: Cols. 581-96.
53 *Hansard :* Vol. 84, No. 13. 26 July 1973: Cols. 989-1004.
54 *op. cit.* See note 43.
55 1960: Creighton, T. R. M.: *The Anatomy of Partnership : Southern Rhodesia and the Central African Federation :* London: Faber and Faber.
56 1964: *Report of the University College Review Commission :* C.S.R. 2-1965.
57 *R.H.* 17 March 1966.
58 The 'supplementary' memorandum to the Birley Report prepared by the staff states that fifteen members of staff refused to lecture.
59 *R.H.* 18, 23 March 1966.
60 *R.H.* 19 March 1966.
61 *R.H.* 19, 21 March 1966.
62 *R.H.* 22 March 1966.
63 *R.H.* 23, 25 March 1966.
64 *R.H.* 29 March 1966.
65 *R.H.* 14, 15, 18 April 1966.
66 The Council's Public Statement outlined five 'freedoms' which it considered must be upheld at the University College:—
   freedom to select and appoint its own staff;
   freedom of the Academic Board to determine the curriculum of teaching and the standards of study, and to decide how its students should be examined;
   freedom of expression in teaching and study by staff and students;
   freedom of the academic staff to publish their professional views and findings without prior approval of other persons or authorities;
and freedom to choose its own research programmes.

67 *University College of Rhodesia : Report by Dr. Robert Birley : April 1966 :* Salisbury: University College of Rhodesia and Nyasaland.
68 As reported in *R.H.* 2, 3 May 1966.
The Principal, Dr. W. Adams, resigned in June 1966 to take up the post of Director at the London School of Economics and Political Science.
69 *The University College in Rhodesia : Background to the events of March to May, 1966.* (unpublished cyclo-styled memorandum).
70 *R.H.* 9 June 1966.
71 As reported by *R.H.* 18, 27 July, 18 November 1966.
72 *Hansard :* Vol. 64. 27 July 1966: Cols. 906-11.
73 *R.H.* 28 July 1966.
74 *R.H.* 1 August 1966.
75 *R.H.* 5, 8, 12 August 1966.
76 *Hansard :* Vol. 64. 17 August 1966: Cols. 1839-43.
R.H. 19 August 1966.
77 *R.H.* 6, 20 September 1966.
78 *R.H.* 4 October 1966.
A brief account of this affair can be found in:
1971: Shay, R. and C. Vermaak: *The Silent War :* Salisbury: Galaxie Press.
79 *Hansard :* Vols. 69, 70. 1, 2 November 1967, 23 January 1968: Cols. 939-65, 998-1021, 39-64.
The new Principal referred to was Professor Terence Miller.
80 *S.M.* 15 March 1970.
81 *R.H.* 14 May 1970.
According to the Land Tenure Act the College (now the University of Rhodesia) is deemed to have been granted a permit for an indefinite period but the Minister of Lands has the power to cancel it at any time or to impose conditions.
82 *R.H.* 18 March 1972.
83 *Hansard :* Vol. 81, No. 6. 13 June 1972: Cols. 417-8.
84 *R.H.* 15 May 1972.
85 *R.F.G.* 14 July 1972.
86 The Triennial Grants Review Committee was appointed by the Rhodesian government as an independent review body to undertake the task of considering the academic planning, with the relevant estimates, of the University for the triennium 1973-75.
87 *Hansard :* Vol. 82, No. 5. 22 August 1972: Col. 423.
88 As reported in *R.H.* 25 August 1972.
89 *R.H.* 26 August 1972.
90 As reported from London by *R.H.* 18 January 1973.
91 *Daily Telegraph* (London) 21 March, *R.H.* 25 March 1973.
92 *The Times Higher Educational Supplement* 29 June, *R.H.* 25 June 1973.
93 *R.H.* 30 June 1973.
94 University of Rhodesia News Release No. 537, 15 March 1973
Comparative figures for the years 1972/1973 were:

	EUROPEAN		AFRICAN		OTHERS		TOTAL	
	1972	*1973*	*1972*	*1973*	*1972*	*1973*	*1972*	*1973*
Full Time								
Students	217	280	170	174	26	35	413	489
Returning								
Students	300	268	214	201	40	38	554	507
Higher Degrees							41	102
Part Time								
Students							299	341
Grand Total							1 307	1 439

95 *Property and Finance* No. 206. April 1973.
96 *R.H.* 5, 12 May, *S.M.* 13 May 1973.

XIV

LABOUR

According to Richard Gray (writing in 1960) labour in Southern
Rhodesia before the First World War was a problem because of
its scarcity. Throughout the twenties, however, there was a gradual
increase in cheap unskilled African labour which, by the end of
the slump years significantly aided the country's recovery. By 1930
economists were warning that dependence on unskilled labour was
causing a dangerous lack of balance in the economy and that every
effort should be made to improve African skills 'as the only means
of permanently securing a high standard of living for the community as a whole.' However, 'a rational use of African labour
challenged the assumptions of ... segregation ... and also seemed
to challenge the vested interests of the European workers.' By this
time European wage earners were well organized and after a very
successful railway strike 'European artisans became less interested
in direct warfare with capital and management... and became
more concerned with preventing the infiltration of lower-paid Africans into skilled or semi-skilled work.'

THE INDUSTRIAL CONCILIATION ACT

According to the Minister of Justice at the time the Industrial
Conciliation Act, passed in 1934, had three objectives: 'to maintain
harmony in industry, to provide for apprenticeship, and to help
to maintain a white standard of living in this country.' As the
Act expressly excluded Africans from being defined by the term
'employee' its effect was 'to introduce a modern and progressive
method of industrial conciliation for European wage-earners and
employees while leaving the mass of the labour force under the
Master and Servant Act.' By 1943 there was 'wide-spread dissatisfaction among urban Africans.'[1]

416

The Native Labour Boards Act was passed in 1947 with the initial purpose of laying down a minimum wage level and other basic conditions for African workers (excluding workers in agriculture and domestic service). The Labour Boards were appointed by the responsible Minister and consisted of an independent chairman and two representatives of employer and employee interests. By 1959 it was reported that the interests of Africans were increasingly being represented by Africans themselves.[2] There remained no provision, however, for direct negotiations between African employees and their employers.

The Industrial Conciliation Act No. 29 of 1959 was, for the first time, made applicable to all races and it remains, with its amendments, the foundation of Rhodesian labour legislation. Its provisions relate to all workers in the country except for those in agriculture and domestic service (who remain under the Master and Servants Act) and public servants and employees of the Rhodesia Railways (who come under the Rhodesia Railways Act).

To control wage determination, two of the Act's principal institutions are industrial boards and industrial councils. Industrial boards are appointed by the government to recommend conditions of employment mainly for unorganized (unskilled) workers, who are largely African and are not represented in the industrial councils. The boards can only make recommendations to the government on conditions of employment.

The pre-requisite for an industrial council is a registered trade union which can invite the employer or employer's organisation to form a council or, should the trade union desire, can apply for establishment of a statutory industrial council with the same powers and duties as a permament council but with its constitution determined by the Minister.

THE POSITION OF TRADE UNIONS

In order to obtain the benefits of the Industrial Conciliation Act a trade union must be registered. Registration gives the union proprietary rights to the classes of occupation for which it is registered, in the area in which it is registered. Once a union is registered all employees falling within the interests for which it is registered are entitled to apply for membership. A registered trade union safeguards its members' interests by applying for the setting up of an industrial council or board. Where no council or board exists the union, or an employee or group of employees, can apply for the establishment of a conciliation board to settle disputes. A conciliation board is an industrial council established by the Minister on an *ad hoc* basis to settle or attempt to settle a particular dispute.

Under the Act, trade unions which had been organized before its introduction were able to register and gain exclusive rights within a number of industries. African workers were entitled to join these unions, but because voting strength was apportioned according to grades of occupation and African workers largely come within those grades which have minimal voting strength, effective control remained with European workers.

INDUSTRIAL COUNCIL AGREEMENTS

When a Council achieves agreement on conditions of employment the agreement must be submitted to the Minister: to be legally binding this must be published and available for public inspection and objection for a period of thirty days. If the Minister is unable to accept the provisions of an agreement (on the grounds that it is not equitable to consumers or to members of the public as a whole) the Minister's proposed amendments must prevail, but if either the Minister or the council are not satisfied with the amendments then the whole matter must be referred to an industrial tribunal.

ARBITRATION

If a council is unable to effect the settlement of a dispute, it may agree to voluntary arbitration. This has the effect of settling the matter for the parties have to accept the award of the arbitrator as final and binding. If a council is unable to settle a dispute and cannot agree to voluntary arbitration the whole matter is automatically referred to arbitration. As arbitration is compulsory the parties to it are not bound by the subsequent award and either party, having given notice of rejection, may within a period of 28 days from the date of publication of the award (and subject to certain conditions) take part in a strike or lock-out. This is the only time when a strike is legal. Employees in essential services however cannot reject an award and employees in other industries may have their rejection of an award overruled by Presidential declaration stating that the terms of the award shall be binding, if the President is satisfied that such a course would be in the public interest.

UNREGISTERED TRADE UNIONS

With the introduction of the 1959 Act all unregistered unions became subject to control for the first time. They have the same obligations as registered unions but are denied the benefits of the use of machinery for negotiation, arbitration, etc.

In March 1971 the Minister of Labour, Mr. I. F. McLean, moved that the Senate take note of the government's policy with regard to the Department of Labour—the instrument of implementing government policy on labour. He also informed Senate that, in view of current needs and in line with changing patterns and the national interest, he was soon going to send to all interested parties a draft amending bill which would have the object of bringing the principal Act up to date.

The Minister prefaced his statement by saying that the essence of government policy was to provide a system of stable relationships based on law and justice. Over the years three broad areas in the implementation of the labour policy had been developed: 'the ensuring of an adequate current and future supply of manpower; the maintenance of a harmonious system of industrial relations; [and] the protection of the safety and health of the worker.'

With regard to manpower, the Minister said that, to meet labour requirements, employment exchanges to serve all races had been established in all main centres of the country, with special sections at the exchanges in Salisbury and Bulawayo to deal with school leavers, the professional man and the new immigrant. A special watch was being kept on young people undergoing higher technical and University training to advise them of employment opportunities throughout the country. In the field of African employment, the Minister said that the large numbers of alien African workers from neighbouring territories (working largely in the farming and mining industries) were progressively being decreased, for the government wished to encourage the employment of indigenous Africans to replace migrant workers. As far as training for the future was concerned, the Minister went on to say that the Department confined its activities to meeting the demand for workers in the skilled trades; other Ministries were responsible for training in other fields.

As far as industrial relations was concerned, the Minister considered that the current figures (27 industrial councils in existence; 39 out of 50 registered trade unions; 20 out of 35 registered employers' organizations being parties to the councils; and 52 industrial agreements achieved during 1970-1971) represented 'a clear indication of the usefulness and the productive end-result of their deliberations.' The Minister also said that there were 59 industrial boards in existence and these covered a wide range of industries and undertakings. During the year 1970 43 industrial board meetings had been held. These had covered 31 industries and their deliberations had led to the publication of 10 new comprehensive employment regulations and amendments to 44 other employment regulations.[3]

AMENDMENTS TO THE INDUSTRIAL CONCILIATION ACT

During mid-November 1971 a number of trade unions condemned certain aspects of the amending bill to the Industrial Conciliation Act, the principal objection being to the section prohibiting the right to a strike (or a lock-out) when the President is satisfied that the strike or lock-out would be against the public interest. Introducing the Second Reading the Minister of Labour said that he considered that a major defect of the Act was that nowhere in it was there any protection of the public interest. He conceded that 'the strike weapon was an admirable tool when used to bring unscrupulous employers to their senses ... but when used, as it is being used almost daily in many countries of the western world, to blackmail whole communities into acceptance of the demands of small, perhaps insignificant, sectors of the community, I suggest that the right to strike becomes less than a right.' Mr. McLean warned that this situation could not be accepted in Rhodesia and that the government would be failing in its responsibilities if it took no steps to protect the public interest against strikes or lock-outs.

Among other proposed amendments the Minister also referred to another measure which he planned to introduce. Any person convicted of a charge under the Law and Order (Maintenance) or Unlawful Organizations Acts and sentenced to a term of imprisonment of three months or more (even if the sentence was suspended) would be debarred from holding office in an employer's association or trade union for a period of seven years. [4]

Commenting upon the new amendments, the *Mail* considered that 'Emasculation is not too strong a word for what the Minister of Labour, Mr. McLean, wants to do to the trade unions with his Industrial Conciliation Bill. The effect of his proposed legislation will be to leave the unions defenceless, at the mercy of the employers and in fear of the Government.' [5]

When the Minister of Labour moved that the Bill be read for the Third time Mr. E. G. Watungwa registered his disappointment that it had passed through the House against 'the wishes of those who have interests in the Industrial Conciliation Act'. He also registered his objection to the amendments 'which give the Minister over-all powers to whittle away the ... Act ... which stabilized industrial relations.' [6] The Act was gazetted in early 1972 as the Industrial Conciliation Amendment Act No. 79 of 1971.

In May 1973 the Minister of Labour announced that the Act was to be further amended because it was considered that as it stood it did not give the government wide enough powers to safeguard the public when it was considered that an industrial agreement might be prejudicial to the public interest. Mr. McLean said that the proposed amendments had already been circulated to all interested parties and organizations.

Among the proposed amendments was one to withdraw, from industrial councils and conciliation boards, the power to choose the method of arbitration which they prefer—a single arbitrator, a panel of arbitrators with an independent umpire, or an industrial tribunal—by withdrawing the first two options and making it obligatory for all disputes to be referred to an industrial tribunal. Another amendment was intended to give the Minister power to 'intervene', prior to publication, to alter the terms of any agreed terms of an arbitrator's award (at the present time only the unresolved clauses in an industrial agreement are forwarded to arbitration). This would prevent agreed clauses from being published, and thus given the force of law, without first being given Ministerial permission. A third amendment affects Section 103 of the existing Act whereby the Minister may amend the terms of an industrial agreement if he considers the operation of such an agreement would be against the interests of consumers or of the public as a whole. If the Minister opposes the terms of an agreement on any other basis the final decision must be left to the Industrial Court. The proposed amendment, however, would give this power of making the final decision to the President if he 'deems it expedient in the public interest.'[7]

Apart from the trade unions, employers' organizations such as the Salisbury City Council, the Confederation of Rhodesian Employers (representing about 90 *per cent* of employers throughout the country), the Associated Chambers of Commerce and the Association of Rhodesian Industries, as well as private employers, were reported to have categorically rejected the proposals, mainly on the grounds that too much power was being vested in the Minister.

Earlier in June the Secretary of the Amalgamated Engineering Union was reported as calling for a shelving of differences between all trade unions so that a united front against the proposed new amendments could be formed. The president of the Rhodesia Railway Workers' Union commented that trade unions were 'virtually in a position where they could not operate'. He added that the Minister could say that all proposed amendments were circulated to interested parties for their views but 'I challenge the Ministry to give one instance of where cognizance was taken of our views to the extent that any material change took place in Government thinking.' The president of the African Trades Union Congress told the general council of the A.T.U.C. that he considered the proposed amendments would be harmful, undesirable and impracticable. He said that he had no doubt that they would be used 'not to promote but to undermine the system of private enterprise and collective bargaining.'[8]

EMPLOYMENT

According to the Report of the Secretary for Labour and Social Welfare for the year ended 31st December 1972, the monthly average of Africans in employment increased from 803 000 in June 1971 to 870 000 in June 1972 (an increase of 8.3 *per cent*) while for Europeans, Asians and Coloureds there was an increase from

107 800 in June 1971 to 113 000 in June 1972 (an increase of 5.1
per cent). With regard to migrant African labour the inflow of African males, mainly from Malawi and Mozambique, decreased from
10 500 to 8 640 while the outflow also decreased from 20 250 to
16 090. Quoting from the Central Statistical Office figures it was
estimated that foreign Africans, during March 1972, in employment in Rhodesia numbered 205 300 males and 17 700 females.
It was noted that the total of 223 000 represented 27 *per cent* of
the total number of Africans in employment; a percentage which
had been progressively declining from 75 *per cent* in 1903; 66 *per
cent* in 1921; 52 *per cent* in 1954; and 34 *per cent* in 1969.[9]

JOB RESERVATION

During the debate on the Presidential speech at the opening of
Parliament in 1971, Mr. R. C. Makaya, M.P. for Lowveld, referred
to the need for racial co-operation and among other things spoke
of 'job reservation' by which 'well qualified ... suitable ... very
able people' were not getting jobs because of their colour. In reply
the Minister of Labour said that he found this statement untenable
for, under the Industrial Conciliation Act, there were no regulations concerning reservation of employment for various racial
groups because 'every employer has the right to employ whom
he likes ... providing he pays the prescribed wages.'[10]

In reply to Mr. J. A. Newington, M.P. for Hillcrest (who had
appealed to Members of the House to appreciate the need for job
guarantees in the European areas to safeguard the skilled worker
from competition from the unskilled), the Minister said that if
Mr. Newington meant job reservation—'as it is generally understood in terms of the Physical Planning Act in South Africa' then
this was not the government's policy.[11]

A later comment on Mr. Newington's contribution to the debate
came from Mr. J. Goldwasser, the president of the Bulawayo
Chamber of Industries, who was reported as warning that 'if we
are going to aim for job reservation for unskilled Europeans it
will have the effect of retarding our growth.' Mr. Goldwasser also
said that Rhodesia could not hold back the continuous progress
of Africans. The ever-increasing population required as many job
opportunities as possible for the large numbers of Africans who
were entering the labour market each year.[12]

During the Budget debate in July 1972 Mr. Newington again returned to the position of the European working man. He said that he believed that 'it is absolutely essential that there should be an overhauling of legislation relating to trade unions to ensure that the European working-man is never pushed into a position where, to protect the financial interests of his family and his job, he is forced to side with dissident and anti-government elements within multi-racial trade unions.' Mr. Newington then outlined the reasons why he thought that trade unions should be separated along racial lines. [13]

Later in the year, during a debate on the Second Reading of the Appropriation (1972-73) Bill, Mr. Newington spoke on the subject of labour. He asked why more fragmentation had taken place under the guidance of the present Minister of Labour than at any other time. He considered that during the past 10 years, 'the mining industry, the building industry and now the motor industry [have been] removed from the sphere of certain all-European employment, and all because of fragmentation' and asked the Minister to give a clear statement of government policy. A number of other M.P's, both European and African, criticized differing aspects of labour policy during the debate, concerning which the *Herald* commented that it 'raised many interesting points. There was emphasis on the oft repeated need for the rate for the job regardless of colour, but against this a tendency to regard certain jobs as reserved for Europeans, or at least deserving of a wage sufficient to maintain a European standard of living.' The editorial concluded by saying that, although the Minister (not present at the debate because of indisposition) had promised replies in writing to those taking part in the debate, this did not go far enough. 'He should make a public statement setting out Government policy clearly for all to see.' [14]

THE PROFESSIONS

Teachers

In June 1971 the new increases in salary scales for teachers not in government service were announced. [15] These were criticized as being a departure from previous government policy which had, up to this time, upheld the policy of equal pay for teachers with similar qualifications and responsibilities. The Education Secretary of the Roman Catholic Bishops' Conference described the introduction of the differing scales as 'unjust discrimination, indefensible and completely unacceptable.'[16]

A spokesman for the Division of African Education explained the new salary scales by saying that the choice had been between granting African standard qualified teachers the same increase as the European teachers employed in the Public Service 'or granting the largest percentage increases to the lowest paid teachers who form the bulk of the African teaching service.' He said that the pay increases had only been made after considerable thought had been given to alternative pay scales within the total amount of money allocated.[17]

In July Mr. J. M. Khabo, M.P. for Pagati, asked a private member's question in the House. He wished to know whether the disparity in teachers' salary scales was a temporary measure, and why there had been such a sudden change. Mr. N. A. Gandanzara, M.P. for Manica, asked the Minister to explain why there were different pay scales for Africans and Europeans, and also why male and female teachers of each race also had differential pay scales.

In reply the Minister of Education, Mr. A. P. Smith, said that two points had emerged from protestations about the teachers' salaries; the rationale behind the review of salaries had been lost or deliberately ignored; and that the issue was being used by 'dissident elements as an excuse for impressing their views on certain visitors to Rhodesia.'[18] He said that there was 'no justification whatsoever for the claim that the pay review discriminated unfairly and unjustly against the African teachers [for] personnel employed in a professional capacity as members of the Public Service of Rhodesia by the Division of African Education holding the same qualifications and having the same responsibilities are on the same salary scales whether they be African or European. European teachers employed by missions... and African teachers in the United African Teaching Service holding standard qualifications and carrying the same responsibilities are also on the same rates of pay.'

The Minister said he was of the opinion that 'in a situation in which finance is limited and where already 80 *per cent* of the total money voted for African Education ... goes on payment of teachers' salaries, it would not only be irresponsible but detrimental to the interests of the African people as a whole to channel more funds into teachers' salaries ... Consequently, I do not regard this as a temporary measure, I believe it is in the long term interests of the African people.'[19]

The Civil Service

In mid-1972 during the debate on the Revenue Vote for Agriculture, Mr. Newington asked the Minister of Agriculture if he would make a statement on the staffing policies of his Ministry. Mr. Newington then quoted from a letter which had been drawn to his attention. The letter had been signed by an under-secretary of the Agricultural Land Settlement Department of the Ministry. It had advised its recipient to look for alternative employment, because he would shortly be placed in the position of having to accept directions from a senior African colleague. The secretary had doubted whether the recipient 'would be amenable' to this arrangement. The recipient of the letter had since resigned from his job. Mr. Newington said that he had brought this matter to the notice of the Minister because 'it is our responsibility to demonstrate that the Government sticks to its policies ... which are that they will not do anything in the form of integration of the races where this could cause friction.'

In his reply the Minister of Agriculture, Mr. D. C. Smith, reminded his questioner that his Ministry had responsibility for two sectors of Agriculture—European and African—and that it was the Ministry's policy 'to take on qualified technicians and scientists in order that they be trained up to a level at which they can ultimately look after the people whom we would wish them to look after.' The following day the Minister returned to the subject and said that he thought all Members would agree 'that there is a role to be played by the qualified African, but I take the point that one must be careful to avoid creating circumstances in which friction can occur. Accordingly I have given instructions that no further such appointments are made without my prior approval, and in considering such cases I will give regard to all the circumstances and to the request that has been made in this House.'[20]

Nurses

During the debate on the Revenue Vote for Health in 1972 African M.P's drew the Minister's attention to the question of employment of trained African nurses in European hospitals and promotion of nurses in African hospitals to senior positions. The Minister replied that it was already a well-canvassed subject and reiterated that it was not government policy to employ African nurses in European hospitals. As far as promotion of African nurses to senior grades was concerned the Minister said that there were several African nurses in the assistant-matron grade who were at present acting as sister-tutors. 'When they are ready on merit for administrative jobs in African hospitals they will get them. The correct professional qualifications are not everything in this regard; the quality of the work and the integrity of the person concerned is very important.'[21]

The Law

During April 1972 African advocates presented a memorandum to the Rhodesian Bar Association stating their arguments for being allowed to defend cases in magistrate's and district commissioner's courts and at tribunals without the necessity of being instructed by attorneys. It was considered that if their proposals were not approved they would put forward an alternative that African advocates only be allowed to act in simple matters without being instructed by an attorney. Failing agreement on either alternative it was thought likely that the African advocates would break away from the Bar Association to form their own organization.

There are only seven practising African advocates in the whole of Rhodesia (although there are several non-practising Africans with the necessary legal qualifications) and there are no African attorneys. The advocates considered that the majority of European attorneys preferred to brief European advocates, even in cases involving African clients, and listed three further reasons they considered relevant to their request for alterations to the Bar Council's ruling; namely, that the system was archaic and had been abandoned by most countries; that it made the cost of legal representation expensive and beyond the reach of most Africans; and that most European firms did not want to article Africans to become attorneys.[22]

In August the Bar Council issued a statement, described by the *Herald* as 'apparently designed to help the African advocate', which read that, for a trial period, an attorney need not be present at consultations nor be obliged to attend court to instruct counsel

(in criminal defence and appeals cases before district commissioner's courts and the appeal court for African Civil Cases) where
counsel is to be instructed in, and consultations between counsel,
client and witnesses conducted in a language with which the attorney is not conversant. The *Herald* reported that 'a lawyer' had
commented that 'this could possibly mean an increase in fees
and/or opportunities for the African advocate.' [23]

The trial period came into effect in July 1972 but by April 1973
African advocates were complaining that the scheme was not working for, they claimed, very few attorneys were fulfilling their part
of the bargain. The advocates urged that their original proposals
be implemented. In order to determine the validity of complaints
and also to investigate other ways of overcoming the difficulties
the Bar Council then instituted an enquiry. The African advocates
however made it clear that any system which differed from the
proposals already made by them would be unacceptable and that
unless their proposals were put into practice by the first week in
July they would break away and form their own African Bar Association. [24]

THE RHODESIA RAILWAYS

During the debate on the President's speech in June 1972 Mr.
J. A. Newington referred (as he had on the same occasion in 1971)
to the government's labour policy. Mr. Newington considered that
the main problem in the future would be jobs for the semi-skilled
or unskilled European working man. He said he was not advocating job reservation but 'was most strongly advocating that protection be given to the unqualified Europeans.' Mr. Newington cited
the case of the Railways in which he considered that the position
of Europeans was being eroded. He thought it was 'significant
to note that something approaching 50 *per cent* of the footplate
staff are non-Europeans, compared with what they were eight years
ago.' Mr. Newington warned the House that 'we would do well
to ponder the fact that there is solid indisputable evidence that
where there is a sphere of traditional European activity and where
there is direct competition by all races for the same job in this
sphere, then gradually the European tends to withdraw and leave
the field uncontested.' [25]

In reply to Mr. Newington's specific mention of the Railways, the Minister of Transport, Mr. R. T. R. Hawkins, said that Mr. Newington in his speech had 'omitted the all-important, and indeed vital consideration... the present non-availability of European recruits to fill vacancies in the categories of employment he mentioned.' Mr. Hawkins queried whether it was being suggested that the operations of the Railways should be reduced and confined to the availability of European recruits and said that Mr. Newington had erred when he had spoken of the increased erosion of European employment on the Railways. He quoted figures to show that the ratio of Europeans to non-Europeans on the Railways was far greater than in agriculture, mining, manufacturing, and construction work. As far as the ratio of non-Europeans to Europeans on the footplate was concerned, the Minister said that the actual figures were 830 Europeans to 289 non-Europeans (with the addition of 170 non-European stokers who were in a separate category).

In conclusion Mr. Hawkins pointed out that the problem was not one confined only to Rhodesia Railways, for 'the South African Railways, for exactly similar reasons, have had to breach their job reservation policy extensively and today the extent of non-European employment in what were once occupations reserved for Europeans is very considerable.'

The Minister of Labour in his reply to the points raised said that he had a good deal of sympathy for the views of Mr. Newington but, in regard to the position of the semi-skilled and unskilled European, he felt that Mr. Newington had confused certain issues and ignored certain facts as far as the government's position was concerned. Firstly, as regards European unemployment, the Minister said that, among the economically active section of the population, Rhodesia's unemployment rate must be one of the lowest in the world. The figures available from government employment exchanges 'showed that the number of adult Europeans who fall into the categories of unskilled or semi-skilled workers and who register at the exchanges remains constant at about 180 each month throughout the whole of Rhodesia.' The Minister reminded his listeners that 'some of our most powerful and influential trade unions' represent large numbers of skilled and unskilled Europeans, and said that he hoped the Hon. Member was 'not implying that these unions are incapable or incompetent to look after the interest of these people.'[26]

In mid-October a departmental draft of the Rhodesia Railways Bill was gazetted 'for general information'. A few days previously it had been announced that 96 resignations had been handed to the Rhodesia Railways Workers' Union (R.R.W.U.) by Coloured, Asian and African workers in the enginemen's grade. The men felt that the Union had not protected their rights in the matter of promotions. A spokesman for the group of enginemen said that three non-European engine drivers had been passed over. when promotion had been given to three Europeans who were junior to them in length of service. [27]

Commenting upon this action the *Mail* said 'the problem is one not only for the whole Government but for every white man in the country. How to solve it? It is a measure of Rhodesia's perplexity on this that, in the same week in which the problem blew up on Rhodesia Railways, the Ministry of Law and Order appointed the first non-white magistrate.' [28]

It was not until late November that the Minister of Transport gave an indication of the official policy of the government towards the question of main line drivers on the Railways. Answering the question put by Mr. L. Masenda, M.P. for Mabvazuma, whether it was government policy to permit only Europeans to drive main line trains, he said 'promotion within the engineman grades of the Railways and thus to the post of main-line driver is by merit and suitability. Government does not lay down the policy in regard to these promotions. It is usual for this to be negotiated between the trade unions and management.' [29]

AGRICULTURAL WORKERS

In early October 1972, following a complaint by workers at a chicken farm near Salisbury that they had been sacked for belonging to the unregistered Agricultural and Plantation Workers' Union, the *Herald* asked the Minister of Labour whether the Industrial Conciliation Act would be amended to cover agricultural workers and so enable their unions to gain official registration. The Minister in reply gave three reasons why the government could not, at the present time, agree to include agricultural workers under the Act. He explained that there was inherent difficulty in prescribing comprehensive conditions of service for the various classes of farm worker; that there would have to be a very large inspectorate to enforce the regulated conditions; and the presence of a large seasonal labour force on the farms would not enable a sufficiently stable combination of employees to meet the requirements for a registered trade union. Agricultural workers' conditions of service are covered by the Master and Servants Act which does not provide for the recognition of trade unions. Asked what legal process was open for farm workers to negotiate terms of service a Ministry spokesman replied that the Act allowed free and voluntary meetings of any persons to consult or discuss any matters arising from the relation of employer and employee. The spokesman considered that the Master and Servants Act was 'the best vehicle... by which certain basic conditions of employment can be prescribed for farm labour.'[30]

The Agricultural and Plantation Workers' Union announced in February 1973 that it had renewed its campaign for amendment to the legislation, which excluded farmworkers from provisions of the Industrial Conciliation Act, by submitting a memorandum to the Minister of Labour. A Union spokesman said that the memorandum called for a change in the law on several grounds. It claimed that as there is no provision for collective bargaining under the Master and Servants Act real earnings had fallen by 16.5 *per cent* during the period 1963-71 and that a 1971 survey showed that 95.7 *per cent* of the work force earned less than $20 a month; there was no machinery to deal with collective negotiations for improved working or living conditions, nor was there a body to which workers could take complaints as it was impossible for the union to register under existing legislation. The memorandum pointed out that one reason for low wages in the industry was that excessive numbers of foreign workers were allowed to enter the agricultural industry and ended by stating that it was because 'we are left unprotected and excluded from the Industrial Conciliation Act that we are unable to even protect and maintain our low standard of living, let alone promote our interests and increase the standard in accordance with the general development experienced in the economy.'[31]

THE TRADE UNIONS

During March 1972 the African Transport Workers' Union called
upon private transport companies to follow the lead of the municipalities and the railways and to drop racial discrimination against
non-Africans. The African Transport Worker's Union is affiliated
to the National African Federation of Unions (N.A.F.U.) and its
Mashonaland Regional Secretary, Mr. P. J. Mpofu, issued a statement reading: 'We very much regret this economic exploitation
of job reservation for Africans only. No European, Coloured or
Indian is allowed to drive these vehicles for fear of disturbing
the wage structure.' [32]

The following month it was reported that a six-man delegation
from the African Trades Union Congress (A.T.U.C.) had met
the Minister of Labour to discuss a statement by the latter when,
in October 1971, he had accused some trade unionists of using
their positions to further political ends. The Minister said that
he had no intention of allowing trade unions to become involved
in politics. The A.T.U.C. delegation led by its National President,
Mr. P. F. Sithole, was quoted as saying that the meeting had been
held in a reasonable atmosphere and 'we are satisfied that we made
our point'. A statement issued by the A.T.U.C. later explained
that its delegation had appealed to the Minister to separate comment on current political developments from political party lines.
The next day the *Herald* commented that the President of the
A.T.U.C. had made a good point, one which 'the Minister should
accept, for it would be folly to bar trade unions from openly discussing legislation or social trends that affect their members. Such
an outlet is especially important ... where the great bulk of trade
unionists have no way of compelling attention, for they have no
vote.' [33]

Early in 1972 further attempts were made to unite the two main
African labour bodies, the A.T.U.C. and N.A.F.U., these two
bodies having been divided since the split in the African nationalist
movement in 1965. A sub-committee to deal with the merger
had been formed in February 1972 but over a year later matters
appeared to be at a standstill. The Chairman of the Salisbury
region of the A.T.U.C. said that the region would shortly meet
to consider ways to pressurize the sub-committee into coming to
an early decision, for individual unions were losing interest in the

central bodies and without unity between the two organizations it would be difficult to unite the already divided unions within the same industry. [34]

At the end of August 1972 it was announced that the R.R.W.U. had adopted a new constitution. The R.R.W.U.'s president, Mr. J. Kinley, described it as a 'system where railway workers in all grades are represented on the executive committee. The old system of national councils falls away ... Under the old constitution the executive committee was elected by the national councillors ... now we have full representation for all members.' Mr. Kinley added that priorities for the new executive committee included pensions and a job rationalization investigation. [35]

Early in November it was reported that the R.R.W.U. was discussing, with the management of the railways, certain changes such as the removal of firemen from diesel goods trains and opportunities for guards to become diesel engine drivers. The General Secretary of the Railway Association of Locomotive Enginemen (R.A.L.E.) was reported as saying that 'these radical changes will mean the erosion of our service conditions and of the grade of enginemen.' The *Herald* said that it was understood that R.A.L.E. would fight the proposed changes, but as it was an unregistered trade union, it could not represent its members at Industrial Council level. [36]

By mid-January 1973 the talks had reportedly broken down, but after a two-day meeting of the R.R.W.U. and an indication that management wanted to continue they were resumed in February. Agreement was eventually reached that diesel main-line trains would have only one man on the foot-plate and that this would not lead to retrenchment. There would also be amended conditions of service for engine-men. [37] At the same time it was announced that R.A.L.E. (with about 800 members), which had been attempting to gain registration for almost two years, had finally been registered as a trade union.

The following month, however, the R.R.W.U. announced its decision to contest R.A.L.E.'s registration and to take the issue to an Industrial Court. The Court hearing opened in Bulawayo on the 28th May. It concerned itself with three issues—whether the R.R.W.U. was sufficiently representative of the interests of engine-men; whether R.A.L.E. was sufficiently representative of that interest; and whether it was expedient to register R.A.L.E.

as representing engine-men's interests. By mid-June the Court handed down its judgement and dismissed the R.R.W.U.'s appeal, finding that R.A.L.E., with the larger percentage of membership of the Railway's engine-men, had adequate numerical strength and expertise to represent them. It had collected dues from its members without the machinery of the R.R.W.U. and had increased its membership by over 100 in less than a year despite the disadvantage of not being able to negotiate, or safeguard the working conditions of its members since its formation. [38]

The report of the Secretary for Labour and Social Welfare for the year ended 31st December 1972 listed 50 registered and 23 unregistered trade unions in existence at the end of 1972. With regard to the unregistered unions the report noted that there had been an increase of three over the previous year and commented that only a few of them 'are capable of reaching the degree of responsibility and the membership necessary to achieve registration. The remainder have a small, fluctuating membership, of which few are in good standing and they are led mainly by inexperienced and itinerant officials.' By the end of 1972 27 industrial councils were registered and arising from their negotiations 31 industrial agreements were published and the periods of operation of 31 other agreements were extended. The approximate number of employees whose conditions of employment were regulated by industrial councils throughout 1972 was given as 162 536. At the end of 1972 there were 62 industrial boards in operation and the number of registered employers' associations remained at 35. [39]

WAGES

Towards the end of 1971 it was reported that the two African labour organizations (the A.T.U.C. and N.A.F.U.) were to press for the introduction of a national minimum wage. In March 1972 the A.T.U.C. president, Mr. P. F. Sithole, said that 'until the wage structure among Africans in Rhodesia was significantly improved to a minimum of $15 per week for general workers, employers would have no incentive to train the abundant African labour now available.' [40]

Throughout the year various authorities called attention to the need for closing the gap between the earnings and standards of

living of Europeans and Africans. In the *Herald's* weekly supplement, *Business and Financial Review,* reporter John Robertson
quoted from the *Monthly Digest of Statistics* to show that the gap
between the average earnings of Europeans, Asians and Coloureds,
on the one hand, and African workers on the other was increasing,
and warned that merely to maintain a constant gap African earnings
would have to increase by 30 *per cent* each year for each employee.
Giving figures of total earnings of $244 400 000 for all employed
Africans for 1971, Mr. Robertson said that this provided individual
employees with an average of $313 *per annum* but if the total was
divided by the total African population it would show that the
average income per head would come to only $46 *per annum.* He
commented 'with incomes at this level, the ability of the Africans
to contribute to the development of the economy is extremely
limited. In fact, the vast majority of the population is an anchor
on the country's progress.'[41]

During 1972 both Salisbury and Bulawayo municipalities
announced increases for their African workers, and it was reported
that the Railway Associated Workers' Union (R.A.W.U.) had
approached the management of the railways with a claim for higher
wages. It was also announced that both the Television and Radio
Workers' and the Rhodesia Transport Workers' Unions were to
submit wage claims to their respective industrial boards.

In September it was reported that, at the annual Rhodesian
Front Congress, a recommendation had been made to undertake
'an intensive investigation ... to establish which jobs should have
high minimum wages—basically to make the job attractive enough
for a white to want.'[42] For there had been much comment on
jobs which were paid at rates which were too low for Europeans
to live on and were thus becoming 'reserved' for other races.

In November a Bulawayo Chartered Accountant, Mr. A. J. L.
Lewis, prepared a private memorandum on African wages which
he distributed to people in industrial and commercial organizations
as well as to the government. Mr. Lewis said that his memorandum
had been written because: 'the country must take action to enable
it to maintain itself in a buoyant economic state and at the same
time to demonstrate to the world at large, and to the Rhodesian
African in particular, its determination to govern wisely, well and
fairly. [For] no Government can claim to be governing fairly if
they are not taking active steps to ensure that all workers are being

paid at least a living wage, which is not the position in Rhodesia today.'[43]

Comments upon the memorandum came from Mr. B. Frewin, president of the Confederation of Rhodesian Employers, who said that it appeared that Mr. Lewis had made 'a sweeping over-simplification of a very complex problem.' He warned that 'An immediate and massive increase in African wages would tend to place many workers on the labour market.' African trade union leaders however supported Mr. Lewis and claimed that thousands of African workers were 'living below the breadline in a country of plenty.' The *Herald* considered that Mr. Lewis' memorandum was 'the type of document that deserves close study by all employers' and warned that 'wages cannot be raised markedly overnight. But there must be a willingness to examine wage levels and act before employers find themselves with their backs to the wall in the face of more extreme demands.'[44]

During the early months of 1973 various newspapers drew attention to the lessons which they considered Rhodesia should be learning from the industrial unrest currently taking place in South Africa. Although it was considered that the position of the African worker in Rhodesia was better than that of his South African counterpart, in that the former was able to belong to or to form a trade union and his voice could be heard through the various industrial councils, the problems of the widening gap between agricultural workers and earnings of African workers in other sectors of the economy; the relationship between wage levels and the poverty datum line; and the rapidly increasing gap between average earnings of African and European (including Asian and Coloured), were subject to examination and recommendations for improvement.

The Economic Survey of Rhodesia for 1972 lists a total of 848 000 Africans in employment during 1972 of which 338 200, or just under 40 *per cent,* are employed in agriculture and forestry. Their average earnings of $135 *per annum* being less than half those of the next lowest paid group of workers (those in private domestic service) and considerably less than the average earnings of the highest paid group of workers (transport and communications). The figure for European, Asian and Coloured employees is given as a total of 112 500. Average annual earnings of this group, during 1972, were $3 632 while the average annual earnings of Africans during this period were $332.[45]

The latest enquiry into the calculation of the cost of living at a defined minimum standard of health and decency for households of a given size and composition (commonly known as the Poverty Datum Line or P.D.L.) was conducted in connection with the Commission on Urban African Affairs (the Plewman Commission) by Dr. David Bettison who, in 1957, conducted a short enquiry as part of a larger socio-economic study of the three capital cities of Northern and Southern Rhodesia and Nyasaland. [46] Using Bettison's figure of just over $31 per month for a married couple with two children and the rise of about 30 *per cent* in the African consumer price index since Bettison's time, a correspondent of the *Financial Gazette* calculated that such a family would now require about $40 per month.

This correspondent pointed out, however, that a number of other factors would 'nullify such a simplistic conclusion.' He instanced the change in African consumer spending as shown by Urban Budget Surveys carried out by the Central Statistical Office and the fact that the urban surveys show a higher standard of living than that estimated by Bettison. He postulated that if one were to take the $40 a month figure 'as a very rough rule of thumb, one would find agriculture, private domestic and mining coming well below this urban P.D.L.' [47]

In June amendments to the employment regulations for workers in the transport industry were announced in the *Government Gazette*. These amendments, giving workers an increase of about 5 *per cent*, followed recommendations made to the Minister of Labour by the Industrial Board for the transport operating industry. The Acting General Secretary for the unregistered Transport Operating Workers' Union was quoted as saying, however, that his union did not consider that the increases were acceptable. [48] Later that same month the chairman of the Central African Textile Manufacturers' Association announced that more than 11 600 workers in the textile industry would receive a 5.4 *per cent* wage increase from the beginning of August. He explained that the current agreement had been to award wage increases in two parts; about half in April 1972 and the remainder, about 4 *per cent*, in October 1973. This latter 4 *per cent* had been raised to 10 *per cent* of the wages for the last agreement providing a net effect of about 5.4 *per cent* extra on current wages. [49]

STRIKES

According to M. W. Murphree the ability of African labour in Rhodesia to strike legally is severely curtailed. Such strikes that occur are illegal and are not instigated by the unions nominally involved but they do, nevertheless, reveal the bargaining power of the African worker. [50]

On 13th January police headquarters in Salisbury confirmed that a labour dispute had occurred at the Shabanie Asbestos Mine (in Shabani) two days previously, involving between three to four hundred workers. It was understood that the dispute had arisen over the dismissal of several workers. By the evening of the 12th January the dispute was reported to have escalated into violence when the strikers were joined by an unruly crowd. A beer-hall was severely damaged and administration offices burnt; police and their vehicles were stoned and a store broken into. To quell the riot, police used tear smoke and were then forced to open fire causing the death of one African man and the wounding of nine others. At this time it seemed that most people believed that mounting political feelings over the arrival of the Pearce Commission 'had escalated, what had started as a labour dispute, into a riot.' [51] By the end of the second week in January it was reported that all was quiet in the area following the arrest of at least 25 people and the grouping of about 50 police and police reservists at the local police camp.

Discussing the strike, the president of the Associated Mineworkers of Rhodesia, Mr. H. Bloomfield, said that while he sympathized with the mine management, he felt it had handled the dispute badly in its initial stages. 'Had my [union] representatives been brought in at the start and an inquiry allowed, I don't think it would have allowed people behind the scenes to escalate it to the present position.' What had started over a misunderstanding had now changed to a demand for higher wages, he added. [52]

Early in the following week it was announced that the two-week strike had come to an end with all the mine's 3 000 African employees returning peacefully to work, except for nine men sentenced in Shabani Magistrate's Court for four to twelve months' imprisonment for public violence.

During the first week in February all 1 600 African mineworkers at the Trojan Nickel Mine near Bindura were reported to be out on strike. A spokesman for the Rhodesian Nickel Corporation (the mine-owners) said that it was impossible to clarify the reasons for the strike because no member of the staff had come forward to put their demands to the mine management. A government spokesman, however, said that the mine workers were demanding pay increases. At the same time it was announced that the police had arrested two men suspected of attempting to intimidate mine workers going on shift at Gaths Mine, Mashaba. [53]

The following day the mine management was reported to have received a letter from the striking workers demanding an extra $1 per shift or $30 per month increase for those paid monthly. Demands were also made for pay increases in lieu of rations. Mr. H. Bloomfield was reported as saying that he had little information about the strike as there was no active National Industrial Council sub-branch at the Trojan Mine. It was noted that the estimated cost of the miners' wage demands represented more than the total net profit declared by the corporation for the first six months of the current financial year. [54] The strikers returned to work the next day after being told that the management could not entertain their claims for pay rises.

The 440 African mineworkers at the Blanket Gold Mine near Gwanda, reportedly on strike, demanded cash in lieu of rations and an extra $5 a month. It was also alleged (but later denied) that workers at the Sandawana Emerald Mine were on strike. The manager of the Chamber of Mines is reported to have said that the demands cropping up around the country had not come up in any of the mines in the past and were obviously associated with political agitation.

In commenting upon these strikes the president of the Associated Mineworkers of Rhodesia, the largest multi-racial union in the country with 6 000 European and 1 000 African members, warned Africans that although they had some genuine grievances they did themselves no good by not negotiating for better pay and conditions through the unions. Mr. Bloomfield also spoke of the new agreement shortly to be negotiated for the mining industry and of the discussions within the national council which would begin in the near future. [55]

In late February it was reported that, following a meeting addressed by Pearce Commissioners at the Hippo Valley Estates near Chiredzi, about 500 sugar mill workers had gone on strike.

By the next day 1 200 workers (out of a total of 6 000) had failed to report for work. Disturbances were reported on part of the estate and several Africans were arrested, one African subsequently being gaoled for contravening the Law and Order (Maintenance) Act and for malicious damage to property.[56] The strike, which lasted six days, ended on the 28th February.

In mid-June 1972 it was reported that about 250 African drivers of the Salisbury United Bus Company had gone on unofficial strike. The men were drivers of one-man operated buses and were demanding that the 45 cent *per diem* allowance for operating ticket machines should be increased immediately to $1 a day.[57] Mr. P. Hornblow, the general manager of the bus company, said that the strike had followed several earlier meetings between the company and representatives of the drivers. The company had told the drivers that it could not meet their demands because such an increase could only be granted through proper arbitration by the Industrial Board of the Transport Operating Industry. Shortly before the strike was announced a meeting had been held with about 120 drivers who had been asked to reconsider their intention to strike; when they still refused to go back to work they had been dismissed. When some refused to leave the premises the police had been called in. The Organizing Secretary of the Mashonaland Region of the Rhodesia Transport Workers' Union, Mr. M. S. Malumisa, was reported later as saying that the strike was unofficial and that he had advised the drivers to return to work.[58]

When a motion for adjournment of the House of Assembly was proposed in mid-June, Mr. R. T. D. Sadomba, M.P. for Nemakonde, raised the issue of the bus drivers' strike and called upon the Minister of Labour to look into the relationship between employer and employees and also the behaviour of the police. In reply the Minister of Labour said that he was aware of the dispute and had already announced that he would be prepared to recall the Industrial Board for the industry in order to consider the drivers' grievances and try to meet them. The fact that the drivers had now indulged in an illegal stoppage of work made this action out of the question. The Minister said that he found the drivers' action 'quite irresponsible' and until such time as there was some rethinking on their part he would support the management. The Minister added that he was considering prosecuting 'those who had inspired this illegal withdrawal of labour.' The Minister of

Justice, Mr. D. W. Lardner-Burke, outlined the events of the morning and said that uniformed members of the police had escorted 80 dismissed drivers from the bus depot but 'no incidents between the strikers and the police have been reported, save for the arrest of one striker for obstruction, and no unnecessary force has been used by members of the police. In escorting the strikers from the depot, the police used dogs but the dogs were not used to attack anyone and, as far as I know, no one was bitten.'[59]

According to a *Herald* reporter, African transport workers get higher wages than most Africans in other jobs, the average earnings for a month being $74. They had last received a pay award increase in November 1971 and had, at the same time, received a raise from 35 to 45 cents a day on the allowance for operating one-man buses. The general manager of the omnibus company was reported as saying that, in addition to the flat rate of pay, drivers were paid time and a half when working over 48 hours a week and double pay for work on rest days, plus a night allowance of time and a quarter if the majority of hours were worked between midnight and 6 a.m. The drivers also received such 'fringe' benefits as free uniforms, laundered free; free travel to and from work; subsidized canteen meals; free services from a company doctor and free medical prescriptions.[60]

The next day it was reported from Bulawayo that the general secretary of the Transport Workers' Union (T.W.U.), Mr. R. R. Bango, had said that despite the high feelings of the men the union was trying to dissuade them from holding an illegal strike. He outlined the history of the negotiations which had taken place since May 1971 and warned that drivers in Bulawayo were threatening to join their Salisbury colleagues. Mr. Bango said that at the previous negotiations the T.W.U. had submitted a reasonable claim for $3 in addition to the basic pay of the driver who operated without a conductor and that the Chairman of the Industrial Board had assured union officials that a recommendation would be made for this sum to be paid. However, according to Mr. Bango, when the Minister of Labour had published the Transport Industry Employment Regulations in November 1971 the sum of $3 had been reduced to $1.70.[61]

At the end of the week the Minister of Labour made a statement in the House on the strike. He said that it was his duty, in the public interest, 'to put straight a record which had been grossly distorted by so-called spokesmen of the drivers of Salisbury United Omnibus Company and by the secretary of the unregistered Transport Workers' Union.' Mr. McLean added that the chairman of the Transport Operating Industry had categorically denied that he had given Mr. Bango any assurances that the Board would recommend a $3 a week allowance to be paid to the one-man bus drivers. The Minister concluded his statement by saying 'I would like to make it quite plain that the strike is illegal. I am no longer prepared to tolerate a situation where people are holding to ransom, not only their own colleagues, but the people of Salisbury as a whole. Accordingly I have to announce that steps are being taken to prosecute certain of the drivers in terms of the Industrial Conciliation Act, under which the penalties for striking illegally are a fine, not exceeding five hundred dollars, or imprisonment of up to three years, or both such fine and imprisonment.'[62]

The following week the striking drivers held a private meeting and afterwards stated that they had agreed to end the strike if the United Omnibus Company accepted their demands before work was resumed. These demands were listed as: No dismissals or arrests of drivers as a result of the strike; drivers to receive either a daily allowance of $1 a day or conductors on their buses; drivers not to pay for repairs to buses or to be dismissed because of an accident; and drivers involved in the strike not to be required to sign new work contracts.[63] The following day it was reported that the management had offered to re-engage all the striking drivers if they agreed to negotiate their remaining claims constitutionally.

On 21st June it was announced that 138 African bus drivers in Bulawayo had joined the strikers in Salisbury in their demands for increased allowances. In Salisbury the bus company decided to recruit new drivers in a bid to end the eight-day-old strike. Advertisements in the local press offered African public service vehicle drivers (first class) an average monthly wage of $70 with several fringe benefits.[64]

By Saturday the government decided to call in Defence Force drivers to ensure the resumption of basic bus services in Salisbury and Bulawayo on the following Monday. According to a government statement this step was being taken because of the illegal strike which had brought to a halt services essential to the community.[65] In the meantime strikers and trade union officials were holding meetings to try and break the deadlock. On the Sunday it was announced by Mr. Bango that the men had decided to accept, in good faith, the assurances given to them by the company and to leave their grievances in the hands of the union. In view of the agreement with the company Mr. Bango called on drivers in both cities to return to work and also requested the authorities to release the 76 Bulawayo drivers who had been arrested. Mr. Bango added that he felt strongly that the Minister of Labour should appoint a commission of enquiry to go into the background of the drivers' 'long-lasting' grievances. [66]

The strike was followed by the government's promulgation of new powers under the Emergency Powers Act—the Emergency Powers (Passenger Transport Services) Regulations 1972—to empower the Commander of the Rhodesian Army to take what steps he considered necessary to maintain public transport in the event of a strike by employees or any other cause of disruption. [67]

In the event, early on the Monday morning, a fleet of 156 army and government trucks carried an estimated 30 000 people to work from Salisbury's four African townships. They were progressively recalled as more of the Salisbury United Omnibus Company's buses took over normal service when 317 of the striking drivers returned to work. It was later reported that four drivers who had pleaded not guilty to contravening the Industrial Conciliation Act by striking were fined $50 in Salisbury Magistrate's Court. In late November, having appealed against their conviction and sentence, the four men had their fines reduced to $20 (or two weeks).

In Bulawayo 62 drivers were found guilty of striking illegally and each fined $30 (or 15 days) at the Western Commonage Magistrate's Court. Army trucks serviced routes between the townships and the industrial area of Bulawayo during peak periods and it was reported that the Omnibus Company expected to organize a full normal service by the following day. [68]

On 1st July it was announced that the Industrial Board for the Transport Operating Industry would be reconvened (on 25th July) to discuss the bus drivers' grievances. The composition of the Board, however, was criticized by Mr. Bango who said that out of the five employees' representatives on the twelve-man Board only two were Africans representing the interests of 12 000 workers. [69]

In Parliament Mr. T. M. Chikonyora, M.P. for Highveld, asked the Prime Minister why it had been found necessary, during the strike, to provide army transport for carrying of bus passengers in Bulawayo and Salisbury. The Prime Minister stated in answer that there had been two reasons for this action: 'firstly to avoid hardship for the Africans living in the townships and secondly, to bring an early end to the illegal strike.' He then said he would take the opportunity of stating that the government would not hesitate to take equally firm action whenever necessary in the future. [70]

In mid-August it was reported that the Minister of Labour was to see representatives of the bus companies and the bus drivers before drawing up new regulations aimed at resolving the difficulties which had led to the strike. The Minister had decided upon this action because the Industrial Board had twice failed to reach agreement on the terms of the recommendations. Under the Industrial Conciliation Act the Minister has the power to make regulations after he has consulted persons in the industry concerned. [71] By the end of August it was announced that the Minister had decided that a national increase in the allowance of drivers of one-man operated buses was justified and recommended that the allowance be raised from 45 to 75 cents a day. The Ministerial spokesman added that the recommendations of the Industrial Board had been accepted—the management would have to prove shortages in fare taking and deductions would only be allowed with the written consent of the driver concerned; pay deductions for damage to vehicles would be limited to no more than $8 provided the driver's negligence was proved. [72]

Reactions to the Minister's decision came both from employers and workers; the drivers were reported to be considering taking legal opinion over the proposals, while the United Transport Group, which owns the bus-operating companies, accused the Minister of abrogating both the spirit and the letter of the Industrial Conciliation Act. [73]

In June 1973 a government spokesman, commenting upon the recently gazetted amendments to the employment regulations for workers in the transport industry, stated that the Minister had referred certain matters, which included an examination of the conditions of service for drivers of one-man operated buses, to the Industrial Board for the Transport Operating Industry which would sit later in the month. [74]

In June it was reported that six clerical workers at Tafara Township had staged a walk-out over their new conditions of service
and loss of seniority when the township was handed over from
Greendale to Salisbury Municipality. The employees returned to
work after being visited by a representative of Salisbury Municipality's African Administration Department, who later refused to
comment.[75] Another dispute took place in August when it was
reported that about 200 employees at the African Lumber Company in Bulawayo had been dismissed after going on
strike.[76]

In September 'pirate' taxi operators in Bulawayo went
on a strike called by the African Action Committee on Bus
Services whose vice-chairman said later that 'we wanted to show
the public that, despite statements by the general manager of the
Rhodesia Omnibus Company, the bus service is not adequate.'[77]

In late September, a four-hour strike by 250 employees at a
chicken farm outside Salisbury led to the dismissal of about 30
workers mainly on the grounds that they belonged to the unregistered Agricultural and Plantation Workers' Union. This led to
the Minister being asked whether the Industrial Conciliation Act
could not be amended to cover agricultural workers (see also pp.
430-1).[78]

The Report of the Secretary for Labour for the year ended 31st
December 1972 stated that during the year there had been an increase in the number of work stoppages caused by disputes between
employers and employees in which the assistance of the Ministry's
Industrial Relations Branch had been sought. It noted, however,
that the number of employees involved and man-days lost relative
to total employees and days worked was insignificant. The report
itemized the number of work stoppages caused by disputes
between employers and employees whose conditions of employment are regulated by the Industrial Conciliation Act as 29, involving 3 203 employees and resulting in a total of 6 984 lost man-days
(eight hours). The figures do not include work stoppages occurring
during the sitting of the Pearce Commission because these were
not caused by disputes between employers and employees. Work
stoppages in employment regulated by the Master and Servants
Act numbered 13, involving 1 120 employees and a loss of 753
man-days, which again did not include work stoppages during the
visit of the Pearce Commission.[79]

At the end of March 1973 twelve African men appeared at the Harare Magistrate's Court on allegations of public violence in connection with a dispute at the Portland Cement Company. The twelve men had been dismissed on the afternoon of 19th March and contrary to instructions regarding wages had demanded their pay immediately and refused to disperse. A crowd had collected and, being joined by the twelve men, had stoned a vehicle belonging to the firm. [80]

In mid-May a labour dispute, at the David Whitehead textile plant near Hartley, involved more than 900 African workers who demanded a 50 *per cent* wage increase. A spokesman for the firm said that the average weekly wage for African workers at the plant— from sweepers to machine operators—was $10. The strike lasted five days and ended with the workers returning to work without their demands being met; 21 men were dismissed. One of the company's directors was later quoted as saying that it was a case of '98 *per cent* of a good work force being intimidated by a 2 *per cent* rabble-rousing element.' [81]

UNEMPLOYMENT

Introducing the 1971 Budget the Minister of Finance, Mr. J. J. Wrathall, made reference to what he considered to be the major problem—growth of employment opportunities. He pointed out that on past evidence it was clear that 'the cash economy cannot expand fast enough to absorb the increasing number of potential work seekers generated by the African population.' Growth figures of the Gross National Product from 1962 to 1970 showed an increase at an average compound rate of about 3.25 *per cent per annum* while during the same period the African population had increased at a rate of 3.5 *per cent per annum*. These figures, said the Minister, would lead one to expect only a moderate increase in the rate of unemployment but this, unfortunately, was not the case.

Mr. Wrathall continued by saying that for various reasons there had been an accelerating pace of substitution of capital for labour. 'In 1961, nearly 17 *per cent* of the African population was employed in the cash economy. By 1970 this ratio had fallen to 14 *per cent*, despite the growth of commerce and the expansion in mining that has taken place since 1965. In numerical terms, 3 100 000 Africans of all ages were not employed in the cash economy in 1961. By 1970 this figure had risen to 4 400 000, and by 1980, assuming the current pattern is unchanged, the figure will be about 6 million.'

Another factor which had exacerbated the situation was the growth of the African population. Mr. Wrathall explained that 'between the Census years, 1962 and 1969, the numbers of Africans in employment in the seven major urban areas had increased by 17 000, but in the same period the number of Africans born in these centres amounted to 187 000. These figures show that the growth of the African urban population contains the seeds of a massive employment problem.'[82]

Following speeches by various members, the Minister of Finance continued the Budget debate by saying that the unemployment problem could be ameliorated to some extent by indigenous Africans taking over jobs that were, at present, being done by alien Africans. On the other hand, the Minister warned that the increasing tendency for African women to enter the employment field could well aggravate the position. He then went on to remind his listeners that although the figures (given the present rate of African population increase) show that the number of employment opportunities in the cash economy will be inadequate to meet the number of work-seekers, this did not mean that those not absorbed in commerce and industry would be unemployed, for ample opportunities remained for them to obtain a livelihood in the rural areas. It was therefore necessary for 'present attitudes towards agricultural pursuits... to undergo a radical transformation.'[83]

It should be noted that the importance of the problem of developing the tribal areas so as to absorb a very rapidly growing African population was emphasized in the White Paper of the Settlement Proposals. However, according to the Pearce Report:

This was widely regarded as sugaring the pill or too little and too late. We were told that Africans would not sell their country for this or that it was a bribe to buy African support. ...
... Others appreciated the value of the development programmes but found it difficult to understand how it could be ensured that aid was spent on the purposes for which it was intended.[84]

Introducing the 1972 Budget, the Minister of Finance referred to the Pearce Commission's verdict and said that for the present, therefore, conditions which had governed Rhodesia's economic development would remain largely unchanged. Referring to unemployment, the Minister said that 'a most satisfying feature of 1971 was the high rate of employment generation for all races. The country was able to absorb the highest net gain of European migrants in 14 years and, in percentage terms, the increase in African employment opportunities exceeded the net increase of the African population. The trend is continuing.' [85]

The Report of the Secretary for Labour for the year ended 31 December 1972 gives the average number of unfilled vacancies for Europeans, Asians and Coloureds as 691 (compared with 892 for 1971) and the average number of registrants remaining on the live register as 890 (as compared with 882 for 1971). For Africans the numbers are 1 038 unfilled vacancies (as compared with 1 200 for 1971) and 4 125 registrants (compared with 5 128 for 1971) registered at the Department's Labour Employment Exchanges. (The figures also include those registered at the Bulawayo Municipal Employment Exchange). The Report also gives figures of 8 579 vacancies notified to the Department's Labour Employment Exchanges for Europeans, Asians and Coloureds (as compared with 9 869 for 1971) and 36 057 vacancies for Africans (as compared with 40 991 for 1971). The numbers of vacancies filled are given as 4 989 for Europeans, Asians and Coloureds (as compared with 5 944 for 1971) and 27 641 for Africans (as compared with 30 974 for 1971). [86]

In early February 1973 new controls on African work seekers were published in the *Government Gazette*. Entitled Africans (Urban Areas) Accommodation and Registration (Employment Bureaux) Regulations 1973, the regulations apply to any local authority in which an employment bureau is established and make it obligatory for any African, except those in possession of a valid identity card in terms of the Africans (Registration and Identification) Act, wishing to obtain employment to register at the labour employment bureau for a specific local authority area. The employment registration would be endorsed on individual identity registration certificates and would be valid for 15 days. An accompanying government notice suspended the regulations until the 30th June to allow time for the government to negotiate with local authorities for the takeover of all government employment exchanges. It was noted that the new regulations were part of an overall government influx control plan for making local authorities responsible for controlling the numbers of African work seekers in their areas. [87]

SCHOOL LEAVERS

With an African population increasing at possibly the highest known rate in the world [88] and with half the population under the age of 17 years, it is hardly surprising that, at the end of each year, much thought and attention is given to the problems associated with the 40 000 to 60 000 school leavers annually entering the labour market.

In early 1971 the *Herald* postulated that in Rhodesia 'a quarter of a million Europeans have gone a long way towards converting five million Africans to their alien way of life. A third of these five million live physically in the European areas of the country. Many more live there "mentally". In political jargon those youngsters, if not their parents, have opted for the Western way of life'. The newspaper asked 'What does white Rhodesia intend should happen to these scores of thousands of young people? [They] have been taught to shun the subsistence life of their parents. To let lack of opportunity and hunger force them back to it would engender the terrifying resentment of dashed hopes.' [89]

APPRENTICESHIP TRAINING

The present system of apprenticeship training was introduced under the Apprenticeship and Skilled Manpower Act of 1968. In terms of the Act the Apprenticeship Training and Skilled Manpower Development Authority was established under the control of the Department of Labour. The Authority is composed of employer and employee respresentatives and it was established to make new and further provision for the training of apprentices and minors and to establish a fund to cover the cost of training. The fund is maintained by a levy paid by employers in respect of each workman employed in the trades designated for apprenticeship. In the period for which figures are available (1961-1970) the registered contracts rose from a total of 308 to 600, the figures for African apprenticeship rising from nil to 100.

To become a registered journeyman an employee must first be indentured (usually for five years) to a registered employer. The employer must provide him with on-the-job training as well as enable him to attend a two-year course at the Salisbury Polytechnic or the Bulawayo Technical College.

As M. W. Murphree points out 'the cost to the employer of indenturing an apprentice is considerable', and with the promise of the official immigration programme to supply immediately available trained manpower, 'it is not surprising that employers have exhibited a certain complacency about the training of local personnel, White and Black.'[90]

In August 1972 African M.P's pressed, in the House of Assembly, for more technical training for Africans. The Minister of Education answered their plea by referring to the establishment of a committee which was studying ways of turning an existing African school in a Tribal Trust Land into a technical training institute which he hoped would come into use in the near future.[91]

The Report of the Secretary for Labour for the year ended 31st December 1972 shows that there were 350 apprenticeships completed in the seven registered industries and trades in 1972 (compared with 261 in 1968) and that apprenticeships due to be completed in 1973, 1974, 1975 and 1976 are 362, 355, 560 and 631 respectively.[92]

In mid-June 1973, during the debate on the Presidential speech in the Senate, Senator G. Fraser brought up the question of technical education, which he considered to be a field where there was a need for urgent expansion. He said that the building up of the range of skilled people was of the utmost importance in sustaining and expanding the growth of the country's economy and that there must be a build-up in the training of Africans. In this respect he said that he considered there was a gap in the educational framework for there was education at the highest level at the University but not enough polytechnic and other facilities for technical training. Senator Chief K. Ndiweni also referred to the question of technical training. He said that 'this question of general education does not seem to fit these young people for anything.' He emphasized that the schools which were helping the people were those at which they were taught trades and farming skills and said that the tribal areas needed young men and women taught various trades and industries to help the tribal people to advance—'where we can have our own people assisting us in our tribal areas—building, improving our actual development—then our tribal areas will progress and we will progress with them.'

In his reply to the debate the Minister of Education said that he agreed with Senator Fraser and he announced that it was the government's intention to increase the vote for technical education by 22.5 *per cent* in the coming year.[93]

NOTES

1 1960: Gray, Richard: *The Two Nations: aspects of the development of race relations in the Rhodesias and Nyasaland:* London: Oxford University Press.
2 1958: Mathews, David and R. Apthorpe (eds.) *Social Relations in Central African Industry:* 12th Conference Proceedings of the Rhodes-Livingstone Institute: Lusaka: Rhodes-Livingstone Institute.
3 1971: *Government's Policy on Labour:* Ministry of Labour and Social Welfare: Salisbury: Government Printer.
4 *Hansard:* Vol. 80, No. 10. 16 November 1971: Cols. 680-733.
5 *S.M.* 21 November 1971.
6 *Hansard:* Vol. 80, No. 16. 25 November 1971: Col. 1112.
7 *R.H.* 28 May 1973.
  The chairman of an industrial tribunal is appointed by the Minister. Members of the tribunal are selected by the chairman from a panel put forward by the Minister.
8 *R.H.* 20 June 1973.
9 *Report of the Secretary for Labour and Social Welfare for the year ended 31 December 1972:* Salisbury: Government Printer.
10 *Hansard:* Vol. 79, Nos. 2, 3. 1, 2 June 1971: Cols. 28-9, 99-108.
11 *Hansard:* Vol. 79, No. 11. 11 June 1971: Col. 559.
12 *R.H.* 4 June 1971.
13 *Hansard:* Vol. 81, No. 13. 18 July 1972: Cols. 1032-7.
14 *Hansard:* Vol. 82, Nos. 14, 15. 6, 7 September 1972. Cols. 1268-88, 1291-1325.
  R.H. 11 September 1972.
15 See also chapter on Education.
16 *R.H.* 23 June 1971.
17 *R.H.* 26 June 1971.
18 At this time representatives of the British government were in Rhodesia to negotiate terms for settlement of the constitutional dispute.
19 *Hansard:* Vol. 79, No. 14. 23 July 1971: Cols. 849-51.

20 *Hansard:* Vol. 81, Nos. 15, 16. 20, 21 July 1972: Cols. 1244-6, 1204-5, 1283.
21 *Hansard:* Vol. 81, No. 25. 8 August 1972: Col. 2207.
22 *R.H.* 26 May 1972.
23 *R.H.* 19 August 1972.
24 As reported in *R.H.* 13 July 1973.
25 *Hansard:* Vol. 81, No. 5. 9 June 1972: Cols. 332-44.
26 *Hansard:* Vol. 81, No. 10. 20 June 1972: Cols. 742-71.
27 *R.H.* 17 October 1972.
28 *S.M.* 29 October 1972.
29 *Hansard:* Vol. 82, No. 2, 22 November 1972: Cols. 104-5.
30 As reported in *R.H.* 2 October 1972.
31 *R.H.* 23 February 1973.
32 *S.M.* 19 April 1972.
   In other words non-African drivers would have to be paid higher wages.
33 As reported in *R.H.* 7, 8 April 1972.
34 *R.H.* 19 April 1973.
35 *R.H.* 31 August 1972.
36 As reported in *R.H.* 6 November 1972.
37 *R.H.* 19, 25 January; 14, 28 February 1973.
38 *R.H.* 28 February; 29, 31 May; 1, 2, 14 June 1973.
39 *op. cit.* See note 9.
40 As reported by *R.H.* 13 March 1972.
41 *R.H.* 13 July 1972.
42 As reported by *R.F.G.* 29 September 1972.
43 Lewis, A. J. L.: *African Wages in Rhodesia: Private Memorandum* (cyclostyled) 23 October 1972.
44 As reported in *R.H.* 21, 22 November 1972.
45 *Economic Survey of Rhodesia:* Ministry of Finance, April 1973: Cmd. R.R. 5-73: Salisbury: Government Printer.
   The Survey notes, with reference to agricultural and forestry workers, that the figure of average earnings is depressed by the figures of earnings of well over 100 000 casual and contract employees in seasonal work. The figures of actual cash earnings are also inclusive of payments in kind.
46 See Bettison, David G.: The Poverty-Datum Line in Central Africa in *Human Problems in Central Africa:* Rhodes-Livingstone Journal No. 27, June 1960: Manchester University Press.
   Also see *Report of the Urban African Affairs Commission 1958* (The Plewman Commission) Salisbury: Government Printer.
47 *R.F.G.* 23 February 1973.
48 *Rhodesia Government Notice No. 615,* 8 June 1973.
   R.H. 12 June 1973.
49 As reported in *R.H.* 28 June 1973.
50 Murphree, M. W.: *Organised Labour and Black Economic Advancement in Rhodesia:* Unpublished Paper read at the 3rd Research Workshop, Abe Bailey Institute of Inter-Racial Studies, Capetown: 29-31 January 1973.
51 As reported in *R.H.* 13, 15 January 1972.

52 As reported in *R.H.* 17 January 1972.
53 *R.H.* 8 February 1972. Gaths Mine is owned by the same company as the Shabanie Asbestos Mine.
54 *R.H.* 9 February 1972.
55 *R.H.* 11 February 1972.
56 *R.H.* 25 February 1972.
57 In Salisbury the bus services are mainly for Africans. Of the 250 buses normally operating daily only 22 are routed through the European suburbs and these are used 40-50 *per cent* by Africans.
58 *R.H.* 15 June 1972.
59 *Hansard :* Vol. 81, No. 7. 14 June 1972: Cols. 561-66.
60 *R.H.* 15 June 1972.
61 *R.H.* 16 June 1972.
62 *Hansard :* Vol. 81, No. 9. 16 June 1972: Cols. 736-40.
63 As reported in *R.H.* 19 June 1972.
64 *R.H.* 22 June 1972.
65 *R.H.* 24 June 1972.
66 *S.M.* 25 June 1972.
67 As reported in *R.H.* 26 June 1972.
68 *R.H.* 27 June 1972.
69 As reported in *R.H.* 5 July 1972.
70 *Hansard :* Vol. 81, No. 16. 21 July 1972: Col. 1273.
71 *R.H.* 16 August 1972.
72 *R.H.* 31 August 1972.
73 *R.H.* 1, 4 September 1972.
74 *R.H.* 8 June 1973.
75 *S.M.* 18 June 1972.
76 *R.H.* 24 August 1972.
77 *R.H.* 12 September 1972.
78 *R.H.* 26 September 1972.
79 *op. cit.* See note 9.
80 *R.H.* 27 March 1973.
81 *R.H.* 18, 22 May 1973.
82 *Hansard :* Vol. 79, No. 10. 15 July 1971: Col. 601.
83 *Hansard :* Vol. 79, No. 21. 5 August 1971: Cols. 1406-7.
84 *Pearce Report*, p. 85.
85 *Hansard :* Vol. 81, No. 12. 13 July 1972: Cols. 961-65.
86 *op. cit.* See note 9.
87 *Rhodesia Government Notices* 134, 135, 2 February 1973.
88 According to the 1969 Census the African birthrate is 52 live births per 1 000 population.
89 *R.H.* 26 January 1971.
90 1973: Murphree, Marshall W.: *Employment Opportunity and Race in Rhodesia :* Vol. 4, No. 2: Studies in Race and Nations: Denver: University of Denver (Quoted by kind permission of the author).
91 *Hansard :* Vol. 82, Nos. 6, 7. 23, 24 August 1972: Cols. 581-96.
92 *op. cit.* See note 9.
93 *Hansard : Senate Debates :* Vol. 4, Nos. 2, 5. 19, 28 June 1973: Cols. 13-14, 33-34, 128.

INDEX

(Where subjects are identified in the table of contents, which is detailed, they are not mentioned separately here)

455

CENTRE FOR INTER-RACIAL STUDIES
UNIVERSITY OF RHODESIA
Members of Academic Staff, 1973